The Grammar of Messianism

The Grammar of
Messianism

*An Ancient Jewish Political Idiom
and Its Users*

MATTHEW V. NOVENSON

OXFORD
UNIVERSITY PRESS

OXFORD
UNIVERSITY PRESS

Oxford University Press is a department of the University of Oxford. It furthers
the University's objective of excellence in research, scholarship, and education
by publishing worldwide. Oxford is a registered trade mark of Oxford University
Press in the UK and certain other countries.

Published in the United States of America by Oxford University Press
198 Madison Avenue, New York, NY 10016, United States of America.

Library of Congress Cataloging-in-Publication Data
Names: Novenson, Matthew V., author.
Title: The grammar of messianism : an ancient Jewish political idiom and its
users / Matthew V. Novenson.
Description: New York : Oxford University Press, [2017] | Includes
bibliographical references and index.
Identifiers: LCCN 2016034957 (print) | LCCN 2016035306 (ebook) |
ISBN 9780190255022 (hardback) | ISBN 9780190053215 (paperback)
ISBN 9780190255039 (updf) | ISBN 9780190255046 (oso)
Subjects: LCSH: Messianism. | Messiah—Judaism. | Jesus Christ—Messiahship. |
Christianity and other religions—Judaism. |
Judaism—Relations—Christianity.
Classification: LCC BL475 .N68 2016 (print) | LCC BL475 (ebook) |
DDC 296.3/36—dc23
LC record available at https://lccn.loc.gov/2016034957

Uxori carissimae

Not all the water in the rough rude sea
Can wash the balm off from an anointed king.
SHAKESPEARE, *Richard II, act 3, scene 2*

Contents

Acknowledgments

IF THIS BOOK has turned out well, as I hope is the case but must leave to the readers and reviewers to decide, it is thanks in large part to the work of many people other than myself. The handsome printed artifact is a credit to the consistently excellent work of editor Cynthia Read and her staff at Oxford University Press in New York—in particular, Marcela Maxfield and Drew Anderla, as well as Kubra Ameen and Cat Ohala on the project team. Most of the research represented here I have presented, piece by piece, in a number of collegial venues, where I have received valuable feedback from very smart people. I note with particular gratitude the following: Aryeh Amihay, Martha Himmelfarb, Jeremy Hutton, Peter Schäfer, Loren Stuckenbruck, and Ross Wagner in Princeton; William Adler, Maria Doerfler, Bart Ehrman, and Joel Marcus in Chapel Hill; Jörg Frey, Benjamin Schliesser, and Samuel Vollenweider in Zurich; Markus Bockmuel, David Lincicum, and Alison Salvesen in Oxford; James Davila and N. T. Wright in St. Andrews; George Brooke in Manchester; Helen Bond, Larry Hurtado, and Timothy Lim in Edinburgh; and my anonymous readers at the Press. Philip Alexander, Andrew Chester, and Annette Reed generously shared prepublication manuscripts with and fielded questions from me. My Edinburgh graduate students Bernardo Cho and Jay Thomas Hewitt have been eager and learned interlocutors; they, along with their colleagues Ryan Collman and Sydney Tooth, also rendered great help in proofing and indexing the manuscript. I could point to places in the book where each of these many good people saved me from error. The same is true, still more so, of John Collins, Martha Himmelfarb, and Robert Kraft—towering scholars and generous human beings, all—who did the supererogatory task of reading and commenting on the entire manuscript. Whatever faults remain in the book are mine alone.

Writing this book while juggling my various other responsibilities took some strategizing and no little help from a phalanx of colleagues and friends. Early on, Mark and Jenny Stirling generously made space for me in their home in St. Andrews for a timely writing retreat. Around the halfway point, a visiting professorship at Dartmouth College afforded me an intensive summer's worth of research, for which I have Susan Ackerman and Randall Balmer to thank. In the later stages, St. John's College and the Department of Theology and Religion, Durham University, provided me a generous research fellowship, beautiful workspace, and good company, for which I am very grateful to John Barclay, Alec Ryrie, and David Wilkinson. In Edinburgh, New College Librarian Christine Love-Rodgers ensured that I lacked for nothing in the way of books, and Head of School Paul Foster demonstrated his commitment to protecting staff research time. My children were, as ever, a welcome source of encouragement and good humor. No one, however, did more to facilitate the research and writing of this book than my wife Michelle. The final product is by no means worthy of her, but it is for her.

Abbreviations

For ancient Near Eastern, biblical, Jewish, and Christian primary sources, I follow the system of abbreviations prescribed by *The SBL Handbook of Style* (ed. Patrick H. Alexander et al.; Peabody, Mass.: Hendrickson, 1999). For classical Greek and Roman primary sources, I follow the system of abbreviations prescribed by *The Oxford Classical Dictionary* (ed. Simon Hornblower and Antony Spawforth; 3d rev. ed.; Oxford: Oxford University Press, 2003). Other abbreviations are as follows:

AB	Anchor Bible
ABD	*Anchor Bible Dictionary.* Edited by D. N. Freedman. 6 vols. New York, 1992
ABRL	Anchor Bible Reference Library
AGJU	Arbeiten zur Geschichte des antiken Judentums und des Urchristentums
ANET	*Ancient Near Eastern Texts Relating to the Old Testament.* Edited by J. B. Pritchard. Princeton, 1969
ANF	Ante-Nicene Fathers
ANRW	*Aufstieg und Niedergang der Römischen Welt: Geschichte und Kultur Roms im Spiegel der neueren Forschung.* Edited by H. Temporini and W. Haase. Berlin, 1972–
ArBib	The Aramaic Bible
ArSt	*Aramaic Studies*
ATANT	Abhandlungen zur Theologie des Alten und Neuen Testaments
Aug	*Augustinianum*
BAR	*Biblical Archaeology Review*
BDAG	Danker, F. W., W. Bauer, W. F. Arndt, and F. W. Gingrich. *Greek-English Lexicon of the New Testament and Other Early Christian Literature.* 3d ed. Chicago, 1999

BDB	Brown, F., S. R. Driver, and C. A. Briggs. *A Hebrew and English Lexicon of the Old Testament*. Oxford, 1907
BETL	Bibliotheca ephemeridum theologicarum lovaniensium
BHS	*Biblia Hebraica Stuttgartensia*. Edited by K. Elliger and W. Rudolph. Stuttgart, 1983
Bib	*Biblica*
BJS	Brown Judaic Studies
BRLJ	Brill Reference Library of Judaism
BSAC	*Bulletin de la Société d'Archéologie Copte*
BZ	*Biblische Zeitschrift*
BZAW	Beihefte zur Zeitschrift für die alttestamentliche Wissenschaft
BZNW	Beihefte zur Zeitschrift für die neutestamentliche Wissenschaft
CAH	Cambridge Ancient History
CBET	Contributions to Biblical Exegesis and Theology
CBQ	*Catholic Biblical Quarterly*
CBT	Cultures, Beliefs, and Traditions
CCSG	Corpus Christianorum: Series graeca. Turnhout, 1977–
CCSL	Corpus Christianorum: Series latina. Turnhout, 1953–
CEJL	Commentaries on Early Jewish Literature
CHJ	*Cambridge History of Judaism*. Edited by W. D. Davies and Louis Finkelstein. Cambridge, 1984–
CJ	*Classical Journal*
CJAS	Christianity and Judaism in Antiquity Series
ConBNT	Coniectanea biblica: New Testament Series
ConBOT	Coniectanea biblica: Old Testament Series
Cont	*Continuum*
COS	*The Context of Scripture*. Edited by W. W. Hallo. 3 vols. Leiden, 1997–
CQ	*Classical Quarterly*
CQS	Companion to the Qumran Scrolls
CRINT	Compendia rerum iudaicarum ad Novum Testamentum
CSHJ	Chicago Studies in the History of Judaism
Danby	Danby, H., trans. *The Mishnah*. Oxford, 1933
DJD	Discoveries in the Judaean Desert
DSD	*Dead Sea Discoveries*
EB	Études bibliques
EJL	Early Judaism and Its Literature
EKK	Evangelisch-katholischer Kommentar
EncJud	*Encyclopedia Judaica*. 16 vols. New York, 1971–1972
ErJb	*Eranos-Jahrbuch*

ESCJ	Études sur le christianisme et le judaïsme
ETL	*Ephemerides theologicae lovanienses*
FAT	Forschungen zum Alten Testament
FRLANT	Forschungen zur Religion und Literatur des Alten und Neuen Testaments
GCS	Die griechische christliche Schriftsteller der ersten Jahrhunderte
HAR	*Hebrew Annual Review*
HAT	Handbuch zum Alten Testament
Hen	*Henoch*
Herm	*Hermathena*
HNT	Handbuch zum Neuen Testament
HSCP	*Harvard Studies in Classical Philology*
HTR	*Harvard Theological Review*
HTS	Harvard Theological Studies
HUCA	*Hebrew Union College Annual*
HUCM	Monographs of the Hebrew Union College
ICC	International Critical Commentary
IEJ	*Israel Exploration Journal*
IJSSJ	IJS Studies in Judaica
Int	*Interpretation*
JAJ	*Journal of Ancient Judaism*
JAJSup	Journal of Ancient Judaism Supplements
JBL	*Journal of Biblical Literature*
JBR	*Journal of Bible and Religion*
JBTh	*Jahrbuch für biblische Theologie*
JCP	Jewish and Christian Perspectives
JCTC	Jewish and Christian Texts in Contexts
JDT	*Jahrbuch für deutsche Theologie*
JECS	*Journal of Early Christian Studies*
JJS	*Journal of Jewish Studies*
JNES	*Journal of Near Eastern Studies*
JPS	Jewish Publication Society
JQR	*Jewish Quarterly Review*
JRelS	*Journal of Religious Studies*
JRS	*Journal of Roman Studies*
JSJ	*Journal for the Study of Judaism*
JSNT	*Journal for the Study of the New Testament*
JSNTSup	Journal for the Study of the New Testament Supplements
JSOT	*Journal for the Study of the Old Testament*
JSOTSup	Journal for the Study of the Old Testament Supplements

JSP	*Journal for the Study of the Pseudepigrapha*
JSPL	*Journal for the Study of Paul and His Letters*
JSPSup	Journal for the Study of the Pseudepigrapha Supplements
JSQ	*Jewish Studies Quarterly*
JSS	*Journal of Semitic Studies*
JTS	*Journal of Theological Studies*
JZWL	*Jüdische Zeitschrift für Wissenschaft und Leben*
KJV	King James Version
KTU	*Die keilalphabetischen Texte aus Ugarit.* Edited by M. Dietrich, O. Loretz, and J. Sanmartin. AOAT 24/1. Neukirchen-Vluyn, 1976
LCL	Loeb Classical Library
LD	Lectio divina
LHBOTS	Library of Hebrew Bible/Old Testament Studies
LNTS	Library of New Testament Studies
LSJ	Liddell, H. G., R. Scott, and H. S. Jones. *A Greek-English Lexicon.* 9th ed. With revised supplement. Oxford, 1996
LSTS	Library of Second Temple Studies
NETS	New English Translation of the Septuagint
NHL	*Nag Hammadi Library in English.* Edited by J. M. Robinson. 4th rev. ed. Leiden, 1996
NHMS	Nag Hammadi and Manichaean Studies
NJahrb	*Neue Jahrbücher für das klassische Altertum*
NovT	*Novum Testamentum*
NovTSup	Novum Testamentum Supplements
NPNF	*Nicene and Post-Nicene Fathers*
NRSV	New Revised Standard Version
NTL	New Testament Library
NTS	*New Testament Studies*
OBO	Orbis Biblicus et Orientalis
OCD	*Oxford Classical Dictionary.* Edited by S. Hornblower and A. Spawforth. 3d ed. Oxford, 1996
OCT	Oxford Classical Texts
OECT	Oxford Early Christian Texts
OTL	Old Testament Library
OTM	Oxford Theological Monographs
OTP	*Old Testament Pseudepigrapha.* Edited by J. H. Charlesworth. 2 vols. New York, 1983, 1985
OTS	Old Testament Studies
OtSt	Oudtestamentische Studiën
PAAJR	*Proceedings of the American Academy of Jewish Research*

PG	Patrologia graeca. Edited by J.- P. Migne. 162 vols. Paris, 1857–1886
PGL	*Patristic Greek Lexicon*. Edited by G. W. H. Lampe. Oxford, 1968
PIASH	Proceedings of the Israel Academy of Sciences and Humanities
PL	Patrologia latina. Edited by J.- P. Migne. 217 vols. Paris, 1844–1864
PMS	Patristic Monograph Series
PO	Patrologia orientalis
RB	*Revue biblique*
RBL	*Review of Biblical Literature*
REJ	*Revue des Études Juives*
RevQ	*Revue de Qumran*
RHR	*Revue de l'histoire des religions*
RRJ	*Review of Rabbinic Judaism*
RSR	*Recherches de science religieuse*
RSV	Revised Standard Version
RThom	*Revue thomiste*
SBAW	*Sitzungsberichte der bayerischen Akademie der Wissenschaften*
SBL	Society of Biblical Literature
SBLSBS	Society of Biblical Literature Sources for Biblical Study
SBT	Studies in Biblical Theology
SBTS	Sources for Biblical and Theological Study
SC	Sources chrétiennes. Paris, 1943–
SECA	Studies on Early Christian Apocrypha
SHR	Studies in the History of Religions
SIJD	Schriften des Institutum Judaicum Delitzschianum
SJOT	*Scandinavian Journal of the Old Testament*
SJT	*Scottish Journal of Theology*
SNTSMS	Society for New Testament Studies Monograph Series
SPAW	*Sitzungsberichte der Preußischen Akademie der Wissenschaften*
SPhA	*Studia Philonica Annual*
SR	*Studies in Religion*
SSEJC	Studies in Scripture in Early Judaism and Christianity
SSN	Studia semitica neerlandica
STDJ	Studies on the Texts of the Desert of Judah
SUNT	Studien zur Umwelt des Neuen Testaments
SVTP	Studia in Veteris Testamenti pseudepigrapha
TAPA	*Transactions of the American Philological Association*
TDNT	*Theological Dictionary of the New Testament*. Edited by G. Kittel and G. Friedrich. Translated by G. W. Bromiley. 10 vols. Grand Rapids, 1964–1976

TENTS	Texts and Editions for New Testament Study
Teubner	Bibliotheca scriptorum graecorum et romanorum teubneriana
ThT	*Theologisch tijdschrift*
TLG	*Thesaurus linguae graecae*
TLL	*Thesaurus linguae latinae*
TLZ	*Theologische Literaturzeitung*
TS	*Theological Studies*
TSAJ	Texte und Studien zum antiken Judentum
TSMEMJ	Texts and Studies in Medieval and Early Modern Judaism
TUGAL	Texte und Untersuchungen zur Geschichte der altchristlichen Literatur
TynBul	*Tyndale Bulletin*
USFISFCJ	University of South Florida International Studies in Formative Christianity and Judaism
VC	*Vigiliae Christianae*
VCSup	Vigiliae Christianae Supplements
VT	*Vetus Testamentum*
VTSup	Vetus Testamentum Supplements
WJK	Westminster John Knox
WUNT	Wissenschaftliche Untersuchungen zum Neuen Testament
YJS	Yale Judaic Studies
ZAC	*Zeitschrift für Antikes Christentum*
ZAW	*Zeitschrift für die alttestamentliche Wissenschaft*
ZKG	*Zeitschrift für Kirchengeschichte*
ZNW	*Zeitschrift für die neutestamentliche Wissenschaft und die Kunde der älteren Kirche*
ZRG	*Zeitschrift der Savigny-Stiftung für Rechtsgeschichte*

I

After the Messianic Idea

AN ANONYMOUS SEVENTH-CENTURY CE Jewish writer tells the story of
a mythical woman named Hephzibah, the mother of the messiah ben
David, who fights alongside the messiah ben David and the messiah
ben Joseph in the final eschatological battle against Armilus. Hephzibah
slays wicked gentile kings with a rod of almond wood that had belonged
to Adam, Moses, Aaron, Joshua, and David in turn and was hidden away
until the last day to be wielded by the mother of the messiah. The text
is the late ancient apocalypse *Sefer Zerubbabel*, and among its contributions to Jewish legend is the striking image of the mother of the messiah as a righteous avenger in the last battle.[1] *Sefer Zerubbabel* falls at the
end of the historical period in view in the present book, but it does as
well as any of its antecedents to illustrate the phenomenon with which
the book is concerned—namely, the participation by ancient Jews and
Christians in a common scriptural discourse in texts about their respective messiahs.

The character of Hephzibah reflects late ancient Jewish familiarity with
the figure of the virgin Mary in Byzantine Christian art and liturgy. As the
Byzantine armies carried the image of the mother of their messiah into
battle with the Sasanian Persians, so, for the author of *Sefer Zerubbabel*, the
mother of the Jewish messiah will one day march into battle on behalf of

---

1. The best text is Israël Lévi, "L'apocalypse de Zorobabel et le roi de Perse Siroès,"
REJ 68 (1914): 131–44, an edition based on Oxford MS 2797. A fine English transla-
tion with critical introduction and notes is John C. Reeves, *Trajectories in Near Eastern
Apocalyptic: A Postrabbinic Jewish Apocalypse Reader* (Atlanta, Ga.: Society of Biblical
Literature, 2005), 40–66.

her own people.[2] But if, in a sense, Hephzibah comes from Jewish experience with Byzantine mariology, in a different sense she also comes from the Bible. Hephzibah is the name of an ancient Judahite queen mother, the wife of king Hezekiah and mother of Manasseh (2 Kgs 21:1).[3] Indeed, if, likely as not, Manasseh was anointed with oil upon his accession to the throne, then this ancient Judahite Hephzibah will have been a mother of a messiah, strictly speaking.[4] Hephzibah also appears in etymologized form in Third Isaiah, where the feminine name is applied figuratively to Zion:

> You [O Zion] shall no more be called Azuvah [עזובה, "forsaken"], and your land shall no more be called Shemamah [שממה, "desolate"]; but you shall be called Hephzibah [חפצי־בה, "my delight is in her"], and your land Beulah [בעולה, "married"]; for YHWH delights [חפץ] in you, and your land shall be married [תבעל]. (Isa 62:4)[5]

Before *Sefer Zerubbabel*, there is no mother of the messiah named Hephzibah.[6] When *Sefer Zerubbabel* undertakes to imagine a mother of the messiah, however, he draws on intelligible biblical imagery—in this case, a queen mother in the ancient Judahite house of David (2 Kgs 21:2) and a poetic picture of a restored Jerusalem (Isa 62:4). In this respect, *Sefer Zerubbabel* illustrates the way that all ancient messiah texts, both Jewish and Christian, typically work. This book comprises a demonstration that this is the case.

---

2. See Martha Himmelfarb, "The Mother of the Messiah in the Talmud Yerushalmi and Sefer Zerubbabel," in *The Talmud Yerushalmi and Graeco-Roman Culture*, vol. 3 (ed. Peter Schäfer; TSAJ 93; Tübingen: Mohr Siebeck, 2002), 369–89; Joseph Dan, "Armilus: The Jewish Antichrist and the Origins and Dating of the Sefer Zerubbavel," in *Toward the Millennium: Messianic Expectations from the Bible to Waco* (ed. Peter Schäfer and Mark R. Cohen; SHR 77; Leiden: Brill, 1998), 73–104.

3. On Hephzibah the queen mother, see Hermann Michael Niemann, "Choosing Brides for the Crown-Prince: Matrimonial Politics in the Davidic Dynasty," *VT* 56 (2006): 225–38.

4. On the ritual anointing of Israelite kings, see Chapters 2 and 3 in this volume.

5. On the name Hephzibah in this oracle, see Baruch Halpern, "The New Names of Isaiah 62:4: Jeremiah's Reception in the Restoration and the Politics of 'Third Isaiah,'" *JBL* 117 (1998): 623–43, especially 637–43. Here and subsequently, translations of primary texts are my own unless otherwise noted.

6. But compare the unnamed mother of the messiah in *y. Ber.* 2:4 (5a), as well as the possibly related myth of the woman, child, and dragon in Rev 12, on which see Israël Lévi, "Le ravissement du Messie à sa naissance," *REJ* 74 (1922): 113–26; and Himmelfarb, "Mother of the Messiah."

After the Messianic Idea

Writing twenty years ago, Shemaryahu Talmon commented, "A renewed examination of messianism in early Judaism can with some justification be likened to carrying coals to Newcastle or balm to Gilead."[7] In view of the steady flow of publications on the topic since the early 1990s, Talmon's sentiment is perhaps even truer now than it was then.[8] And yet, Talmon justified his own study by appealing to new evidence from recently published manuscripts

---

7. Shemaryahu Talmon, "The Concept of *Masiah* and Messianism in Early Judaism," in *The Messiah: Developments in Earliest Judaism and Christianity* (ed. James H. Charlesworth; Minneapolis, Minn.: Fortress, 1992), 79–115 at 79.

8. To speak only of monographs, leaving aside for the moment the many journal articles and edited volumes, major contributions in the two decades since Talmon's essay include Gerbern Oegema, *Der Gesalbte und sein Volk: Untersuchungen zum Konzeptualisierungsprozess der messianischen Erwartungen von den Makkabäern bis Bar Koziba* (SIJD 2; Göttingen: Vandenhoeck & Ruprecht, 1994); ET *The Anointed and His People: Messianic Expectations from the Maccabees to Bar Kokhba* (JSPSup 27; Sheffield: Sheffield Academic, 1998); John J. Collins, *The Scepter and the Star: Messianism in Light of the Dead Sea Scrolls* (2d ed.; Grand Rapids, Mich.: Eerdmans, 2010 [1st ed. Doubleday, 1995]); Kenneth E. Pomykala, *The Davidic Dynasty Tradition in Early Judaism: Its History and Significance for Messianism* (EJL 7; Atlanta, Ga.: Scholars Press, 1995); Dan Cohn-Sherbok, *The Jewish Messiah* (London: T. & T. Clark, 1997); William Horbury, *Jewish Messianism and the Cult of Christ* (London: SCM, 1998); Harris Lenowitz, *The Jewish Messiahs: From the Galilee to Crown Heights* (New York, N.Y.: Oxford University Press, 1998); Johannes Zimmerman, *Messianische Texte aus Qumran: Königliche, priesterliche und prophetische Messiasvorstellungen in den Schriftfunden von Qumran* (WUNT 2.104; Tübingen: Mohr Siebeck, 1998); Michael O. Wise, *The First Messiah: Investigating the Savior before Jesus* (San Francisco, Calif.: Harper, 1999); Israel Knohl, *The Messiah before Jesus: The Suffering Servant of the Dead Sea Scrolls* (trans. David Maisel; Berkeley, Calif.: University of California Press, 2000); Stefan Schreiber, *Gesalbter und König: Titel und Konzeptionen der königlichen Gesalbtenerwartung in frühjüdischen und urchristlichen Schriften* (BZNW 105; Berlin: De Gruyter, 2000); Timo Eskola, *Messiah and the Throne: Jewish Merkabah Mysticism and Early Christian Exaltation Discourse* (WUNT 2.142; Tübingen: Mohr Siebeck, 2001); Ernst-Joachim Waschke, *Der Gesalbte: Studien zur alttestamentliche Theologie* (BZAW 306; Berlin: De Gruyter, 2001); William Horbury, *Messianism among Jews and Christians* (London: T. & T. Clark, 2003); Andrew Chester, *Messiah and Exaltation: Jewish Messianic and Visionary Traditions and New Testament Christology* (WUNT 207; Tübingen: Mohr Siebeck, 2007); Joseph A. Fitzmyer, *The One Who Is to Come* (Grand Rapids, Mich.: Eerdmans, 2007); Adela Yarbro Collins and John J. Collins, *King and Messiah as Son of God* (Grand Rapids, Mich,: Eerdmans, 2008); Eric F. Mason, *You Are a Priest Forever: Second Temple Jewish Messianism and the Priestly Christology of the Epistle to the Hebrews* (STDJ 74; Leiden: Brill, 2008); Albert L. A. Hogeterp, *Expectations of the End: A Comparative Traditio-Historical Study of Eschatological, Apocalyptic, and Messianic Ideas in the Dead Sea Scrolls and the New Testament* (STDJ 83; Leiden: Brill, 2009); Israel Knohl, *Messiahs and Resurrection in "The Gabriel Revelation"* (London: Continuum, 2009); Shirley Lucass, *The Concept of the Messiah in the Scriptures of Judaism and Christianity* (LSTS 78; London: T. & T. Clark, 2011); James Waddell, *The Messiah: A Comparative Study of the Enochic Son of Man and the Pauline Kyrios* (JCTC 10; London: T. & T. Clark, 2011); Daniel Boyarin, *The Jewish Gospels: The Story of the Jewish Christ* (New York, N.Y.: New Press, 2012); and Matthew V. Novenson, *Christ among the Messiahs: Christ Language in Paul and Messiah Language in Ancient Judaism* (New York, N.Y.: Oxford University Press, 2012).

from Qumran.[9] In my case, the justification is not so much new evidence (although there are several recently published primary texts to be discussed here), but rather an alternative model for understanding a familiar set of primary texts. The modern study of ancient messianism has suffered from a lamentable naiveté with respect to theory—that is, meta-level reflection on what we talk about when we talk about messianism. Most modern studies engage in no such reflection at all, but a praiseworthy minority do bring conceptual questions to bear.

R. J. Zwi Werblowsky, for instance, suggests:

> Messianism should be, and in fact has been, studied from two perspectives: that of the historian of ideas, and that of the social historian. In other words, a distinction must be made between messianism as a complex of ideas, doctrines, hopes and expectations on the one hand, and messianic movements on the other. Messianism is the potentiality of messianic movements; messianic movements are messianism in action.[10]

If Werblowsky conceives of two basic approaches to the study of messianism—the history of ideas and social history—Moshe Idel identifies at least four approaches and imagines the possibility of others, as well:

> Messianism may be approached from various vantage points. The sociological approach emphasizes the expressions of messianism that appear in various strata of the population, particularly the masses, while the psychological approach is ideal for analyzing the messianic consciousness of the masses and the extraordinary personality of a Messiah. Messianism may also be studied as part of a complex of religious concepts, with the aim of integrating them into a certain theology

---

Reflecting in 2007 on the state of research on the question since 1991, Andrew Chester aptly comments:

> It is striking ... that the main questions I focused on then [in 1991] are still [in 2007] seen as central, not least whether messianism appears to be a significant and coherent phenomenon, or whether it is merely peripheral and disparate. There is still no consensus, and the issues remain very contested. (Chester, *Messiah and Exaltation*, 191)

9. Talmon, "Concept of *Masiah*," 79–80.

10. R. J. Zwi Werblowsky, "Jewish Messianism in Comparative Perspective," in *Messiah and Christos: Studies in the Jewish Origins of Christianity* (ed. Ithamar Gruenwald et al.; TSAJ 32; Tübingen: Mohr Siebeck, 1992), 7.

or placing them within the framework of the history of ideas. Yet it is also possible to investigate the relationship between messianic aware-ness and an individual's private mystical experience.[11]

Despite the notional plurality of approaches to the study of messianism, how-ever, in actual practice modern research on the topic has tended overwhelmingly to take what Werblowsky calls the history-of-ideas approach.[12] Consequently, as William Scott Green has shown, most modern studies of ancient messiah texts are actually studies not of the texts themselves, but of a concept abstracted from them—a concept most often called the messianic idea.[13]

The messianic idea is a firmly established trope in biblical studies and Jewish studies from the mid nineteenth century to the present.[14] The particu-lars vary from one writer to the next, but the common core is the notion that ancient messiah texts belong in an extraordinary way to *Geistesgeschichte* or *Ideengeschichte*, the history of ideas.[15] On this model, the pertinent texts in

---

11. Moshe Idel, *Messianic Mystics* (New Haven, Conn.: Yale University Press, 1998), 1.

12. Thus rightly Idel, *Messianic Mystics*, 17: "Though the great variety of literatures under inspection would invite an assumption that many sorts of messianic ideas would compete, the phrase *messianic idea* looms too prominently in the titles of many books and articles."

13. See William Scott Green, "Introduction: Messiah in Judaism: Rethinking the Question," in *Judaisms and Their Messiahs at the Turn of the Christian Era* (ed. Jacob Neusner et al.; Cambridge: Cambridge University Press, 1987), 7: "The standard works on the topic typically devote less attention to concrete textual references than to discussion of a religious attitude allegedly at the core of Israelite and Jewish experience: the so-called 'future hope.'"

14. See the survey of nineteenth- and twentieth-century scholarship in Horbury, *Messianism among Jews and Christians*, 1–22. Representatives of this trope include Heinrich Julius Holtzmann, "Die Messiasidee zur Zeit Jesu," *JDT* (1867): 389–411; David Castelli, *Il Messia secondo gli Ebrei* (Florence: Le Monnier, 1874); Maurice Vernes, *Histoire des idées messian-ique depuis Alexandre jusqu'à l'empereur Hadrien* (Paris: Sandoz et Fischbacher, 1874); James Drummond, *The Jewish Messiah: A Critical History of the Messianic Idea among the Jews from the Rise of the Maccabees to the Closing of the Talmud* (London: Longman, 1877); James Scott, "Historical Development of the Messianic Idea," *The Old Testament Student* 7 (1888): 176–80; Julius H. Greenstone, *The Messiah Idea in Jewish History* (Philadelphia, Pa: JPS, 1906); W. O. E. Oesterley, *The Evolution of the Messianic Idea: A Study in Comparative Religion* (New York, N.Y.: Dutton, 1908); Ernest F. Scott, "What Did the Idea of Messiah Mean to the Early Christians?" *JR* 1 (1921): 418–20; Joseph Klausner, *The Messianic Idea in Israel: From Its Beginning to the Completion of the Mishnah* (trans. W. F. Stinespring; New York, N.Y.: Macmillan, 1955); Gershom Scholem, *The Messianic Idea in Judaism and Other Essays on Jewish Spirituality* (New York, N.Y.: Schocken, 1971); Isaiah Tishby, "The Messianic Idea and Messianic Trends at the Beginning of Hasidism," *Zion* 32 (1967): 1–45 (in Hebrew); Dov Schwartz, "The Neutralization of the Messianic Idea in Medieval Jewish Rationalism," *HUCA* 64 (1993): 37–58 (in Hebrew).

15. On the notion of *Geistesgeschichte*, see Richard Rorty, "The Historiography of Philosophy: Four Genres," in *Philosophy in History* (ed. Richard Rorty et al.; Cambridge: Cambridge University Press, 1984), 49–75, especially 56–61. On the

Daniel, or the *Psalms of Solomon*, or the *Parables of Enoch*, or the Talmud Bavli are so many instantiations of a single suprahistorical idea that exists independently of them all. This idea itself is not just—as the word *messiah* might suggest—an anointed ruler, but rather a uniquely and characteristically Jewish hope for a utopian future.

Thus Heinrich Graetz, writing in the mid nineteenth century, comments, "The messianic idea, that constant hope for a better and more beautiful future, is the elixir of life which has granted the Jewish people its remarkable tenacity."[16] Julius Hillel Greenstone, writing at the turn of the twentieth century, claims:

> The Messianic idea is characteristically Jewish. The nations of antiquity, despairing of the present and heedless of the future, gloried in their past, in which they saw the perfection of all happiness, social and national.... The Jew looks for happiness and virtue, not to a past golden age, but to the future, to "the end of days," a favorite phrase with prophet and sage.[17]

Writing in the same vein some twenty years later, Joseph Klausner praises "the greatness and loftiness of the Messianic idea, that original Hebrew idea which has influenced all humanity so much."[18] Klausner's messianic idea is "the summation of the most exalted hopes for a shining future, which our greatest and most venerated dreamers await," and, more precisely, "the prophetic hope for the end of this age, in which there will be political freedom, moral perfection, and earthly bliss for the people Israel in its own land, and also for the entire human race."[19] A generation later and still more famously, Gershom Scholem undertakes to explain how "the Messianic idea ... became an effective force after its crystalization in historical Judaism";[20] and how

---

Geistesgeschichte motif in the academic study of messianism, see David Biale, *Gershom Scholem: Kabbalah and Counter-History* (2d ed.; Cambridge, Mass.: Harvard University Press, 1982), 35–50.

16. Heinrich Graetz, "Stages in the Evolution of the Messianic Belief," in idem, *The Structure of Jewish History, and Other Essays* (trans. Ismar Schorsch; Moreshet 3; New York, N.Y.: Jewish Theological Seminary, 1975), 152; German original in *Jahrbuch für Israeliten 5625*, vol. 11 (ed. Josef Wertheimer and Leopold Kompert; Vienna: Engel, 1864–1865).

17. Greenstone, *Messiah Idea*, 22–23.

18. Klausner, *Messianic Idea*, 2.

19. Klausner, *Messianic Idea*, 6, 9.

20. Gershom Scholem, "Toward an Understanding of the Messianic Idea in Judaism," in idem, *Messianic Idea*, 1–36 at 2.

"the Messianic idea appears as a living force in the world of Judaism."[21] On Scholem's account, "The magnitude of the Messianic idea corresponds to the endless powerlessness in Jewish history during all the centuries of exile, when it was unprepared to come forward onto the plane of world history."[22]

More recent writers on ancient messianism have criticized the synthesizing tendencies of their nineteenth- and twentieth-century forebears, who of course did not have the benefit of the scores of newly discovered and published texts that we now have.[23] But despite this significant shift in opinion in favor of the diversity of ancient messianism, many of these same recent interpreters perpetuate the older history-of-ideas approach in other respects. James Charlesworth, for instance, has documented thoroughly the diversity of messiah figures in the Second Temple-period pseudepigrapha and the Dead Sea Scrolls;[24] but he nevertheless writes in a *geistesgeschichtlich* vein about how "Jewish messianology exploded into the history of ideas in the early first century B.C.E."[25] And elsewhere how "in the history of western culture no concept has been more crucial than messianism."[26] More polemically, in a 2007 monograph Joseph Fitzmyer sharply criticizes other recent writers on ancient messianism for "failing to respect the history of ideas."[27] For Fitzmyer, the important question about the messiah in ancient texts is "when and how the idea emerged in Jewish history."[28] As he sees it, his bibliographical predecessors offer inadequate readings of the primary texts because they are not sufficiently attuned to the history of ideas. In short, despite the major

---

21. Scholem, "Messianic Idea," 4.

22. Scholem, "Messianic Idea," 35.

23. See Morton Smith, "What Is Implied by the Variety of Messianic Figures?" *JBL* 78 (1959): 66–72; Marinus de Jonge, "The Use of the Word 'Anointed' at the Time of Jesus," *NovT* 8 (1966): 132–48; Jacob Neusner, "Preface," in *Judaisms and Their Messiahs*, ix–xiv; Green, "Messiah in Judaism"; James H. Charlesworth, "From Messianology to Christology: Problems and Prospects," in *The Messiah*, 3–35; Pomykala, *Davidic Dynasty Tradition*, 1–9, 265–71.

24. See James H. Charlesworth, "The Concept of the Messiah in the Pseudepigrapha," *ANRW* II.19.1:188–218; idem, "From Jewish Messianology to Christian Christology," in *Judaisms and Their Messiahs*," 225–64; idem, "From Messianology to Christology"; idem, "Introduction: Messianic Ideas in Early Judaism," in *Qumran Messianism: Studies on the Messianic Expectations in the Dead Sea Scrolls* (ed. James H. Charlesworth et al.; Tübingen: Mohr Siebeck, 1998), 1–8.

25. Charlesworth, "From Messianology to Christology," 35.

26. Charlesworth, "Messianic Ideas in Early Judaism," 1.

27. Fitzmyer, *One Who Is to Come*, viii, ix, 7.

28. Fitzmyer, *One Who Is to Come*, 7, 182.

developments in the last generation of research on ancient messianism, the messianic idea trope is still very much with us.

Even so, recent research has seen increasing discontent with the dominant paradigm, as well as halting steps in creative new directions. A leading figure in this development is Jacob Neusner, who introduced a 1987 collection of state-of-the-art essays in this way:

> People have written books on the messianic doctrine in Judaism, but this is the first book on the Messiah-theme in Judaisms.... What is wrong with the established view is simple. People join together books that do not speak the same language of thought, that refer to distinctive conceptions and doctrines of their own.[29]

Neusner's own distinction between "the messianic doctrine" and "the messiah theme" is arguably imprecise and, to just that extent, unpersuasive, but his criticism of previous research is to the point. For the most part, the modern study of ancient messianism has been organized around an artificial concept, not a corpus of texts, and the result has been a kind of interpretive anarchy.[30] Neusner rightly notes the need for an alternative model, but his principal contribution is the deconstruction of the dominant model, not the articulation of a new one.[31]

More recently, several other scholars have made ad hoc observations that point in the direction of a more excellent way. John Collins has introduced a crucial distinction between messianic expectations as such and the cluster of scriptural texts that provided that language in which such expectations were expressed. He writes:

> Whether we may therefore speak of a "general messianic expectation" is another matter. We do not know how important these traditions were to the populous at large; interest probably fluctuated with historical

---

29. Neusner, "Preface," xii.

30. On this diagnosis, see Green, "Messiah in Judaism."

31. Elsewhere, similarly, Neusner writes:

    We find in the rabbinic canon no such thing as the messianic idea.... Klausner and Scholem provide portraits of a composite that, in fact, never existed in any one book, time, or place, or in the imagination of any one social group, except an imagined "Israel" or a made-up "Judaism." (Jacob Neusner, *Messiah in Context: Israel's History and Destiny in Formative Judaism* [Philadelphia, Pa.: Fortress, 1984], 227)

    On the subsequent influence of Neusner's deconstruction, see Chester, *Messiah and Exaltation*, 276–84.

circumstances. When interest in messianic expectation arose, however, there was at hand a body of tradition which could be used to articulate it.[32]

Peter Schäfer has challenged the conventional premise that it is possible to plot ancient messiah texts as points on an arc running from the early Iron Age to late antiquity. He writes:

> It is tempting to view the various facets of the Messianic expectation as stages of a certain historical development, and I confess that I couldn't resist this temptation completely. However, I should like to re-emphasize that the different Messianic figures cannot be reduced to a uniform underlying pattern; they are to be described adequately only as the dynamic interaction of various and changing configurations within different historical constellations.[33]

John Gager and Loren Stuckenbruck, among others, have questioned the methodological convention of taking only non-Christian Jewish texts as evidence for Jewish messianism in antiquity.[34] Gager writes, "The presence of the term *christos* in a first-century [CE] text, even attached to one put to death by his enemies, does not place that figure outside or even at the periphery of messianic Judaism."[35] Similarly Stuckenbruck: "If we allow for such diversity in both early Christian and Jewish communities, there is no reason to suppose that, beyond the reconciliation of 'Messiah' by Christians to the experiences of Jesus, Jewish and Christian ideas were necessarily very distinct from one another."[36]

The present book picks up where these interpreters leave off. My project is not simply to do what the classic surveys (e.g., Klausner, Mowinckel, Scholem, and, more recently, Collins and Fitzmyer) have done, only a bit more critically or more up-to-date, but rather to ask a different set of questions altogether.

---

32. John J. Collins, "Messiahs in Context: Method in the Study of Messianism in the Dead Sea Scrolls," *Annals of the New York Academy of Sciences* 722 (1994): 213–27 at 222.

33. Peter Schäfer, "Diversity and Interaction: Messiahs in Early Judaism," in *Toward the Millennium*, 15–35 at 35.

34. On this complicated issue, see Chapter 6 in this volume.

35. John G. Gager, "Messiahs and Their Followers," in *Toward the Millennium*, 37–46 at 38.

36. Loren T. Stuckenbruck, "Messianic Ideas in the Apocalyptic and Related Literature of Early Judaism," in *The Messiah in the Old and New Testaments* (ed. Stanley E. Porter; Grand Rapids, Mich.: Eerdmans, 2007), 90–113 at 113n44.

I take it that the two questions that have dominated modern research on the subject—first, where is the phenomenon of messianism attested in antiquity? and second, what are the major types of messiah figures represented in the sources?—are more or less settled.[37] Before the discovery of the Dead Sea Scrolls, scholars of ancient Judaism tended to claim that messianism was widespread in antiquity and that it centered on a single mythical ideal: the future king from the house of David.[38] After the discovery of the Dead Sea Scrolls, a reactionary trend in scholarship argued that, in fact, messianism is attested only very sparsely in antiquity and that, even where we do find it, there is no consistency in the forms it takes.[39] In the past quarter century, several interpreters have suggested that this post-Dead Sea Scrolls reaction was an overreaction, and consequently the discussion of these two classic questions has arrived at, if not a consensus, at least a moderate common ground.[40]

Regarding the first question, as Collins writes, "We cannot be sure just how widespread messianic expectation was. Our sources do not permit us to speak with confidence about the majority of the Jewish people."[41] With this caveat, however, he notes, "The evidence suggests that messianism was virtually dormant from the early fifth to the late second century BCE."[42] Regarding the second question, as Schäfer writes, "The respective traditions range mainly within the triangle (Davidic) Messiah-king, priestly Messiah, and Son of Man."[43] Or, slightly differently, per Collins's summary, "We shall find four basic messianic paradigms (king, priest, prophet, and heavenly messiah), and they were not equally widespread."[44] Of course, it may be that new primary

---

37. As Chester (*Messiah and Exaltation*, 191) rightly notes, one still finds these questions contested in the secondary literature, but not, in my view, in ways that advance the discussion significantly.

38. For example, Drummond, *Jewish Messiah*; Greenstone, *Messiah Idea*; Klausner, *Messianic Idea*; and similarly Emil Schürer, *The History of the Jewish People in the Age of Jesus Christ* (rev. and ed. Geza Vermes et al.; 3 vols.; Edinburgh: T. & T. Clark, 1973–1987 [1st German ed., 1885]), 2:488–554; George Foot Moore, *Judaism in the First Centuries of the Christian Era* (3 vols.; Cambridge, Mass.: Harvard University Press, 1927–1930), 2:323–76.

39. For example, Smith, "What Is Implied"; de Jonge, "Use of the Word 'Anointed'"; Neusner, "Preface"; Green, "Messiah in Judaism"; Charlesworth, "From Messianology to Christology."

40. See Chester, *Messiah and Exaltation*, 191–205, 324–27; Collins, *Scepter*, 1–20.

41. Collins, *Scepter*, 18.

42. Collins, *Scepter*, 50–51.

43. Schäfer, "Diversity and Interaction," 35.

44. Collins, *Scepter*, 18.

sources will come to light and necessitate a serious reevaluation, but for the present these two questions have been answered as satisfactorily as they are likely to be answered.[45]

One might get the impression from the secondary literature that these are the only questions worth asking about the primary sources.[46] In fact, however, they represent only the beginning, not the end, of a historical study of early Jewish and Christian messiah texts. Granted that we can sketch a rough timeline of the production of ancient messiah texts and identify a taxonomy of types of messiahs, we are now in a position to ask a whole range of potentially enlightening interpretive questions, especially questions about the inner logic of each text, why it makes the particular choices it does—questions, that is, about the grammar of messianism.

The Grammar of Messianism

In speaking of the grammar of messianism, I am taking methodological cues from a number of scholars in related subfields. One immediate influence is Nils Dahl, who—in an incisive 1977 lecture—drew attention to the conceptual models presupposed by scholars in their discussions of early Christian Christology.[47] Dahl observes that many mid-twentieth-century writers on early Christology share the curious habit of talking in fluminous terms of "streams" or "tributaries" of tradition that "flow" into christological doctrine,[48] and he raises the sensible question why the metaphor of a river basin holds such sway over this particular scholarly discussion. In fact, Dahl suggests, the metaphor is poorly suited to the subject matter, since it is not the case that early Christology becomes increasingly homogeneous over time or that any particular motif, once combined with others, disappears from the literary record. Dahl, therefore, proposes an alternative conceptual model:

> Several works on the origins of Christology speak about sources and influences in a manner that evokes the image of a complicated

---

45. Knohl, *Messiahs and Resurrection*, has argued that the Hazon Gabriel stone does necessitate such a reevaluation, but in my view this is not the case. See the discussion in Chapter 5 in this volume.

46. A few creative exceptions notwithstanding. Among recent studies, one such exception is Yarbro Collins and Collins, *King and Messiah as Son of God*.

47. Nils A. Dahl, "Sources of Christological Language," in idem, *Jesus the Christ* (ed. Donald H. Juel; Minneapolis, Minn.: Fortress, 1991), 113–36.

48. The most prominent example is Rudolf Bultmann, *Theology of the New Testament* (trans. Kendrick Grobel; 2 vols.; New York, N.Y.: Scribner, 1951–1955).

watershed. . . . It might be wise to exchange this image for the notion of a "language game," to use the term of Wittgenstein. . . . What really matters . . . are the rules of the game. They allow for innumerable moves, so that one game of chess [for example] is never like any other. But if the basic rules are changed, it becomes a different game.[49]

Dahl refers here to the tremendously influential *Philosophical Investigations* of the Cambridge philosopher Ludwig Wittgenstein, which appeared posthumously in 1953.[50] The term "language game" (*Sprachspiel*) encapsulates the later Wittgenstein's theory that human language is best conceived not as a set of symbols corresponding to things in the world, but rather as a set of rules for participation in various kinds of discourse (e.g., giving a command, deliberating about a course of action, telling a joke, reporting an experience, making up a story, and so on). As he famously puts it, "For a large class of cases—though not for all—in which we employ the word 'meaning' it can be defined thus: the meaning of a word is its use in the language."[51] If the meaning of its word is its use, then the implicit rules according to which people communicate in various concrete situations constitute the single most significant factor in determining meaning. Wittgenstein writes:

How many kinds of sentence are there? . . . There are countless kinds: countless different kinds of use of what we call "symbols," "words," "sentences." And this multiplicity is not something fixed, given once for all; but new types of language, new language-games, as we may say, come into existence, and others become obsolete and get forgotten. . . . The term "language-game" is meant to bring into prominence the fact that the speaking of a language is part of an activity, or of a form of life.[52]

Clearly, Dahl's use of the term *language game* is a reappropriation of Wittgenstein's. Whereas the latter is giving an account of the phenomenon of human language as such, the former is simply identifying a conceptual model suitable for describing a particular cluster of ancient texts. In fact,

---

49. Dahl, "Sources of Christological Language," 132–33.

50. The standard German–English diglot edition is Ludwig Wittgenstein, *Philosophical Investigations* (trans. G. E. M. Anscombe; Oxford: Blackwell, 1953).

51. Wittgenstein, *Philosophical Investigations* 1.§43.

52. Wittgenstein, *Philosophical Investigations* 1.§23.

Dahl's invocation of language games is just one moment in the late twentieth-century reception history of Wittgenstein in religious studies circles.[53] At about the same time, but more famously and on a grander scale, Dahl's Yale colleague George Lindbeck appropriated the notion of language games by way of articulating a general theory of the function of doctrines in religions. Lindbeck writes:

> A religion can be viewed as a kind of cultural and/or linguistic framework or medium that shapes the entirety of life and thought. . . . Like a culture or language, it is a communal phenomenon that shapes the subjectivities of individuals rather than being primarily a manifestation of those subjectivities. It comprises a vocabulary of discursive and nondiscursive symbols together with a distinctive logic or grammar in terms of which this vocabulary can be meaningfully employed.[54]

On Lindbeck's model, religions are like languages in that they prescribe a set of rules for communicating successfully within a particular community. Being a practitioner of any given religion means learning and abiding by the grammar of that religion. For example, I can use the phoneme *dog* to mean "an aquatic animal with bones, gills, and scales," but in that case it is clear I am not speaking English. By the same token, I can use the phoneme *Jesus* to mean "a merely human prophet who came after Moses and before Muhammad," but in that case it is clear I am not speaking Christian, as it were. Being a proper English speaker or a proper Christian means consenting to use the relevant terms according to the communal rules.

The discussion of the Lindbeckian and other cultural–linguistic theories of religion proceeds apace;[55] but that larger theoretical discussion lies beyond the purview of this book and my own professional competency. Nevertheless, although I have no stake in the debate whether whole religions are best conceived on an analogy to languages, I do take the view (analogous to Dahl's) that ancient messiah texts comprise a body of evidence very well suited for

---

53. On which, see Fergus Kerr, "The Reception of Wittgenstein's Philosophy by Theologians," in *Religion and Wittgenstein's Legacy* (ed. D. Z. Phillips and Mario von der Ruhr; Surrey: Ashgate, 2005), 253–72; I. U. Dalferth, "Wittgenstein: The Theological Reception," in *Religion and Wittgenstein's Legacy*, 273–302.

54. George Lindbeck, *The Nature of Doctrine: Religion and Theology in a Postliberal Age* (Philadelphia, Pa.: Westminster, 1984), 33.

55. See, for example, Paul Dehart, *The Trial of the Witnesses: The Rise and Decline of Postliberal Theology* (Hoboken, N.J.: Wiley, 2008); John Allan Knight, *Liberal versus Postliberal: The Great Divide in Twentieth-Century Theology* (New York, N.Y.: Oxford University Press, 2013).

cultural–linguistic analysis. Although one might not know it from the modern history of research, what we call messianism is most basically a way of talking about the world, a set of linguistic resources—and, equally important, linguistic constraints—inherited from the Jewish scriptures. Ancient Jewish and Christian texts about "messiahs"—from Second Isaiah to the Talmud Bavli, and at myriad points in between—are participants in one great ancient Mediterranean language game. As different as these texts are from one another in many other respects, they are all involved in negotiating a common set of social realities by using a common set of scriptural source texts to solve a common set of interpretive puzzles (which are themselves generated by the same scriptural source texts). If messianism is a language game, then what I am calling "the grammar of messianism" is the rules of the game: the way messiah language worked for the ancient authors who chose to use it, the discursive possibilities it opened up, as well as the discursive constraints it entailed.

To say ancient discourse about messiahs is a language game is not to say it is frivolous. Indeed, many of the pertinent primary texts reflect very serious circumstances. The first-century BCE *Psalms of Solomon*, for instance, invokes the idea of the messiah by way of earnest protest against both the Hasmonean ruling dynasty in Jerusalem and their Roman successors.[56] The psalmist prays:

> Because of our sins, sinners rose up against us; they attacked us and thrust us out, to whom you did not promise; they took possession by force, and they did not glorify your honorable name. They set up in glory a palace corresponding to their loftiness; they laid waste the throne of David in arrogance leading to change. But you, O God, will overthrow them and will remove their offspring from the earth, when there rises up against them a person that is foreign to our race. . . .. See, O Lord, and raise up for them their king, the son of David [Ἰδέ, κύριε, καὶ ἀνάστησον αὐτοῖς τὸν βασιλέα αὐτῶν υἱὸν Δαυιδ], at the time which you chose, O God, to rule over Israel your servant. . . . He shall be a righteous king, taught by God, over them, and there shall be no injustice in his days

56. On the targets of the psalmist's protest, see George W. E. Nickelsburg, *Jewish Literature between the Bible and the Mishnah* (Philadelphia, Pa.: Fortress, 1981), 195–230; Kenneth Atkinson, *I Cried to the Lord: A Study of the Psalms of Solomon's Historical Background and Social Setting* (JSJSup 84; Leiden: Brill, 2003). Compare Johannes Tromp, "The Sinners and the Lawless in Psalm of Solomon 17," *NovT* 35 (1993): 344–61; and Kenneth Atkinson, "Herod the Great, Sosius, and the Siege of Jerusalem (37 B.C.E.) in *Psalm of Solomon* 17," *NovT* 38 (1996): 313–22.

in their midst, for all shall be holy, and their king the Lord's messiah [βασιλεὺς αὐτῶν χριστὸς κυρίου]. (*Ps. Sol.* 17:5–7, 21, 32)[57]

The psalmist is distressed by the polity of which he finds himself a part, and a messiah from the house of David represents the ideal divine solution to his plight. Likewise serious, but for altogether different reasons, is the messiah language in the Gospel of John. Writing at the turn of the second century CE, the evangelist fears an apparently very real prospect of estrangement from the Jewish community for the crime of taking a certain controversial view of the identity of the messiah: "The Jews agreed that if anyone should confess him [Jesus] as messiah, that person would be put out of the synagogue [ἐὰν τις αὐτὸν ὁμολογήσῃ χριστόν, ἀποσυνάγωγος γένηται]" (John 9:22; cf. 12:42; 16:2).[58] For the Gospel of John, as for the *Psalms of Solomon*, the stakes of this particular language game are very high, indeed.

Having made this caveat, however, we should also note there are some ancient messiah texts in which the language game (in the technical sense) is also a game (in the popular sense). An example is the account in the Bavli of a debate among several rabbinical schools about the name of the messiah:

> What is his [the messiah's] name? The school of R. Shila said: His name is Shiloh, for it is written, *Until Shiloh comes* [Gen 49:10]. The school of R. Yannai said: His name is Yinnon, for it is written, *His name shall endure for ever; e'er the sun was, his name is Yinnon* [Ps 72:17]. The school of R. Haninah maintained: His name is Haninah, as it is written, *Where I will not give you Haninah* [Jer 16:13]. Others say: His name is Menahem ben Hezekiah, for it is written, *For Menahem, who would relieve my soul, is far* [Lam 1:16]. The rabbis said: His name is "the leper scholar," as it is written, *Surely he has borne our griefs and carried our sorrows; yet we regarded him as him a leper, smitten by God and afflicted* [Isa 53:4]. (*b. Sanh.* 98b)[59]

---

57. Trans. mod. from NETS.

58. See the seminal study of J. Louis Martyn, *History and Theology in the Fourth Gospel* (3d ed.; Louisville, Ky.: WJK, 2003 [1st ed., 1968]). Significant objections to Martyn's reconstruction have been raised, for example, by Adele Reinhartz, "The Johannine Community and Its Jewish Neighbors: A Reappraisal," in *What Is John? Readers and Readings of the Fourth Gospel* (ed. Fernando F. Segovia; Atlanta, Ga.: Scholars Press, 1996), 111–38. But a formidable defense of a modified version of Martyn's thesis is provided by Joel Marcus, "Birkat Ha-Minim Revisited," *NTS* 55 (2009): 523–51.

59. Trans. mod. from Soncino.

The latter part of the dialogue relates two unprovenanced proposals for the name of the messiah: Menahem ben Hezekiah (from מנחם, "comforter," in Lam 1:16) and "the leper scholar" (from נגוע, the "leper," of Isa 53:4). In the first part of the dialogue, however, in which proposals are offered by three rabbinical schools in turn, each proposal is actually a midrashic argument that the name of the messiah corresponds to the name of the teacher of that particular school: Shiloh for the school of R. Shila, Yinnon for the school of R. Yannai, and, closest of all, Haninah for the school of R. Haninah. These proposals are doubly clever, because they have to work both as midrashim on scripture and also as puns on the respective teachers' names. In this case, the language game of messiah discourse is also a *jeu de mots*.[60]

Another playful example of ancient messiah language is an exegetical riddle attributed to Jesus in the Synoptic tradition (Mark 12:35–37; Matt 22:41–46; Luke 20:41–44).[61] The three versions of the riddle differ slightly, but the oldest version reads as follows:

> As Jesus taught in the temple, he said, "How can the scribes say that the messiah is the son of David? David himself, inspired by the Holy Spirit, said, *The Lord said to my lord: Sit at my right hand until I put your enemies under your feet.* [Ps 110:1]. David himself calls him lord; so how is he his son [αὐτὸς Δαυὶδ λέγει αὐτὸν κύριον, καὶ πόθεν αὐτοῦ ἐστιν υἱός]?" And the great throng heard him with pleasure. (Mark 12:35–37)

In its wider Markan literary context, this saying has a genuine theological point—namely, that Jesus himself is the messiah son of God (cf. Mark 1:1; 3:11; 5:7; 9:7; 14:61–62; 15:39).[62] But the logion itself is a riddle, a question that identifies and exploits a contradiction in the biblical text in order to confound its hearers. The Markan narrative frame even preserves something of the genre of the saying, commenting after the punch line that "the crowd heard him with pleasure [ἡδέως]" (Mark 12:37). Here, as in the previous example, the postbiblical messiah text makes an actual word game of the biblical source text. Some ancient messiah texts are playful, others gravely serious, but they are all participants in a common language game.

---

60. On this passage, see further Klausner, *Messianic Idea*, 463–65.

61. On this passage, see in particular Joel Marcus, *The Way of the Lord: Christological Exegesis of the Old Testament in the Gospel of Mark* (London: T. & T. Clark, 2004 [1st ed., 1992]), 130–52.

62. See W. R. Telford, *The Theology of the Gospel of Mark* (Cambridge: Cambridge University Press, 1999), 30–54.

Viewed from this angle, ancient messiah texts constitute one example—an excellent example—of the vast, sprawling ancient Jewish and Christian project of scriptural interpretation. As the last generation of scholarship, especially, has shown, in antiquity, virtually all Jewish discourse—and, *mutatis mutandis*, Christian discourse—consisted of scriptural interpretation of one kind or another. To speak about anything significant was to speak in the language of scripture.[63] As James Kugel writes, for Persian- and Hellenistic-period Jews, "the past was everywhere. It was what explained the present, and was the standard by which the present was to be judged and upon which future hopes were to be based; and it was legitimacy."[64] For these ancient interpreters, "the past was not approached in the spirit of antiquarianism but for what message it might yield, and this is necessarily predicated on an interpretive stance, indeed, a willingness to deviate from the texts' plain sense."[65] Again, as Donald Juel puts it:

> By the first century, biblical interpretation had become an essential feature of Jewish intellectual life. . . . [Interpreters] had developed an elaborate hermeneutical mechanism with which to make sense of sacred texts, to fit them into a harmonious whole, and to apply them to the realities of life in the Greco-Roman world. . . . Exegesis had become a primary mode of intellectual discourse.[66]

Or again, as Shaye Cohen writes:

> All Jews knew at least something of the Tanak, especially the Torah. The educated knew it by heart, studied it closely, cited it liberally in their

---

63. I say "scripture" as opposed to "Bible" to signify a phenomenon that was current long before the late ancient advent of canons and pandect codices. On this point, see Robert A. Kraft, "Para-mania: Beside, Before, and Beyond Bible Studies," *JBL* 126 (2007): 5–27; and Eva Mroczek, "The Hegemony of the Biblical in the Study of Second Temple Literature," *JAJ* 6 (2015): 2–35. On the phenomenon in general, see Geza Vermes, *Scripture and Tradition in Judaism* (2d ed.; Leiden: Brill 1973 [1st ed., 1961]); Michael Fishbane, *Biblical Interpretation in Ancient Israel* (Oxford: Clarendon, 1985); Marc Hirshman, *A Rivalry of Genius: Jewish and Christian Biblical Interpretation in Late Antiquity* (trans. Batya Stein; Albany, N.Y.: SUNY Press, 1996); and the recent state-of-the-art collection edited by Matthias Henze, *A Companion to Biblical Interpretation in Early Judaism* (Grand Rapids, Mich.: Eerdmans, 2012).

64. James L. Kugel, "Early Interpretation: The Common Background of Later Forms of Biblical Exegesis," in idem and Rowan A. Greer, *Early Biblical Interpretation* (Philadelphia, Pa.: Westminster, 1986), 9–106 at 36.

65. Kugel, "Early Interpretation," 38.

66. Donald H. Juel, *Messianic Exegesis: Christological Interpretation of the Old Testament in Early Christianity* (Philadelphia, Pa.: Fortress, 1988), 32.

conversations, drew inspiration from it in their writings, and labored long and hard to establish its correct text and to clarify its numerous obscurities.[67]

This is true not only of Jews in the homeland who encountered the scriptures in the ancestral language, but also of their hellenophone countrymen in the Mediterranean diaspora.[68] As Tessa Rajak has pointed out:

> [In the diaspora,] a language for self-expression was forged by the Greek Bible. The translators devised a vocabulary and with it a range of concepts that could not, in the nature of things, represent exactly their Hebrew prototypes.... It is often when we explore that basic level of individual lexical units that we are struck by the pervasive influence of the Greek Bible on its communities of Jewish users.[69]

And again, "The mental furniture of literate Jews was biblical when they expressed themselves in Greek at moments of crisis and drama."[70] In sum, the scriptures, whether in Hebrew or in Greek, functioned not only as a holy book but also as a mode of expression for literate Jews throughout the ancient world.[71]

This is the historical context within which ancient messiah texts become intelligible. They represent so many creative reappropriations of an archaic scriptural idiom to talk about matters of contemporary concern to their latter-day authors and audiences. As Martin Karrer has pointed out, in Judaism of the Hellenistic and Roman periods, the actual performance of ritual anointing was associated primarily not with persons (and, in any case, certainly not with kings) but with sacred artifacts, especially the altar and related cultic

---

67. Shaye J. D. Cohen, *From the Maccabees to the Mishnah* (2d ed.; Louisville, Ky.: WJK, 2006), 193.

68. See John M. G. Barclay, *Jews in the Mediterranean Diaspora* (Edinburgh: T. & T. Clark, 1996), 399–444, especially 424–26.

69. Tessa Rajak, *Translation and Survival: The Greek Bible of the Ancient Jewish Diaspora* (Oxford: Oxford University Press, 2009), 225.

70. Rajak, *Translation and Survival*, 230.

71. For an illuminating modern analogy, see Robert Alter, *Canon and Creativity: Modern Writing and the Authority of Scripture* (New Haven, Conn.: Yale University Press, 2000).

paraphernalia in the Jerusalem temple.[72] Despite this fact, however, almost without exception Hellenistic- and Roman-period Jewish texts use the language of anointing in a manner that reflects the archaic Israelite practice, not the contemporary one.[73] It is deliberately antiquarian usage; that is precisely the point. To borrow Kugel's idiom, ancient messiah texts interpret, order, and legitimate the present by using the language of the past, which is to say, the scriptures.

To speak of the grammar of messianism is not to turn back the clock on recent, salutary developments in the social history of ancient messianism. Since the 1980s, well-placed discontent with the long-dominant *Geistesgeschichte* approach has yielded efforts to describe ancient messianism as a social phenomenon among the nonliterate Jewish majority. A groundbreaking study in this regard is the 1985 monograph of Richard Horsley and John Hanson, who complain: "As a field whose principal purpose has been to interpret sacred literature, [biblical studies] has generally focused almost exclusively on literature, with corresponding attention to the ruling elites and other literate groups that produced or appeared in the literary records."[74] In contrast, Horsley and Hanson's approach to messianism is "to analyze and present some of the movements and leaders among the common people in the late second temple period."[75] More recently, John Gager has likewise argued that ancient messianism is best understood from the perspective of social history:

> There is little need to trace new furrows in the well-plowed field of semantic studies; the terms *maschiach* and *christos* have received more than their fair share of scholarly attention. . . . Many of these semantic studies have limited themselves to literary manifestations of messianic titles and thus fall prey to the abstractness and rigidity that beset all forms of the history of ideas. . . . Few studies have bothered to look at what constitutes 99% of all messianic movements—whether in first-century Palestine or anywhere else—the followers of the movement.[76]

---

72. Martin Karrer, *Der Gesalbte: Die Grundlagen des Christustitels* (FRLANT 151; Göttingen: Vandenhoeck & Ruprecht, 1990), 95–213.

73. *Pace* Karrer, *Gesalbte*, 214–67.

74. Richard A. Horsley and John S. Hanson, *Bandits, Prophets, and Messiahs: Popular Movements at the Time of Jesus* (Minneapolis, Minn.: Winston, 1985), xiii.

75. Horsley and Hanson, *Bandits, Prophets, and Messiahs*, xiii.

76. Gager, "Messiahs and Their Followers," 37.

Gager's point is well taken, and this development in research is all for the good. There is, however, one obstinate problem having to do with the possibility of epistemic access—to wit: What evidence do we modern historians have for the messianism of the ancient ninety-nine percent? Granted, most ancient messianic movements will have consisted largely of nonliterate low-status people, but with a very few exceptions there simply are no extant sources for messianism as experienced by these people.[77] On the other hand, we do have a respectable corpus of primary texts attesting ancient messianism, but these texts only directly reflect the ideologies of their elite authors, not of the non-literate majority. How, then, to proceed? One sophisticated solution to this problem is that of William Horbury, who isolates strands in the literary record that might plausibly be taken to reflect ancient popular piety—for instance, folklore traditions such as Tobit, synagogue liturgies such as the Amidah, and widely adopted scripture translations like the Septuagint and Targumim.[78] But even with a suitably refined methodology, there remain serious questions about how close these sources can take us to the piety of the ancient Jewish laity, as Horbury's critics have rightly pointed out.[79]

Research into the social history of ancient messianism can and should go on, but it awaits a methodological innovation (or, better still, an archeological discovery) that can put it on a surer footing.[80] My point in this book is that there is a way of handling the pertinent literary texts that does not, to borrow Gager's phrase, "fall prey to the abstractness and rigidity that beset all forms of the history of ideas."[81] In other words, if one response to the failures of the

---

77. Horsley and Hanson acknowledge this problem but remain methodologically optimistic: "We moderns have almost no access to what the peasants were doing and thinking. . . . [But] they did gather together in certain types of groups and movements, as we know from the Jewish historian Josephus, the Christian gospel tradition, and other fragmentary reports" (*Bandits, Prophets, and Messiahs*, xiii).

78. For example, regarding the LXX: "Not long after Alexander the Great, messianism was sufficiently prominent in communal Jewish understanding of the scriptures to find its place in interpretation of the Pentateuch, the 'book of Moses' which was central and universally revered in the Jewish community" (Horbury, *Jewish Messianism and the Cult of Christ*, 47).

79. See, for example, Judith Lieu, review of Horbury, *Jewish Messianism and the Cult of Christ*, in *JTS* n.s. 50 (1999): 673: "We need to know how far what we are seeing is a literary, exegetical, conceivably scribal, exercise, or, on the other hand, how far it is the literary deposit of considerable currents of popular expectation: how do these texts relate to the wider society?"

80. Yigael Yadin's excavations at Masada and at the Bar Kokhba caves (ca. 1960–1965) are extremely important in this respect, although in both cases there are difficulties interpreting the material remains alongside the corresponding literary texts. For a basic overview, see Yigael Yadin, *Bar Kokhba: The Rediscovery of the Legendary Hero of the Second Jewish Revolt against Rome* (New York, N.Y.: Random House, 1971).

81. Gager, "Messiahs and Their Followers," 37.

traditional *Geistesgeschichte* approach is to abandon literary texts in favor of material history, then another response is to demonstrate a more satisfactory reading strategy for the pertinent literary texts.[82] This is what I propose to do here. What follows is a demonstration of an alternate, better way of conceiving what it is that ancient messiah texts do. My title, *The Grammar of Messianism*, is not a promise of a survey of terrain, but rather a thesis statement with a suppressed verb. That is to say, my goal in this book is not to map exhaustively the rules of ancient messiah discourse (to do so would be painfully tedious, even if it were possible), but to show that the relevant primary texts do amount to such a discourse, that messianism is effectively a grammar. To this end, each chapter of the book takes up a classic problem in the modern study of ancient messianism—for example, the messianic vacuum hypothesis, the quest for the first messiah, and the Jewish messiah–Christian messiah distinction, among others—and shows how the problem dissolves when viewed from the revisionist angle advocated here. The book thus takes the form of a proof, by means of a series of related studies, that in antiquity the messiah was not an article of faith but a manner of speaking.

An Idiom and Its Users

I have already broached the not uncontroversial subject of the range of primary texts that are allowed to count as evidence for messianism. In my view, a proper study of messiah language in antiquity ought to account for all the texts that use the pertinent language, and these, significantly, include both Jewish and Christian texts.[83] These two corpora, however, have often not been read together in this connection, because the prevailing view has been that early Christian texts redefine "messiah" to mean just "Jesus" and so effectively recuse themselves from ancient Jewish discourse about messiah figures.[84] In

---

82. Thus rightly Wayne A. Meeks, review of Horbury, *Messianism among Jews and Christians*, in *JQR* 95 (2005): 336–40, following Nils A. Dahl, "Eschatology and History in Light of the Qumran Texts," in idem, *Jesus the Christ*, 49–64.

83. On this point, see Annette Yoshiko Reed, "Messianism between Judaism and Christianity," in *Rethinking the Messianic Idea in Judaism* (ed. Michael L. Morgan and Steven Weitzman; Bloomington, Ind.: Indiana University Press, 2014), 23–62.

84. See, for example, Nils A. Dahl, "The Messiahship of Jesus in Paul," in idem, *Jesus the Christ*, 15–25 at 17: "The name 'Christ' does not receive its content through a previously fixed conception of messiahship but rather from the person and work of Jesus Christ. An *interpretatio christiana* is carried out completely." Similarly Klausner, *Messianic Idea*, 519–31; George MacRae, "Messiah and Gospel," in *Judaisms and Their Messiahs*, 169–85; Charlesworth, "From Jewish Messianology to Christian Christology"; idem, "From Messianology to Christology"; Lenowitz, *Jewish Messiahs*, 32–47; Fitzmyer, *One Who Is to Come*, 182–83.

Chapter 6, I advance a full-fledged argument against this Jewish messiah–
Christian messiah distinction, but for now it is enough to give a more general
indication of my approach to the issue.

It has often been noted that much modern scholarship on ancient messianism, being preoccupied consciously or unconsciously with explaining
the origins of Christianity, has failed to give sufficient attention to Jewish
messiah texts in their own right or for their own sake.[85] This indictment is
probably accurate, and the situation it describes is probably explicable in
terms of the social history of the discipline of biblical studies in European
and North American universities.[86] Happily, the decades since World War
II have witnessed the flourishing of the discipline of Jewish studies, as a
result of which we now have many valuable studies of ancient messianism
that are not influenced disproportionately by the concerns of Christian theology. Meanwhile, the admonition to give attention to ancient Jewish messiah texts in their own right, as appropriate as it undoubtedly is, has had
one unfortunate side effect in the secondary literature—namely, the artificial
quarantining of Jewish evidence from Christian evidence. What we need is
an approach that is not blinkered by the single-minded quest for the origins
of Christianity but that can nevertheless accommodate pertinent ancient
Christian texts as well as Jewish ones.

Such an approach has been pioneered, for instance, by Geza Vermes, who
calls for a "Schürer-type religious history of the Jews from the Maccabees to
AD 500 that fully incorporates the New Testament data . . . a reliable guide to
the diverse streams of post-biblical Judaism in all their manifestations and

---

85. See, for example, Klausner, *Messianic Idea*, 3: "Thus do all Christian theologians. And no
wonder; for they investigate the Messianic idea of the Jews not as a scientific end in itself, but
as a means of becoming acquainted with the Messianic ideas which prevailed in the time of
the rise of Christianity"; Green, "Messiah in Judaism," 4:

> One may wonder . . . how so much has come to be written about an allegedly
> Jewish conception in which so many ancient Jews manifest such little interest.
> The primacy of "the messiah" as a subject of academic study derives not from
> ancient Jewish preoccupation, but from early Christian word-choice, theology, and
> apologetics.

Such complaints lie behind the apt insistence of Chester, *Messiah and Exaltation*, 192: "I
would want to stress again . . . that the Jewish evidence (as also Jewish belief and practice
more generally) are intrinsically important in their own right, and should very much not just
be seen as a backdrop to the New Testament."

86. See Michael C. Legaspi, *The Death of Scripture and the Rise of Biblical Studies*
(New York, N.Y.: Oxford University Press, 2010); Stephen Moore and Yvonne Sherwood,
The Invention of the Biblical Scholar: A Critical Manifesto (Minneapolis, Minn.: Fortress,
2011).

reciprocal influences."[87] Similarly, with particular reference to messianism, Alan Segal has suggested:

> The New Testament is ... much better evidence for the history of Judaism than is rabbinic Judaism for the origins of Christianity. This is precisely the converse of standard methodology. Instead of producing scholarly documents like Strack-Billerbeck ... we should be writing a commentary on the Mishnah which includes Christian and other first-century sectarian evidence.[88]

In other words, we ought to think of ancient Christianity as a chapter in the history of ancient Judaism rather than think of ancient Judaism as the antecedent of ancient Christianity. Note that this alternative model, like the crypto-Christian model to which it is a response, implies that the history and literature of ancient Judaism and ancient Christianity are deeply interrelated. The way forward is not to deny this interrelation in the interest of "interpreting the Jewish texts in their own right," but rather to describe it in a more accurate way.

In this connection, recent research has seen no little discussion—both for and against—of the notion of an ancient "parting of the ways" between Judaism and Christianity.[89] The term is a recent coinage, but the idea for which it is a shorthand has a long history. James Dunn, perhaps the most formidable recent proponent of an early second-century parting of the ways, rightly points to the nineteenth-century precedent of F. C. Baur and J. B. Lightfoot, who, for all their considerable disagreements, both speak in terms of the emergence of Christianity from Judaism around the time of Ignatius of Antioch.[90] There is, however, significant second-, third-, and even fourth-century evidence of close interaction, both friendly and hostile, between Jews and Christians around the

87. Geza Vermes, "Jewish Literature and New Testament Exegesis: Reflections on Method," in idem, *Jesus and the World of Judaism* (London: SCM, 1983), 88.

88. Alan F. Segal, "Conversion and Messianism: An Outline for a New Approach," in *The Messiah*, 296–340 at 299.

89. On the "for" side, see in particular James D. G. Dunn, *The Partings of the Ways: Between Judaism and Christianity and Their Significance for the Character of Christianity* (London: SCM, 2006 [1st ed., 1991]); idem, ed., *Jews and Christians: The Parting of the Ways, A.D. 70 to 135* (Grand Rapids, Mich.: Eerdmans, 1999 [1st ed., 1992]).

90. See F. C. Baur, *Paul the Apostle of Jesus Christ* (2 vols.; London: Williams & Norgate, 1873–1875 [German original, 1845]); J. B. Lightfoot, *Saint Paul's Epistle to the Galatians* (London: Macmillan, 1865).

Mediterranean, and scholars such as Robert Kraft, Judith Lieu, Daniel Boyarin, Annette Reed, and Adam Becker have recommended scuttling the "parting of the ways" rubric altogether.[91] Reed and Becker write in a programmatic essay, "We wish to call attention to the ample evidence that speaks against the notion of a single and simple 'Parting of the Ways' in the first or second century CE and, most importantly, against the assumption that no meaningful convergence ever occurred thereafter."[92]

It is the case that rabbinic and patristic orthodoxies established themselves over the course of the first four centuries CE, and it is the case that this late ancient process had certain discernible roots in the first century CE. But the creation of Judaism and Christianity as discrete religions was a centuries-long discursive exercise, and the subject matter of this book (namely, ancient messiah texts) was part of the warp and woof of that exercise, so that to quarantine the Jewish and Christian texts from one another would be to miss the historical context altogether.[93] A few recent interpreters, Segal among them, have offered new analyses of messianism from this alternative perspective.[94] Gerbern Oegema, for instance, adduces all messiah texts, both Jewish and Christian, from the Maccabees (160s BCE) to Bar Kokhba (130s CE) by way of arguing for an analogy between messiah myths and the political circumstances of their respective authors.[95] William Horbury, although concerned partly with explaining the origins of the Christ cult, also takes both Jewish and Christian messiah texts as evidence for the more general phenomenon of messianism in antiquity.[96] As will become clear, I have some not insignificant disagreements with these scholars regarding their particular conclusions, but I think their methodological outlook on the whole range of relevant primary texts is profoundly correct, and I intend this book as a contribution to the very productive research project begun by them.

---

91. See in particular Adam H. Becker and Annette Yoshiko Reed, eds., *The Ways That Never Parted* (TSAJ 95; Tübingen: Mohr Siebeck, 2003); Daniel Boyarin, *Border Lines: The Partition of Judaeo-Christianity* (Philadelphia, Pa.: University of Pennsylvania Press, 2004).

92. Annette Yoshiko Reed and Adam H. Becker, "Introduction," in *Ways That Never Parted*, 22.

93. On the interaction between the two developing religious traditions, compare the recent proposals of Daniel Boyarin, *Jewish Gospels*, and Peter Schäfer, *The Jewish Jesus: How Judaism and Christianity Shaped Each Other* (Princeton, N.J.: Princeton University Press, 2012).

94. Segal, "Conversion and Messianism."

95. Oegema, *Anointed and His People*.

96. Horbury, *Jewish Messianism and the Cult of Christ*; idem, *Messianism among Jews and Christians*.

The time frame of this study is antiquity, broadly understood. I consider texts spanning roughly a millennium from the Judahite exile in the sixth century BCE to the redaction of the Talmud Bavli in the sixth century CE. The medieval and modern Jewish and Christians traditions carried on using messiah language, of course;[97] but the end of the classical rabbinic and patristic periods forms a natural endpoint for our purposes. This is, of course, a long period of time, and it subsumes a large number of primary texts, but as a heuristic it suits the subject matter. At the one end, before the composition of the texts that comprise the Hebrew Bible, there simply was no discourse about "messiahs" in ancient literature;[98] and at the other end, after late antiquity, there was no longer the production of the kind of formative Jewish and Christian literature that there had been during the days of the rabbis and church fathers.[99] For the millennium between, say, Second Isaiah and *Sefer Zerubbabel*, however, it is possible to identify, both within and between Jewish and Christian scribal circles, an ongoing, often spirited project of scriptural interpretation surrounding the ancient Israelite trope of an anointed ruler.

Of course, a number of historical events along the way—the building of the Second Temple, the accession of the Hasmoneans, the execution of Jesus of Nazareth, the destruction of the Second Temple, the Bar Kokhba revolt, and the accession of Constantine, to name some of the most important—marked this discourse in decisive ways.[100] Contrary to the *Geistesgeschichte* model, however, none of these events entailed the supersession of one form of the messianic idea by another. On the contrary, what the primary texts actually suggest is the resilience of literary features of messiah texts from one epoch to subsequent ones. Granted, a certain feature (e.g., a gentile messiah or a suffering messiah) may only come about in the first place because of a certain historical development (e.g., the decree of Cyrus or the crucifixion of Jesus), but ever after that feature remains part of the trove of discursive resources on which the exegetical project draws.[101] But—this is the main point—the whole thing

97. On medieval and modern messiah texts, see Klausner, *Messianic Idea*; Wim Beuken et al., eds., *Messianism through History* (London: SCM, 1993); Idel, *Messianic Mystics*; Lenowitz, *Jewish Messiahs*; Schäfer and Cohen, eds., *Toward the Millennium*; Morgan and Weitzman, eds., *Rethinking the Messianic Idea*.

98. See Franz Hesse, "χρίω κτλ.," *TDNT* 9:493–509; Sigmund Mowinckel, *He That Cometh: The Messiah Concept in the Old Testament and Later Judaism* (Grand Rapids, Mich.: Eerdmans, 2005 [1st ed., 1956]), 23–56; and Chapter 2 in this volume.

99. See Peter Brown, *The World of Late Antiquity* (London: Thames and Hudson, 1971); Boyarin, *Border Lines*.

100. Thus rightly Oegema, *Anointed and His People*.

101. Thus rightly Schäfer, "Diversity and Interaction."

is an exegetical project, a centuries-long discussion within and between the two religious communities about their common scriptures, their overlapping polities, and what the former has to do with the latter.

Where to Begin

It is standard procedure in modern treatments of ancient messianism to begin by establishing a working definition of *messiah* and then to use that definition as a rubric for classifying ancient texts as either properly messianic or not. Definitions of *messiah* vary from one scholar to the next. For Joseph Klausner, *messiah* means "a strong Redeemer [who], by his power and his spirit, will bring complete redemption, political and spiritual, to the people Israel, and along with this, earthly bliss and moral perfection to the entire human race."[102] For H. L. Ginsberg, "a charismatically endowed descendant of David who the Jews of the Roman period believed would be raised up by God to break the yoke of the heathen and to reign over a restored kingdom of Israel to which all the Jews of the exile would return."[103] For Sigmund Mowinckel, succinctly, "an eschatological figure. He belongs 'to the last time'; his advent lies in the future."[104] For Marinus de Jonge, *messiah* "denotes the special relationship to God of various figures which are expected in God's future."[105] R. J. Zwi Werblowsky defines *messiah* in a broad sense as "a person with a special mission from God" and in a technical sense as "the expected king of the Davidic line who would deliver Israel from foreign bondage and restore the glories of its golden age."[106] Jacob Neusner writes programmatically, "A Messiah in a Judaism is a man who at the end of history, at the eschaton, will bring salvation to the Israel conceived by the social group addressed by the way of life and world view of that Judaism."[107] William Scott Green appeals to the popular definition: "Israel's eschatological redeemer."[108] For James Charlesworth, *messiah* means "God's eschatological Anointed One."[109] For J. J. M. Roberts, more

---

102. Klausner, *Messianic Idea*, 9.

103. H. L. Ginsberg, "Messiah," *EncJud* (New York, N.Y.: Macmillan, 1971–1972), 11:1407.

104. Mowinckel, *He That Cometh*, 3.

105. De Jonge, "Use of the Word 'Anointed,'" 147.

106. Werblowsky, "Jewish Messianism in Comparative Perspective," 1.

107. Neusner, "Preface," ix.

108. Green, "Messiah in Judaism," 1.

109. Charlesworth, "From Messianology to Christology," 4.

specifically, "an expected figure of the future whose coming will coincide with the inauguration of an era of salvation."[110] Similarly, for Shemaryahu Talmon, "a unique superterrestrial savior who will arise in an indeterminably distant future."[111] For Gerbern Oegema, "a priestly or royal figure, or one that can be characterized otherwise, who will play a liberating role at the end of time."[112] For John Gager, "a human or human-like figure who, in the final days of history, would restore the fortunes of Israel to the imagined conditions of Israel's ideal past."[113] William Horbury's definition specifies "a coming pre-eminent ruler—coming, whether at the end, as strictly implied by the word 'eschatology,' or simply at some time in the future."[114] Andrew Chester's, "a figure who acts as the agent of the final divine deliverance, whether or not he is specifically designated as 'messiah' or 'anointed.' "[115] John Collins defines *messiah* as "an eschatological figure who sometimes, but not necessarily always, is designated as a משיח in the ancient sources."[116] And Joseph Fitzmyer, responding to Collins's definition, "an awaited or future anointed agent of God."[117] This is just a sample; further examples of definitions of *messiah* by modern historians and exegetes might be multiplied many times over. Chester exaggerates only slightly when he writes, "It can easily appear that there are as many different definitions of messianism as there are those who write about it."[118]

Not all of these scholars presume to establish their respective definitions as governing criteria for classifying ancient messiah texts. Some simply report on conventional usage.[119] Others reject any definition of *messiah* that does not accommodate all and only ancient instances of the lexeme.[120] Also, none of these modern definitions is entirely arbitrary, because each one is based on its author's awareness of certain features of the primary texts. These caveats

---

110. J. J. M. Roberts, "The Old Testament's Contribution to Messianic Expectations," in *The Messiah*, 39–51 at 39.

111. Talmon, "Concept of *Masiah*," 82.

112. Oegema, *Anointed and His People*, 26.

113. Gager, "Messiahs and Their Followers," 38.

114. Horbury, *Jewish Messianism and the Cult of Christ*, 7.

115. Chester, *Messiah and Exaltation*, 201.

116. Collins, *Scepter*, 17–18.

117. Fitzmyer, *One Who Is to Come*, 4.

118. Chester, *Messiah and Exaltation*, 193.

119. For example, Green, "Messiah in Judaism."

120. For example, de Jonge, "Use of the Word 'Anointed.' "

aside, however, it is the case that the prevailing approach in modern research has been to establish a definition for *messiah* and then to sift through the ancient texts judging each one either a match or a mismatch for the definition stipulated. As one might expect, some scholars find more matches than mismatches, while other scholars find vice versa, and for any particular ancient text there are some scholars who call it messianic and others who call it not so. Such disputes, however, are not actually about the ancient texts. They are about the modern definitions, which enjoy a kind of functional immunity from criticism. The logic of this approach is such that each author's findings are more or less true by definition, but also—to just that extent—more or less trivial. Once one defines a term to one's satisfaction, it is a easy enough to sift through a body of data, sorting items into "in" and "out" columns. The really interesting question, of course, is whether the definition proposed actually illuminates the evidence.

In the case of ancient messiah texts, most of the definitions on offer do not illuminate the evidence very well. Or, more generously, they illuminate a particular subset of the evidence reasonably well. Nevertheless, the prevailing definition-first approach has frequently resulted in the bizarre spectacle wherein a modern interpreter claims that a figure called *messiah* in an ancient text is actually not a messiah *sensu stricto*,[121] while another ancient character is indeed a messiah despite never being so called in the primary sources.[122] The reason for this spectacle is clear enough. It comes about because scholars are keen to identify the origins of the concept "eschatological redeemer" (or equivalent), and because of the weight of tradition they insist on using the word *messiah* for this concept.[123] The glaring problem with doing so is that *messiah* is an ancient word with its own ancient range of meaning, so to assign it a definition as a modern technical term is, *ipso facto*, to obscure its meaning in any given ancient text.[124] Modern scholarship has been so preoccupied with

---

121. Frequently cited examples include Cyrus of Persia in Isa 45:1, the anonymous "anointed one" in Dan 9:26 (probably Onias III), and Shimon bar Kosiba in *y. Taʿan.* 4:8 (68d); *Lam. Rab.* 2:2 §4.

122. Frequently cited examples include the white bull in the *Animal Apocalypse* (1 En. 90.37), the Interpreter of the Law in the Damascus Document (CD 7:18) and 4QFlorilegium (4Q174 1:11–12), and the man from heaven in *Sib. Or.* 5:414.

123. See Green, "Messiah in Judaism"; Fitzmyer, *One Who Is to Come*, 1–7, 182–83.

124. Thus rightly Helmer Ringgren, "Mowinckel and the Uppsala School," *SJOT* 2 (1988): 39, on the dispute between Ivan Engnell, *Studies in Divine Kingship in the Ancient Near East* (Uppsala: Almqvist & Wiksell, 1943) and Mowinckel, *He That Cometh*:

> [Mowinckel] defines the Messiah in eschatological terms, while Engnell understood messianism as "elaborate kingship ideology." In a way it may be said that

the quest for the origins of the eschatological redeemer myth that we some-times seem to have lost the capacity simply to interpret ancient messiah texts in their own right.

This felt compulsion to classify ancient texts as either "properly mes-sianic" or not often leads, understandably, to a kind of taxonomic anxiety. Charlesworth, for instance, worries, "How can we be convinced that we have translated משׁיח or χριστός correctly as 'the Messiah,' rather than as 'a messiah,' or 'the Anointed One,' rather than 'an anointed one?'"[125] How, indeed? The reader will note the contrasts between the uses of the definite article ("the") and indefinite article ("a"), capital initial letter ("Messiah") and lowercase ini-tial letter ("messiah"), transliteration ("messiah") and translation ("anointed one"). These are so many ways of representing the self-same academic dis-tinction between "properly messianic" and not. It is telling, however, that the primary sources themselves make none of these distinctions. Neither capital-ization of initial letters nor the choice to transliterate rather than translate is a feature of ancient messiah texts. The definite article is a feature of some such texts (in languages that have a definite article), but it does not carry the signifi-cance in those texts that it does in Charlesworth's usage here. This taxonomic anxiety, then, is misplaced. It is a manufactured problem.

In a departure from the prevailing approach, I opt not to begin this book by assigning a definition to *messiah* or *messianism*.[126] Because my goal is to describe the grammar of messiah language, I count as evidence any and all uses of such language.[127] By "messiah language," I simply mean

---

Engnell uses the term in accordance with the Old Testament itself, for there "the anointed one" always refers to the actual king of Israel.

125. Charlesworth, "From Messianology to Christology," 10.

126. *Pace* R. J. Zwi Werblowsky, "Messianism in Jewish History," in *Essential Papers on Messianic Movements and Personalities in Jewish History* (ed. Marc Saperstein; New York, N.Y.: NYU Press, 1992 [orig. pub., 1968]), 35–52 at 35: "The least that can reasonably be asked of a writer on messianic ideas and messianic movements in Jewish history is to pro-vide an adequate definition of the term 'messianism.'" For as Werblowsky himself rightly complains, "The term . . . seems to mean all things to all men—or at least, to all theologians" (Werblowsky, "Messianism in Jewish History," 35).

127. See Morton Smith, "Historical Method in the Study of Religion," in idem, *Studies in the Cult of Yahweh* (2 vols.; ed. Shaye J. D. Cohen; Leiden: Brill, 1996), 1:3:

Nothing is more wearisome than to have some philosopher invent his own mean-ing for the word religion and then go through history, either distinguishing "true religion," which fits his definition, from "religion falsely so called," which does not, or, even worse, trying to force all religion whatever into his own mold. By contrast with this philosophical procedure, the normal philological—and that is, historical—way of finding out what a word means is to determine what it has been used to mean and then describe the range and distribution of its uses.

discourse that uses the Hebrew word משׁיח (transliterated "messiah," translated "anointed one") and its translation equivalencies (Aramaic משׁיחא, Greek
μεσσίας and χριστός, Latin christus and unctus, and so on). As John Collins
has rightly noted, this does not entail examining only those sentences that
use the pertinent words; many figures called *messiah* go by other names, as
well, in their respective texts, and these wider literary contexts are relevant to
the study of messiah language per se.[128] It does, however, entail examining
only those texts that use the pertinent words. For the purposes of this book,
I am methodologically uninterested in eschatological redeemers in general.
Eschatological redeemers are fascinating, to be sure, and we encounter some
of them in what follows, but they have received their fair share of scholarly
attention. My goal, in contrast, is to seek to understand the discursive possibilities and constraints that presented themselves to ancient Jews and
Christians who chose to write about "messiahs." If this is the goal, then the
only hope of success is to refuse steadfastly to assign *messiah* a definition in
advance.[129]

At just this point, a potential objection looms. One important strand of
recent research has challenged the premise that *messiah* is an analyzable category at all. According to this objection, which was raised during the 1980s by
Burton Mack and has been developed further by Merrill Miller, ancient Jewish
messiahs are simply instances of the broader taxon of ideal figures, which are
commonplace in Greco-Roman literature, religious and otherwise. An impli-
cation of this objection is that modern research on ancient Jewish messianism,
because it naively takes the category *messiah* to represent something unique,
is fundamentally wrongheaded. In a provocative 1987 essay, Mack takes issue
with what he calls "the magical word messiah."[130] About the use of that word

---

128. See Collins, *Scepter*, 16–18.

129. Compare James D. G. Dunn, *Christology in the Making* (London: SCM, 1980), 9, on the
analogous problem with the concept *incarnation*:

> I have not attempted to define "incarnation" at the outset. This neglect is deliber-
> ate. There is considerable risk that any such definition would pre-set the terms and
> categories of the investigation and prevent the NT authors speaking to us in their
> own terms. He who defines too closely what he is looking for at the start of a NT
> study in most cases will find it soon enough, but usually in his wake will be left
> elements which were ignored because they were not quite what he was looking for,
> and material and meaning will often have been squeezed out of shape in order to
> fit the categories prescribed at the outset.

130. Burton L. Mack, "Wisdom Makes a Difference: Alternatives to 'Messianic'
Configurations," in *Judaisms and Their Messiahs*, 15–48 at 15; see also idem, *A Myth of
Innocence: Mark and Christian Origins* (Minneapolis, Minn.: Fortress, 1988), 51–52; idem,
"Why Christos? The Social Reasons," in *Redescribing Christian Origins* (ed. Ron Cameron and
Merrill P. Miller; Atlanta, Ga.: SBL, 2004), 365–74.

in modern scholarship, he writes, "The singular notion of 'the' messiah is disclosed for what it has always been—a scholarly assumption generated by the desire to clarify Christian origins."[131] On this premise, studies of messiahs or messianism simply will not do. Mack proposes an alternative: "I suggest the use of a formal pattern of characterization that can be used to control comparative studies of the so-called messianic texts with other ideal figures of high office imagined during our period."[132] For Mack, in other words, there are no messiahs, only ideal figures.

More recently, Merrill Miller has argued a similar point at greater length:[133]

Messianic expectations and messiahs as categories for comparison and analysis may be quite problematic, especially when they tend to shift the focus away from what can be seen as more fundamental structures and issues.... Different ways of casting and relating leadership roles entail the sort of intellectual effort concerned with how a society works.[134]

For Miller, as for Mack, ancient texts about ideal leaders are really literary efforts to justify certain social structures. Messiah texts might be considered one subset of this category, but they do not share any pertinent features with one another that they do not also share with other texts about ideal figures. There is, then, no such category as *messiah*.

Both Mack's and Miller's objections to the category *messiah* are expressly dependent on Jonathan Z. Smith's criticism of the notion of religious uniqueness. In one influential treatment of the topic, Smith writes, "The 'unique' is an attribute that must be disposed of, especially when linked to some notion of incomparable value, if progress in thinking through the enterprise of comparison is to be made."[135] Smith's problem with the notion of uniqueness is that it excludes, by definition, any comparison:

---

131. Mack, "Wisdom Makes a Difference," 15.

132. Mack, "Wisdom Makes a Difference," 18.

133. See Merrill P. Miller, "How Jesus Became Christ: Probing a Thesis," *Cont* 2 (1993): 243–70; idem, "The Problem of the Origins of a Messianic Conception of Jesus," in *Redescribing Christian Origins*, 301–36; idem, "The Anointed Jesus," in *Redescribing Christian Origins*, 375–416.

134. Miller, "The Anointed Jesus," 383.

135. Jonathan Z. Smith, *Drudgery Divine: On the Comparison of Early Christianities and the Religions of Late Antiquity* (Chicago, Ill.: University of Chicago Press, 1994), 36.

The "unique" ... expresses that which is *sui generis*, *singularis*, and, therefore, incomparably valuable. "Unique" becomes an ontological rather
than a taxonomic category; an assertion of a radical difference so absolute that it becomes "Wholly Other," and the act of comparison is perceived as both an impossibility and an impiety.[136]

Smith's point about the concept of uniqueness in the academic study of
religion is well taken; the concept is effectively a conversation-stopper and so,
to that extent, hinders rather than helps understanding. What is more, Mack
and Miller are right to say that in much modern research the category *messiah* has been liable to precisely this kind of abuse. But their cynicism is too
thoroughgoing. It is simply not the case that all modern research on ancient
messianism is complicit in a subtle apology for Christianity; there are at least
as many exceptions to this trend as there are instances of it. And even if there
were no exceptions, that would not resolve the question of what categories
are appropriate to the ancient texts, for that question stands regardless of the
modern ideological ends to which those ancient texts may have been put.[137] It
is right to say that interpreters ought not to use the word *messiah* to smuggle in
notions of religious uniqueness, but it is a mistake to say that the word *messiah*
does not admit of analysis at all and to throw it out of court.

In fact, ancient messiah texts are intelligible both as messiah texts and as
ideal figure texts, and indeed, as instances of other heuristic categories as well
(e.g., liturgical texts, exegetical texts, political texts, religious texts, and so on),
relative to the particular questions and interests of the modern interpreter.
This is the crucial point. Taxons have value only relative to particular questions
and interests.[138] There is no single correct taxon to which ancient messiah
texts belong. To be sure, there are some taxons that would be entirely inap-
propriate to the evidence, but there are many that are conceivably appropriate, relative to certain questions and interests. The present book is concerned
with the relatively narrow category of messiah texts as such—that is, texts that
use the word *messiah* and its translation equivalencies. The reason for this
focus is not that this is the only appropriate category for these texts, but that it
is one patently appropriate category that, surprisingly, has not been explored
adequately.

---

136. Smith, *Drudgery Divine*, 38.

137. Thus rightly Horbury, *Jewish Messianism and the Cult of Christ*, 117, in response to Smith,
Drudgery Divine, 66–84, 134–43.

138. See Jeffrey Stout, "What Is the Meaning of a Text?" *New Literary History* 14 (1982): 1–12.

Of course, scholars are free to define their objects of inquiry as they please, but some objects of inquiry are more epistemically accessible and more heuristically fruitful than others. If we want to know where in antiquity a given scholar's definition of *messiah* is attested, then the conventional approach will surely lead us to an answer. But why (except in the cases of a few exceptionally interesting scholars) would we want to know such a thing? For historians and exegetes, a more productive question is: How do ancient writers actually use the word *messiah* and its attendant concepts?[139] If we want to know that, then the conventional approach actually begs the question entirely. A more fitting course of action is to eschew all definitions of *messiah*, return to the pertinent ancient texts, and follow the way the words run.

---

139. Thus rightly Charlesworth, "From Jewish Messianology to Christian Christology," 248: "The major discrepancies [in the primary sources] ... must not be ignored in an attempt to construct a content for Jewish messianism. Definitions of messianism must be rewritten to absorb the aforementioned complexities."

2

Oil and Power in Ancient Israel

THE BABYLONIAN TALMUD preserves an interpretation—attributed to the fourth-century Babylonian amora R. Nahman b. R. Hisda—of the curious oracle of Second Isaiah in which the prophet speaks of the Persian king Cyrus II as YHWH's own רעה, "shepherd" (Isa 44:28), and משיח, "messiah" or "anointed one" (Isa 45:1). The passage in Bavli Megillah reads as follows:

> R. Nahman b. R. Hisda gave the following exposition: What is the meaning of the verse, *Thus says YHWH to his messiah, to Cyrus* [כה־אמר יהוה למשיחו לכורש], *whose right hand I have grasped* [Isa 45:1]? Now, was Cyrus the messiah? Rather, what it means is: The Holy One, blessed be He, said to the messiah: I have a complaint for you against Cyrus [א"ל הקב"ה למשיח קובל אני לך על כורש]. I said, *He shall build my city and send forth my exiles* [Isa 45:13], but he said, *Whoever is among you of all his people, let him go up* [Ezra 1:3=2 Chr 36:23]. (b. Meg. 12a)[1]

Most modern Bible versions render משיח in Isa 45:1, quite reasonably, with "anointed" or "anointed one."[2] In the Isaiah citation in this passage from the Bavli, however, I have transliterated it "messiah" to highlight the puzzle that R. Nahman's interpretation is attempting to solve—namely, that the word used by the prophet for Cyrus is the same word used by the rabbis for an eschatological redeemer: "Thus says YHWH to his משיח, to Cyrus." Was Cyrus therefore the משיח? On the surface of it, the oracle might seem to suggest so, but R. Nahman knows this cannot be the case. He therefore reinterprets the two ל prepositional phrases, which are more naturally read in apposition to

---

1. Text from and trans. mod. from Soncino.

2. Thus, for example, KJV, RSV, NRSV, and JPS; and, similarly, Luther Bibel: *Gesalbten*.

one another ("YHWH says to his messiah, [that is,] to Cyrus"), as expressing two different relations to two different persons ("YHWH says *to* his messiah *about* Cyrus").[3] Thus, on R. Nahman's reading, God actually complains to the messiah about Cyrus's unsatisfactory performance in his role as deliverer of the exiles. This is obviously not the original sense of the oracle,[4] but it is a characteristically clever piece of rabbinic exegesis, wrangling a rogue text of scripture back in line with the orthodox assumptions of the ancient interpreter.[5]

If it is fanciful in certain respects, this talmudic interpretation nevertheless faces head-on the historical and philological problem that arises from the use of the same Hebrew word by the Achaemenid-period prophet on the one hand and the Sasanian-period rabbis on the other. Significantly, modern exegetes have not always faced this problem as forthrightly as the rabbis do. Thus, for instance, Sigmund Mowinckel, in his massively learned study of messiah texts in the Hebrew Bible, comments on our Isaiah text as follows:

> It is quite exceptional for a prophet like Deutero-Isaiah, in the exuberant enthusiasm of his faith, to call a heathen king like Cyrus "Yahweh's Anointed," because Yahweh has made him king in order to fulfill His plan for Israel. This use does not help us to define the meaning of the term.[6]

Mowinckel is, of course, right that the use of משיח in Isa 45:1 for a Persian rather than a Judahite ruler is anomalous within the corpus of the Hebrew Bible, where the word typically signifies indigenous kings and priests.[7] But he draws the arbitrary and in fact mistaken conclusion that Second Isaiah's usage

---

3. On this talmudic passage, see further Shai Secunda, *The Iranian Talmud: Reading the Bavli in Its Sasanian Context* (Philadelphia, Pa.: University of Pennsylvania Press, 2014), 66–70, who notes the Bavli's use of Persian characters from the Bible to make sense of the redactors' own situation in Sasanian Persia.

4. On the original sense of the oracle, about which there is still debate, see in particular Lisbeth S. Fried, "Cyrus the Messiah? The Historical Background to Isaiah 45:1," *HTR* 95 (2002): 373–93; Jacob Stromberg, "Deutero-Isaiah's Restoration Reconfigured," in *Continuity and Discontinuity: Chronological and Thematic Development in Isaiah 40–66* (ed. Lena-Sofia Tiemeyer and Hans M. Barstad; Göttingen: Vandenhoeck & Ruprecht, 2014), 195–218.

5. On this impulse in ancient biblical interpretation, both Jewish and Christian, see James L. Kugel, *How to Read the Bible: A Guide to Scripture, Then and Now* (New York, N.Y.: Free Press, 2007), 14–17.

6. Mowinckel, *He That Cometh*, 6.

7. Isa 45:1 is the only biblical instance of the word משיח used of a gentile. We may compare Isa 10:5 ("Assyria, the rod of my anger, the staff of my fury") and Jer 25:9; 27:6; 43:10 ("Nebuchadnezzar, king of Babylon, my servant"), but in those texts the pagan king is

is therefore irrelevant to an account of the meaning of the word in antiquity. In stark contrast to Wittgenstein's axiom that the meaning of a word is its use in the language, Mowinckel begins by establishing a formal definition of "messiah" and then rules particular instances either relevant or not according as they agree with that definition. On this theory of meaning, however, R. Nahman b. R. Hisda's interpretation in *b. Meg.* 12a becomes not just fanciful, as it undoubtedly is, but completely unintelligible. If, per Mowinckel's claim, "messiah" in Second Isaiah does not mean "messiah" at all, then there simply is no puzzle here. But a puzzle there clearly is. The Bavli text begins from the unassailable observation that Isa 45 does in fact use the word "messiah" and then proceeds to explain how such a usage is possible. Its explanation may be strained, but its interpretive starting point is sound. Why this difference? How is it that Mowinckel can pass over without comment a messiah text that the rabbis found so very interesting? The answer lies in the modern history of research of which Mowinckel was part.

Messianic Prophecy
in Hebrew Bible Scholarship

The question of the messiah in the Hebrew Bible is a classic set piece in modern biblical scholarship, the subject of many big, ambitious books from the eighteenth century to the present.[8] Its classic status is an inheritance from the premodern polemical and apologetic traditions,[9] represented, for instance, by the famous Barcelona Disputation of 1263, in which the great Sephardi rabbi Nahmanides was summoned to debate the converso Dominican friar Pablo Christiani on precisely this question.[10] In scholarship since the European Enlightenment, the interpretive methods with which scholars approach the question are more critical than before, but the sense of the uniquely high

---

the instrument of YHWH's wrath, whereas in Isa 45:1 the pagan king is the instrument of YHWH's salvation (thus rightly H. G. M. Williamson, *Variations on a Theme: King, Messiah, and Servant in the Book of Isaiah* [Carlisle, U.K.: Paternoster, 1998], 6; Roberts, "Old Testament's Contribution," 40).

8. On the history of this tradition of research, see R. E. Clements, "The Messianic Hope in the Old Testament," *JSOT* 43 (1989): 3–19.

9. See Reed, "Messianism between Judaism and Christianity."

10. See Cecil Roth, "The Disputation of Barcelona (1263)," *HTR* 43 (1950): 117–44; Robert Chazan, *Barcelona and Beyond: The Disputation of 1263 and Its Aftermath* (Berkeley, Calif.: University of California Press, 1992); Günter Stemberger, "Die Messiasfrage in den christlich-jüdischen Disputationen des Mittelalters," *JBTh* 8 (1993): 239–50.

stakes of the question persists.[11] So the American Hebraist Charles Augustus Briggs, in his 1886 opus *Messianic Prophecy: The Prediction of the Fulfillment of Redemption through the Messiah: A Critical Study of the Messianic Passages of the Old Testament in the Order of Their Development*, writes, "Messianic prophecy is the most important of all themes; for it is the ideal of redemption given by the Creator to our race at the beginning of its history, and it ever abides as the goal of humanity until the divine plan has been accomplished."[12] Strikingly similar, despite his very different social location, are the comments of Jewish historian Joseph Klausner in his *The Messianic Idea in Israel*, addressing the same topic in the first decade of the twentieth century:

> Even in my youth, the greatness and loftiness of the Messianic idea, that *original* Hebrew idea which has influenced all humanity so much, thrilled my soul; and I vowed in my heart to dedicate to it the labor of years, in order to examine it from every side and to grasp its essence.[13]

In this venerable tradition of scholarship, messianic prophecy is the greatest and worthiest theme to which scholars of the Bible may apply their learning.

In his 2007 study on the topic, Andrew Chester organizes contributions to research on the messiah in the Hebrew Bible around the twin poles of minimalism and maximalism—that is, studies that find little or no evidence of a messiah in the Hebrew Bible on the one hand and studies that find a great deal of such evidence on the other.[14] One might think that this twofold rubric seems overly simplistic, but it actually maps onto the history of scholarship quite neatly. If there is oversimplification here, as I think there certainly is (as discussed later in this chapter), the fault lies not with Chester's summary but with the history of scholarship itself. That is to say, when scholars have addressed the question of the messiah in the Hebrew Bible, a few exceptions

---

11. Consequently, as John Barton notes, "The question of the Messiah [is] the topic *par excellence* where Christian scholars may be expected to distort the natural contours of the Hebrew Scriptures" (John Barton, "The Messiah in Old Testament Theology," in *King and Messiah in Israel and the Ancient Near East* [ed. John Day; London: T. & T. Clark, 2013 (1998)], 365). Nor, I would add, are Jewish scholars immune from this temptation.

12. Charles Augustus Briggs, *Messianic Prophecy: The Prediction of the Fulfillment of Redemption through the Messiah: A Critical Study of the Messianic Passages of the Old Testament in the Order of Their Development* (New York, N.Y.: Scribner, 1886), vii.

13. Klausner, *Messianic Idea*, 2; emphasis in original.

14. See Chester, *Messiah and Exaltation*, 205–30.

notwithstanding, they have tended to frame the question in binary terms, as a for-or-against proposition.

For most of the modern history of research, it was emphatically a "for" proposition. The maximalist interpretation was manifestly the dominant one from the eighteenth century to the mid twentieth century. It is represented by the studies of Briggs and Klausner, just cited, and many others beside. These include classic studies by Christoph Friedrich Ammon, Johann Christian Konrad von Hofmann, Johann Jakob Stähelin, Jules Steeg, David Castelli, Franz Delitzsch, Frants Buhl, and Eduard König, among others.[15] The high-water mark of this school, as Chester notes, is the massive three-volume work of Ernst Wilhelm Hengstenberg, *Christologie des Alten Testaments und Commentar über die messianischen Weissagungen der Propheten.*[16] Hengstenberg summarizes his own position as follows:

> When we observe that the Messianic announcements, which are pecu-liar to Israel alone, have their origin in the primeval age, that for many successive centuries they continue to reappear again and again, that they do not occur merely incidentally and in an isolated form, in the midst of other prophecies, but constitute the very centre and soul of all prophecy, that they stand out in great prominence even in the Psalms, in which utterance is given to the living faith of the people of God, under the quickening influence of the law and the prophets, we cannot for a moment doubt, that to the people of the ancient covenant the anticipa-tion of a Messiah must have been one of all-absorbing importance.[17]

---

15. See Christoph Friedrich Ammon, *Entwurf einer Christologie des Alten Testaments* (Erlangen: Palm, 1794); Johann Christian Konrad von Hofmann, *Weissagung und Erfüllung im alte und im neue Testamente* (2 vols.; Nördlingen: Becksche, 1841–1844); Johann Jakob Stähelin, *Die messianischen Weissagungen des Alten Testaments* (Berlin: Reimer, 1847); Jules Steeg, *Le Messie d'après les Prophètes* (Strasbourg: Treuttel et Wurtz, 1867); David Castelli, *Il messia secondo gli Ebrei* (Florence: Le Monnier, 1874); Franz Delitzsch, *Messianische Weissagungen in geschichtlicher Folge* (Leipzig: Faber, 1890); Frants Buhl, *De messianske Forjaettelser i det gamle Testamente* (Copenhagen: Gyldendal, 1894); Eduard König, *Die mes-sianische Weissagungen des Alten Testaments vergleichend, geschichtlich und exegetisch behandelt* (3d ed.; Stuttgart: Belser, 1925).

16. Ernst Wilhelm Hengstenberg, *Christologie des Alten Testaments und Commentar über die messianischen Weissagungen der Propheten* (3 vols.; Berlin: Oehmigke, 1829–1835); ET *Christology of the Old Testament, and a Commentary on the Messianic Predictions* (trans. Theodore Meyer and James Martin; 4 vols.; Edinburgh: T. & T. Clark, 1854–1858); abridged ET *Christology of the Old Testament, and Commentary on the Messianic Predictions of the Prophets* (trans. R. Keith; ed. T. K. Arnold; London: Rivington, 1847; repr. Kregel, 1970).

17. Hengstenberg, *Christology*, 4:259.

For Hengstenberg and the like-minded interpreters who dominated the nineteenth- and early-twentieth-century discussion, the conviction that "to the people of the ancient covenant the anticipation of a Messiah must have been one of all-absorbing importance" justified the enormous scholarly energy devoted to explicating the theme of the messiah in the Hebrew Bible.

During the first quarter of the twentieth century, arguably the most important authority on the topic was Hugo Gressmann, who published his *Der Ursprung der israelitisch-jüdischen Eschatologie* in 1905.[18] The material comprising the latter half of that book Gressmann thoroughly rewrote and supplemented for publication as *Der Messias*. Gressmann died prematurely in 1927, but Hans Schmidt finished editing the manuscript, and *Der Messias* appeared posthumously in 1929.[19] Although from Mowinckel's perspective Gressmann shares in the guilt of the old maximalists for speaking too loosely of biblical figures as "messianic,"[20] relative to his own predecessors and contemporaries, Gressmann's thoroughgoing *religionsgeschichtlich* approach was considered radical.[21] Gressmann argues that the messianic idea in ancient Israel derives from and belongs to a very ancient, pan-Near Eastern mythology of kingship, and he is content to call all the various local forms of this mythology "messianic hope."[22] On the reception of this argument, Brevard Childs rightly comments, "Gressmann ... derived messianism from ancient mythological patterns, but in spite of the early dating for the origins of the concept, it

---

18. Hugo Gressmann, *Der Ursprung der israelitisch-jüdischen Eschatologie* (FRLANT 6; Göttingen: Vandenhoeck & Ruprecht, 1905).

19. Hugo Gressmann, *Der Messias* (ed. Hans Schmidt; FRLANT 26; Göttingen: Vandenhoeck & Ruprecht, 1929). William Creighton Graham said of it, "Without question, *Der Messias* is the most thorough and searching examination of the messianic problem in the Old Testament yet produced" (William Creighton Graham, review of Gressmann, *Der Messias*, in *JR* 10 [1930]: 412).

20. See Mowinckel, *He That Cometh*, 4n2: "In his *Der Messias* Gressmann does not seem to adhere so strictly to this manifestly correct terminology"; Mowinckel, *He That Cometh*, 15: "It is therefore bad scientific method to do as Gressmann, Sellin, and others have done, and to base our inquiry into the origin of the conception of the Messiah on an assumed oriental Messianic theology of which we know nothing."

21. See Horbury, *Jewish Messianism and the Cult of Christ*, 15–21; Magne Saebo, "On the Relationship between 'Messianism' and 'Eschatology' in the Old Testament: An Attempt at a Terminological and Factual Clarification," in idem, *On the Way to Canon: Creative Tradition History in the Old Testament* (JSOTSup 191; Sheffield: Sheffield Academic, 1998), 197–231 at 197–209.

22. For example, Gressmann, *Messias*, 415–45 on *die ägyptische Messiashoffnung*. Compare also the similar, roughly contemporary English-language account of Oesterley, *Evolution of the Messianic Idea*.

certainly offered little comfort to the traditional interpretation."[23] Indeed, this feature of Gressmann's work partly explains Mowinckel's choice of him as a worthy opponent.[24]

With this history of research in view, one can understand why, when Mowinckel wrote it in the 1940s, the following claim was both thinkable and also sharply controversial:

> In later Judaism the term "Messiah" denotes an eschatological figure. He belongs to "the last time"; his advent lies in the future. To use the word "Messiah" is to imply eschatology, the last things. It is, therefore, a misuse of the words "Messiah" and "Messianic" to apply them, for instance, to those ideas which were associated in Israel or in the ancient near east with kings who were actually reigning, even if, as we shall see, these ideas were expressed in exalted and mythical terms. The word "Messiah" by itself, as a title and a name, originated in later Judaism as the designation of an eschatological figure; and it is therefore only to such a figure that it may be applied.[25]

And again, more tersely still, "The expression 'the Anointed One' does not occur in the Old Testament as a technical term for the Messiah."[26] Mowinckel's *Han som kommer* (1951; ET *He That Cometh* [1956]) took to task not only the grand old maximalists such as Hengstenberg, Briggs, and Klausner, but even (and, in fact, more pointedly) scholars such as Ernst Sellin and Hugo Gressmann, who were their more critical counterparts. Even the latter, on Mowinckel's account, allow far too much talk of messianism in the Hebrew Bible. Mowinckel draws an absolute distinction between ancient Israel, where מָשִׁיחַ signifies the sitting king, and later Judaism, where the same word signifies an eschatological redeemer. Between the two discursive contexts there is no passage to or fro. Although, as Mowinckel acknowledges, the lexeme is the same,[27] for him the putative *spätjüdisch* usage is determinative and, what is more, binding on modern scholars: "It is a misuse of the words to apply them

---

23. Brevard Childs, *Biblical Theology of the Old and New Testaments: Theological Reflection on the Christian Bible* (Minneapolis, Minn.: Fortress, 1992), 453.

24. Gressmann is the author cited most frequently by Mowinckel in *He That Cometh*, rivaled only by Willy Staerk and Wilhelm Bousset.

25. Mowinckel, *He That Cometh*, 3.

26. Mowinckel, *He That Cometh*, 7.

27. Mowinckel, *He That Cometh*, 7: "The eschatological Messiah derived his name from the sacral title of the ancient kings of Israel."

to [kings in Israel]"; "It is only to such a[n eschatological] figure that it may be applied."[28] Those scholars who speak of a messiah in the Hebrew Bible are guilty of a semantic transgression.

This acute terminological anxiety is frankly rather strange, but it is intelligible relative to the history of research to that point, which we have just sketched. In addition to its enduring value as a contribution to biblical exegesis, *He That Cometh* is a sophisticated piece of counterapologetics—a 500-page scolding of the many modern scholars who find in the Hebrew Bible a *praeparatio evangelica*. Mowinckel briefly addresses the problem of the messiahship of Jesus in the last part of the book, but for him Jesus represents a marked departure from all antecedents. He writes, "Jesus understood and fulfilled the thought of the unknown Messiah on earth in a manner entirely different from its presentation in the Jewish legend."[29] And again:

> For Jesus, the Jewish Messianic idea was the temptation of Satan, which
> He had to reject. The new conception of a saviour, which Jesus created,
> unites in itself the loftiest elements in both the Jewish and the "Aryan"
> spirit, and fuses them into a true unity, which is realized in Jesus Himself.[30]

Mowinckel, for his part, has no need of a *praeparatio evangelica*.[31]

Mowinckel won the day decisively. *He That Cometh* was well received in its own day and in time earned classic status, effectively supplanting Gressmann.[32] Scholars writing on the issue since Mowinckel have overwhelmingly favored his conclusion that there are no messiahs in the Bible

---

28. Mowinckel, *He That Cometh*, 3.

29. Mowinckel, *He That Cometh*, 447.

30. Mowinckel, *He That Cometh*, 450.

31. On this aspect of *He That Cometh*, see John J. Collins, "Mowinckel's *He That Cometh* in Retrospect," in Mowinckel, *He That Cometh*, xv–xxviii at xxiv–xxv. On the social history of this strand of biblical research, see Guy G. Stroumsa, "Jewish Myth and Ritual and the Beginnings of Comparative Religion: The Case of Richard Simon," in *Religions and Cultures* (ed. Adriana Destro and Mauro Pesce; Binghamton, N.Y.: Global Publications, 2001), 27–48.

32. On its early reception, see, for example, the enthusiastic reviews by A. J. B. Higgins in *SJT* 10 (1957): 304–9; H. Neil Richardson in *JBR* 26 (1958): 135–37; and James Muilenburg in *JBL* 76 (1957): 243–46, here 246: "It is one of the great books of OT scholarship in our generation." S. H. Hooke, reviewing it in *NTS* 4 (1958): 227–30, objects that the author "appears, like Saturn, to be devouring his own children"—that is, scholars such as Hooke who were influenced by the comparative ritual emphasis of Mowinckel's *Psalmenstudien* but now come under criticism in *He That Cometh*. On the book's subsequent legacy, see the retrospectives of D. R. Ap-Thomas, "An Appreciation of Sigmund Mowinckel's Contribution to Biblical Studies," *JBL* 85 (1966): 315–25; Collins, "*He That Cometh* in Retrospect"; and the articles

and, relatedly, no place in *Bibelwissenschaft* for the proof from messianic prophecy. To wit: H. L. Ginsberg writes in the 1972 edition of the *Encyclopedia Judaica*, "[The messiah] is a strictly postbiblical concept. . . . One can, therefore, only speak of the biblical pre-history of messianism"; and his assessment is reprinted unchanged in the 2007 edition.[33] J. J. M. Roberts articulates a similar position: "In the original context not one of the thirty-nine occurrences of משיח in the Hebrew canon refers to an expected figure of the future whose coming will coincide with the inauguration of an era of salvation." And again, "Nowhere in the Old Testament has the term משיח acquired its later technical sense as an eschatological title."[34] Similarly Paul Hanson: "[משיח] in scriptural usage does not normally refer to an eschatological figure whose coming would inaugurate a new era of salvation, rather to contemporary kings and priests."[35] And Shemaryahu Talmon: "I distinguish between the epithet משיח, which is preponderantly used in the Hebrew Bible in reference to an actual ruling king or his immediate successor, and the concept messianism, which . . . transcends the original terrestrial signification of the term *masiah*."[36] Even more succinctly, James Charlesworth: "The term 'the Messiah' simply does not appear in the Hebrew Scriptures."[37] Likewise John Barton: "No-one in ancient Israel believed in the Messiah, and the texts they wrote which would later come to be taken as messianic were not so intended."[38] And John Day: "The term *masiah*, 'Anointed' (whence the word 'Messiah') is applied in the Old Testament to the current Israelite king, not the future eschatological one."[39] And Susan Gillingham: "Although the psalms provided the soil for Messianic eisegesis, they were certainly not written as Messianic compositions."[40] And more recently, Joseph Fitzmyer: "[In] the original literal and religious sense of

---

collected in *SJOT* 2, in particular Nils A. Dahl, "Sigmund Mowinckel, Historian of Religion and Theologian," *SJOT* 2 (1988): 8–22.

33. H. L. Ginsberg et al., "Messiah," *Encyclopedia Judaica* (2d ed.; Detroit, Mich.: Thomson Gale, 2006), 14:110.

34. Roberts, "Old Testament's Contribution," 39, 51, respectively.

35. Paul D. Hanson, "Messiahs and Messianic Figures in Proto-Apocalypticism," in *The Messiah*, 67–75 at 67.

36. Talmon, "Concept of *Masiah*," 80.

37. Charlesworth, "From Messianology to Christology," 11.

38. Barton, "Messiah in Old Testament Theology," 375.

39. John Day, "The Canaanite Inheritance of the Israelite Monarchy," in *King and Messiah*, 72–90 at 80.

40. S. E. Gillingham, "The Messiah in the Psalms," in *King and Messiah*, 209–37 at 237.

these Old Testament passages . . . a 'messianic' meaning is still out of place."[41] And more recently still, John Collins: "As is well known, the word מׁשיח simply means 'anointed' and is not used in the Hebrew Bible in an eschatological sense."[42] And so on, but this is enough to make the point.

Despite this substantial weight of opinion, maximalist accounts of the messiah in the Hebrew Bible did not disappear altogether. Several such accounts, representing quite different approaches, have challenged the *communis opinio* from the 1950s to the present. Immediately on the heels of Mowinckel, Helmer Ringgren used the Scandinavian school's comparative approach to ancient Near Eastern divine kingship to revive the theme of the messiah in Old Testament theology. Ringgren writes:

> From earliest days the Christian Church has seen in many Old Testament passages prophecies which have been fulfilled in Jesus Christ. Modern biblical research has not always been of the same opinion, and has often interpreted those messianic passages in quite a different way. Many good Christians have been offended by this, and the consequence has been the opening of a broad gulf between scholarly and practical interpretation of the Bible. . . . Consequently it must be hailed with satisfaction that there is a certain tendency in more recent research to defend the messianic import of those biblical passages in quite a new manner. Thus, the traditional Christian interpretation of those passages seems to have received some support from historical exegesis.[43]

It is doubtful, to my mind, whether *Religionsgeschichte* can in fact yield the kind of theological results that Ringgren wants, but one can see how the mythical language of ancient kingship texts appeals to him in this respect.

Joachim Becker's 1977 monograph, *Messiaserwartung im Alten Testament*, undertakes to salvage the Old Testament messiah as a matter of urgency for Catholic faith.[44] Becker acknowledges that "there was not even such a thing as

---

41. Fitzmyer, *One Who Is to Come*, 25.

42. Yarbro Collins and Collins, *King and Messiah as Son of God*, 1.

43. Helmer Ringgren, *The Messiah in the Old Testament* (SBT 18; Chicago, Ill.: Allenson, 1956 [Swedish original, 1954]), 7.

44. Joachim Becker, *Messiaserwartung im Alten Testament* (Stuttgart: Katholisches Bibelwerk, 1977); ET *Messianic Expectation in the Old Testament* (trans. David E. Green; Philadelphia, Pa.: Fortress, 1980).

messianic expectation until the last two centuries B.C."[45] But for him, this conclusion induces theological anxiety: "Such a conclusion would contradict one
of the most central concerns of the New Testament, which insists with unprecedented frequency, intensity, and unanimity that Christ was proclaimed in
advance in the Old Testament."[46] Becker's solution is to propose a synthesis of
the historical–critical and canonical approaches;[47] but, in practice, this means
privileging the latter. He writes, "Above all, we must remember that the messianic interpretation of the Old Testament, arbitrary as it may appear, is nevertheless based on the highest authority [viz. the New Testament]."[48] Guided
by this authority, the interpreter can see how "the Old Testament itself and
even the history that lies behind it possess a unique messianic luminosity."[49]
Becker's argument is not unsophisticated, but in the nature of the case it can
only be fully persuasive among his own coreligionists.

Another Catholic exegete, the eminent Leuven Old Testament scholar
Joseph Coppens,[50] marshals a less overtly theological argument in defense of
messianism in the Hebrew Bible. In a number of studies, most significantly
his 1968 monograph, *Le messianisme royal*, Coppens argues for a deep continuity between preexilic Judahite royal ideology and postexilic messianism, even
happily adopting the latter word for the former phenomenon.[51] More recently,
Finnish scholar Antti Laato has argued along similar lines.[52] Although he

---

45. Becker, *Messianic Expectation*, 93. And again, "It is on the threshold of the New Testament
itself that we first encounter a real messianism. It is not the seamless continuation of the
restorative monarchism of the exilic and early postexilic period; it is a new outgrowth of anti-
Hasmonean, anti-Roman, and anti-Herodian tendencies" (Becker, *Messianic Expectation*, 87).

46. Becker, *Messianic Expectation*, 93.

47. Following a proposal by Hans Urs von Balthasar, *Herrlichkeit: Eine theologische Ästhetik*
(Einsiedeln: Johannes Verlag, 1961–1969), 3/2:371–82.

48. Becker, *Messianic Expectation*, 95.

49. Becker, *Messianic Expectation*, 96.

50. On whom see Johan Lust, "Msgr. J. Coppens: The Old Testament Scholar," *ETL* 57
(1981): 241–65.

51. Joseph Coppens, *Le messianisme royal: Ses origines, son développement, son accomplissement*
(LD 54; Paris: Cerf, 1968). See further idem, *Le messianisme et sa relève prophétique: Les anticipations vétérotestamentaires: Leur accomplissement en Jésus* (BETL 38; Gembloux: Duculot,
1974); and idem, *La relève apocalyptique du messianisme royal* (3 vols.; BETL 50, 55, 61;
Leuven: Peeters, 1979–1983).

52. Antii Laato, *A Star Is Rising: The Historical Development of the Old Testament Royal
Ideology and the Rise of the Jewish Messianic Expectations* (USFISFCJ 5; Atlanta, Ga.: Scholars
Press, 1997). This book is Laato's programmatic statement. For his interpretation of some
of the contested texts, see further idem, *Who Is Immanuel? The Rise and the Foundering of
Isaiah's Messianic Expectations* (Åbo, Finland: Åbo Academy Press, 1988); idem, *Josiah and*

formally concedes Mowinckel's terminological point—"The term מָשִׁיחַ, the Messiah, with the absolute meaning 'the Anointed One' (=the coming, ideal, king), never appears in the Old Testament"[53]—Laato, like Coppens, nevertheless argues that Judahite kings like Hezekiah are indeed messiahs and that their enthronement psalms and succession oracles are messianic texts, once allowances are made for synchronic diversity and diachronic change. He writes, "When the term 'Messiah' is adopted to describe the (ideal) king in the Old Testament it should be noted that the Israelite royal and 'messianic' ideology developed and was transformed over a period of many hundred years."[54]

Perhaps the most sophisticated version of the neomaximalist position is that developed by William Horbury, especially in his *Jewish Messianism and the Cult of Christ* (1998).[55] Horbury writes:

> Although the lengthy development of messianism *from* the Old Testament is obvious … , it has also become clear that messianism is important *within* the Old Testament. It flourished especially in the period of the collecting and editing of the books … , [but] from the inception of the Davidic monarchy and the Israelite capture of Jerusalem it was bound up with the traditions of kingship in Zion.[56]

Horbury's argument focuses especially on the collection and redaction of the biblical books during the Persian and Hellenistic periods, but he traces messianism back to the origins of the Judahite monarchy. He does this by flatly rejecting the strict Mowinckelian definition of "messianism" in favor of a more capacious one: "Messianism is taken in the broad sense of the expectation of a coming preeminent ruler—coming, whether at the end, as strictly implied by the word 'eschatology,' or simply at some time in the future."[57] Horbury is right to challenge the post-Mowinckel scholarly orthodoxy about "messianism in the strict sense," but it is not clear

---

David Redivivus: The Historical Josiah and the Messianic Expectations of Exilic and Postexilic Times (ConBOT 33; Stockholm: Almqvist & Wiksell, 1992); idem, *The Servant of YHWH and Cyrus: A Reinterpretation of the Exilic Messianic Programme in Isaiah 40–55* (ConBOT 35; Stockholm: Almqvist & Wiksell, 1992).

53. Laato, *A Star Is Rising*, 394.

54. Laato, *A Star Is Rising*, 3.

55. Horbury, *Jewish Messianism and the Cult of Christ*; also idem, *Messianism among Jews and Christians*.

56. Horbury, *Jewish Messianism and the Cult of Christ*, 35.

57. Horbury, *Jewish Messianism and the Cult of Christ*, 7.

to me that his alternate definition actually advances the discussion. It lets more count as evidence, naturally, but it operates in roughly the same way that Mowinckel's does. As I argued in Chapter 1 and illustrated from Bavli Megillah at the beginning of this chapter, the really interesting thing is not any interpreter's definition of messianism, but rather the way the ancient sources use the words. If we want to understand the latter, then we must take into account not only *Psalms of Solomon* and *Parables of Enoch*, but Psalms and Leviticus as well.

Oil and Power in Ancient Israel

In the fraught history of research just discussed, "messiah" and "messianism" function as ciphers for political utopianism, pious optimism, a linear view of history, and other philosophical or psychological categories. In the biblical sources themselves, however, the discourse of "messiahs"— "anointed persons"—is predicated on a simple symbolic relation between oil and power. The basic but very important point is that the ritual smearing of oil on objects and persons was a widely recognized means of conferring sacredness in ancient Israel as well as in other, older ancient Near Eastern cultures: Egyptian, Hittite, Canaanite, and otherwise.[58] We often think of ritual anointing in connection with the installation of kings and priests, and rightly so, but there are of course biblical stories of the consecration of inanimate objects with oil. In one important example from the patriarch cycle in Genesis, the smearing of oil on a stone makes that stone a *massebah* or a *betyl*, a dwelling for or embodiment of a god (Gen 28:16–19; 31:13; 35:14).[59]

The ritual application of oil to persons is another instantiation of the same principle; anointing a person with oil according to certain protocols makes the person sacrosanct. Indeed, analogously to the case of the *massebah*, anointing a person with oil can effectively make him an embodiment of a god, as in the psalmist's address to the king: "Your throne, O god, endures forever and ever; your royal scepter is a scepter of equity. . . . Therefore God, your God, has

---

58. See especially Ernst Kutsch, *Salbung als Rechtsakt im Alten Testament und im Alten Orient* (BZAW; Berlin: Töpelmann, 1963); and more recently and more specifically Stephanie Dalley, "Anointing in Ancient Mesopotamia," in *The Oil of Gladness: Anointing in Christian Tradition* (ed. Martin Dudley and Geoffrey Rowell; London: SPCK, 1993), 19–25; Stephen E. Thompson, "The Anointing of Officials in Ancient Egypt," *JNES* 53 (1994): 15–25.

59. On this practice, see Benjamin D. Sommer, *The Bodies of God and the World of Ancient Israel* (New York, N.Y.: Cambridge University Press, 2009), 49–54.

anointed you with the oil of gladness beyond your companions" (Ps 45:6–7).[60] In sum: oil, properly applied, confers divinely sanctioned power. Mowinckel himself makes this point well:

> In the ancient east both persons and things were anointed by having sweet-smelling oil poured or smeared over them. . . .. The act had a sacral significance. The original idea was, no doubt, that the oil possessed an abnormal, "holy" power, or "mana," to use the familiar term from the phenomenology of religion. In the act of anointing, this power and holiness were transmitted to the person anointed, or the holiness and supernatural power with which he was already endowed were renewed and strengthened. Practical experience of the power and usefulness of oil, both as a food and as a medicine, readily explains this belief in its sacral, mana-like character.[61]

The appeal to the Polynesian concept of *mana* (a commonplace in mid-twentieth-century religion scholarship) is problematic,[62] and the concluding anthropological claim is speculative, but the core of Mowinckel's comment is to the point: Behind the whole discourse of messianism lies a very ancient Near Eastern complex of oil rituals.

In this connection, there has been considerable discussion of the question whence the Israelites got the custom of anointing their kings with oil. Martin Noth, for instance, argued that it came over to Israel from Hittite precedent.[63] The Hittite custom is attested, for example, in a magical text instructing how the king can avert an evil omen by installing a decoy for himself: "They anoint the prisoner with the fine oil of kingship and [he speaks] as follows: This man [is] the king. To him [have I given] a royal

---

60. Thus rightly Yarbro Collins and Collins, *King and Messiah as Son of God*, 56: "The Hebrew text [of Psalm 45] . . . preserved a remnant of an early Israelite conception of divine kingship."

61. Mowinckel, *He That Cometh*, 4–5.

62. See Jonathan Z. Smith, "Manna, Mana Everywhere and /_/_/," in idem, *Relating Religion* (Chicago, Ill.: University of Chicago Press, 2004), 117–44.

63. Martin Noth, "Office and Vocation in the Old Testament," in idem, *The Laws in the Pentateuch and Other Essays* (trans. D. R. Ap-Thomas; Edinburgh: Oliver & Boyd, 1966), 229–49, here 239:

> If such a practice existed in Syria and Palestine during the late Bronze Age, but is found neither in Egypt nor in Mesopotamia, then we are inclined to search for its origins in Hurrian or Hittite civilizations, unless we accept that it arose spontaneously in Syria and Palestine. There is even some evidence that the anointing of kings was known to the Hittites.

name."[64] The parallel is reasonably close, but Hittite civilization lay in the distant past by the time the Israelites were pouring oil on their kings. Alternatively, Roland de Vaux argued that the Israelite anointing of kings was a modification of the Egyptian anointing of vassals and court officials.[65] An example of Egyptian practice is El-Amarna letter 51, in which Addu-nirari writes to the Pharaoh:

> Manahpiya [i.e., Thutmose III], the king of Egypt, your ancestor, made [T]a[ku], my ancestor, a king in Nuhasse, he put oil on his head and [s]poke as follows: "Whom the king of Egypt has made a king, [and on whose head] he has put [oil], [no] one [shall]."[66]

Unlike the Hittites, the Egyptians were still a force to be reckoned with at the time of the Israelite monarchy, although they had fewer dealings with Israel than the Mesopotamian empires had. The latter would be promising candidates, but there is no reliable evidence that either the Assyrians or the Babylonians anointed their kings with oil. Consequently, John Day, among others, has argued that the anointing of kings was an indigenous Canaanite custom, which naturally therefore became an Israelite custom.[67] Judges 9:7–15, the parable of the trees who "anoint a king over themselves" (representing the rivalry between the chieftains Jerubbaal and Abimelech), might point in this direction, but the passage could be a retrojection of Israelite custom into an earlier period. There is some evidence from Ugarit for royal anointing among non-Israelite Canaanites. Day cites *KTU²* 1.22.II.15–18, a Ugaritic Rephaim text:[68] "Oil . . . He vowed, If at (my?) command, he shall tak[e] the throne of

---

64. Text ed. M. Vieyra, "Rites de purification hittites," *RHR* 119 (1939): 121–53 at 129; trans. James B. Pritchard in *ANET*.

65. Roland de Vaux, "The King of Israel, Vassal of Yahweh," in idem, *The Bible and the Ancient Near East* (trans. Damian McHugh; London: Darton, Longman & Todd, 1972 [French original, 1967]), 152–66, especially 165; idem, *Ancient Israel: Its Life and Institutions* (trans. John McHugh; London: Darton, Longman & Todd, 1980 [French original, 1961]), 104: "These facts suggest an Egyptian practice rather than a native [Levantine] custom: we know from other sources that the high officials in Egypt were anointed on appointment to office, but the Pharaohs were not."

66. Trans. William L. Moran, *The Amarna Letters* (Baltimore, Md.: Johns Hopkins University Press, 1992), 122.

67. Day, "Canaanite Inheritance," here 73: "The clearest evidence of Canaanite, indeed Jebusite Jerusalemite, influence on Israel's monarchy is indicated by the coronation Psalm 110. . . . There is therefore here explicit evidence of the fusion of Israel's royal ideology with that of the Jebusites."

68. And also less certainly *KTU²* 1.6.I.50–52.

his kingship, the resting place of the seat of [his] domin[ion]."[69] Perhaps, then, the anointing of Israelite kings perpetuated a custom that had long been current among the tribes of the Levant,[70] although there is no evidence that any of these older cultures derived a title of office, "anointed one," from the custom.

Thus far Israelite kings. But what about Israelite priests? In a number of biblical texts, they, too, are said to be consecrated by anointing with oil (e.g., Exod 28:41; 30:30; 40:13, 15; Lev 16:32). Many historians, however, have thought this to be a retrojection from the Second-Temple period, when the high priesthood effectively supplanted the kingship.[71] Martin Noth gives classic expression to this view:

> It is clear that the act of anointing was transferred from the kingship to the high priesthood, because in the Old Testament tradition of the earlier period only the anointing of kings is mentioned—not of priests; this anointing only recurs afterward with respect to the post-exilic High Priest. Initially the anointing was intended for the High Priest alone, and not for the rest of the priests as well. Only later, in the course of making the office more "democratic," were they included in the circle of the anointed.[72]

The literary–critical evidence arguably does point in this direction. The anointing of priests is only mentioned in the Priestly Torah, not anywhere in the numerous biblical stories of priests.[73] Against this view, however, Daniel

---

69. Text in *KTU*²; trans. in *COS*.

70. *Pace* Talmon, "Concept of *Masiah*," 87: "The practice of anointing a secular–political leader with oil was an innovation which has no roots whatsoever in the socioreligious tradition or premonarchic Israel." See further Gerhard von Rad, "Royal Ritual in Judah," in idem, *The Problem of the Hexateuch and Other Essays* (trans. N. W. Porteous; Edinburgh: Oliver & Boyd, 1965), 222–31; Frank Moore Cross, "The Judaean Royal Theology," in idem, *Canaanite Myth and Hebrew Epic* (Cambridge, Mass.: Harvard University Press, 1997 [1973]), 241–73; Nicholas Wyatt, "Royal Religion in Ancient Judah," in *Religious Diversity in Ancient Israel and Judah* (ed. Francesca Stavrakapoulou and John Barton; London: T. & T. Clark, 2010), 61–81.

71. In Dan 9:25–26 we find two uses of מָשִׁיחַ for a high priest of the Second Temple: Joshua ben Jehozadak (the contemporary of Zerubbabel) in 9:25 (cf. Zech 4:14) and Onias III in 9:26 (cf. 2 Macc 4:30–38). The genre of Dan 9 is an apocalypse, but here the "messiahs" do not feature prominently as they do in later apocalypses such as *Parables of Enoch*, Revelation, *4 Ezra*, and *2 Baruch*. See further Fitzmyer, *One Who Is to Come*, 56–64; and, more accurately, Collins, *Scepter*, 17, 42.

72. Noth, "Office and Vocation," 237.

73. With the one late exception of Zadok in 1 Chr 29:22: "They made Solomon son of David king a second time, and they anointed him as prince for YHWH and Zadok as priest [וַיִּמְשְׁחוּ לַיהוה לְנָגִיד וּלְצָדוֹק לְכֹהֵן]."

Fleming has objected, first, that anointing of priests was a Near Eastern commonplace, so that nothing would be more natural than for Israelites to do it and, second, that the biblical protocol for anointing rank-and-file priests is, in fact, altogether different from that for anointing kings and high priests.[74] He writes:

> Exodus 29 and Leviticus 8 merge the customs for anointing the high priest and all the sons of Aaron in one narrative for their installation, and these texts preserve two very dissimilar rites. The high priest is anointed by pouring oil on the head, while the priest family as a whole is anointed by splashing oil and blood on men and garments together.[75]

And again, "Where the anointing of Aaron suggests a natural origin in the Jerusalem Temple heritage of the Priestly Torah, the anointing of his sons may have roots in a more widespread practice from the old towns, villages, and shrines of the countryside."[76] Perhaps, then, there was a protocol for anointing priests in preexilic Israel, even if the form of the ritual as we have it in Leviticus reflects the postexilic attraction of royal paraphernalia to the office of high priest.

It is because of these archaic oils rituals that other biblical texts can take for granted the use of מָשִׁיחַ for their respective kings and priests.[77] The prayer of Habakkuk (Hab 3), a divine warrior psalm in the midst of a collection of prophetic oracles,[78] uses מָשִׁיחַ after the pattern of the Psalms for the unnamed Judahite king, whom YHWH delivers from his enemies:[79]

> You [YHWH] strode across the earth in fury, you trampled the nations in anger. You went forth for the salvation of your people, for the salvation

---

74. Daniel E. Fleming, "The Biblical Tradition of Anointing Priests," *JBL* 117 (1998): 401–14.

75. Fleming, "Anointing Priests," 401.

76. Fleming, "Anointing Priests," 414.

77. And in a few, exceptional instances, prophets: Ps 105:15=1 Chr 16:22; cf. 1 Kgs 19:16; Isa 61:1. On this anomaly, see Jean Giblet, "Prophétisme et attente d'un messie prophète dans l'Ancien Testament," in *L'Attente du Messie* (ed. Lucien Cerfaux; Bruges: Desclée de Brouwer, 1958), 85–129.

78. On the literary–critical problem, see J. H. Eaton, "The Origin and Meaning of Habakkuk 3," *ZAW* 76 (1964): 144–71; J. J. M. Roberts, *Nahum, Habakkuk, and Zephaniah* (OTL; Louisville, Ky.: WJK, 1991), 148–49; Francis I. Andersen, *Habakkuk* (AB; New York, N.Y.: Doubleday, 2001), 259–64.

79. Thus Roberts, *Nahum, Habakkuk, and Zephaniah*, 156; but compare the different explanation of Andersen, *Habakkuk*, 335.

of your anointed one [לִישַׁע אֶת־מְשִׁיחֶךָ; OG τοῦ σῶσαι τοὺς χριστούς σου].
You crushed the head of the wicked, laying him bare from thigh to
neck. (Hab 3:12–13)

There is a poetic parallelism between the lines "for the salvation of your
people" and "for the salvation of your anointed" in the sense that the fate of the
king is, in effect, the fate of the people. Interestingly, though, the Greek translator takes the parallel as strictly synonymous, so that מָשִׁיַח (singular) becomes
χριστούς (plural): the people of the Lord are his anointed ones.[80]

Lamentations 4, an alphabetic acrostic poem mourning the atrocities committed during the sack of Jerusalem by the Babylonians in 586 BCE,[81] includes
a description from the perspective of the people of the capture and humilia-
tion of the Judahite king (Zedekiah, although he is not named in the poem)
(cf. 2 Kgs 25:1–17; Jer 32:1–5; 34:2–3; 39:1–7; 52:1–11; Ezek 12:12–13):[82]

Our pursuers were swifter than the vultures in the heavens; they
chased us on the mountains, they lay in wait for us in the wilderness.
The breath of our nostrils, the anointed of YHWH [רוּחַ אַפֵּינוּ מְשִׁיחַ יהוה;
OG πνεῦμα προσώπου ἡμῶν χριστὸς κυρίου], was taken in their pits, he
of whom we said, "Under his shadow we shall live among the nations."
(Lam 4:19–20)

"The anointed of YHWH" is the familiar Deuteronomistic title for the
king, and the poet here uses it in apposition with "the breath of our nostrils,"
illustrating the praise of the king typical of Judahite royal ideology (also "we
shall live under his shadow"), which has, however, been sorely chastened by
recent events.[83]

A generation after Lamentations, another Judahite poet used the same
figure of speech for another king, but, strikingly, a foreign rather than an

---

80. On the text-critical puzzle posed by Hab 3, see Joshua L. Harper, *Responding to a Puzzled
Scribe: The Barberini Text of Habakkuk 3 Analyzed in the Light of the Other Greek Versions*
(LHBOTS 608; London: T. & T. Clark, 2015), and on our verse pp. 119–25.

81. On the acrostic form, see R. B. Salters, *Lamentations* (ICC; London: T. & T. Clark,
2010), 17–21. On the poem as a whole, see Delbert R. Hillers, *Lamentations* (AB; New York,
N.Y.: Doubleday, 1972), 86–93.

82. See Hillers, *Lamentations*, 92; Salters, *Lamentations*, 330–33.

83. Thus rightly Hillers, *Lamentations*, 92:

> He deliberately uses somewhat exaggerated language in speaking of the king, in order
> to sharpen the contrast between their hopes in the king and the bitter actuality.…
> [This event] is given prominent place as the climax of the tragic fall of the nation.

indigenous one. In the passage with which we began this chapter, Deutero-Isaiah writes about Cyrus II of Persia:

Thus says YHWH to his anointed, to Cyrus [כה־אמר יהוה למשיחו לכורש; OG Οὕτως λέγει κύριος ὁ θεὸς τῷ χριστῷ μου Κύρῳ], whose right hand I have grasped, to subdue nations before him and ungird the loins of kings, to open doors before him that gates may not be closed: "I will go before you and level the mountains, I will break in pieces the doors of bronze and cut asunder the bars of iron, I will give you the treasures of darkness and the hoards in secret places, that you may know that it is I, YHWH, the god of Israel, who call you by your name. For the sake of my servant Jacob, and Israel my chosen, I call you by your name, I surname you, though you do not know me." (Isa 45:1–4)

Deutero-Isaiah's use of "anointed" here is purely figurative, because Cyrus of Persia will not have undergone any Judahite oil ritual. Cyrus is, by the prophet's lights, the anointed of YHWH because he effects what the prophet considers the will of YHWH—namely, the toppling of the neo-Babylonian power and the return of the deported Judahites to the homeland.[84] *Mirabile dictu*, the messiah is a gentile.

Messiahs within and without the Hebrew Bible

Thus far ritual anointing in the Hebrew Bible. As noted earlier, a great deal of post-World War II scholarship has insisted loudly that none of this is "messianic" in a certain maximalist sense stipulated by the scholars who make this point. But this seems to me obviously true, and therefore not worth repeating as if it were a significant conclusion. An equally true and much more interesting observation is that oftentimes Hellenistic- and Roman-period messiah texts, too, fall short of the maximalist sense of "messiah" invented by scholars, effectively just reproducing the idiom of the Hebrew Bible unchanged. Such cases undermine the bright line drawn by scholars between biblical

---

84. See Williamson, *Variations on a Theme*, 6: "The single most important conclusion to be drawn is the negative point that the agent of the anticipated restoration will not be an Israelite or Davidic king. But then, in Deutero-Isaiah we should not expect it to be"; Joseph Blenkinsopp, *Isaiah 40–55* (AB; New Haven, Conn.: Yale University Press, 2006), 248–49:

and postbiblical usage.[85] We may cite several cases to illustrate the point. One instructive example, which features prominently in the narrative of 1–2 Samuel, is the scene of messianic recognition or identification. The crucial assumption of the narrative is that there is such a person as a משיח יהוה, an anointed of YHWH, a king sanctioned by the deity, on which assumption, in several scenes, one character in the story recognizes another character as that figure.[86] Thus, for instance, when the prophet Samuel meets the sons of Jesse, we read, "When they came, he looked on Eliab and thought, 'Surely YHWH's messiah is before him [אך נגד יהוה משיחו; OG ἀλλὰ καὶ ἐνώπιον κυρίου χριστὸς αὐτοῦ]'" (1 Sam 16:6). Or later, when David, hiding from Saul in the wilderness of En-gedi, passes up the opportunity to kill his pursuer, he says, "Some bade me kill you, but I spared you. I said, 'I will not put forth my hand against my lord; for he is the YHWH's messiah [כי-משיח יהוה הוא; OG ὅτι χριστὸς κυρίου οὗτός ἐστιν]'" (1 Sam 24:10).

Modern interpreters have pointed out that the "messiah" or "anointed" in these stories is simply the divinely approved king, not any kind of mythical archetype. And this is clearly the case. But if we look ahead to messiah texts from the Roman period, ostensibly the heyday of the messiah-as-mythical-archetype, we find scenes of recognition or identification very much like those in 1–2 Samuel. One such is the scene in the Gospel of Mark in which the disciple Peter identifies Jesus: "He asked them, 'Who do you say that I am?' Peter answered him, 'You are the messiah [σὺ εἶ ὁ χριστός]'" (Mark 8:29; and cf. Matt 16:16; Luke 9:20). Another is the scene in Yerushalmi Ta'anit in which R. Akiba recognizes Shimon bar Kosiba: "R. Shimon b. Yohai taught: My teacher Akiba used to expound, *A star* [כוכב] *goes out from Jacob* [Num 24:17], 'Koziba [כחבא] goes out from Jacob.' When R. Akiba saw Bar Koziba, he said, 'This is the king messiah [דין הוא מלכא משיחא]'" (*y. Ta'an.* 4:8 [68d]; and cf. *Lam. Rab.* 2:2 §4).[87]

Cyrus is introduced at once and surprisingly, even shockingly, as Yahveh's anointed one.... What this implies in concrete historical terms is that Cyrus has taken the place of the Davidic royal house, at least for the time being, an affirmation that we suspect not all of the prophet's audience would have agreed with.

85. A point well made by Clements, "Messianic Hope in the Old Testament." See also, in this connection, Hindy Najman, "The Vitality of Scripture within and beyond the 'Canon,'" *JSJ* 43 (2012) 497–518; Mroczek, "Hegemony of the Biblical."

86. On these scenes, see Noth, "Office and Vocation," 240–42.

87. This and other formal parallels between Jesus stories and Bar Kosiba stories are a consequence not of the dependence of one upon the other (contra J. C. O'Neill, "The Mocking of Bar Kokhba and of Jesus," *JSJ* 31 [2000]: 39–41), but of the dependence of both upon scriptural precedents.

About these Roman-period texts, one might say, and many have said, that the title משיח or χριστός here no longer means what it did in the Deuteronomistic History, that whereas Samuel is merely identifying Eliab as the king-in-waiting, R. Akiba is identifying Bar Kosiba as the eschatological redeemer. But this is by no means obvious,[88] and in any case it begs the question. If we want to say that the Gospels and the Talmud use "messiah" in a technical, eschatological sense, then we owe an account of how they can predicate messiahship of flesh-and-blood, historical persons just as easily as the Deuteronomistic History can. Or perhaps we are better off doing away with the hypothesis of a late, eschatological technical term altogether. Of course, words are not semantically static; they accumulate various shades of meaning with the passage of time and use.[89] But in the case of משיח or χριστός, there is no *geistesgeschichtlich* flip of a switch from an earlier, Israelite, mundane sense ("anointed one") to a later, *spätjüdisch*, eschatological sense ("messiah").[90] Aharon Oppenheimer makes just this point in relation to Bar Kosiba and, *mutatis mutandis*, to R. Judah the Patriarch.[91] Oppenheimer writes, "Just as the *nasi* or the exilarch was not expected to bring the Final Redemption, so it is likely that when Rabbi Aqiva called Bar Kokhva 'the King Messiah,' he really intended to stress Bar Kokhva's status as king, and the term 'Messiah' should be understood simply in its original Hebrew meaning of 'Anointed.' Calling Bar Kokhva by this term is then not very different from the coronations of biblical times when the kings were

---

88. Thus, for example, Leo Mildenberg, *The Coinage of the Bar Kokhba War* (Zurich: Schweizerische Numismatische Gesellschaft, 1984) understandably but mistakenly refuses to classify Shimon bar Kosiba as a messiah, on the (true) premise A that Bar Kosiba was a political and military authority, and the (false) premise B that such persons may not be called "messiahs."

89. See Regine Eckardt et al., eds., *Words in Time: Diachronic Semantics from Different Points of View* (Berlin: De Gruyter, 2003).

90. Thus rightly Clements, "Messianic Hope in the Old Testament," 16: "We are no longer faced with a simple and clear-cut contrast between one original literal meaning and a later expanded, or spiritual, one"; and Peter Schäfer, "Bar Kokhba and the Rabbis," in *The Bar Kokhba War Reconsidered* (ed. Peter Schäfer; TSAJ 100; Tübingen: Mohr Siebeck, 2003), 1–22 at 17:

> I do not have any problem with attaching the label "Messianic" to Bar Kokhba and his rebellion, and I do not quite understand the trend in much of the relevant scholarship to distinguish neatly between merely a "down-to-earth" military leader/warrior on the one hand and a utopian figure with "divine and supernatural qualities" on the other.

91. On both Bar Kosiba and R. Judah the Patriarch, see my discussion in Chapter 3 in this volume.

anointed with oil."[92] Not very different, indeed. Of course 1 Samuel does not attest the putative late, technical sense of "messiah," but then, neither do the Gospel or the Talmud passages. If our goal is to understand any of these texts on their own terms, then the putative late, technical sense of "messiah" is simply a red herring.

Or consider the case of Jewish psalm literature from the Second-Temple period. The biblical Psalter (both MT and OG) is, together with 1–2 Samuel, the foremost source of "messiah" references in the Tanakh (see Pss 2; 18; 20; 28; 84; 89; 105; 132). With the lone exception of Ps 105:15 (OG Ps 104:15) (=1 Chr 16:22), which figures the patriarchs Abraham, Isaac, and Jacob as prophets (נביאים, προφῆται) (cf. Gen 20:7) and anointed ones (משיחים, χριστοί), all of the numerous biblical "messiah" psalms are royal psalms, where משיח is a title of the Judahite or Israelite king.[93] Thus, for instance, Ps 2, which has as strong a claim as any to be a coronation hymn, a poem for the occasion of the installation of a new monarch:[94] "The kings of the earth set themselves, and the rulers take counsel together, against YHWH and against his messiah [עלי-יהוה ועל-משיחו; OG κατὰ τοῦ κυρίου καὶ κατὰ τοῦ χριστοῦ αὐτοῦ].... [YHWH] will speak to them in his wrath, and terrify them in his fury, saying, 'I have set my king on Zion, my holy hill.' I will tell of the decree of YHWH: He said to me, 'You are my son, today I have begotten you'" (Ps 2:2, 5–7). Here, then, the "messiah" or "anointed" (2:2) is the sitting king, or rather, the king who is being installed on the occasion of the psalm's performance.

Other royal "messiah" psalms have different genres and *Sitzen im Leben*, but they serve equally well to illustrate our point. Psalm 132, for instance, is an encomium on the house of David and on the state-sponsored shrine to YHWH on Mount Zion.[95] The psalmist wishes that both institutions should exist in perpetuity, invoking certain oracles of YHWH to this effect

---

92. Aharon Oppenheimer, "Leadership and Messianism in the Time of the Mishnah," in *Eschatology in the Bible and in Jewish and Christian Tradition* (ed. Henning Graf Reventlow; JSOTSup 243; Sheffield: Sheffield Academic, 1997), 157.

93. See Gillingham, "Messiah in the Psalms."

94. See Sigmund Mowinckel, *The Psalms in Israel's Worship* (2 vols.; Grand Rapids, Mich.: Eerdmans, 2004 [1962]), 1:62–63; Gillingham, "Messiah in the Psalms," 212–13; William M. Schniedewind, *Society and the Promise to David* (New York, N.Y.: Oxford University Press, 1999), 69–70.

95. See Gillingham, "Messiah in the Psalms," 216–17; Yarbro Collins and Collins, *King and Messiah as Son of God*, 32–33.

(see 2 Sam 7; and cf. Ps 89).[96] He writes, "YHWH has chosen Zion; he has desired it for his habitation: 'This is my resting place forever; here I will dwell, for I have desired it.... There I will make a horn to sprout for David; I have prepared a lamp for my anointed [שָׁם אַצְמִיחַ קֶרֶן לְדָוִד עָרַכְתִּי נֵר לִמְשִׁיחִי; OG ἐκεῖ ἐξανατελῶ κέρας τῷ Δαυιδ, ἡτοίμασα λύχνον τῷ χριστῷ μου]'" (Ps 132:13–17). Here, again, the מָשִׁיחַ of the psalm is the king from the house of David, although not, in this case, a particular office-holder but rather the office itself. The phrase "prepare a lamp for the messiah" means that the deity endorses the current dynasty against would-be usurpers, whether foreign or domestic. Thus, "messiah" in the Psalms, like "Caesar" in the early Roman Empire, can signify not just the current incumbent but the institution, including successors yet to come.

Now compare the first-century BCE *Psalms of Solomon*, a *locus classicus* for modern theories of early Jewish messianism.[97] This corpus of 18 psalms, attested in Greek and Syriac but possibly going back to a Hebrew *Vorlage*,[98] gives a pious interpretation of the turbulent events in Judea in the mid first century BCE: the siege of Jerusalem by Pompey and the end of a century of Hasmonean rule (cf. Josephus, *War* 1.131–58).[99] All eighteen psalms include pleas that God will intervene to resolve matters to the psalmist's satisfaction. Two psalms, in particular, ask God to do so by appointing a legitimate χριστός (rendering מָשִׁיחַ, if there was indeed a Hebrew *Vorlage*), an indigenous king from the house of David. Thus *Ps. Sol.* 17 prays: "See, O Lord, and raise up for them their king, the son of David, at the time which you choose, O God, to rule over Israel your servant.... He shall be a righteous king, taught by God, over them, and there shall be no injustice in his days in their midst, for all shall be holy, and their king shall be the Lord's messiah [βασιλεὺς αὐτῶν χριστὸς

---

96. See J. J. M. Roberts, "The Davidic Origin of the Zion Tradition," in idem, *The Bible and Ancient Near East* (Winona Lake, Ind.: Eisenbrauns, 2002), 313–30; idem, "Zion in the Theology of the Davidic–Solomomic Empire," in *The Bible and Ancient Near East*, 331–47; Schniedewind, *Society and the Promise to David*, 44–46.

97. See, for example, Schürer-Vermes, *History*, 2:503: "The figure of the messianic King is encountered in fuller colour and sharper outline in the Psalms of Solomon"; also Klausner, *Messianic Idea*, 317–24; Collins, *Scepter*, 52–60; Fitzmyer, *One Who Is to Come*, 115–17; and many others.

98. Thus the majority view, but it may be that the Greek text is the original, as recently argued by Jan Joosten, "Reflections on the Original Language of the Psalms of Solomon," in *The Psalms of Solomon: Language, History, Theology* (ed. Eberhard Bons and Patrick Pouchelle; EJL 40; Atlanta, Ga.: SBL, 2015), 31–47.

99. On the historical background, see Atkinson, *I Cried to the Lord*; and the essays in Bons and Pouchelle, eds., *Psalms of Solomon*.

κυρίου]" (*Ps. Sol.* 17:21, 32).[100] And similarly *Ps. Sol.* 18: "May God cleanse Israel for the day of pity with blessing, for the day of election when he brings up his messiah [ἐν ἀνάξει χριστοῦ αὐτοῦ]. Happy are those who shall live in those days, to see the good things of the Lord, which he will perform for the coming generation. Under the rod of discipline of the Lord's messiah in fear of his God [ὑπὸ ῥάβδον παιδείας χριστοῦ κυρίου ἐν φόβῳ θεοῦ αὐτοῦ], in wisdom of spirit and of righteousness and strength" (*Ps. Sol.* 18:5–7).[101] *Psalms of Solomon* is writing centuries after the fall of the house of David, so of course by χριστός the psalmist does not mean a particular, incumbent Judahite king—there being no such person. By χριστός, the psalmist means, roughly, the office of the Judahite king, which he eagerly hopes will soon be occupied once again. Yes, this usage points to the future rather than present, but so does the prayer of Ps 132 that YHWH will ensure the franchise of the house of David in perpetuity. We could create a difference by calling *Pss. Sol.* 17–18 eschatological, but what is eschatology if not just another word for the future?[102]

One more example. There is a less familiar but no less important cluster of biblical משיח texts in the Priestly Torah, in the protocols for sacrifices in Lev 1–7 (Lev 4:3, 5, 16; 6:15). In these texts, משיח is used not as a substantive ("anointed one") but as an adjective with כהן, "priest," thus "the anointed priest."[103] For example, the instructions for the sin offering for the priest are as follows:

> If it is the anointed priest [הכהן המשיח; LXX ὁ ἀρχιερεὺς ὁ κεχρισμένος] who sins, thus bringing guilt on the people, then let him offer for the sin which

---

100. Trans. mod. from NETS.

101. Trans. mod. from NETS.

102. It is standard, of course, to stipulate that eschatology signifies only the very last things, which is etymologically precise, but artificial and ill-suited for many of our primary texts. On this issue, see John Barton, *Oracles of God* (London: Darton, Longman & Todd, 1986), 214–23; Saebo, "Messianism and Eschatology." Gillingham, "Messiah in the Psalms," 210, writes, "The future the psalmists point to, even in postexilic times, appears to be that of the present or the next generation, rather than any great and golden age breaking in from beyond." Yes, but, first, the same is true of *Psalms of Solomon* and many other Roman-period messiah texts, and, second, the notional distinction between the next generation and the golden age is frequently collapsed in the primary sources. Thus rightly Aage Bentzen, *King and Messiah* (London: Lutterworth, 1955 [German original, 1948]), 37: "The difference between the 'cultic' and the 'eschatological' interpretations of the Enthronement Psalms is not very great."

103. On this P material, see Deborah W. Rooke, "Kingship as Priesthood: The Relationship between the High Priesthood and the Monarchy," in *King and Messiah*, 198–206, here 199:

> Of P's seven references to the high priest as "anointed," four of them come in the context of his officiation on behalf of the community as a whole ... thereby apparently underlining the correspondence of the high priesthood with the monarchy as a vocational position that is vital for the well-being of the whole sacral community.

he has committed a young bull without blemish to YHWH for a sin offering. He shall bring the bull to the door of the tent of meeting before YHWH,
and lay his hand on the head of the bull, and kill the bull before YHWH.
And the anointed priest [הכהן המשיח; LXX ὁ ἱερεὺς ὁ χριστός] shall take some
of the blood of the bull and bring it to the tent of meeting; and the priest
shall dip his finger in the blood and sprinkle part of the blood seven times
before YHWH in front of the veil of the sanctuary. (Lev 4:3–6)[104]

In this context, the כהן המשיח is the high priest, in particular (thus the Greek
translator's choice of ἀρχιερεύς for כהן in v. 3). The basic participial sense of
משיח remains live, so that the LXX can use either the standard equivalency
χριστός (v. 5) or the perfect-tense form κεχρισμένος (v. 3). These instructions
for "the anointed priest" either presuppose or are presupposed by the narrative of the consecration by anointing of Aaron and his sons in Lev 8–9.[105]
This P material purports to legislate for the cult of YHWH in the wilderness
tent–shrine and, *mutatis mutandis*, in Solomon's temple. If P was working in
the Persian period,[106] then its purpose may have been to legislate for the cult of
YHWH in the Second Temple. In any case, the כהן המשיח or ἱερεὺς ὁ χριστός of
Lev 1–7 is an officiant in the liturgy, not an eschatological savior figure of any
sort. And yet, he is a template for some Roman-period messiahs.

1QSa (=1Q28a), the much-discussed Rule of the Congregation (*Serekh Ha-
'Edah*) from Qumran, gives instructions for a ritual meal to be attended by the
anointed high priest, the other sons of Aaron, the messiah of Israel, and the
chiefs of the clans of Israel. The text has sometimes been called "the Messianic
Rule" on account of its *dramatis personae* and its stated time frame ("This the
Rule for all the congregation of Israel in the last days" [1QSa 1:1]),[107] but in terms

104. Trans. mod. from RSV.

105. For example, Lev 8:12: "[Moses] poured some of the anointing oil on Aaron's head, and
anointed him, to consecrate him [וימשח אתו לקדשו; LXX ἔχρισεν αὐτὸν καὶ ἡγίασεν αὐτόν]."

106. Which question remains much disputed. See, for example, Joseph Blenkinsopp,
"An Assessment of the Alleged Pre-exilic Date of the Priestly Material in the Pentateuch,"
ZAW 108 (1996): 495–518; and compare Jacob Milgrom, "The Antiquity of the Priestly
Source: A Reply to Joseph Blenkinsopp," *ZAW* 111 (1999): 10–22.

107. Thus, for example, Geza Vermes, *The Complete Dead Sea Scrolls in English* (7th ed.;
London: Penguin, 2011). Likewise Lawrence H. Schiffman, "The Eschatological Community
of the *Serekh Ha-'Edah*," *PAAJR* 51 (1984): 105–29, here 105:

> The text describes the nature of the eschatological community which is structured
> to reflect the ultimate purity and perfection following the dawning of the escha-
> ton. In the present age, the sect's way of life was structured to accord as much as
> possible with their aspirations for the future. *Serekh Ha-'Edah* is a Messianic docu-
> ment picturing the ideal constitution of the sect in the end of days.

of content the text is actually very quotidian. The relevant part of column 2 reads as follows:

> When God engenders (the Priest-) Messiah [יוליד אל את המשיח], he shall come with them [at] the head of the whole congregation of Israel with all [his brethren, the sons] of Aaron the Priests [בני אהרון הכוהנים], [those called] to the assembly, the men of renown; and they shall sit [before him, each man] in the order of his dignity. And then [the Mess]iah of Israel [משיח ישראל] shall [come], and the chiefs of the [clans of Israel] shall sit before him, [each] in the order of his dignity. . . . And [when] they shall gather for the common [tab]le, to eat and [to drink] new wine, when the common table shall be set for eating and the new wine [poured] for drinking, let no man extend his hand over the firstfruits of bread and wine before the Priest [הכוהן]; for [it is he] who shall bless the firstfruits of bread and wine, and shall be the first [to extend] his hand over the bread. Thereafter, the Messiah of Israel [משיח ישראל] shall extend his hand over the bread, [and] all the congregation of the Community [shall utter a] blessing. (1QSa 2:11–21)[108]

Much of the discussion of this text has centered on the verb in the subordinate clause of the first sentence, which Vermes translates "engenders," reading יוליד, from the root ילד, "to beget." This reading is contestable on paleographic grounds, but both early and recent interpreters have tended to support it.[109] For our purposes, it does not matter. The important thing is the cast of characters and the scene. We have, first, the messiah of Israel, who is not a priest but a lay ruler; he is coordinated with the chiefs of the clans of Israel. And we have, second, the (high) priest, who is coordinated with his brothers, the sons of Aaron, the priests. He is not here called the messiah of Aaron (see 1QS 9:9–11; and cf. CD 12:22–13:1; 14:18–19; 19:10–11; 19:33–20:1); but he is apparently identical with the messiah begotten (or sent) by God in line 1. Hence Vermes's gloss "(Priest-) Messiah" is on the right track. Because we have here both a (priest) messiah and the messiah of Israel, it seems to me that 1QSa presupposes the Qumranite motif of the two messiahs of Aaron and Israel.[110]

---

108. Text ed. D. Barthélemy in D. Barthélemy and J. T. Milik, eds., *Qumran Cave I* (DJD 1; Oxford: Clarendon, 1955), 107–18; trans. Vermes, *Complete Dead Sea Scrolls*.

109. On this issue, see Collins, *Scepter*, 81–82.

110. Thus rightly Collins, *Scepter*, 81–82; see also Johannes Zimmermann, *Messianische Texte aus Qumran* (WUNT 2.104; Tübingen: Mohr Siebeck, 1998), 33–34.

In this Rule text, their job is to preside (the priest messiah at the head, the messiah of Israel his attaché) at the ritual meal in the last days.[111]

Morton Smith comments on this and several other related Qumran messiah texts: "There are a number of passages [in the Scrolls] where the word 'messiah' does appear, but refers to some anointed functionary who may have nothing whatever to do with the End, and in any case owes his title to a position quite other than that normally, in modern usage, called messianic."[112] This is to the point. In my view, 1QSa does envision an ideal future state of affairs (which is to say, eschatology)—a state of affairs that includes at least one and probably two persons called messiah. But the particular role that 1QSa assigns to these messiahs is not, say, descending on the clouds to Mount Zion or slaying the wicked with swords from their mouths, but rather presiding at a properly ordered temple meal. In fact, the *mise en scène* has a great deal in common with Lev 1–7. As Smith notes, it is not the kind of thing that we moderns usually call messianic, but it is messianic by Qumran standards and, for that matter, by the standards of the Priestly writer in the Pentateuch.

We might adduce still more examples, but this is enough to make the point. The post-World War II scholarly axiom that in the Hebrew Bible we find mundane "anointed ones" but after the Hebrew Bible eschatological "messiahs" is, well, partly true. To the extent that it rebutted the grand old triumphalist accounts of messianic prophecy (Hengstenberg, Delitzsch, Briggs, and the like), it did a valuable service. But as an analytical tool, it is virtually useless. If we set aside, as we must do, the apologetic and counterapologetic projects handed down to us by our disciplinary forebears, we can see myriad fine points of continuity and change among messiah texts from the Persian, Hellenistic, Roman, and Byzantine periods.[113] As Peter Schäfer has commented, "We are not dealing here with evolutionary stages which can be derived 'genetically' from one another, but with themes or motifs which are

---

111. See Émile Puech, "Préséance sacerdotale et Messie-Roi dans la Règle de la Congrégation (1QSa ii 11–22)," *RevQ* 16 (1995): 351–65; Zimmermann, *Messianische Texte*, 26–34.

112. Smith, "What Is Implied," 67.

113. As rightly highlighted by the mid-twentieth-century Scandinavian Myth and Ritual School (especially Aage Bentzen, *King and Messiah*), about whom John Barton writes:

> In the Scandinavian tradition, as I see it, there is a concern not to lose sight of the wood by concentrating too much on the trees, to avoid the minimalism which might lead an English-speaking or German-speaking critic to note that the developed Messiah concept is not yet present in pre- and most post-exilic literature, and so to declare the idea simply post-biblical. (Barton, "Messiah in Old Testament Theology," 372)

in many ways intertwined and emphasized differently in different periods."[114] And again, "They are to be described adequately only as the dynamic interaction of various and changing configurations within different historical constellations."[115] This is every bit as true of those messiah texts that are now part of the Bible as it is of those that are not.[116]

Conclusion

When is a messiah not a messiah? The answer, according to much of the past half century of research, is when it appears in the Hebrew Bible. Relative to the theologically loaded history of interpretation up to that point, this judgment was a welcome and perhaps necessary corrective. Against the dominant narrative of the smooth evolution of a single messianic idea from premonarchic Israel to a magnificent acme (whether at the time of Jesus, of R. Yohanan b. Zakkai, of Bar Kokhba, of Theodor Herzl, or otherwise), post-World War II scholars rightly pointed out that משיח in the Hebrew Bible does not mean all that it means in many Roman-period and later texts. But if this was a welcome corrective, it also introduced seven other spirits more wicked than the first, or, if not more wicked, at least wicked in a different way. Where before there was precisely one very capacious concept "messiah," now there were precisely two: the mundane, political, ancient Israelite "anointed one" and the *spätjüdisch*, mythical, eschatological "messiah." Hebrew Bible scholars secured their disciplinary jurisdiction over the former at the cost of accepting uncritically the status of the latter.

Perhaps it was a cost worth paying, but it was not necessary to pay it. The conspicuous flaw at the heart of the dominant, Mowinckelian approach is the ubiquitous appeal to a supposed late, technical sense of the word "messiah." In Mowinckel's formulation: "As a title and name for the eschatological king, Messiah does not occur in the Old Testament, but appears first in the literature of later Judaism."[117] Likewise Roberts: "Nowhere in the Old Testament has the term משיח acquired its later technical sense as an eschatological

---

114. Schäfer, "Diversity and Interaction," 20.

115. Schäfer, "Diversity and Interaction," 35.

116. Thus rightly Clements, "Messianic Hope in the Old Testament," 15–16:

> The type of interpretation of these royal prophecies which is found in later Judaism and in the New Testament does not stand isolated and distinct from what has preceded it. Rather it marks the end of a long process of what we have come to describe as "inner-biblical exegesis."

Except that these late Second Temple-period texts do not, in fact, mark the end of the process.

117. Mowinckel, *He That Cometh*, 7.

title."[118] And Fitzmyer: "It is significant that the title משיח does not appear, for it is still too early (520–518 B.C.) for 'Messiah' in the narrow sense."[119] All point to an ostensibly late technical term "messiah," the status of which they take for granted, and the burden of the argument is simply to show that none of the biblical instances of the word משיח means that. Already in 1959, Morton Smith identified and deconstructed this methodological stratagem: "Faced with this embarrassment of messianic riches, the Christian exegete will probably try to define the object of his interest as 'the Messiah'— the one whose coming is to be the major event in the End. But this brings us to the fact that just as there are messiahs without Ends, so there are Ends without messiahs."[120]

In other words, the supposed late, technical sense of messiah is an entirely artificial construct. This might perhaps be excusable, but it is not even a well-formed artificial construct. David Reimer, in a passing comment in an essay on the subject, puts his finger on this issue. Reimer writes, "We agree that 'full blown messianism' (we all know intuitively what we mean by that) is not to be found until very late in the day."[121] Just so. In practice, ostensibly, we all know intuitively what we mean by full-blown messianism, and we all agree that it is not in the Bible. But what exactly do we mean? Intuition can of course be deceptive, and in this case, our intuition that we know what we mean is, in fact, deceptive. Not that we do not articulate definitions; indeed, there are scores of formal definitions of "messiah" on offer, some of which overlap with some others at various points.[122] But such definitions, almost without exception, are entirely arbitrary. They take the form: Let "messiah" mean x. They are stipulated rather than defended. We are of course free to stipulate such definitions, but we should recognize that to do so is to beg the question.

Interestingly, at one key moment in his own argument, Mowinckel comes very close to conceding this criticism. He writes, "All the genuinely Messianic passages in the Old Testament date from the time after the fall of the monarchy and the destruction of the Israelite states. Of those passages which are commonly held to be Messianic, only Isa. vii and ix, 1ff. can with certainty be

118. Roberts, "Old Testament's Contribution," 51.

119. Fitzmyer, One Who Is to Come, 52.

120. Smith, "What Is Implied," 68. Compare the exact opposite statement of Mowinckel, He That Cometh, 8: "An eschatology without a Messiah is conceivable, but not a Messiah apart from a future hope." Smith, who has the better side of this argument, does not indicate whether he is responding to Mowinckel, who had written just a few years prior.

121. David J. Reimer, "Old Testament Christology," in King and Messiah, 380–400 at 384.

122. See the discussion in Chapter 1 in this volume.

referred to the pre-exilic age, but they are not Messianic in the strict sense. This may seem to the reader to be a *petitio principii*, but it is not."[123] But no explanation follows. Mowinckel denies the charge of question-begging, but he does not defend himself from it. In fact, his argument at this point is a text-book example of *petitio principii*. The whole thing hangs on how one defines "genuinely messianic" or "messianic in the strict sense," which Mowinckel does literally on page 1. The balance of the book, although it is a gold mine of incisive exegetical observations, is preoccupied with showing systematically that no preexilic text fits the definition stipulated on the first page. Mowinckel succeeds in proving his thesis, but the thesis itself is, strictly speaking, trivial.

James Muilenburg, giving due praise to *He That Cometh* in a review in *JBL* in 1957, wrote, "Once the definitions of Mowinckel are accepted, it is difficult to resist the force and persuasiveness of his arguments."[124] Indeed. "Once the definitions of Mowinckel are accepted." Muilenburg, for his part, is happy to accept Mowinckel's definitions and thus all that follows, but as I have argued in this chapter, there are good reasons for challenging Mowinckel's definitions. And if we do so, then the resultant picture turns out to be quite different. We can see, with Mowinckel, how Hellenistic- and Roman-period Jewish writers added creative new layers of mythology to their source texts. But we can also see how they often reused or imitated those source texts, adding little or nothing in the way of innovation.[125] In these latter cases, the difference between an ancient Israelite "anointed one" and an early Jewish "messiah" is effectively nil. This may be a disappointment for the historian of ideas, but it is an essential piece of evidence for the exegete.

For the exegete, it is entirely possible and methodologically far preferable to describe the various ancient uses of the word "messiah" and the pertinent differences among them without artificially privileging one as the ostensibly real, proper, strict, fully evolved definition.[126] We can appreciate how, in their historical context, interpreters like Mowinckel made a genuine advance over

---

123. Mowinckel, *He That Cometh*, 20.

124. Muilenburg, review of Mowinckel, *He That Cometh*, in *JBL* 76 (1957): 244.

125. Thus rightly Smith, "What Is Implied," 68: "The state of affairs in the [Qumran] scrolls is a heritage from the OT and a parallel to the pseudepigrapha and the rabbinic literature."

126. Thus rightly Bentzen, *King and Messiah*, 37:

> When we know what we mean, and are sure that we shall not be misunderstood by readers and listeners, it will be much more in tune with the material which we have to investigate and describe to use the expressions "Messiah" and "Messianic" of a figure which changes through the ages, but still retains certain essential characteristic features even through changed circumstances.

the powerful legacy of interpreters like Hengstenberg.[127] But it is no credit to us twenty-first-century interpreters if we carry on repeating Mowinckel's point for emphasis, as many of us continue to do. We ought to have found more interesting things to say by now. To be fair, some have found more interesting things to say. (May their tribe increase.) The messiah texts in the Hebrew Bible are fascinating in their own right and historically generative out of all proportion to their small number. Sixty years after *He That Cometh*, there is no longer any point in showing what these texts do not mean. Whatever worthwhile research remains lies in showing what they do mean.

---

127. Again, rightly, Bentzen, *King and Messiah*, 37: " That some people want to restrict the word 'Messiah' to the Saviour of Eschatology is based only on a praiseworthy desire for clarity of expression."

3

Messiahs Born and Made

WRITING NEAR THE end of the first century CE, the author of the
Gospel of Matthew takes from his source and revises a curious dialogue between Jesus and the Pharisees in which he asks them, "What
do you think about the messiah? Whose son is he [τίνος υἱός ἐστιν]?"
to which the Pharisees respond, quite sensibly, "David's" (Matt 22:42).
Jesus objects to this answer, however, with a dexterous interpretation
of Psalm 110, suggesting that the messiah is not the son of David at all
but, perhaps, the son of God (Matt 22:43–45; cf. Mark 12:35–37).[1] Some
three centuries later, working perhaps not far from where Matthew
wrote his Gospel, the editors of the Talmud Yerushalmi relate a story
about a Jew living in Israel during the late first century CE who one
day receives news both that the temple has been destroyed and that
the king messiah has been born. The Jew responds by questioning
the Arab who brought the news: "The Jew asked, 'What is his name?'
'Menahem,' he said. 'And what is his father's name [ומה שמיה דאבוי]?'
he asked. 'Hezekiah,' he said. 'Where is he from?' he asked. 'From the
royal city, Bethlehem in Judah,' he said" (*y. Ber.* 2:4 [5a]).[2] Just as Jesus
in Matthew asks the Pharisees, "Whose son is the messiah?" so the Jew
in *y. Ber.* 2:4 asks the Arab, "What is the name of the messiah's father?"
In these texts, the issue of the ancestry of the messiah—Whose son
is he?—is at the forefront. For them, at least part of what makes the

---

1. This passage is discussed later in this chapter.

2. Trans. Himmelfarb, "Mother of the Messiah"; text per Peter Schäfer and Hans-Jürgen
Becker, eds., *Synopse zum Talmud Yerushalmi* (7 vols.; Tübingen: Mohr Siebeck, 1991–2001).

messiah the messiah is the identity of his father, the family from which he comes.[3] Other messiah texts (e.g., *Parables of Enoch, 2 Baruch*), in contrast, give no indication of any interest in the matter of the messiah's ancestry. They characterize their messiahs in other ways and justify them on other grounds.

There is a related puzzle in the secondary literature on messianism. In light of the importance accorded to ancestry in many messiah texts, modern interpreters have tried to explain how the genealogies of certain historical persons will have contributed to their being called messiahs, or not, in the ancient sources. So, for instance, Joseph Klausner goes to some lengths explaining why there are in antiquity some non-Davidides who merit the title messiah and other non-Davidides who do not, even though they might seem to us like promising candidates. For instance, regarding the sons of Mattathias who led the Jewish revolt against the Seleucids in the 160s BCE, Klausner writes, "Neither Judas Maccabeus nor any other member of the Hasmonean house could have been considered in their time as the Messiah, because the first generations could not have conceived of a man not of the house of David sitting on the royal throne of Israel."[4] In other words, Judah Maccabee is never called messiah in the sources because he was not a Davidide,[5] and second-century BCE Jewish writers knew better than to call a non-Davidide the messiah.

Some three centuries later, however, another non-Davidide Judean, Shimon bar Kosiba,[6] led a rather less successful revolt against the Seleucids' imperial successors, the Romans, and he, Bar Kosiba, does enjoy the title messiah in the literary record. Why this difference? Referring to the passage in the Talmud Yerushalmi where the tanna R. Akiba hails Bar Kosiba as the messiah, Klausner writes:

---

3. In the texts with which we are concerned, by and large, a patrilineal logic is presupposed (see Caroline Johnson Hodge, *If Sons Then Heirs: A Study of Kinship and Ethnicity in the Letters of Paul* [New York, N.Y.: Oxford University Press, 2007], 19–42). The well known rabbinic matrilineal principle for determining Jewishness is another matter, on which see Shaye J. D. Cohen, *The Beginnings of Jewishness: Boundaries, Varieties, Uncertainties* (Berkeley, Calif.: University of California Press, 1999), 263–307. In a few texts from the late first century CE and later, the mother of the messiah becomes an important character in her own right (see Himmelfarb, "Mother of the Messiah"; Markus Bockmuehl, "The Son of David and His Mother," *JTS* n.s. 62 [2011]: 476–93).

4. Klausner, *Messianic Idea*, 250.

5. But rather (probably) a Levite (1 Macc 2:1–5), although see the discussion later in this chapter.

6. Whose genealogy is simply unknown.

R. Akiba proclaimed Bar-Cochba as Messiah, even though he was not of the house of David, had done no miracles, and was not even distinguished for great piety. Bar-Cochba's great spirit of heroism was enough in itself to make him Messiah in the eyes of one of the greatest of the Tannaim.[7]

For Klausner, in other words, Bar Kosiba's distinction on the field of battle was so great as to warrant a bending of the rules, so that despite his lack of ancestral qualifications, he was able to earn for himself the title messiah—in the eyes of R. Akiba, if not in fact. I disagree with Klausner on the details (see the discussion later in this chapter), but he is quite right in identifying this literary phenomenon and in posing the question how we ought to explain it.

Not a few scholars have tried to explain it by appealing to the relative strength or weakness of messianism as an ideological force at the time of the composition of the relevant texts. Thus Claude Reignier Conder, writing in the late nineteenth century, comments on the Maccabean revolt,

It is not a little important to understand clearly what was the general Jewish expectation at this time with regard to a future Messiah, or anointed King, temporal or spiritual. If, at the time of the revolt, such an expectation had been general, there would no doubt have been a strong party which would have recognised in the appearance of Judas the fulfillment of their hopes. Yet in the history of the Hasmoneans we find no hint that he was ever so regarded.[8]

For Conder, in other words, Judah Maccabee is not called a messiah because in the second century BCE messianism had ebbed low among the Jewish people.

In contrast, Julius Hillel Greenstone, writing at the beginning of the twentieth century, cites Conder in order to contradict him:

Some writers would conclude that the hope for a personal Messiah had died out in the minds of the people, because there is no reference in

---

7. Klausner, *Messianic Idea*, 395.

8. Claude Reignier Conder, *Judas Maccabaeus and the Jewish War of Independence* (new ed.; London: Watt, 1894 [1st ed., 1879]), 68. In contrast, Conder writes about the early Roman period, "The expectation of a future native King, which had perhaps first sprung up at the time of the quarrel between Hyrcanus and the Pharisees, waxed stronger and stronger, until, by the time of Christ, it had completely taken possession of the heart of the people" (197). For a similar account, see Drummond, *Jewish Messiah*, 196–99.

contemporary literature to the belief that Judah Maccabee, the redeemer of his people, the beloved general of his army, and the adored hero of his nation, was the long-expected Messiah—a belief most natural in the circumstances. . . . To my mind, the opposite is proved. The Messianic ideal was so firmly rooted and so clearly defined, and its association with the personal Messiah, the king of the house of David, so obvious, that the people would regard no one as a Messiah except a scion of the Davidic dynasty. Since Judah was a priest, he could not be the Messiah.[9]

Greenstone agrees with Conder that there is such a thing as the messianic idea, and that our primary texts attest its relative strength or weakness at this or that point in Jewish history. For Greenstone, however, it is a sign of the strength of the messianic idea if the primary sources adhere strictly to biblical rules of dynastic succession, even if that means their abstaining from messiah discourse altogether. Here is an illustration, if ever there was one, of the axiom that evidence does not interpret itself. Depending whether one asks Conder or Greenstone, the fact that pro-Hasmonean texts never call Judah Maccabee a messiah is proof either of the frailty of messianism during the second century BCE or, conversely, of its vigor. This way of thinking about the problem is especially common in older treatments, but it is amply represented in recent scholarship as well.[10] Per my argument in Chapter 1, I find this way of thinking about the problem gravely problematic. The purpose of the present chapter, therefore, is to give a more satisfactory account of how ancestry and merit work in ancient messiah texts,[11] how some messiahs are born and others made. Or, to put it differently, a better answer to Klausner's question why Shimon bar Kosiba is called messiah while Judah Maccabee is not.

From as far back as we have texts about messiahs, many of them attest a preoccupation with the issue of ancestry. In line with the haggadic questions posed by Matthew ("Whose son is he?") and Yerushalmi Berakhot ("What is his father's name?"), messiahs in early Jewish and Christian texts are, in fact, frequently identified by patronyms. In sources from the Hellenistic, Roman, and Byzantine periods, we encounter a cast of characters including messiah son of David, messiah son of Aaron, messiah son of Israel, messiah son of Joseph,

---

9. Greenstone, *Messiah Idea*, 64–65.

10. See, for example, Charlesworth, "From Jewish Messianology to Christian Christology"; idem, "From Messianology to Christology"; Fitzmyer, *One Who Is to Come*.

11. I take the rubric of ancestry and merit from Martha Himmelfarb, *A Kingdom of Priests: Ancestry and Merit in Ancient Judaism* (Philadelphia, Pa.: University of Pennsylvania Press, 2006).

messiah son of Ephraim, and messiah son of God.[12] Understandably, texts that imagine future messiahs often attribute to them whatever genealogy they like, while texts that have to reckon with particular historical messiahs are more constrained in this respect.[13] In particular, some messiah texts that reckon with the careers of particular persons are entirely silent regarding questions of ancestry, while others in this category are pointedly concerned with such questions. As George Foot Moore put it, "There were times when the deliverance was of greater moment than the lineage of the deliverer."[14] In short, the issue of proper ancestry—one's having it or not having it, precisely what counts as proper, and the implications for one's eligibility for office—is a bone of contention in not all but many early Jewish and Christian messiah texts. It behooves us, therefore, to try to understand why each respective text makes the particular choices it does in marshaling credentials for its messiah or messiahs.

Zerubbabel ben Shealtiel

Chronologically, the first historical figure who warrants our attention here is Zerubbabel, the late sixth-century governor of the Persian province of Yehud (פחת יהודה in Hag 1:1), who was instrumental in the construction of the Second Temple.[15] The principal sources for Zerubbabel are biblical (Chronicles, Ezra, Nehemiah, Haggai, Zechariah) rather than postbiblical, but he is the first in a series of figures in the Second-Temple period who were, in the eyes of some of their contemporaries, candidates for the role of messiah. Zerubbabel is not called משיח in the biblical sources, but he and his attendant high priest Joshua are called the שני בני־היצהר, "two sons of oil" in Zech 4:14, which is generally and rightly taken as an idiom for ritual anointing (cf. NRSV: "two anointed ones").[16] It is no accident, then, that some centuries later *Targum Jonathan* to Zechariah (at Zech 3:8; 4:7; 6:12–13) makes the identification of Zerubbabel with the messiah explicit.

---

12. On this commonplace, see Joel Marcus, "Are You the Messiah-Son-of-God?" *NovT* 31 (1989): 125–41.

13. On the latter phenomenon, see the discussion in Chapter 6 in this volume.

14. Moore, *Judaism*, 2:327.

15. In this connection, we might also discuss, if we had not already done so in Chapter 2, Cyrus II of Persia, whom Second Isaiah calls a messiah (Isa 45:1) despite his being a gentile, thus bypassing ancestral qualifications of even the most general sort (on which phenomenon see Lemaire, "Messies non-israélites").

16. Thus rightly Collins, *Scepter*, 34–46; contra Wolter H. Rose, *Zemah and Zerubbabel: Messianic Expectations in the Early Postexilic Period* (JSOTSup 304; Sheffield: Sheffield Academic, 2000), 200–6, who argues that the two sons of oil are not human leaders but divine attendants in the heavenly court.

Thus, for instance, *Tg.* Zech 4:7: "Of what worth are you before Zerubbabel, you foolish kingdom? Are you not like a plain? For he shall reveal his messiah, whose name was called from the beginning, and he shall have dominion over all the kingdoms."[17] If, from the perspective of the Deuteronomistic History, the preexilic political ideal was an anointed king like David and an anointed high priest like Zadok (see 2 Sam 15; 1 Kgs 1), then Zerubbabel and Joshua are the first, best approximations of this ideal in the postexilic period.

The glaring difference, of course, is that Zerubbabel was not a king. Zechariah, however, may still reflect the hope that he would be:

> Thus says YHWH of hosts: Behold, the man whose name is Branch [הנה־איש צמח שמו], for he shall grow up in his place and shall build the temple of YHWH. It is he who shall build the temple of YHWH, and shall bear majesty, and shall sit and rule upon his throne [והוא יבנה את־היכל יהוה והוא־ישא הוד וישב ומשל על־כסאו]. And there shall be a priest by his throne, and peaceful understanding shall be between them both. (Zech 6:12–13)[18]

The title צמח, "branch," is frequently an idiom for a dynastic successor (so the gloss "scion" in some modern translations)[19] and is used in Jeremiah with reference to the house of David (Jer 23:5: "I will raise up for David a צמח צדיק"; Jer 33:15: "I will cause a צמח צדקה to spring forth for David").[20] The Zechariah 6 oracle presents some difficulties, but in its original context it most likely refers to Zerubbabel as the branch who grows, builds the temple, attains royal honor, and is attended by a high priest.[21]

Zechariah's colleague, the prophet Haggai, seems to have shared a similar optimism for the political prospects of the governor:

> Speak to Zerubbabel, governor of Judah, saying, I am about to shake the heavens and the earth, and to overthrow the throne of kingdoms;

---

17. Trans. mod. from Samson H. Levey, *The Messiah: An Aramaic Interpretation* (HUCM 2; Cincinnati, Ohio: HUC Press, 1974), 98, who comments, "Zerubbabel seems to be taken as the name of the Messiah, for it is in comparison with him that the high mountain is like a plain. In the course of the evolution of the Messiah idea Zerubbabel was considered a Messianic personality" (98).

18. Trans. mod. from RSV.

19. See BDB, s.v. צמח; Moore, *Judaism*, 2:325.

20. But the latter oracle, which is unattested in OG Jeremiah, is probably a later addition, indeed, perhaps from the time of Zerubbabel, on which possibility see Y. Goldman, *Prophétie et royauté au retour de l'exil* (OBO 118; Göttingen: Vandenhoeck & Ruprecht, 1992).

21. Thus rightly Collins, *Scepter*, 34–36.

I am about to destroy the strength of the kingdoms of the nations, and overthrow the chariots and their riders; and the horses and their riders shall go down, every one by the sword of his fellow. On that day, says YHWH of hosts, I will take you, O Zerubbabel my servant, son of Shealtiel, says YHWH, and make you like a signet ring [חותם]; for I have chosen you, says YHWH of hosts. (Hag 2:21–23)[22]

If some of his Judean partisans, such as Haggai, hoped that the throne of the Persians would be thrown down and replaced by the throne of Zerubbabel, this was, unfortunately, not to be. These prophetic oracles, however, probably reflect a moment during the last quarter of the sixth century when it looked to some as though such a thing might indeed be possible.[23]

In view of these texts, we might well ask what about Zerubbabel was cause for such enthusiasm. What qualified him to be the "royal branch" or one of the "two sons of oil" in Zechariah's visions? Here the reader will recall that, according to the Chronicler, Zerubbabel was a Davidide, the grandson of king Jehoiachin (that is, Jeconiah) of Judah (1 Chr 3:19). Ezra, Nehemiah, and Haggai consistently call him Zerubbabel son of Shealtiel (who is named as one of the sons of Jehoiachin in 1 Chr 3:17), while Zechariah only ever refers to him *sans* patronym.[24] It has been suggested—by Kenneth Pomykala, in particular—that Zerubbabel's Davidic ancestry is a fiction invented by the Chronicler, that Zerubbabel was simply a Judean of unremarkable ancestry whom the Persians happen to have appointed as governor.[25] If so, then whatever prophetic excitement there was was occasioned only by the political events of which Zerubbabel was part. This is not impossible, but it seems to me that that the primary texts are better accounted for on the supposition

---

22. Trans. mod. from RSV.

23. See Joachim Schaper, "The Persian Period," in *Redemption and Resistance: The Messianic Hopes of Jews and Christians in Antiquity* (ed. Markus Bockmuehl and James Carleton Paget; London: T. & T. Clark, 2007), 3–14 at 6:

> Zerubbabel is possibly best understood as a figure of potential resistance against the new Achaemenid order: while he was the governor appointed by the Persians to run the Yehud province, he was also a Davidide and thus an obvious focus of attention and hope to all those who were expecting a restoration of Davidic rule.

24. See Ezra 2:2; 3:2, 8; 4:2; 5:2; Neh 7:7; 12:1, 47; Hag 1:1, 12, 14; 2:2, 4, 21, 23; Zech 4:6, 7, 9, 10.

25. See Pomykala, *Davidic Dynasty Tradition*, 45–60, here 46:

> Zerubbabel's status as a davidic descendant rests on very fragile grounds. . . . It may be that the Chronicler has secondarily grafted Zerubbabel, a non-davidic post-exilic leader, into the davidic family tree to emphasize the continuity between the post-exilic temple built by Zerubbabel and pre-exilic traditions.

that Zerubbabel was indeed descended from Jehoiachin, as Chronicles says he was.[26] Such a dynastic claim would best explain the title צמח and the image of the anointed king alongside an anointed priest.[27] If this is the case, then Zerubbabel is a parade example of what we might call a born messiah, a blue-blood candidate for the Judean monarchy. He was a son of David who seemed, briefly, to be in a position to restore the glory of the house of David until cold, hard imperial reality intervened.

The Hasmoneans

After Zerubbabel, apparently, the provincial governorship passed from Davidic hands, and eventually it passed away altogether, giving way to imperial government via an indigenous hierocracy.[28] With respect to our focal question, the next significant development is the second- and first-century BCE discussion among several Jewish texts concerning the ancestry of Judah Maccabee and his brothers. The Hasmonean family had led a revolt expelling the Seleucid rulers and their Jewish sympathizers from Judea. In the wake of the revolt, the sons of Mattathias naturally set about establishing a measure of Judean self-rule, but doing so involved navigating certain archaic Israelite protocols regarding ancestral credentials for high office. The Hasmoneans were a priestly family (1 Macc 2:1), but there is some dispute whether they were Zadokites, the priestly clan that apparently had held the high priesthood in Jerusalem for the entire Second-Temple period to that point.[29]

---

26. In agreement with Sara Japhet, "Sheshbazzar and Zerubbabel against the Background of the Historical and Religious Tendencies of Ezra-Nehemiah, Part 1," in eadem, *From the Rivers of Babylon to the Highlands of Judah* (Winona Lake, Ind.: Eisenbrauns, 2006), 58; Schniedewind, *Society and the Promise to David*, 120, 133–35; H. G. M. Williamson, "Early Post-Exilic Judaean History," in idem, *Studies in Persian Period History and Historiography* (FAT 38; Tübingen: Mohr Siebeck, 2004), 3–24, especially 14; Collins, *Scepter*, 34–36.

27. Thus rightly David Goodblatt, *The Monarchic Principle* (TSAJ 38; Tübingen: Mohr Siebeck, 1994), 58:

> [Zerubbabel's genealogy] is not explicitly mentioned by either Haggai or Zechariah, but both use terminology and imagery with Davidic royalist associations. And clearly it was Zerubbabel's inner-Judean sources of legitimation, not his appointment to office by the Persians, that mattered for Haggai and Zechariah.

28. On this period, see H. G. M. Williamson, "The Governors of Judah under the Persians," *TynBul* 39 (1988): 59–82.

29. The Zadokite priesthood itself is elusive in the sources and controversial in recent discussion. See Deborah W. Rooke, *Zadok's Heirs: The Role and Development of the High*

Even if they were Zadokites (as Alison Schofield and James VanderKam have argued),[30] and all the more so if they were not,[31] the Hasmoneans were newcomers to the Jerusalem high priesthood—that is, they were not Oniads[32]—and consequently they found themselves having to defend their legitimacy.[33] The book that has come down to us as 1 Maccabees is largely an exercise in doing just this. The author narrates the accession of Simon Maccabee to the high priesthood as follows:

> The Jews and their priests decided that Simon should be their leader and high priest for ever [ἡγούμενον καὶ ἀρχιερέα εἰς τὸν αἰῶνα], until a trustworthy prophet should arise [ἕως τοῦ ἀναστῆναι προφήτην πιστόν], and that he should be governor [στρατηγόν] over them and that he should take charge of the sanctuary (1 Macc 14:41–42).

Simon is declared to be high priest "forever," or rather, the author clarifies, "until a trustworthy prophet should arise," where the latter clause is best understood as a concession to the irregularity of the arrangement.[34] Rather

---

Priesthood in Ancient Israel (Oxford: Clarendon, 2000); James C. VanderKam, *From Joshua to Caiaphas: High Priests after the Exile* (Minneapolis, Minn.: Fortress, 2004); Alice Hunt, *Missing Priests: The Zadokites in Tradition and History* (LHBOTS 452; London: T. & T. Clark, 2006); Maria Brutti, *The Development of the High Priesthood during the Pre-Hasmonean Period* (JSJSup 108; Leiden: Brill, 2006).

30. Alison Schofield and James C. VanderKam, "Were the Hasmoneans Zadokites?" *JBL* 124 (2005): 73–87; and similarly Regev Eyal, *The Hasmoneans: Ideology, Archaeology, Identity* (JAJSup 10; Göttingen: Vandenhoeck & Ruprecht, 2013), 103–28.

31. Thus, for example, Lawrence H. Schiffman, *The Halakhah at Qumran* (Leiden: Brill, 1975), 75; L. Dequeker, "1 Chronicles XXIV and the Royal Priesthood of the Hasmoneaons," in *Crises and Perspectives: Studies in Ancient Near Eastern Polytheism, Biblical Theology, Palestinian Archaeology, and Intertestamental Literature* (Leiden: Brill, 1986), 94–106; Hanan Eshel, *The Dead Sea Scrolls and the Hasmonean State* (Grand Rapids, Mich.: Eerdmans, 2008), 29–61; Rooke, *Zadok's Heirs*, 280–81.

32. See Daniel R. Schwartz, *2 Maccabees* (CEJL; Berlin: De Gruyter, 2008), 13: "Jonathan's acceptance of the high priesthood meant a parting of the ways between the Hasmoneans and the Oniads; it was effectively a Hasmonean announcement that to the victors go the spoils and that they would not content themselves with fighting and concede the high priesthood."

33. On this burden, see Morton Smith, "Were the Maccabees Priests?" in idem, *Studies in the Cult of Yahweh*, 1:320–25; Tessa Rajak, "Hasmonean Kingship and the Invention of Tradition," in eadem, *The Jewish Dialogue with Greece and Rome: Studies in Cultural and Social Interaction* (Leiden: Brill, 2001), 58: "The rediscovery, or invention of native tradition is . . . a central preoccupation, pervading the Hasmonean high priesthood and kingship. This process is a key to interpreting the mentality and the image of these rulers."

34. Compare the similar account of the purification of the temple in 1 Macc 4:44–46:

than simply claim that Simon is the rightful heir to the office, the author demurs, citing exceptional circumstances. He knows there are some who would challenge Simon's right to the high priesthood,[35] and the reference to a distant future when a trustworthy prophet will sort things out is a way of preempting any such objections.[36]

Another way of doing the same thing is to appeal straightforwardly to merit rather than ancestry as a qualification. In this connection, it is noteworthy that 1 Maccabees makes such a great deal of the figure of Phinehas, the grandson of Aaron, who famously proved his zeal by executing an offending member of the Israelite congregation at Baal Peor in the wilderness of Moab, thereby earning for himself and his descendants a "covenant of perpetual priesthood [MT ברית כהנת עולם; LXX διαθήκη ἱερατείας αἰωνία]" (Num 25:1–13). This episode in Numbers betrays a source or redactional seam, because in the Pentateuchal narrative, God had already granted the priesthood to Aaron's family (Exod 28:1–5; 29:1–9; Lev 9). The Phinehas story, however, supplies a reason for the priestly covenant: It is no mere dynastic heirloom; rather, it is a divine reward for exceptional merit.[37] Significantly, 1 Maccabees makes no mention of Zadok and only one mention of Aaron (1 Macc 7:14), but the author expressly portrays the Maccabees as imitators of and heirs to Phinehas at the outset of the revolt (1 Macc 2:23–26)[38] and in the

---

They deliberated what to do about the altar of burnt offering, which had been profaned. And they thought it best to tear it down, lest it bring reproach upon them, for the gentiles had defiled it. So they tore down the altar, and stored the stones in a convenient place on the temple hill until there should come a prophet [μέχρι τοῦ παραγενηθῆναι προφήτην] to tell what to do with them.

35. Including, perhaps, the Qumran covenanters, if the "wicked priest" who opposes the "teacher of righteousness" (see 1QpHab 8:4–11; 9:8–12; 11:3–16) is to be identified with one or more of the Hasmonean high priests, about which see the recent discussion of John J. Collins, *Beyond the Qumran Community: The Sectarian Movement of the Dead Sea Scrolls* (Grand Rapids: Eerdmans, 2010), 88–121.

36. Thus rightly Goodblatt, *Monarchic Principle*, 75–76:

Clearly the advent of a true prophet was not assumed to be imminent. In the meantime Simeon and his descendants could serve as high priests. Nor was Simeon to be disappointed, for his descendants held the office for a century. And when they were displaced, it was not by a true prophet but by *force majeure* exercised by King Herod.

37. On this anomaly in the Pentateuch, see Jacob Milgrom, *Numbers* (Philadelphia, Pa.: JPS, 1990), 476–80; Baruch A. Levine, *Numbers 21–36* (AB; New York, N.Y.: Doubleday, 2000), 297–300.

38. 1 Macc 2:24–26: "When Mattathias saw it, he burned with zeal and his heart was stirred. He gave vent to righteous anger; he ran and killed him upon the altar.... Thus he burned with zeal for the law, as Phinehas did against Zimri son of Salu."

deathbed testimony of Mattathias (1 Macc 2:54).[39] The message is that the Hasmoneans, like Phinehas of old, are worthy to hold the high priesthood on account of their pious zeal, despite any genealogical objections that might be raised.[40] As Morton Smith comments, "They [the Hasmoneans] might have claimed the 'eternal priesthood' promised him [Phinehas] (Num 25:13), just as they claimed the eternal priesthood exercised by Melchizedek, where they saw yet another opportunity to appeal to a standard of priesthood other than that by which they were excluded."[41]

Some sixty years after the revolt, a Hasmonean high priest, Aristobulus I, took the additional step of assuming the title of king of Judea (see Josephus, *Ant.* 13.301).[42] Relative to ancient Mediterranean political norms, this was not an absurd thing to do, but here again the Hasmonean dynasty bumped clumsily into another archaic rule of ancestry and succession.[43] According to one strand of scriptural tradition encapsulated in the divine promise of 2 Sam 7, the Judahite kingship could only ever be occupied by a son of David.[44] Throughout the Persian and Hellenistic periods, of course, this dynastic rule had been obsolete and therefore, strictly speaking, not in a state of contravention. Aristobulus I was the first Judean king in nearly five hundred years, but he was also not a Davidide, so some of his traditionally minded countrymen

---

39. 1 Macc 2:54: "Phinehas our father, because he was deeply zealous, received the covenant of everlasting priesthood."

40. Thus rightly Schwartz, *2 Maccabees*, 13n30: "As for Phinehas ... , so too for the Hasmoneans, zealotry entitled them to the high priesthood."

41. Smith, "Were the Maccabees Priests?" 325.

42. On this turn of events, see Rajak, "Hasmonean Kingship," 47–48:

> It is ... unclear whether internal caution alone prevented Hyrcanus from calling himself king: it may well be that so big a step still required Seleucid approval. Josephus certainly regards it as a major landmark in post-exilic history when finally, in 104 B.C., the diadem is adopted by Aristobulus, Hyrcanus' son and short-lived successor (*AJ* XIII 301). Interestingly, the technical phrase, διάδημα πρῶτος περιτίθεται, is used here by the historian.

43. See Arie van der Kooij, "The Greek Bible and Jewish Concepts of Royal Priesthood and Priestly Monarchy," in *Jewish Perspectives on Hellenistic Rulers* (ed. Tessa Rajak et al.; Berkeley, Calif.: University of California Press, 2007), 255–64.

44. Granted, it is only one strand of scriptural tradition, as rightly noted by David Flusser, "Judaism in the Second Temple Period," in idem, *Judaism of the Second Temple Period* (2 vols.; trans. Azzan Yadin; Grand Rapids, Mich.: Eerdmans, 2007–2009), 2:6–2:43 at 2:33: "Even when the Maccabees did assume the crown, this would not necessarily have caused their opponents to deny the legitimacy of Hasmonean rule since, halakhically, the kings of Israel do not have to be from the House of David." But as Flusser himself acknowledges, this one strand of scriptural tradition was disproportionately influential in some quarters.

were not as happy with his accession as they might have been.[45] The Qumran covenanters, it appears, took offense at the conflation of the royal and priestly offices, which may explain why they take care to distinguish the messiah of Aaron and his duties from the messiah of Israel and his duties (1QS 9:11; cf. CD 12:23; 14:19; 19:10; 20:1).[46]

The first-century BCE *Psalms of Solomon* are equally critical of Aristobulus and his successors, but for a rather different reason. *Psalms of Solomon* rails against the Hasmonean dynasty for usurping the Judean kingship, which in the psalmist's view may only be held by a legitimate descendant of David:

> Because of our sins, sinners rose up against us; they attacked us and thrust us out, to whom you did not promise [οἷς οὐκ ἐπηγγείλω]; they took possession by force, and they did not glorify your honorable name. They set up in glory a palace corresponding to their loftiness; they laid waste the throne of David in arrogance, introducing change [ἠρήμωσαν τὸν θρόνον Δαυιδ ἐν ὑπερηφανίᾳ ἀλλάγματος]. But you, O God, will overthrow them and will remove their offspring from the earth, when there rises up against them a person foreign to our race. (*Ps. Sol.* 17:5–7)[47]

The Hasmoneans are "sinners to whom God did not promise" the kingship. They "laid waste the throne of David" and "arrogantly introduced change" to the institution of the monarchy. But not with impunity. As the last clause of this passage suggests, the psalmist knows that the Hasmonean dynasty was brought to an end by a pagan enemy—namely Rome. Indeed, *Psalms of Solomon* interprets Pompey's desecration of the Jerusalem temple in 63 BCE as divine judgment on the Hasmonean interlopers: "Foreign nations went up

---

45. See Moore, *Judaism*, 2:328: "It is very unlikely that the biblical scholars of the time as a class, and the party of the Pharisees, were inclined to bestow upon the priests who had mounted the throne the predictions of the restoration of the legitimate monarchy"; and more recently Rooke, "Kingship as Priesthood," 207: "It may well be that the perceived usurpation of the monarchy was a far more heinous crime than the illegitimate assumption of the high priesthood. After all, a priest is basically a religious functionary, and at least the Hasmonaeans were of priestly descent."

46. Thus rightly A. S. van der Woude, *Die messianische Vorstellungen der Gemeinde von Qumran* (SSN 3; Assen: van Gorcum, 1957), 32–33, 60–61; K. G. Kuhn, "The Two Messiahs of Aaron and Israel," in *The Scrolls and the New Testament* (ed. Krister Stendahl; New York, N.Y.: Crossroad, 1992 [1957]), 54–64; Joseph Liver, "The Doctrine of the Two Messiahs in Sectarian Literature in the Time of the Second Commonwealth," *HTR* 52 (1959): 149–85; Schürer-Vermes, *History*, 2:550–54; Talmon, "Concept of *Masiah*"; Collins, *Scepter*, 79–109; *pace* Martin Abegg, "The Messiah at Qumran: Are We Still Seeing Double?" *DSD* 2 (1995): 125–44.

47. Trans. mod. from NETS.

to your altar; in pride they trampled it with their sandals, because the sons of Jerusalem had defiled the sanctuary of the Lord, had profaned the gifts of God with acts of lawlessness" (*Ps. Sol.* 2:2–3). This anti-Hasmonean sentiment, in turn, becomes a crucial factor in the psalmist's fervent prayer for a righteous messiah who is a legitimate descendant of the house of David (*Pss. Sol.* 17–18).[48]

Herod the Great

The authors of the *Psalms of Solomon* were no doubt glad to see the end of the Hasmonean kingship; but, unhappily for them, what came next (following an interregnum of direct Roman rule) was not the renewal of the house of David, but the rise of the house of Herod,[49] which itself provides another instructive example of literary disputes over ancestry.[50] Like the first kings of the Hasmonean dynasty to which he was successor, Herod was, strictly speaking, an interloper.[51] He attained the throne as a result of the goodwill of Octavian (Josephus, *War* 1.386–92; *Ant.* 15.187–201),[52] not any dynastic claim of his own, because by all accounts he had none. Unsurprisingly, then, Herod's ancestral deficiencies soon became a favorite trope of his critics.[53]

---

48. Thus rightly Schniedewind, *Society and the Promise to David*, 154. Samuel Rocca has recently argued that the righteous messiah of *Ps. Sol.* 17 is actually Herod the Great (Samuel Rocca, "Josephus and the Psalms of Solomon on Herod's Messianic Aspirations: An Interpretation," in *Making History: Josephus and Historical Method* [ed. Zuleika Rodgers; JSJSup 110; Leiden: Brill, 2007], 313–33). This interpretation is certainly wrong, it seems to me, but I suspect that Herod would have liked to be written about in such terms and perhaps was written about in similar terms by Nicolaus of Damascus, on which possibility see my discussion later in this chapter.

49. Indeed, Atkinson, "Herod the Great, Sosius, and the Siege of Jerusalem"; and Matthew Thiessen, *Contesting Conversion: Genealogy, Circumcision, and Identity in Ancient Judaism and Christianity* (New York, N.Y.: Oxford University Press, 2011), 99–101, argue that *Ps. Sol.* 17 is actually referring to Herod, not Pompey, when it speaks of the "person alien to our tribe" (*Ps. Sol.* 17:7) and "lawless one" (*Ps. Sol.* 17:11), which is admittedly possible but seems to me less likely than the alternative.

50. For this section, I owe a debt of thanks for a helpful conversation with Ross Wagner.

51. Sean Freyne, "The Herodian Period," in *Redemption and Resistance*, 29–43 at 31: "If the Hasmoneans could not develop a Davidic lineage, Herod, as an Idumean, certainly was in no position to do so."

52. On Herod's standing with Octavian, see the essays collected in *Herod and Augustus* (ed. David Jacobson and Nikos Kokkinos; IJSSJ 6; Leiden: Brill, 2009), especially Anthony A. Barrett, "Herod, Augustus, and the Special Relationship: The Significance of the Procuratorship," 281–302.

53. At first, Herod's outsider status may have worked in his favor, as rightly noted by Freyne, "Herodian Period," 29: "His Idumean pedigree was an advantage, especially since the young

In one well-known passage, Josephus relates how Herod's Hasmonean rival Antigonus petitioned the Romans to install himself rather than Herod as client king in Judea:

> Antigonus in answer to Herod's proclamation [to the citizens of Jerusalem] told Silo and the Roman army that it would be contrary to their own notion of right if they gave the kingship to Herod, who was a commoner [ἰδιώτης] and an Idumaean, that is, a half-Jew [ἡμιουδαῖος], when they ought to offer it to those who were of the [ruling] clan, as was their custom (*Ant.* 14.403).[54]

Herod, Antigonus objects, is an ἰδιώτης, "commoner," and moreover a ἡμιουδαῖος, "half-Jew," whereas Antigonus can boast that he comes from οἱ ἐκ τοῦ γένους, "those of the [ruling] clan," that is, the Hasmoneans.[55]

Josephus himself corroborates the report that Herod was Idumean on the side of his father Antipater (*Ant.* 14.8). There was, however, another Herodian genealogy on offer at the time, which Josephus cites and to which he responds:

> Nicolaus of Damascus, to be sure, says that his family belonged to the leading Jews who came to Judea from Babylon [γένος ἐκ τῶν πρώτων Ἰουδαίων τῶν ἐκ Βαβυλῶνος εἰς τὴν Ἰουδαίαν ἀφικομένων]. But he says this in order to please Antipater's son Herod, who became king of the Jews by a certain turn of fortune (*Ant.* 14.9).[56]

According to Nicolaus, Antipater was not an ethnic Idumean at all, but rather a descendant of Jewish nobility who were displaced during the Babylonian exile. Nicolaus, however, was a court historian to Herod (as Josephus himself was to the Flavian dynasty in Rome), and Josephus says here and elsewhere that Nicolaus's cliency leads him to write in such as way as to

---

Hasmonean pretender-king, Antigonos, had in fact invited the Parthians to invade Palestine, and he [Herod] had widespread popular support among the Judaean population." Once he was established, however, Herod's ancestry became, in many respects, a political liability.

54. Greek text ed. Ralph Marcus in the LCL; trans. mod.

55. On this passage and the controversy surrounding Herod's Jewishness, see Albert Baumgarten, "On the Legitimacy of Herod and His Sons as Kings of Israel," in *Jews and Judaism in the Second Temple, Mishnah, and Talmud Period* (ed. Isaiah Gafni et al.; Jerusalem: Yad Ben-Zvi, 1993), 31–37 (in Hebrew); Cohen, *Beginnings of Jewishness*, 13–24; Thiessen, *Contesting Conversion*, 97–99.

56. Greek text ed. Ralph Marcus in the LCL; trans. mod.

flatter his patron without regard for veracity (see *Ant.* 16.184–86).[57] Josephus has his own biases, of course, no less corrupting than those of Nicolaus. On the particular question of Herod's ancestry, however, Josephus's biases are less relevant and so his report more trustworthy than Nicolaus's. If Josephus is right, then what we have is an attempt on the part of Nicolaus of Damascus to manufacture a more advantageous ancestry for Herod.[58] It is an unsuccessful attempt, however, as Josephus's countergenealogy demonstrates. The problem for Nicolaus is that Herod's ancestry was a matter about which other parties, too, had information, so that it could not easily be rewritten, at least not persuasively.[59]

In this connection, there are ancient reports not only that Herod had his own ancestry falsified, but also that he attempted to erase the ancestries of those who might have had a counterclaim. The early-third-century Christian chronographer Julius Africanus is cited by Eusebius as saying:

> Herod, inasmuch as the lineage of the Israelites contributed nothing to his advantage, and since he was goaded with the consciousness of his own ignoble extraction, burned all the genealogical records, thinking that he might appear of noble origin if no one else were able, from the public registers, to trace back his lineage to the patriarchs or proselytes and to those mingled with them, who were called Georae. (Julius Africanus, *Epistle to Aristides*, apud Eusebius, *Hist. eccl.* 1.7.13)[60]

According to Africanus, there were, in Herodian-period Judea, official archives of the genealogical records of aristocratic Jewish families, not only priests but noble laity as well.[61] On the premise that Herod's own family would not have been among these, Africanus claims that Herod burned the archives in order to preempt criticisms from those who did come from royal or priestly

57. See Mark Toher, "Herod, Augustus, and Nicolaus of Damascus," in *Herod and Augustus*, 65–82.

58. A noble ancestry, but not, contra Abraham Schalit, *König Herodes* (Berlin: De Gruyter, 1969), a specifically Davidic ancestry, a point rightly made by Menahem Stern, "A. Schalit's Herod," *JJS* 11 (1960): 49–58.

59. See Cohen, *Beginnings of Jewishness*, 17: "What is important about the fabrication is that it reveals that Herod realized that his real pedigree was inadequate to assure him of an unassailable claim to the epithet *Ioudaios*."

60. Trans. Arthur Cushman McGiffert in *NPNF*.

61. This claim is debatable, but it is defended at length by Joachim Jeremias, *Jerusalem in the Time of Jesus* (Philadelphia, Pa.: Fortress, 1969), 275–90.

Jewish families.[62] The rationale would seem to be that if you cannot prove your own ancestral credentials, you can at least make it impossible for your enemies to disprove them. This report may or may not be true. A number of recent interpreters have found it plausible, and not without reason.[63] Even if the report is not true, however, its existence is further evidence of the literary dispute over Herod's ancestral right to the Judean kingship.

Herod's best hope for cementing his legacy as a legitimate king of Judea was not to rewrite his family tree (which turns out to be rather more difficult than one might think), but to prove himself by his accomplishments. And in fact, the problems posed for Herod by his family of origin may help make sense of certain other aspects of his reign. As Abraham Schalit and William Horbury, especially, have emphasized, Herod's tremendous building program at the temple complex in Jerusalem is an eloquent statement of Herodian royal ideology.[64] In one influential strand of scriptural and later Jewish tradition, the king messiah is he who builds the temple and fortifies Mount Zion.[65] Thus the oracle at Zech 6:12: "Behold the man whose name is Branch [צמח; cf. OG ἀνατολή, "Dawn"]; for he shall grow up in his place, and he shall build the temple of YHWH"; and similarly the *Parables of Enoch*: "After this, the Righteous and Chosen One will cause the house of his congregation to appear" (1 *En.* 53.6).[66] Herod may not be a son of David and Solomon; but, like David and Solomon—who themselves did not have a prior dynastic right

---

62. Africanus further claims that some of these records were saved from burning by the families concerned, including the Davidic family of which Jesus was part (see Eusebius, *Hist. eccl.* 1.7.14).

63. See Robert M. Grant, *Jesus after the Gospels: The Christ of the Second Century* (Louisville, Ky.: WJK, 1990), 16–17; Richard Bauckham, *Jude and the Relatives of Jesus in the Early Church* (Edinburgh: T. & T. Clark, 1990), 359–61; Aryeh Kasher, *King Herod: A Persecuted Persecutor* (with Eliezer Witztum; trans. Karen Gold; Berlin: De Gruyter, 2007), 222–24; but compare the skeptical assessments of Marshall D. Johnson, *The Purpose of the Biblical Genealogies* (2d ed.; Cambridge: Cambridge University Press, 1969), 103–4; and William Adler, "Christians and the Public Archive," in *A Teacher for All Generations: Essays in Honor of James C. VanderKam* (2 vols.; JSJSup 153; Leiden: Brill, 2012), 1:917–38.

64. See Schalit, *König Herodes*, 328–403, especially 372–97; Horbury, "Herod's Temple and 'Herod's Days,'" in idem, *Messianism among Jews and Christians*, 83–122, here 100:

> In Nicolas' account the rebuilding shows Herod as a Jewish king piously restoring the temple to its Solomonic glory, and as a victor who has conquered the Jews' traditional enemies.... He appears, therefore, as a Jewish king touched by the aura of messianism.

65. See Jostein Ådna, *Jesu Stellung zum Tempel* (WUNT 2.119; Tübingen: Mohr Siebeck, 2000), 50–87.

66. Trans. George W. E. Nickelsburg and James C. VanderKam, *1 Enoch: A New Translation* (Minneapolis, Minn.: Fortress, 2004).

to the throne—he is the builder of God's temple on Mount Zion. Herod could not be the king the son of David, so he did what he could. He became a king like David.[67]

Herod is not called a messiah in any contemporary sources, but, like Zerubbabel in the *Targum Jonathan* to Zechariah, he gains the title in subsequent tradition. Thus Epiphanius and Jerome, among other ecclesiastical writers, attest the view that the Ἡρῳδιανοί (Mark 3:6; 12:13; Matt 22:16), Latin *Herodiani*, are a sect of Jews who revere Herod as the messiah.[68] Further down this interpretive path, the Slavonic Josephus, of thirteenth-century Christian provenance,[69] relates the story of a group of priests in the Second Temple weighing and ultimately rejecting the possibility that Herod might be the messiah. The passage reads:

Herod spent little (time) in Jerusalem, and marched against the Arabs. At that time the priests mourned and grieved one to another in secret. They dared not (do so openly for fear of) Herod and his friends. For (one Jonathan) spoke: "The law bids us have no foreigner for king. Yet we wait for the Anointed, the meek one, of David's line. But of Herod we know that he is an Arabian, uncircumcised. The Anointed will be called meek, but this (is) he who has filled our whole land with blood. Under the Anointed it was ordained for the lame to walk, and the blind to see, (and) the poor to become rich. But under this man the hale have become lame, the seeing are blinded, the rich have become beggars. What is this? or how? Have the prophets lied?" ... But Ananus the priest answered and spake to them: "I know all books. When Herod fought beneath the city wall, I had never a thought that God would allow him to rule over us. But now I understand that our desolation is nigh." ... But one of them, by name Levi, wishing to outwit them, spake to them what he got with his tongue, not out of books, but in fable. They, however, being learned in the Scriptures, began to search for the time when the Holy one would come; but the speeches of Levi they execrated. ... He, overcome with shame, fled to Herod and informed him of the speeches

---

67. This point is well made by Tal Ilan, "King David, King Herod and Nicolaus of Damascus," *JSQ* 3 (1998): 195–240.

68. Epiphanius, *Pan.* 1.20; Jerome, *Lucif.* 23. On this tradition, see H. H. Rowley, "The Herodians in the Gospels," *JTS* 41 (1940): 14–27; Horbury, "Herod's Temple"; Joan E. Taylor, *The Essenes, the Scrolls, and the Dead Sea* (Oxford: Oxford University Press, 2012), 124–26.

69. On Slavonic Josephus, see Elias Bickerman, "Sur la version vieux-russe de Flavius Josephe," in idem, *Studies in Jewish and Christian History, Part 1* (AGJU 9; Leiden: Brill, 1976), 172–95.

of the priests which they had spoken against him. But Herod sent by
night and slew them all.[70]

The priests in the story reject the notion that Herod is the messiah, but
the instructive point for our purposes is that the story raises the possibility at
all. His humble birth notwithstanding, Herod's distinguished tenure as king
of the Jews put his name in circulation in the literary body of messiah legend.
As Cohen writes:

> Depending on whom you ask, Herod was either a *Ioudaios* (that is, a
> Judaean and Jew), a blue-blooded Judaean, an Idumaean and therefore
> not a Judaean, an Idumaean and therefore also a Judaean, an Idumaean
> and therefore a half-Judaean, an Ascalonite, a gentile slave, or—the
> Messiah![71]

Jesus of Nazareth

Although no text from Herod's own lifetime calls him a messiah, one nearly
contemporary text does paint him as a ψευδόχριστος, a counterpart of and
rival to another messiah. The Gospel of Matthew, written within a century of
Herod's death, narrates the birth of Jesus of Nazareth as a threat to Herod's
hold on the Judean kingship:

> When Jesus was born in Bethlehem of Judea in the days of Herod the
> king [Ἡρῴδου τοῦ βασιλέως], behold, wise men from the East came to
> Jerusalem, saying, "Where is he who has been born king of the Jews
> [ὁ τεχθεὶς βασιλεὺς τῶν Ἰουδαίων]? For we have seen his star in the East,
> and have come to worship him." When Herod the king heard this, he
> was troubled, and all Jerusalem with him; and assembling all the chief
> priests and scribes of the people, he questioned them where the mes-
> siah was to be born [ποῦ ὁ χριστὸς γεννᾶται]. (Matt 2:1–4)[72]

According to Matthew, Jesus, in contrast to Herod, has a rightful dynastic
claim to the office of messiah, king of the Jews, and the conflict between their

---

70. In the manuscripts of Slavonic Josephus, this passage replaces the Greek text of
War 1.364–70. An English translation is given by Thackeray in the LCL Josephus, vol. 3,
pp. 438–40.

71. Cohen, *Beginnings of Jewishness*, 23.

72. Trans. mod. from RSV.

respective claims can be resolved only by the death of the one or the other (Matt 2:13–23). For Matthew, in other words, Jesus is born to the office of messiah (Matt 1:1–17).

In making this claim, Matthew has a considerable weight of early tradition on his side.[73] Our earliest witness to the Jesus movement, the apostle Paul, says that Jesus is the messiah from the house of David, and this in contexts reflecting traditions antecedent to himself, such as Rom 1:3, where Jesus is "God's son, who came from the seed of David according to the flesh [τοῦ υἱοῦ αὐτοῦ τοῦ γενομένου ἐκ σπέρματος Δαυὶδ κατὰ σάρκα]." Further on in the same letter, Paul identifies Jesus with the ideal Davidide of Isaiah 11, "the root of Jesse, he who rises to rule the gentiles" (Rom 15:12).[74] Although they differ on other points, all three Synoptic Gospels agree on the Davidic ancestry of Jesus. Mark is most circumspect about the idea (see Mark 10:47–48; 11:10), perhaps lest it undermine his insistence that Jesus is the son of God (Mark 1:1; 3:11; 15:39).[75] Matthew titles his work "the book of the genealogy of Jesus Christ, the son of David, the son of Abraham" (Matt 1:1) and traces the Judahite royal line through Judah, David, and Zerubbabel to Jesus (Matt 1:2–17).[76] Luke goes to still greater lengths weaving the theme into his work, not only in his own genealogy (Luke 3:23–38),[77] but also in the poems in his birth narrative (Luke 1:32, 68–69) and the speeches in Acts (Acts 2:25–36; 13:32–37; 15:13–18).[78] Despite its many idiosyncrasies, the Apocalypse of John likewise attests the

---

73. See Rom 1:3–4; 15:12; 2 Tim 2:8; Mark 10:47–48; 11:10; 12:35–37; Matt 1:1–17; 1:20; 9:27; 12:23; 15:22; 20:30–31; 21:9, 15; 22:41–45; Luke 1:27, 32, 69; 2:4, 11; 3:31; 18:38–39; 20:41–44; Acts 2:25–36; 13:32–37; 15:13–18; Heb 7:14; Rev 3:7; 5:5; 22:16.

74. See Dahl, "Messiahship of Jesus in Paul"; Matthew V. Novenson, "Jewish Messiahs, the Pauline Christ, and the Gentile Question," *JBL* 128 (2009): 357–73. The deutero-Pauline tradition develops christological emphases of its own, but it also preserves Paul's affirmation of the Davidic ancestry of Jesus, as in 2 Tim 2:8: "Remember Jesus Christ, risen from the dead, descended from David, as preached in my gospel."

75. See Marcus, *Way of the Lord*, especially 130–52.

76. See Krister Stendahl, "Quis et Unde? An Analysis of Mt. 1–2," in *Judentum, Urchristentum, Kirche* (ed. Walther Eltester; BZNW 26; Berlin: Töpelmann, 1964), 94–105; Jack Dean Kingsbury, "The Title 'Son of David' in Matthew's Gospel," *JBL* 95 (1976): 591–602; Yigal Levin, "Jesus, 'Son of God' and 'Son of David': The 'Adoption' of Jesus into the Davidic Line," *JSNT* 28 (2006): 415–42.

77. A comparison of Matthew's and Luke's genealogies of Jesus suggests that, although minor ancestors can be selected or invented with relative impunity, major ancestors (such as Abraham, Judah, Jesse, David, and Zerubbabel) have a greater degree of obstinacy in the tradition.

78. See Mark L. Strauss, *The Davidic Messiah in Luke-Acts: The Promise and Its Fulfillment in Lukan Christology* (JSNTSup 110; Sheffield: Sheffield Academic, 1995).

messiahship of Jesus and his genealogical claim thereto. John's heavenly Jesus identifies himself as "the root and the offspring of David [ἡ ῥίζα καὶ τὸ γένος Δαυίδ], the bright morning star" (Rev 22:16; cf. Rev 3:7), and the elders in the divine throne room acclaim him as "the lion of the tribe of Judah, the root of David [ὁ λέων ὁ ἐκ τῆς φυλῆς Ἰούδα, ἡ ῥίζα Δαυίδ]" (Rev 5:5).[79] In these and other first-century CE sources, Jesus of Nazareth, like Zerubbabel before him, is a messiah by virtue of his royal pedigree.[80]

This genealogical tradition, however, has looked suspicious to modern critics as far back as David Friedrich Strauss in the early nineteenth century. Strauss writes:

> The phrase υἱὸς Δαβίδ ["son of David"] is a predicate that may naturally have been applied to Jesus, not on historical, but on dogmatic grounds. According to the prophecies, the Messiah could only spring from David. When therefore a Galilean, whose lineage was utterly unknown, and of whom consequently no one could prove that he was not descended from David, had acquired the reputation of being the Messiah; what [could be] more natural than that tradition should under different forms have early ascribed to him a Davidical descent?[81]

For Strauss, the motif of Jesus's Davidic ancestry came about because Jesus's earliest followers, convinced that he was the messiah, were carried on by the logic of the messiah myth—"According to the prophecies, the Messiah could only spring from David"—to conclude that he must also have been a Davidide. This account has long been and remains very influential.[82] Even so, other interpreters have rightly pointed out, first, that it is not in fact mythologically necessary that the messiah be a son of David and, second, that there are at least some mundane, nonmythical claims of Davidic ancestry among

---

79. See Richard Bauckham, *The Theology of the Book of Revelation* (Cambridge: Cambridge University Press, 1993), 66–108; John W. Marshall, *Parables of War: Reading John's Jewish Apocalypse* (ESCJ 10; Waterloo, Ont.: Wilfrid Laurier University Press, 2001), 76–82.

80. On this point, see Bockmuehl, "Son of David and His Mother."

81. D. F. Strauss, *The Life of Jesus, Critically Examined* (trans. George Eliot; London: Sonnenschein, 1892 [German original, 1835]), 117–18.

82. Other important proponents include William Wrede, "Jesus als Davidssohn," in idem, *Vorträge und Studien* (Tübingen: Mohr, 1907), 147–77; Christoph Burger, *Jesus als Davidssohn* (FRLANT 98; Göttingen: Vandenhoeck & Ruprecht, 1970); Dennis C. Duling, "The Promises to David and Their Entrance into Christianity—Nailing Down a Likely Hypothesis," *NTS* 20 (1973): 55–77; Anthony Le Donne, *The Historiographical Jesus: Memory, Typology, and the Son of David* (Waco, Tex.: Baylor University Press, 2009).

Jews in the early Roman period.[83] There is, for instance, a first-century CE Jerusalemite ossuary, excavated in 1971 by Amos Kloner, bearing the inscription שלבידוד, "of the house of David,"[84] and the passage in Mishnah Ta'anit instructing members of certain Jewish clans, including the family of David, to contribute wood offerings on designated feast days (*m. Ta'an.* 4:5).[85]

These contextual factors are a counterweight to Strauss's too-easy assumption that the Gospel writers would inevitably have invented a Davidic ancestry for Jesus. There are, however, some early Gospel texts that themselves challenge the claim that Jesus was from the family of David. The first of these is a triply attested Synoptic tradition, the so-called *Davidssohnfrage*:[86]

> As Jesus taught in the temple, he said, "How can the scribes say that the messiah is the son of David? David himself, inspired by the holy spirit, declared, *The lord said to my lord: Sit at my right hand, until I put your enemies under your feet* [Ps 110:1]. David himself calls him lord; so how is he his son?" And the great throng heard him gladly. (Mark 12:35–37; cf. Matt 22:41–46; Luke 20:41–44)[87]

This passage presents an ancient exegetical puzzle. There is a tradition (attributed in Mark to the scribes) that says the messiah is a son of David, but Jesus challenges this tradition by quoting a psalm. Psalm 110 is superscribed

---

83. See in particular David Flusser, "Jesus, His Ancestry, and the Commandment of Love," in *Jesus' Jewishness: Exploring the Places of Jesus within Early Judaism* (ed. James H. Charlesworth; New York, N.Y.: Crossroad, 1991), 153–76; Raymond E. Brown, *The Birth of the Messiah: A Commentary on the Infancy Narratives in the Gospels of Matthew and Luke* (rev. ed.; London: Chapman, 1993), 505–12; James D. G. Dunn, *Jesus Remembered* (Grand Rapids, Mich.: Eerdmans, 2003), 340–48.

84. Plates and transcription in Hannah M. Cotton et al., eds., *Corpus Inscriptionum Iudaeae/ Palestinae*, vol. 1, part 1 (Berlin: De Gruyter, 2010), 88–90.

85. *m. Ta'an.* 4.5:

> The wood-offering of the priests and the people was brought nine times [in the year]: on the 1st of Nisan by the family of Arah of the tribe of Judah; on the 20th of Tammuz by the family of David of the tribe of Judah [בני דוד בן יהודה]; on the 5th of Av by the family of Parosh of the tribe of Judah; on the 7th of the same month by the family of Jonadab the son of Rechab. (trans. mod. from Danby)

86. On which see R. P. Gagg, "Jesus und die Davidssohnfrage," *TZ* 7 (1951): 18–30; Gerhard Schneider, "Die Davidssohnfrage," *Bib* 53 (1972): 65–90; Fritz Neugebauer, "Die Davidssohnfrage und der Menschensohn," *NTS* 21 (1974): 81–108; Bruce Chilton, "Jesus ben David: Reflections on the Davidssohnfrage," *JSNT* 14 (1982): 88–122.

87. Matthew's and Luke's redactional changes are relatively minor and not relevant for our purposes. Their respective decisions to preserve and include the saying virtually unchanged is their most striking feature.

"a psalm of David" (MT לדוד מזמור; OG τῷ Δαυιδ ψαλμός), so most ancient readers will have taken it as a word spoken by David. Moreover, the psalm comprises a divine oath to prosper the king on Mount Zion, so some ancient readers (including Mark) will have taken it as an oracle about the messiah.[88] Jesus presupposes the truth of both these premises and shows how together they result in an apparent contradiction. To paraphrase: The Lord (God) said to my (David's) lord (that is, the messiah): Sit at my right hand, and so on. If David is the speaker and "my lord" is the messiah, then how can the messiah be both David's lord (as the psalm says) and David's son (as the scribes say)?

This is a clever piece of scriptural interpretation in its own right, but from the perspective of the Evangelists it poses a problem—namely, that Jesus, who according to all three Synoptic Gospels is both messiah and son of David— appears to deny that the messiah is a son of David. Perhaps, then, the passage is an apologia for a non-Davidide Jesus: It explains how he can be called the messiah despite his lack of genealogical qualifications.[89] Indeed, it is conceiv- able that Mark 12:35–37 betrays a very early layer of tradition in which it had not yet occurred to anyone to think that Jesus was a Davidide. And yet, all three Synoptic Gospels preserve the passage virtually unchanged. Why? Because although Mark, Matthew, and Luke all attest the son of David tradition, they all also make other, even more loaded christological claims for Jesus (espe- cially the categories "lord" and "son of God"). All three, consequently, exploit a potential way of reading the *Davidssohnfrage*. Read in isolation, the passage suggests that the messiah is not a son of David. Read as part of any of the three Gospel narratives, however, the passage suggests that the messiah is not merely a son of David, that he is more than a son of David. It is possible that the passage had a prehistory in which it was evidence for a non-Davidide Jesus, but in all the actual texts of which it is a part it presents a supra-Davidide Jesus.[90]

The second passage comes from the Gospel of John, which nowhere identi- fies Jesus as a Davidide, even though it does identify him as the messiah (John

---

88. See Juel, *Messianic Exegesis*, 135–50.

89. Like *Lamentations Rabbah*'s apologia for the non-Davidide Bar Kosiba, discussed later in this chapter.

90. On this point, see Nils A. Dahl, "The Crucified Messiah," in idem, *Jesus the Christ*, 27–47 at 41:

> The answer to the problem of the seemingly self-contradictory statements of Scripture lies in the concrete messiahship of Jesus, who, as a man, is son of David but, as the Exalted One, is his Lord. Here the Christian concept of Messiah is indeed presupposed. And for precisely this reason the pericope is probably a prod- uct of Christian scriptural interpretation.

1:41; 4:25–26; 7:26; 9:22; 11:27; 20:31). In John 7, a festival crowd in Jerusalem argue among themselves about Jesus:

> When they heard these words, some of the people said, "This is really the prophet." Others said, "This is the messiah." But some said, "Is the messiah to come from Galilee? [μὴ γὰρ ἐκ τῆς Γαλιλαίας ὁ χριστὸς ἔρχεται;] Has not the scripture said that the messiah is descended from David, and comes from Bethlehem, the village where David was? [οὐχ ἡ γραφὴ εἶπεν ὅτι ἐκ τοῦ σπέρματος Δαυὶδ καὶ ἀπὸ Βηθλέεμ τῆς κώμης ὅπου ἦν Δαυὶδ ἔρχεται ὁ χριστός;]" So there was a division among the people over him. Some of them wanted to arrest him, but no one laid hands on him. (John 7:40–44)[91]

The anonymous skeptics question Jesus's fitness for the office of messiah on the grounds that he is known to come from Galilee whereas, according to the tradition they report, scripture says that the messiah would be a Davidide and would come from the city of David—namely, Bethlehem. This report is striking because the Gospel of John does not mention either David or Bethlehem anywhere else. Some interpreters have suggested that this is dramatic irony on John's part—that he knows, and expects his audience to know, that Jesus is a Davidide from Bethlehem and so has the crowd unwittingly testify to the truth.[92] This is possible, although elsewhere John is rather more heavy-handed with his use of dramatic irony (e.g., John 11:49–52; 18:14), so this instance would be remarkable for its subtlety.

Complicating the matter further still, earlier in the same chapter John has a crowd quote a different, conflicting tradition about the provenance of the messiah:

> Some of the people of Jerusalem therefore said, "Is not this the man whom they seek to kill? And here he is, speaking openly, and they say nothing to him! Can it be that the authorities really know that this is the messiah? Yet we know where this man comes from; and when the messiah appears, no one will know where he comes from [τοῦτον οἴδαμεν πόθεν ἐστίν· ὁ δὲ χριστὸς ὅταν ἔρχηται οὐδεὶς γινώσκει πόθεν ἐστίν]." (John 7:25–27)[93]

---

91. Trans. mod. from RSV.

92. For example, F. F. Bruce, *The Gospel of John* (Grand Rapids, Mich.: Eerdmans, 1983), 183–84.

93. Trans. mod. from RSV.

This crowd opinion concurs with the previous one on the provenance of Jesus ("We know where he comes from"—namely, Galilee) but not on the provenance of the messiah ("No one knows" and "Bethlehem," respectively). Indeed, John includes in his narrative a hodgepodge of popular opinion about the messiah,[94] and it is not entirely clear which bits of it—if any—also represent John's own view. The same may be said of the matter of Jesus's ancestry. John's only comment on the issue appears in the mouth of the (unreliable) crowd of John 7:41–42. He might be ironically affirming the son of David tradition, although it would be a very ironic affirmation. It is too much to say, as Christoph Burger does, that John knows and roundly rejects the tradition that Jesus is descended from David.[95] It may be, however, that all John knows about Jesus's family background is that he comes from Galilee, which by itself would not suggest a Davidic pedigree.[96] Because John's Christology is happily unconcerned with Jesus's family tree anyway, this is no loss for him. What we have, then, is a majority tradition to the effect that Jesus is descended from David, and a minority report that appears to be ignorant of this tradition.

It is remarkable that, aside from these passages in Mark and John, the first-century claim of Davidic ancestry for Jesus goes mostly uncontested. There is, of course, an ancient tradition, attested first in Celsus (apud Origen, *Cels.* 1.28, 32) and subsequently in the Talmud (*b. Šabb.* 104b; *b. Sanh.* 67a) and the medieval *Toledot Yeshu*, to the effect that Jesus was the child of an illicit union between his mother Mary and a Roman soldier (whose name Celsus gives as Pantera),[97] but this tradition does not appear until the end of the second century and, more important for our purposes, it does not specifically dispute Jesus's Davidic ancestry. As we have it, the Jesus son of Pantera tradition presupposes and satirizes the virgin conception stories in Matthew and Luke, whereas the

---

94. On this feature, see Marinus de Jonge, "Jewish Expectations about the 'Messiah' according to the Fourth Gospel," *NTS* 19 (1973): 246–70.

95. Burger, *Jesus als Davidssohn*, 158. Compare John P. Meier, "From Elijah-like Prophet to Royal Davidic Messiah," in *Jesus: A Colloquium in the Holy Land* (ed. James D. G. Dunn and Doris Donnelly; London: Continuum, 2001), 54: "The 'from the seed of David' tradition . . . is witnessed in a back-handed way even in John, though whether it is accepted, ignored, or rejected by John remains uncertain."

96. If correct, this would corroborate the view that John is independent of the Synoptics. On this difficult question, see D. Moody Smith, *John among the Gospels* (2d ed.; Columbia, S.C.: University of South Carolina Press, 2001).

97. On which story see Peter Schäfer, *Jesus in the Talmud* (Princeton, N.J.: Princeton University Press, 2007), 15–24; Philip Alexander, "Jesus and His Mother in the Jewish Anti-Gospel (the *Toledot Yeshu*)," in *Infancy Gospels: Stories and Identities* (ed. Claire Clivaz et al.; WUNT 281; Tübingen: Mohr Siebeck, 2011), 588–616.

Davidic ancestry tradition is older than all of these. Granted, there are two possible hints of the illegitimacy charge in first-century sources: Mark 6:3, where
Jesus is called "son of Mary," and John 8:41, where Jesus's interlocutors say
angrily, "We were not begotten from fornication."[98] Even if these passages do
imply a charge of illegitimacy, which is disputable, they do not address themselves to the Davidic ancestry tradition any more than Celsus does. In short,
despite a robust tradition of anti-Christian polemic from the second century
onward, we find no genealogical challenge to the Davidic ancestry of Jesus.
Ancient critics deny the messiahship of Jesus on a variety of grounds (as, for
example, in Justin, *Dialogue*), but not on genealogical grounds.

An oblique but valuable piece of evidence is provided by the anonymous
Epistle to the Hebrews, which for its part has little christological stake in the
messiahship of Jesus.[99] Hebrews is peculiar among the New Testament texts
for its insistence that Jesus holds the office of high priest (Heb 2:17; 3:1; 4:14–15;
5:1, 5–6, 10; 6:20; 7:11, 15–26; 8:1–4; 9:11, 25; 10:21).[100] The obvious problem with
this claim is that, according to the P source in the Pentateuch, the Israelite
priesthood is reserved exclusively for descendants of Aaron (Exod 28–29;
Lev 8–9), whereas there is no evidence in Hebrews or any contemporary text
that Jesus belonged even to the tribe of Levi, much less the family of Aaron.
Consequently, Jesus would seem to be not even minimally qualified for the
office of priest.

The author of Hebrews acknowledges this difficulty: "For the one of whom
these things are spoken belonged to another tribe, from which no one has ever
served at the altar. For it is evident that our lord was descended from Judah, and
in connection with that tribe Moses said nothing about priests" (Heb 7:13–14).
Undeterred, however, Hebrews proposes an ingenious solution. The ideal high
priest, he explains, "does not take the honor upon himself, but he is called by

---

98. On the theme of illegitimacy in these passages, see Morton Smith, *Jesus the Magician*
(San Francisco, Calif.: Hampton Roads, 2014 [1st ed., 1978]), 33–38.

99. On the Christology of Hebrews, see C. K. Barrett, "The Christology of Hebrews," in
Who Do You Say That I Am? Essays on Christology (ed. Mark Allen Powell and David R. Bauer;
Louisville, Ky.: WJK, 1999), 110–27; David Flusser, "Messianology and Christology in the
Epistle to the Hebrews," in idem, *Judaism and the Origins of Christianity* (Jerusalem: Magnes,
1988), 246–79; Hugh Anderson, "Jewish Antecedents of the Christology in Hebrews," in
The Messiah, 512–35.

100. On which see especially Mason, *You Are a Priest Forever*, 8–39. The idea of the priesthood of Jesus would become a commonplace in medieval and early modern Christologies,
but in a first-century text it is an anomaly. On subsequent developments, see Anna Maria
Schwemer, "Jesus Christus als Prophet, König und Priester: Das munus triplex und die frühe
Christologie," in *Der messianische Anspruch Jesu und die Anfänge der Christologie* (WUNT 138;
ed. Martin Hengel and Anna Maria Schwemer; Tübingen: Mohr Siebeck, 2001), 165–230.

God, just as Aaron was" (Heb 5:4). That is to say, priesthood can be, and ideally should be, attained not in the normal manner by descent from Aaron, but by direct divine vocation after the pattern of Aaron—that is, not by ancestry but by merit. On this tenuous but ingenious premise, the author reasons, "So also Christ did not exalt himself to be made a high priest, but was appointed by him who said to him, *You are my son, today I have begotten you* [Ps 2:7]; as he says also in another place, *You are a priest forever, after the order of Melchizedek* [Ps 110:4]" (Heb 5:5–6).

The "he who says" both of these sayings is God, and the sayings themselves are citations from the Psalter, and from royal enthronement psalms, in particular. The first, "You are my son; today I have begotten you" (Ps 2:7) is an address from God to his royal anointed one (χριστός in Ps 2:2) on the day of the king's enthronement. The second, "You are a priest forever, in the order of Melchizedek" (Ps 110:4), is likewise an address from God to the king authorizing his rule: "YHWH said to my lord, Sit at my right hand until I make your enemies your footstool," and so on. The author of Hebrews takes for granted that both of these are words spoken by God to Jesus, and there is reason to think that his audience will have granted him this interpretive move.[101] The upshot is that Melchizedek solves, for Hebrews, the genealogical objection to the claim that Jesus is high priest. Lacking any claim to Aaronic or at least Levite ancestry, Jesus would seem to be disqualified by definition; but the Melchizedek of Psalm 110 provides for the author of Hebrews a paradigm of the otherwise oxymoronic Davidic priest,[102] and thus grounds for the assertion that Jesus has a rightful claim to the high priesthood.[103] It is striking, when we consider Nicolaus's ersatz genealogy of Herod the Great, that Hebrews does not try to manufacture an Aaronic genealogy for Jesus. The author reckons that to do so would be a vain undertaking (Heb 7:14). Like the Gospel of Mark (for whom Jesus is son of God), Hebrews (for whom Jesus is high priest) is stuck with the fact that Jesus was widely thought to be a Davidide from the

---

101. These two royal psalms are widely cited in the New Testament as oracles about Jesus on the premise that he is the "messiah" spoken of by the psalmist (see Matt 22:44; Mark 12:36; Luke 20:42–43; Acts 2:34–35; 4:25–26; 13:33; 1 Cor 15:25; Rev 2:26). On this phenomenon, see Harold W. Attridge, "Giving Voice to Jesus: Use of the Psalms in the New Testament," in idem, *Essays on John and Hebrews* (WUNT 264; Tübingen: Mohr Siebeck, 2010), 320–30. On this and other early Christian uses of Ps 110, see David Hay, *Glory at the Right Hand: Psalm 110 in Early Christianity* (SBLMS 18; Nashville, Tenn.: Abingdon, 1973).

102. Which model may in fact go back to ancient Canaanite, and specifically Jebusite, precedent, as suggested by Day, "Canaanite Inheritance."

103. See Richard N. Longenecker, "The Melchizedek Argument of Hebrews," in *Unity and Diversity in New Testament Theology* (ed. Robert Allison Guelich; Grand Rapids, Mich.: Eerdmans, 1978), 161–85.

tribe of Judah. Also like Mark, therefore, Hebrews negotiates this obstinate genealogical tradition in creative ways that allow him to make his own christological points.

A few much later Christian sources do manufacture a Levite ancestry for Jesus—in particular, the twelfth-century Byzantine Suda Lexicon (s.v. Ἰησοῦς ὁ χριστὸς καὶ θεὸς ἡμῶν)—with a parallel Arabic account in the *History of the Patriarchs of the Coptic Church in Alexandria*.[104] These medieval accounts relate a dialogue, set in the sixth-century reign of Justinian, between a Christian named Philip and a Jew named Theodosius, in which Theodosius informs Philip of a secret codex kept for centuries by the Jews of Tiberias since its rescue from the destruction of the Jerusalem temple by Titus in 70 CE. The codex is a register of Jewish priests of the Second Temple, with their respective genealogies, and among them is listed one "Jesus, son of the virgin Mary and the living God." Jesus, according to the Suda, had legitimate priestly ancestry and was actually installed as a priest before his baptism by John. But even this medieval story, radically innovative as it is, concedes the axiom that Jesus was a Davidide. Its solution is to appeal to a very ancient mingling of the royal and priestly lines in Aaron's marriage to Elisheba (Exod 6:23).[105] In this medieval story, Jesus becomes both the messiah of Aaron and the messiah of Israel, so to speak.[106] In ancient sources, however, he is spoken of consistently as a blueblood Davidide messiah, although a few sources—Christian sources, not hostile ones—question that genealogy.

Shimon bar Kosiba

A century after Jesus, there was another important Levantine Jewish messiah of disputable pedigree: Shimon bar Kosiba. Bar Kosiba famously led the

---

104. The Greek text of the Suda is given by Ada Adler, ed., *Suidae Lexicon* (Leipzig: Teubner, 1931), here 2:620–25. A. Vassiliev collates this Suda story with some fragmentary Greek parallels in his *Analecta Graeco-Byzantina* (Moscow: Imperial University, 1893), 1:58–72. The Arabic version is translated into English by B. Evetts, "The Priesthood of Christ," in *History of the Patriarchs of the Coptic Church in Alexandria* (PO 1; Paris: Firmin-Didot, 1907), 120–34. The Suda account is translated into English, with commentary, by William Adler, "The Suda and the 'Priesthood of Jesus,'" in *For a Later Generation: The Transformation of Tradition in Israel, Early Judaism, and Early Christianity* (ed. Randal A. Argall et al.; Harrisburg, Pa.: Trinity, 2000), 1–12. Another valuable recent discussion is Pieter Willem van der Horst, "Jesus and the Jews According to the Suda," *ZNW* 84 (1993): 268–77.

105. Perhaps following Christian precedent, for example, Africanus, *Epistle to Aristides* 1. See further Adler, "Suda," 8.

106. See further Simon C. Mimouni, "Jésus: Messie Fils de David et Messie Fils d'Aaron," in *Aux origines des messianismes juifs*, 145–72.

initially successful but finally disastrous second Jewish war against Rome in the 130s CE.[107] Having no grounds for claiming Davidic ancestry, he seems never to have claimed it, nor do any of the numerous ancient sources about him manufacture a Davidic genealogy for him.[108] In the documentary sources, Bar Kosiba uses the title נשיא, "prince" or "chief."[109] In the literary record, however, he is overwhelmingly associated with the title "messiah," although the late ancient rabbis who preserve the accounts strenuously deny him the title.[110] Perhaps the most well-known talmudic passage reads:

> R. Shimon b. Yohai taught: My teacher Akiba used to expound, *A star* [כוכב] *goes forth from Jacob* [Num 24:17], "Koziba [כוזבא] goes out from Jacob." When R. Akiba saw Bar Koziba, he said, "This is the king Messiah [דין הוא מלכא משיחא]." R. Yohanan b. Torta said to him, "Akiba, grass will come up between your cheeks and still the son of David [בן דוד] will not have come." (*y. Ta'an.* 4:8 [68d])

At the very least, this passage implies stern rabbinic disapproval of misplaced messianic hope—in particular, messianic hope in the leader of the second Jewish–Roman war. A case can be made that this passage more likely reflects the late ancient rabbis' hindsight than it does an actual event in the life of R. Akiba.[111] But, whatever one's view on that historical question, the rhetorical effect of the logion of R. Yohanan b. Torta is surely to chasten messianic fervor on the part of the pious.

---

107. On which, see in particular Peter Schäfer, *Der Bar Kokhba-Aufstand: Studien Zum Zweiten Jüdischen Krieg Gegen Rom* (TSAJ 1; Tübingen: Mohr Siebeck, 1981); idem, ed., *Bar Kokhba War Reconsidered*; Menahem Mor, *The Second Jewish Revolt: The Bar Kokhba War, 132-136 C.E.* (BRLJ 50; Leiden: Brill, 2016).

108. But some medieval sources do; see the later in this chapter.

109. See the edition of Yigael Yadin et al., eds., *The Documents from the Bar Kokhba Period in the Cave of Letters* (Jerusalem: Israel Exploration Society, 2002).

110. On these accounts, see G. S. Aleksandrov, "The Role of Aqiba in the Bar Kokhba Rebellion," trans. Sam Driver, in *Eliezer ben Hyrcanus*, vol. 2 (ed. Jacob Neusner; Leiden: Brill, 1973), 422–36; Peter Schäfer, "Rabbi Aqiva and Bar Kokhba," in *Approaches to Ancient Judaism*, vol. 2 (ed. William S. Green; Chico, Calif.: Scholars Press, 1980), 113–30; idem, "Bar Kokhba and the Rabbis"; David Goodblatt, "Did the Tannaim Support Bar-Kokhba?" *Cathedra* 29 (1983): 6–12 (in Hebrew); Adele Reinhartz, "Rabbinic Perceptions of Simeon bar Kosiba," *JSJ* 20 (1989): 171–94; Matthew V. Novenson, "Why Does R. Akiba Acclaim Bar Kokhba as Messiah?" *JSJ* 40 (2009): 551–72.

111. For this case, see Schäfer, "Rabbi Aqiva and Bar Kokhba"; Novenson, "Why Does R. Akiba."

There may be more, however. It may be significant that R. Akiba acclaims Shimon bar Kosiba as מלכא משיחא, "the king messiah," whereas R. Yohanan b. Torta replies that the coming of בן דוד, "the son of David," is still a long way off. These two titles could be read simply as synonyms, as they are sometimes used in the Talmud (e.g., *b. Sanh.* 97a). In this case, R. Yohanan b. Torta would simply be flatly denying R. Akiba's claim.[112] But it is also possible, and in my view more likely, that R. Yohanan b. Torta's reply is actually a counterargument, not simply a denial. R. Akiba acclaims Bar Kosiba as messiah by identifying him with the star of the oracle of Balaam in Num 24:17, but that oracle only specifies an Israelite ruler, not a Davidide: דרך כוכב מיעקב וקם שבט מישראל, "A star goes forth from Jacob, a scepter arises from Israel."[113] The late ancient rabbis knew as well as modern historians do that Shimon bar Kosiba apparently neither had nor made any claim to Davidic ancestry. This being the case, perhaps the logion of R. Yohanan b. Torta is pointing out Bar Kosiba's ancestral ineligibility for the office. Some may call him the king messiah, but he is no son of David.[114]

This interpretation is corroborated by another talmudic Bar Kosiba text at *b. Sanh.* 93b, the fictional story of Bar Kosiba's trial before the rabbis. It reads:

> Bar Koziba reigned two and a half years and then said to the rabbis, "I am the messiah." They answered, "Of the messiah it is written that he smells and judges [דמורח ודאין] [cf. Isa 11:3]. Let us see whether he [Bar Kosiba] smells and judges." When they saw that he could not smell and judge, they killed him. (*b. Sanh.* 93b)

In fact, it is virtually certain that Bar Kosiba was killed in battle by the Romans, probably at Betar during the last days of the revolt (see *Lam. Rab.*

---

112. Thus, for example, Oppenheimer, "Leadership and Messianism," 156: "It is probable that R. Aqiva is relating Bar Kokhva to the Royal House of David. This at any rate is what appears from the contradiction voiced by R. Yohanan b. Torta, which is intended to disqualify Bar Kokhva's leadership."

113. This is rightly noted by Graetz, "Stages," 162: "It is worth noting that R. Akiba did not ask about the genealogy of the Messiah-king Bar-Kokhba!"

114. This possibility is considered by Moore, *Judaism*, 2:329 and n5:

> Whether Davidic descent was claimed in his own time for Bar Cocheba, whom Akiba recognized as the Messiah ... is unknown. In fact his antecedents are wrapt in complete obscurity, and the assertion frequently made that he was not even of the tribe of Judah seem[s] to have no other foundation than the silence of the sources.... Johanan ben Torta, who did not acknowledge him, is reported to have told Akiba that he would be long in his grave and still the *Son of David* would not come; but it would not be wise to lay much weight on the verbal exactness of the report [emphasis original].

2:2 §4).[115] This scene of a messianic trial in a rabbinic court is not a historical report but a narrative expression of the rabbis' verdict on Bar Kosiba and
his war: He was not the messiah, and his death was a just outcome.[116] The
test imposed in the story, however, is a curious one. Judging cases by smell
alone would of course be a remarkable feat, but the story itself highlights the
scriptural warrant for the test.[117] "He smells and judges" is a reading of the
curious phrase in Isa 11:3: והריחו ביראת יהוה ולא־למראה עיניו ישפוט, "His delight is in
the fear of YHWH, and he judges not by the sight of his eyes." The noun ריח
here is idiomatic (so rightly "delight"), but "smelling" is a good literal rendering, and the Talmud reads it in this way, as a contrast for the sense of sight in
the following clause: The messiah judges not by the sight of his eyes, but by a
divinely inspired sense of smell.

The reason why the rabbis can cite Isa 11:3 as a test for messianic office is
because that verse is part of a classic prophetic expression of Davidic royal
ideology:

> There shall come forth a shoot from the stump of Jesse, and a branch
> shall grow out of his roots, and the spirit of YHWH shall rest upon him. . . .
> In that day the root of Jesse shall stand as a sign to the peoples; him shall
> the nations seek, and his dwellings shall be glorious. (Isa 11:1–2, 10)

There is some dispute regarding the dating of this oracle. In my view, it is
more likely a preexilic royal propaganda text than an exilic or postexilic wish
for a utopian future.[118] In any case, however, by the time of the rabbis, Isaiah
11 was a messiah text because it had been a biblical house of David text.[119]
Consequently, here in *b. Sanh.* 93b, as in the Akiba-Ben Torta scene in *y. Ta'an.*
4:8, Bar Kosiba's messianic claim is challenged on the grounds of Davidic
dynastic ideology. Bar Kosiba cannot do what Isaiah says the root of Jesse must
do, so he is no son of David and therefore no messiah. Of course, Bar Kosiba

---

115. See Aharon Oppenheimer, "Betar als Zentrum vor dem Bar-Kochba-Aufstand," in idem,
Between Rome and Babylon (TSAJ 108; Tübingen: Mohr Siebeck, 2005), 303–19.

116. Thus rightly Schäfer, "Bar Kokhba and the Rabbis," 5.

117. Contra O'Neill, "Mocking of Bar Kokhba," who argues ingeniously but mistakenly that
the trial of Bar Kokhba story is actually a stray Jesus tradition.

118. See J. J. M. Roberts, "Old Testament's Contribution," 44–45; Collins, *Scepter*, 27–28;
Williamson, "Messianic Texts in Isaiah 1–39," in *King and Messiah*, 258–64, here 264: "[Isaiah]
11.1–5 originally expressed a comparatively modest hope by Isaiah that the new society which
he anticipated would be led both judiciously and more broadly by a righteous Davidide."

119. On this interpretive dynamic, see Roberts, "Old Testament's Contribution," 41–49.

had a remarkably impressive claim to messiahship on charismatic grounds. He did what David had done, so to speak, liberating Israel from oppression by its pagan neighbors.[120] He was not a son of David, however, and his later detractors pointed to this genealogical deficiency as an explanation for his eventual failure.

The rabbinic corpus recognizes the problem of having an eminent sage like R. Akiba acclaim a non-Davidide as the messiah and suggests an explanation for the anomaly.[121] "What did Bar Koziba do? He would catch the missiles from the enemy's catapults on one of his knees and hurl them back, killing many of the foe. On that account R. Akiba made his remark" (*Lam. Rab.* 2:2 §4). According to this account, R. Akiba acclaimed Bar Kosiba as messiah on charismatic, not ancestral grounds. That is, even if Bar Kosiba was not a Davidide, so great was his success as a warrior that it alone was reason enough for thinking that he was the messiah. He was a second David rather than a son of David, a messiah made rather than born. This illustrates the point: Bar Kosiba was acclaimed as messiah despite the fact that he was known not to be a Davidide. Those who thought he was the messiah had other reasons for thinking so, and those who did not think he was the messiah were quick to point out his lack of ancestral credentials.

Not until well into the Middle Ages does one find anything in the sources suggesting that Bar Kosiba might have had ancestral claim to the office of messiah.[122] Rashi, in his eleventh-century commentary on Bavli Sanhedrin, makes but does not substantiate the claim that "Bar Koziva was one of the kings of Herod."[123] On Rashi's authority, Isaac Abravanel, writing in the late fifteenth century, reasons as follows:

> Perhaps, too, Ben Koziva had said that he was of the seed of David; and if he were of the seed of Herod, as Rashi says in his commentary, then

---

120. Thus rightly Oppenheimer, "Leadership and Messianism," 160, 162:

> In order to decide finally on the quality of Bar Kokhva's messianism, we must first answer the question of what it was that qualified him in the eyes of the sages and the people to head the Revolt as sole leader, almost unquestioned. In the period we are discussing there were three criteria which qualified a man for leadership— wisdom, family and economic status. There is no certain evidence that Bar Kokhva had any of these qualities.... [Rather,] he was a charismatic leader, the sort that comes to the fore in a time of crisis, when it is characteristic that such a man does not belong to the group of legal, rational leaders.

121. This function of this text is rightly noted by Reinhartz, "Rabbinic Perceptions," 185.

122. See Moore, *Judaism*, 2:329n4: "Mediaeval statements ... that he was of the house of David, are probably inferred from the conviction that otherwise Akiba would not have proclaimed him the Messiah."

123. Trans. Richard G. Marks, *The Image of Bar Kokhba in Traditional Jewish Literature: False Messiah and National Hero* (University Park, Pa.: Penn State University Press, 1993), 109.

> there would be grounds for his [Bar Kosiba's] claim, because Antipater,
> the father of Herod, was of the Judean nobility, according to what Joseph
> ben Gorion wrote, although Antipater's wife was an Idumean. . . . The
> second [possibility] is that R. Akiba did not think that Ben Koziva would
> be king over Israel. . . . R. Akiba was aware that the King Messiah would
> be of the seed of David and that Ben Koziva in truth was not. (Isaac
> Abravanel, *Yeshu'ot Meshiho* 30b–31a)[124]

Abravanel knows the tradition, discussed earlier, that Herod the Great was
descended from Jewish nobility displaced in the Babylonian exile. He knows
it via Joseph ben Gorion (that is, *Josippon*),[125] but we know that it goes back to
the court history of Nicolaus of Damascus (Josephus, *Ant.* 14.9). Abravanel
generously interprets this vague tradition to imply that Herod could have been
a Davidide, and because Rashi says that Bar Kosiba was "one of the kings
of Herod," it follows that Bar Kosiba could have been a Davidide. Abravanel
recognizes, however, what a tenuous string of conjectures that is, so he also
considers it possible that Bar Kosiba had no royal blood and that R. Akiba
never actually endorsed him as messiah. Abravanel does not consider what
is in fact the most likely scenario, that Bar Kosiba's messianic claim was not
genealogical at all, but charismatic. For Bar Kosiba, as for Jesus of Nazareth,
Herod the Great, and their forebears, one could claim the Judean kingship
intelligibly either on the grounds of ancestry, as a rightful son of David, or on
the grounds of merit, as one divinely appointed like David was. Those who
could claim Davidic ancestry often did or, alternatively, their followers or biographers claimed it for them. Those who could not claim it typically did not. For
upstarts like Herod and Bar Kosiba, the more convincing course was to prove
oneself worthy of David's office by, for instance, subduing Israel's enemies or
building God's temple.

Patriarch and Exilarch

The conventional wisdom has it that, after the Bar Kokhba revolt, messianism effectively ceased in Israel, at least until the rise of Islam, so great was

---

124. Trans. Marks, *Image of Bar Kokhba*, 109. On Abravanel's *Yeshu'ot Meshiho*, see
Marks, *Image of Bar Kokhba*, 99–134; Eric Lawee, "The Messianism of Issac Abarbanel,"
in *Jewish Messianism in the Early Modern Period* (ed. Matt Goldish and Richard Popkin;
Dordrecht: Kluwer, 2001), 1–39.

125. On *Josippon*, see Schürer-Vermes, *History*, 1:117–18; Solomon Zeitlin, "Josippon," *JQR* 53
(1963): 273–97; David Flusser, "Josippon," *EncJud*, 10:296–98.

the trauma of this last Jewish–Roman war.[126] There is a grain of truth in this, inasmuch as late antiquity saw no further violent uprisings among the Jews, but the language of messianism remained an important discursive resource throughout the amoraic period, especially in connection with the offices of the patriarch (נשיא) in the land of Israel and the exilarch (ריש גלותא) in Babylonia.[127] The seminal figure here is R. Judah I the Patriarch, who flourished during the late second century and is traditionally credited with compiling the Mishnah. About his tenure, Peter Schäfer writes:

> R. Judah was officially recognized as Patriarch by the Romans and ruled almost like a king. Prayers were offered in the synagogue for his well-being, and incense was burned after his death as if for royalty. The fact that he was accorded equivalent status to a king not only indicates the political power of the Patriarch, but also points to quasi-Messianic ambitions (albeit in a diluted, "secularized" form that had come to terms with Roman supremacy). The claim that, as a descendant of Hillel, the Patriarch could trace his lineage to the House of David, would also date from this period. This was no doubt nothing but propaganda for a patriarchal dynasty whose Davidic claim was intended to secure power at home while opposing similar claims to power made elsewhere, and particularly those of the head of the Babylonian Diaspora (the exilarch).[128]

"Nothing but propaganda," indeed, but propaganda has a way of becoming hallowed tradition, and so it is in this case.[129] It is not clear by what sequence of events R. Judah I came to be revered as patriarch. In the sources, he just

---

126. See, for example, Philip Alexander, "The King Messiah in Rabbinic Judaism," in *King and Messiah*, 456–73 at 469–70:

> There were very good political reasons why the Rabbis would have attempted to suppress messianism. The Talmudic period opens with two bitter and disastrous wars, both of which took on a messianic tinge.... The Rabbis were level-headed enough to realize that messianism spelt trouble.

127. On these institutions, see Martin Jacobs, *Die Institution des jüdischen Patriarchen* (TSAJ 52; Tübingen: Mohr Siebeck, 1995); Geoffrey Herman, *A Prince without A Kingdom: The Exilarch in the Sasanian Era* (TSAJ 150; Tübingen: Mohr Siebeck, 2012); Alan Appelbaum, *The Dynasty of the Jewish Patriarchs* (TSAJ 156; Tübingen: Mohr Siebeck, 2013).

128. Peter Schäfer, *The History of the Jews in Antiquity: The Jews of Palestine from Alexander the Great to the Arab Conquest* (Luxembourg: Harwood, 1995 [German original, 1983]), 168.

129. Thus rightly Richard Kalmin, "Midrash and Social History," in *Current Trends in the Study of Midrash* (ed. Carol Bakhos; JSJSup 106; Leiden: Brill, 2006), 15n49: "Patriarchal and exilarchic claims of Davidic descent were almost certainly fictional. I have no doubt, however, that ancient rabbis accepted the validity of these claims."

is.[130] But somewhere early in the process, his claim to the office became entwined with a claim to descent from king David by way of Hillel (see *b. Hor.* 11b; *Gen. Rab.* 98:8). And from that point on, the Davidic ancestry of the patriarch in Israel and of his counterpart the exilarch in Babylonia (see later in this chapter) is a fixture in the literature of the amoraic period. What is more, as Schäfer notes, in the sources this genealogical claim is tied, none too subtly, to the discourse of messianism—"diluted," "secularized," or "quasi-" messianism, perhaps, if we accept a conventional definition of messianism, but messianism nonetheless. Thus, for instance, the passage in Yerushalmi Shabbat in which R. Hiyya, a disciple of R. Judah the Patriarch, identifies him as the משיח יהוה, "anointed of YHWH," of Lam 4:20:[131]

> There was the incident in which Rabbi, R. Hiyya the Elder, and R. Ishmael b. R. Yose were in session and reviewing the scroll of Lamentations on the eve of the ninth of Ab which coincided with the Sabbath, doing so from the time of the afternoon offering and onward. They omitted one alphabetical letter, saying, "Tomorrow we will go and complete it." Now when [Rabbi] was leaving for his house, he fell and injured his finger, and he recited in his own regard the following verse: *Many are the sufferings of the wicked* [Ps 32:10]. R. Hiyya said to him, "These things happened to you on our account, for so it is written, *The breath of our nostrils, the anointed of the Lord, was caught for their corrupt deeds* [Lam 4:20]." (*y. Šabb.* 16:1 [15c])[132]

---

130. See Catherine Hezser, *The Social Structure of the Rabbinic Movement in Roman Palestine* (TSAJ 66; Tübingen: Mohr Siebeck, 1997), 411–12:

> One may only hypothesize about the reasons why (some) rabbis of the early third century considered one of them to be the nasi, that is, to have a relatively higher status and more power than they and their colleagues and friends. In all likelihood the reasons for the emergence of the patriarchal dynasty were not much different from the reasons for the emergence of other prominent rabbis.... R. Yehudah ha-Nasi probably surpassed his colleagues in a number of areas. He had the reputation of being a great scholar and a righteous man. He was probably wealthy. Although the stories about Rabbi's meetings with Antoninus are probably fictitious, it is conceivable that he had friends amongst high standing Romans. While he may not have claimed Davidic descent, he may nevertheless have come from a distinguished family.

On these obscure developments, see also Martin Goodman, *State and Society in Roman Galilee, A.D. 132–212* (2d ed.; London: Valentine Mitchell, 2000).

131. See also the parallel accounts at *Lev. Rab.* 15:4, ed. Margulies, pp. 328–29; *Lam. Rab.* 4:23.

132. Trans. mod. from Jacob Neusner, *The Talmud of the Land of Israel* (Chicago, Ill.: University of Chicago Press, 1982–1993).

In this story, R. Judah, scolding himself, interprets his injury as one of those misfortunes that befall the wicked. R. Hiyya, however, suggests that, in fact, R. Judah suffered vicariously for his companions, identifying him with the משיח of Lam 4:20. In that scriptural text, "the breath of our nostrils, the anointed of YHWH" is the beloved but disgraced king of Judah, scion of the house of David.[133] R. Hiyya's exegesis rests on the premise that R. Judah is a latter-day scion of the house of David, a counterpart to Zedekiah of old (see 2 Kgs 25:1–7).[134]

If Yerushalmi Shabbat speaks of R. Judah in terms of the messiah, other rabbinic texts speak of the messiah in terms of R. Judah.[135] An example is the dialogue about the identity of the messiah in *b. Sanh.* 98b:

> R. Nahman said: If he [the messiah] is of those living, it might be one like myself, as it is written, *And their nobles shall be of themselves, and their governors shall proceed from the midst of them* [Jer 30:21]. Rav said: If he is of the living, it would be our holy master [R. Judah the Patriarch]; if of the dead, it would have been Daniel the most desirable man. (*b. Sanh.* 98b)[136]

This passage presents a thought experiment: Suppose the messiah were someone who has already lived or is presently living. Who would he be? The lattermost opinion is a reference to the biblical Daniel, the ancient seer, whose angelic interpreter addresses him as "most desirable man" (איש־חמדות) (Dan 10:11; cf. Ezek 14:14, 20).[137] But the former two opinions, about the messiah

---

133. Lam 4:19–20:

> Our pursuers were swifter than the vultures in the heavens; they chased us on the mountains, they lay in wait for us in the wilderness. The breath of our nostrils, the anointed of YHWH, was taken in their pits, he of whom we said, "Under his shadow we shall live among the nations."

On this passage, see my discussion in Chapter 2 in this volume.

134. See Goodblatt, *Monarchic Principle*, 161:

> At the very least, by applying Lamentations 4:20 to Judah I the narrator implies that the latter was a Davidide. And he has Hiyya assert that Judah suffers vicariously for the sins of Israel. And he may suggest that Judah I should be seen in messianic terms.

135. On the motif of R. Judah I as the messiah, see further E. E. Urbach, *The Sages: Their Concepts and Beliefs* (2 vols.; trans. Israel Abrams; Jerusalem: Magnes, 1979), 1:678–79.

136. Trans. mod. from Soncino.

137. Perhaps owing to the much older image of Daniel the folk hero, on which see John Day, "The Daniel of Ugarit and Ezekiel and the Hero of the Book of Daniel," *VT* 30 (1980): 174–84.

being among the living, refer to the exilarchate and patriarchate, respectively. Rav says, "If he is of the living, it would be our holy master," *Rabbenu ha-qadosh*—that is, R. Judah the Patriarch. Here, as in R. Hiyya's interpretation of Lam 4:20 in *y. Šabb.* 16:1 noted earlier, R. Judah is the messiah. R. Nahman, on the other hand, says, "If he is of those living, it might be one like myself." Significantly, this R. Nahman b. Jacob was a high-ranking official in and related to the family of the exilarchate,[138] so his opinion is best understood not simply as an expression of narcissism, but as a Babylonian counterpart to Rav's about the patriarch in Palestine. Neusner comments:

> Nahman inferred that the rule of the exilarchate certified, and might in time mark the fulfillment of, that particular Messianic promise. Such a saying reflected the political theology of the exilarch. Being both scion of David and recognized governor of the Jews, the exilarch represented the fulfillment of prophetic hopes for the restoration of a Jewish monarch of the Davidic line.[139]

Thus, in a twist on the old Jewish idea of dual messiahs—messiah of Aaron and messiah of Israel, messiah ben David and messiah ben Joseph—the rabbis can speak of the patriarch and the exilarch as a messianic pair, both of them, however, from the same tribe. We find this notion again in a passage in Bavli Horayot, in which R. Judah I, whose own title is נשיא ("patriarch" or "ruler"), inquires whether the law for the sin-offering by the biblical נשיא ("ruler") in Lev 4:22–24 applies to him.[140] The passage in the Bavli reads:

> Rabbi enquired of R. Hiyya: "Is one like myself to bring a he-goat [Lev 4:22-24]?" "You have your rival in Babylon," the other replied. "The kings of Israel and the kings of the house of David," the first objected, "bring sacrifices independently of one another!" "There they were not subordinate to one another," the other replied, "but here we are subordinate to them." R. Safra taught thus: Rabbi enquired of R. Hiyya, "Is

---

138. See Jacob Neusner, *History of the Jews in Babylonia*, vol. 3 (Leiden: Brill, 1968), 61–75.

139. Jacob Neusner, *There We Sat Down: Talmudic Judaism in the Making* (Nashville, Tenn.: Abingdon, 1978), 56.

140. Lev 4:22–24:

> When a ruler [נשיא] sins, doing unwittingly any one of all the things which YHWH his God has commanded not to be done, and is guilty, if the sin which he has committed is made known to him, he shall bring as his offering a goat, a male without blemish, and shall lay his hand upon the head of the goat, and kill it in the place where they kill the burnt offering before YHWH; it is a sin offering.

one like myself to bring a he-goat [Lev 4:22–24]?" "There [Babylonia] is
the scepter," the other replied, "here [Palestine] is only the law giver," as
it was taught: *The scepter shall not depart from Judah* [Gen 49:10] refers
to the exilarch in Babylonia who rules Israel with the scepter. *Nor the
ruler's staff from between his feet* [Gen 49:10] refers to the grandchildren
of Hillel [i.e., the patriarchs in Palestine] who teach the Torah to Israel
in public. (*b. Hor.* 11b)

The main point here is that there is not one but two chief executives in
rabbinic circles at the time: one in the homeland and the other in Babylonia.
And, what is more, the two are not equal in authority. In both versions of the
dialogue, R. Hiyya, who is himself a disciple of the patriarch, concedes that the
exilarch is the greater of the two: "We are subordinate to them." "There is the
scepter, here only the law-giver."[141]

In R. Safra's version of the dialogue, R. Hiyya parses the two parallel clauses
of Jacob's blessing upon Judah in Gen 49:10 as referring to the exilarch and
patriarch, respectively. The scriptural text, part of the deathbed testament of
Jacob in Gen 49, reads: "The scepter [שבט] shall not depart from Judah, nor the
ruler's staff [מחקק] from between his feet, until he comes to whom it belongs;
and to him shall be the obedience of the peoples" (Gen 49:10). This text, which
gives voice to the official ideology of the ancient Judahite monarchy,[142] unsurprisingly became fodder for messianic exegesis in antiquity.[143] It is interpreted
thusly, for example, in a fragmentary commentary on Genesis at Qumran:

Whenever Israel rules there shall [not] fail to be a descendant of David
upon the throne. For the ruler's staff is the covenant of kingship, [and
the clans] of Israel are the feet, until the Messiah of Righteousness
comes, the Branch of David. For to him and to his seed was granted the
covenant of kingship for everlasting generations. (4Q252 frg. 1, col. 5)[144]

Whereas 4Q252 interprets the scepter and staff of Gen 49:10 as two ways of
signifying the same thing (namely, the covenant of kingship), R. Hiyya in *b. Hor.*

---

141. On the power differential, see Goodblatt, *Monarchic Principle*, 277–311; Hezser, *Social
Structure*, 405–49; Herman, *Prince without a Kingdom*, 112–17.

142. See Raymond de Hoop, *Genesis 49 in Its Literary and Historical Context* (OtSt 39;
Leiden: Brill, 1998), 114–47.

143. See Emmanouela Grypeou and Helen Spurling, *The Book of Genesis in Late Antiquity*
(Leiden: Brill, 2013), 361–435.

144. Trans. Vermes, *Complete Dead Sea Scrolls.*

11b interprets them as two different things: the scepter is the exilarchate, the ruler's staff the patriarchate.[145] Perhaps inevitably in light of the Jewish population distribution in late antiquity, the two executive offices wrestled over spheres of influence, but *b. Hor.* 11b makes this Realpolitik out to be a fulfillment of scripture.

In all of this, there is—to paraphrase David Biale—a conceptual continuity between the myth of the messiah and the politics of the rabbinic executives. What is the messiah if not the ideal of a legitimate scion of the house of David? And what is the patriarch (or the exilarch) if not the best present approximation of that ideal? Biale writes:

> [A] doctrine of continuity between the rabbis and the Messiah can already be found in talmudic times. In [*b. Sanh.* 98b], there are messianic sayings about figures from the courts of the Exilarch (*Resh Galuta*), the political leader of the Babylonian Jewish community, and the Patriarch, the leader of the Palestinian community.... Both the Exilarchs and the Patriarchs traced their ancestry to the House of David, which not only conferred legitimacy on their power, but gave credence to such messianic theories. For these authorities, the coming of the Messiah was guaranteed by the continuity of Jewish government in exile. Instead of sitting disguised as a beggar at the gates of Rome waiting to redeem his powerless people (a theme in some of the rabbinical legends), the Messiah reflected in this theory would emerge out of the institutions of Jewish power in the Diaspora.[146]

This continuity is a two-edged sword, however. On the one hand, it can function, in an obvious way, to legitimate the executive offices, to lend them a halo of authority from the kings of old and the messiah who is to come. As Isaiah Gafni comments, "Both [patriarch and exilarch] claim Davidic lineage, and thereby represent a type of monarchic remnant from the past as well as potential for the future."[147] On the other hand, the same glorious past and

---

145. The Scrolls themselves use this same strategy elsewhere, notably at CD 7:19:

> The star is the Interpreter of the Law who shall come to Damascus, as it is written: *A star shall come forth out of Jacob, and a scepter shall rise out of Israel* [Num 24:17]. The scepter is the Prince of the whole congregation, and when he comes *he shall smite all the children of Sheth* [Num 24:17]. (trans. mod. from Vermes, *Complete Dead Sea Scrolls*)

146. David Biale, *Power and Powerlessness in Jewish History* (New York, N.Y.: Schocken, 1986), 42.

147. Isaiah M. Gafni, "The Political, Social, and Economic History of Babylonian Jewry, 224–638 CE," in *CHJ*, vol. 4 (ed. Steven T. Katz; New York, N.Y.: Cambridge University Press, 2006), 792–820 at 802.

utopian future that lend their halo of authority can also be held up as standards against which to judge the current incumbents.

This latter dynamic is at work in a story in Bavli Sanhedrin in which the sons of R. Hiyya, fortified with liquid courage, challenge R. Judah the Patriarch:

> Judah and Hezekiah, the sons of R. Hiyya, once sat at table with Rabbi and uttered not a word. Whereupon he said: Make the wine strong for the young men, so that they may say something. When the wine took effect, they began by saying: The son of David cannot appear until the two ruling houses in Israel—the exilarchate in Babylon and the patriarchate in Palestine—have come to an end, for it is written, *And he shall be for a sanctuary, for a stone of stumbling and for a rock of offence to both houses of Israel* [Isa 8:14]. Thereupon he [Rabbi] exclaimed: You throw thorns in my eyes, my children! (*b. Sanh.* 38a)

This saying of the sons of R. Hiyya is both a political criticism—hence the wine to loosen their tongues as well as R. Judah's aggrieved response—and a theological argument. The theological argument is that the messianic ideology of the patriarchate (and the exilarchate) contains the seeds of its own destruction. If the two ruling houses in Israel are proxy sons of David, then they must eventually give way to the great and final son of David. By borrowing his authority, they delay rather than hasten his arrival. As Philip Alexander rightly comments:

> The political purpose of [the Davidic ancestry claim] is obvious: it is intended to bolster the authority of the House of the Patriarch, who claimed descent from Hillel. But its theological implications should not be missed. What it suggests is: Don't look for a future ruler of the House of David. You are already living under a scion of his house. This is as good as it gets! ... The message [of the story in *b. Sanh.* 38a] may be that so long as the Jewish people accept the Davidic pretensions of the Nasiʾ and the Resh Galuta the true son of David can never come.[148]

The patriarchate was abolished by the Byzantine Christian emperor Theodosius II in the fifth century, while the exilarchate endured for several centuries more, but the association of Davidic lineage with political legitimation outlasted them both. In a recent study, Arnold Franklin has shown how,

---

148. Philip Alexander, "The Rabbis and Messianism," in *Redemption and Resistance*, 227–44 at 236.

for Jewish communities in the medieval Islamic East, even in the absence of
the old rabbinic institutions, claims to Davidic ancestry functioned in such a
way as to justify a variety of ad hoc authority structures. Franklin writes:

> The almost complete overlap of Davidic ancestry and Davidic authority
> found in rabbinic literature disintegrates in sources from the Middle
> Ages as claims to Davidic ancestry are no longer tied exclusively to
> particular authority structures in the Jewish community. If previously
> the social value of royal lineage was restricted to those individuals who
> succeeded in winning appointments as either exilarchs or patriarchs,
> during the Middle Ages the value of a Davidic pedigree could be actual-
> ized by a much wider pool of dynasts, most of whom would never hold
> a Davidic post.[149]

But this takes us well beyond our current focus. In late antiquity, as we
have seen, the authority of the royal house of David was thought to inhere in
the offices of the patriarch and exilarch, who could, in this historical context,
plausibly be interpreted as the "scepter" and "staff" promised by father Jacob
to the tribe of Judah (Gen 49:10; *b. Hor.* 11b). Like Zerubbabel in the Persian
period, R. Judah the Patriarch and his successors were born messiahs, so to
speak—dynastic claimants to the leadership of the Jewish people, even though,
also like Zerubbabel, they served at the pleasure of their imperial overlords.[150]

The Legend of the Rise of David

It is of course understandable—predictable, even—that an aspiring ruler who
happens to descend from an illustrious family would claim ancestral qualification,
whereas an aspiring ruler who comes from an ignoble family would instead claim
to be qualified by virtue of his own accomplishments. In many of our ancient

---

149. Arnold E. Franklin, *This Noble House: Jewish Descendants of King David in the Medieval Islamic East* (Philadelphia, Pa.: University of Pennsylvania Press, 2013), 43.

150. See Hayim Lapin, *Rabbis as Romans: The Rabbinic Movement in Palestine, 100–400 CE* (New York, N.Y.: Oxford University Press, 2012), 23:

> If Judah and his successors began to claim some sort of "royal" status in 200 or
> later in the third century, the apparent lack of political repercussions for the claim
> is notable: Patriarchs were not, as Jesus reportedly was, crucified for claiming to
> be king of the Jews. This is because the Patriarch was not in any significant way
> the "ruler" of the Jews. It may be tempting to view the Patriarchs against other
> third-century Syrians who claimed royal or imperial prerogatives [e.g., Abgar IX of
> Edessa, Odenathus of Palmyra]. But . . . Patriarchs did not issue coins. . . . [nor did
> they] field armies against Persians or Romans.

messiah texts, however, there is more to it than that. In these texts, both kinds of messiahs—upstarts as well as bluebloods—are able to ground their claims to legitimacy in the scriptural story of king David.[151] This is possible because, although the notion of the messiah came to be associated with ancestral right (in the tropes "son of David," "house of David," and so on), ritual anointing in ancient Israel—not least in the story of David himself—actually signified quite the opposite.[152]

In the biblical narrative, ritual anointing of priests is a conservative act (e.g., Exod 30:30: "You shall anoint Aaron and his sons, and consecrate them, that they may serve me as priests"),[153] but ritual anointing of kings is anticonservative— a symbol of usurpation or, indeed, open rebellion.[154] The first mention of royal anointing in the Deuteronomistic History comes in the "parable of the trees" told by Jotham son of Jerubbaal in Judg 9:7–21, in which the trees figuratively "anoint a king over themselves" (למשח עליהם מלך in Judg 9:8, 15) just as the chiefs of Shechem had "made Abimelech king" (וימליכו את־אבימלך למלך in Judg 9:6). Abimelech's coronation, however, was the result of a bloody coup, so "anointing" here signifies the bestowal of kingship precisely not under circumstances of regular dynastic succession.[155] And in fact, this is the standard use of the verb משח, "to anoint," in the subsequent narrative of Samuel–Kings. Leaving aside Abimelech, the first person to be anointed king in Israel is Saul son of Kish. By ritually pouring a vial of oil on his head (1 Sam 10:1), the prophet Samuel anoints Saul as king (מלך in 1 Sam 15:1, 17) or ruler (נגיד in 1 Sam 9:16; 10:1) over Israel. Therefore Saul is called the משיח יהוה, "anointed one of YHWH" (1 Sam 24:6, 10; 26:9, 11, 16, 23; 2 Sam 1:14, 16), but not, obviously, by means of dynastic succession. This is in the nature of the case. The first king cannot be a rightful heir to the throne.[156]

---

151. Here I have royal messiah texts specifically in view, but there is a conspicuous analogy among priestly messiah texts, as well (especially with regard to the figures of Melchizedek, Aaron, and Phinehas), as I argued earlier in the case of the Hasmoneans. See further Himmelfarb, *Kingdom of Priests*, 1–10.

152. I owe this important observation to a helpful conversation with Jeremy Hutton.

153. See Noth, "Office and Vocation," 237–38; Fleming, "Anointing Priests."

154. Thus rightly Horsley and Hanson, *Bandits, Prophets, and Messiahs*, 96: "From Saul and David at the end of the eleventh century to Jehoahaz at the end of the seventh, it is clear that the anointing of a king by people or prophet was generally a revolutionary act." On this pattern, see Z. Weisman, "Anointing as a Motif in the Making of a Charismatic King," *Bib* 57 (1976): 378–98.

155. See Baruch Halpern, "The Rise of Abimelek ben-Jerubbaal," *HAR* 2 (1978): 79–100.

156. See J. M. Miller, "Saul's Rise to Power," *CBQ* 36 (1974): 157–74; Tomoo Ishida, *The Royal Dynasties in Ancient Israel* (BZAW 142; Berlin: De Gruyter, 1977), 26–54; James W. Flanagan, "Chiefs in Israel," *JSOT* 20 (1981): 47–73.

The second king, however, ought to be a rightful heir to the throne, but in the Deuteronomistic History, of course, he is not. David, who becomes the prototypical מְשִׁיחַ יהוה, is anointed as king under circumstances as irregular as Saul's or, rather, more so. David is actually anointed several times over, first, famously, by Samuel when he, David, is just a youth tending his father's sheep (1 Sam 16:3, 12, 13). At the time of this ritual anointing, however, Saul is still very much alive and very much king, notwithstanding the Deuteronomistic Historian's verdict to the effect that "YHWH had repented of making Saul king over Israel" (1 Sam 15:35). The irregularity of this arrangement is not lost on Saul, who rightly recognizes the threat posed by the young upstart: "What more is there for him but the kingdom itself?" (1 Sam 18:8). From the perspective of 1–2 Samuel, of course, David is scrupulously deferential to Saul's authority: "YHWH forbid that I should lay a hand on YHWH's anointed one" (1 Sam 24:6, 10; 26:9, 11, 16, 23; 2 Sam 1:14, 16). And yet. The next we hear about ritual anointing, Saul has been killed and it is David who is being anointed king again, this time by the men of Judah (2 Sam 2:4, 7), while Saul's son Ishbaal has become king over the territories to the north (2 Sam 2:8–10). There is, in other words, a rightful successor, Ishbaal, who does not need to be anointed, and there is his rival, David, who is anointed precisely because he is not the rightful successor.[157] If you are the oldest surviving son of recently deceased Israelite king, the worst news you could receive is that someone else has just gone and gotten himself anointed. Anointing is the last resort of those who are not next in line for the throne.

After the accession-of-David cycle, this pattern of usage persists. Royal anointing happens only when regular dynastic succession goes awry. The next person said to be anointed as king is Absalom (2 Sam 19:11; cf. 2 Sam 15:10), whose problem is not pedestrian ancestry but bad timing. He is David's son, but he sets himself up as king during the lifetime of and in revolt against his father.[158] After Absalom, the next person anointed as king is another son of David—namely, Solomon (1 Kgs 1:34, 39, 45; 5:1). Granted, the circumstances of Solomon's anointing are rather more auspicious than those of Absalom's, but even Solomon's anointing is an act of desperation intended to supersede the prior claim of his older brother Adonijah (1 Kgs 1:22–27), whom Solomon finally has to assassinate in order to consolidate his own hold on the throne

---

157. On David's *coup d'état*, see A. S. Kapelrud, "König David und die Söhne des Saul," *ZAW* 67 (1955): 198–205; Ishida, *Royal Dynasties*, 55–80; P. Kyle McCarter, "The Apology of David," *JBL* 99 (1980): 489–504; Baruch Halpern, *David's Secret Demons: Messiah, Murderer, Traitor, King* (Grand Rapids, Mich.: Eerdmans, 2001), 280–94.

158. On Absalom's revolt, see Halpern, *David's Secret Demons*, 357–81.

(1 Kgs 2:13–25).[159] So even Solomon, who in subsequent tradition becomes the archetypal son of David (e.g., *Pss. Sol.* 17–18), is actually anointed because he does not have a presumptive right to the throne.

Throughout 1–2 Kings, regular dynastic succession is not marked by ritual anointing, but the interruption of dynasties is.[160] So, in 1 Kgs 19:16, God instructs the prophet Elijah to anoint Jehu son of Nimshi as king over Israel, supplanting Joram of the house of Omri, and in 2 Kings 9 Elisha does so. Jehu must be anointed because he is an upstart. He is not a member of the ruling dynasty, so he has no claim to the monarchy save the anointing itself.[161] By the same token, we do not read of another anointing in the southern kingdom of Judah until the child king Joash in 2 Kings 11. Joash had been secreted away to the temple as an infant when his grandmother Athaliah (daughter of Ahab and Jezebel of Israel) slaughtered all the other children of her son, king Ahaziah of Judah, and took the throne for herself. After some seven years, the priest Jehoiada, in collusion with the captains of the army, brings the child out of hiding and ceremonially presents Joash with heirloom weapons from the house of David, puts a crown on his head, and anoints him (2 Kgs 11:10–12). If the meaning of this ritual anointing were not clear enough, when Athaliah comes upon the scene she cries out: קֶשֶׁר קָשֶׁר, "Conspiracy! Conspiracy!" (2 Kgs 11:14). The anointing of Joash is a coup. In this case, the anointed one actually has a prior dynastic claim, but relative to the then-current regime he is a usurper.[162] We get an anointing story because there is an irregularity in the process of succession.[163]

Interestingly, the Talmud recognizes this anomaly, that although by late antiquity the term "anointed one" had come to signify the rightful heir to the throne of David, in the Bible the anointing of kings happens in the cases

---

159. On Solomon and Adonijah, see Leonhard Rost, *The Succession to the Throne of David* (trans. M. D. Rutter and D. M. Gunn; London: Bloomsbury, 2015 [German original, 1926]), 65–114; Timo Veijola, "Solomon: Bathsheba's Firstborn," in *Reconsidering Israel and Judah: Recent Studies on the Deuteronomistic History* (ed. Gary N. Knoppers and J. Gordon McConville; SBTS 8; Winona Lake, Ind.: Eisenbrauns, 2000), 340–57; Halpern, *David's Secret Demons*, 391–406.

160. On crises of succession, see Ishida, *Royal Dynasties*, 151–82.

161. On this episode, see Marsha C. White, *The Elijah Legends and Jehu's Coup* (BJS 311; Atlanta, Ga.: Scholars Press, 1997).

162. On this episode, see Patricia Dutcher-Walls, *Narrative Art, Political Rhetoric: The Case of Athaliah and Joash* (JSOTSup 209; Sheffield: Sheffield Academic, 1996).

163. The one other mention of royal anointing in the Deuteronomistic History is in the account of the death of Josiah at the hand of Pharaoh Neco of Egypt, at which time "the people of the land took Jehoahaz son of Josiah, anointed him, and made him king in place

of persons who are not rightful heirs. Thus the discussion in Yerushalmi Horayot:

> A king at the beginning [of a dynasty] requires anointing. A king who is a son of a king does not require anointing, for it is said, *Rise, anoint him, for this is he* [1 Sam 16:12]—This one requires anointing, but his descendants do not require anointing.... They anoint kings only on account of controversy. Why then was Solomon anointed? Because of the controversy with Adonijah, and Joash because of Athaliah, and Jehu because of Joram. Is it not written: *Rise, anoint him, for this is he* [1 Sam 16:12], meaning that this one requires anointing, but the kings of Israel do not require anointing? (*y. Hor.* 3:2 [47c])[164]

This perceptive observation notwithstanding, it is likely that in actual practice, ancient Judahite kings who succeeded their fathers through regular means were ritually anointed at their enthronements, as some royal psalms may suggest.[165] Psalm 2, for instance, has been interpreted widely since Hermann Gunkel as an enthronement hymn:[166] "YHWH said to me: You are my son; today I have begotten you" (Ps 2:7); and it speaks of the anointing of the sitting king: "The kings of the earth set themselves ... against YHWH and his anointed one" (Ps 2:2). No doubt this psalmic usage, in combination with the common psalm superscription לדוד, contributed to the tradition according to which the messiah is a son of David. As we have seen, however, the Deuteronomistic History, which supplies most of the scriptural legend of king David, reserves the verb משׁח for instances of usurpation, including David's own divinely sanctioned usurpation of the throne of Saul. It is understandable, then, that this latter usage will have provided a useful scriptural paradigm for certain Hellenistic- and Roman-period Jewish upstarts, people who

---

of his father" (2 Kgs 23:30). There is no narrative of intrigue here, but the anointing may fit the pattern on the assumption that the crown ought to have passed to Jehoahaz's older brother Eliakim.

164. Trans. mod. from Neusner, *Talmud of the Land of Israel*. Compare the parallel passages at *y. Šeqal.* 6:1 (49c); *y. Sotah* 8:3 (22c).

165. Thus rightly de Vaux, *Ancient Israel*, 103–4; Ishida, *Royal Dynasties*, 76n87. See further my discussion in Chapter 2 in this volume.

166. See Hermann Gunkel, *An Introduction to the Psalms* (trans. James D. Nogalski; Macon, Ga.: Mercer University Press, 1998 [German original, 1933]), 99–120; Mowinckel, *Psalms in Israel's Worship*, 1:61–65; and recently Yarbo Collins and Collins, *King and Messiah as Son of God*, 10–15.

were long on zeal but short on pedigree.[167] In the words of Morton Smith, "The most likely way to become a messiah was to begin as a robber. . . . After all, David had made it."[168]

Writing in a different context, Shemaryahu Talmon has commented:

> The image of the anointed king, scion of a dynastic line, as realized in the Davidic house, contained two essentially contradictory principles: the concept of inspired leadership deriving its power from personal charisma, which by definition is non-consecutive, coalesced with the idea of an automatically continuous government drawing its strength from an institutionalized charisma of office. The principle of election by the divine spirit was grafted on to the system of dynastic government, which in essence is void of any religious and ideological dimension. This unexpected amalgam of seemingly contradictory concepts raised the dynastic monarchy to the level of a basic principle of biblical ideology.[169]

Talmon alludes here to Max Weber's *Theory of Social and Economic Organization*—in particular, the famous chapter titled "The Routinization of Charisma"—which rubric Weber himself applied to a discussion of ancient Israel in one of his last works.[170] Talmon's essay is concerned with the preexilic

---

167. Thus rightly Horsley and Hanson, *Bandits, Prophets, and Messiahs*, 88–102, here 91: "The future Davidic king was not necessarily a *son* of David. . . . The imagery of a Davidic king symbolized substantively what this agent of God would do: liberate and restore the fortunes of Israel, as had the original David" (emphasis in original). John Gager has made an analogous case for the influence of

> the myth of the Maccabees, preserved (I suspect) not just in oral legend but in the widely circulated books that have come down to us as [1–2] Maccabees. At the heart of this myth lies the unlikely story of a small band of brothers who turn aside the might of the Seleucid army and restore sovereignty to the land of Israel. If they did—so the thinking must have run—so can we. (Gager, "Messiahs and Their Followers," 45)

This may well be so, but the David story is older, more widely circulated, and more often cited in Roman-period messiah texts.

168. Morton Smith, "Messiahs: Robbers, Jurists, Prophets," in idem, *Studies in the Cult of Yahweh*, 2:42.

169. Shemaryahu Talmon, "Kingship and the Ideology of the State," in idem, *King, Cult and Calendar in Ancient Israel: Collected Studies* (Jerusalem: Magnes, 1986), 9–38 at 37.

170. Max Weber, *The Theory of Social and Economic Organization* (trans. A. M. Henderson and Talcott Parsons; New York, N.Y.: Free Press, 2009 [1st English ed., 1947; German original, 1920]), 363–85; idem, *Ancient Judaism* (New York, N.Y.: Free Press, 1952 [German original, 1921]).

Judahite monarchy,[171] whereas I am interested here in the postexilic *Nachleben* of the David story. If we entertain Talmon's Weberian rubric, then we can say that, in the ancient *Nachleben* of the David story, at least, the charismatic model of leadership is never fully routinized. Rather, the two models, charisma and institution, upstart and blueblood, coexist side by side, each one always susceptible of appropriation in new circumstances. David is the progenitor of the foremost blueblood institution in ancient Israel, the Judahite monarchy, but he is also the archetypal upstart, a man who rises from utter obscurity to the heights of power with nothing more than personal charisma and divine favor. Consequently, both bluebloods like Zerubbabel and upstarts like Shimon bar Kosiba can, with some plausibility, cast themselves—or be cast by their biographers—as Judean kings after the pattern of the greatest Judean king.[172]

This account of things gives the lie to one oft-cited theory in the secondary literature—namely, that messianic partisans invented Davidic genealogies for their messiahs as a matter of course. As Yehezkel Kaufmann, for instance, writes about the Second-Temple period:

> The Messiahs that appeared in those times staked their claims in their own right. Of course, they and their followers believed implicitly that they were Sons-of-David, but their genealogy was not a condition of their Messianism. They were Messiahs not because they were descended from David, but were sons-of-David because they were Messiahs.[173]

Kaufmann's claim is prima facie plausible, but in fact it is doubly mistaken. For one thing, there is evidence that some messiahs (e.g., Zerubbabel) did come to the job with blueblood credentials, and for another, we know of upstarts (e.g., Bar Kosiba) who were messiahs but not therefore sons of David. Davidic ancestry was not the mythical *sine qua non* it has often been made out to be.[174]

---

171. In dialogue with the likes of Albrecht Alt, "The Monarchy in the Kingdoms of Israel and Judah," in idem, *Essays in Old Testament History and Religion* (trans. R. A. Wilson; New York, N.Y.: Doubleday, 1967), 239–59, 311–35; and J. A. Soggin, "Charisma und Institution im Königtum Sauls," *ZAW* 75 (1963): 54–65.

172. See Ilan, "King David"; and relatedly Dahl, "Eschatology and History in Light of the Qumran Texts," 56–57: "At the beginning of messianic doctrine both royal ideology and the peculiar history of David were already in place."

173. Yehezkel Kaufmann, "The Messianic Idea: The Real and the Hidden Son of David," *Jewish Bible Quarterly* 22 (1994 [1st pub., 1961]): 141–50 at 146.

174. Contra Graetz, "Stages," 153:

Jon Levenson has made a closely related point with reference to the Hebrew Bible:

> Even in the religious consciousness of an Israelite for whom kingship was of central importance, the entitlement of the House of David could remain peripheral. That is why, despite the presence of a great quantity of material bearing on royal theology, the specific covenant with David is expounded in clear form so very rarely. Not all royal theology was Davidic, and not all Davidic theology was covenantal.[175]

Kenneth Pomykala, too, has demonstrated a similar dynamic in early Jewish texts:

> Writers in the early Jewish period would be under no obligation to make use of davidic dynasty tradition, or to use it in service of monarchical or messianic ideologies. They would be free to use it or ignore it, and if they used it, to employ it and adapt it for whatever purpose the author chose.... [Therefore] one must ask *how* early Jewish writers employed and adapted the biblical traditions about davidic figures and the davidic dynasty.[176]

This is just right. Repurposing Levenson's turn of phrase, we might say that not all Jewish leaders are messiahs, not all messiahs are royal, not all royal messiahs are Davidic, and not all Davidic messiahs are sons of David.

It may be helpful, finally, to return to Joseph Klausner's assessments of Judah Maccabee and Shimon bar Kosiba, which we noted at the beginning of the chapter. The reader will recall that Klausner raises the question why Bar Kosiba is called messiah in the ancient sources while Judah Maccabee is not so called, if neither of them was a Davidide. Hasmonean sources, Klausner

---

Once David, "a king after God's heart," had been chosen as the leader of the Israelite nation securing national independence, and Solomon had added a good deal of splendor and a central sanctuary, the messianic hope attached itself permanently to a scion from the house of David, without whom the glory of the future could no longer be imagined.

175. Jon D. Levenson, "The Davidic Covenant and Its Modern Interpreters," *CBQ* 41 (1979): 205–19 at 217.

176. Pomykala, *Davidic Dynasty Tradition*, 68 (emphasis original). See further Thomas Römer, "Les interrogations sur l'avenir de la dynastie davidique aux Époques babylonienne et perse et les origines d'une attente messianique dans les textes de la Bible hébraïque," in *Aux origines des messianismes juifs*, 47–59.

proposes, do not call Judah Maccabee messiah because they know better, but rabbinic sources call Bar Kosiba messiah because he was exceptionally heroic.[177] On closer inspection, however, this explanation is liable to the charge of special pleading. After all, by any objective standard, Bar Kosiba was not measurably more heroic than the Maccabees. And if not, then why does the Talmud not also know better, as 1 Maccabees does, than to call a non-Davidide the messiah? Other scholars such as Conder, Greenstone, Charlesworth, and Fitzmyer avoid this difficulty, but they do so by postulating a dubious extra-textual force ("the messianic idea" or "messianism") whose relative strength or weakness supposedly accounts for the occurrence or nonoccurrence of the term in the pertinent texts.[178]

If the account that I have offered here is compelling, then Klausner's dilemma simply dissolves. Judah Maccabee is not called "messiah" either because it never occurred to his biographers to call him that or because it did occur to them but seemed implausible or unhelpful for their purposes. Bar Kosiba is called a messiah because, although he was not a Davidide, he was in the eyes of some, at least, Davidesque. He arose in a time of great distress to fight Israel's enemies and restore the glory of Jerusalem. To cite Morton Smith again:

> A man who wanted to be thought a messiah usually could not do everything with which his model was credited, he would imitate only such traits as he could. Similarly, when trying to decide whether or not a man was a messiah, his contemporaries would find that he matched their favorite picture in some points, but not in others.[179]

Just so. We might say that, because of the tension built into the biblical legend of David (and, *mutatis mutandis*, of the priests Melchizedek, Aaron, and Phinehas), all subsequent messiah language inherits the twin ideological poles of ancestry and merit, rightful succession and divine inspiration. Messiahs could be either born or made. All early Jewish and Christian messiah texts, therefore, have to navigate both these poles, and in practice each text does so in creative ways that suit its own rhetorical ends. For persons who

---

177. Klausner, *Messianic Idea*, 250, 395.

178. Conder, *Judas Maccabaeus*; Greenstone, *Messiah Idea*; Charlesworth, "From Jewish Messianology to Christian Christology"; idem, "From Messianology to Christology"; Fitzmyer, *One Who Is to Come*.

179. Smith, "Robbers, Jurists, Prophets," 41–42.

had a plausible claim to Davidic descent, the texts could say: *Behold the son of David*. And for persons who had no such claim, the texts could say: *David did it. Why not our man?* In this respect, the conflicted scriptural portrait of David proved to be a boon to prospective messiahs of both types, born as well as made.

4

Messiahs Present and Absent

WRITING IN YEHUD in the mid fifth century BCE, the prophet Malachi (whether that is his name or an epithet, מלאכי, "my messenger")[1] warns the priests of the recently reestablished temple of YHWH in Jerusalem, who he thinks are rendering improper cult (Mal 1:6–2:9), that the deity will shortly call them to account:

> The Lord whom you seek will suddenly come to his temple.... But who can endure the day of his coming, and who can stand when he appears? For he is like a refiner's fire and like fullers' soap; he will sit as a refiner and purifier of silver, and he will purify the sons of Levi and refine them like gold and silver, till they present right offerings to YHWH. (Mal 3:1–3)

What is more, Malachi (or his redactor, depending on the date of the these lines)[2] envisions a role for a messenger who will precede this day of reckoning: "Behold, I send my messenger [מלאכי] to prepare the way before me.... The messenger of the covenant [מלאך הברית] in whom you delight, behold, he is coming" (Mal 3:1). And again:

---

1. An ambiguity debated already in antiquity by the rabbis, as, for example, in *b. Meg.* 15a: "It has been taught: R. Joshua b. Korha said: Malachi is the same as Ezra. But the Sages say that Malachi was his proper name" (trans. Soncino).

2. On the redaction-critical problem, see Rainer Kessler, "The Unity of Malachi and Its Relation to the Book of the Twelve," in *Perspectives on the Formation of the Book of the Twelve* (ed. Rainer Albertz et al.; BZAW 433; Berlin: De Gruyter, 2012), 223–36; Russell Fuller, "The Sequence of Malachi 3:22–24 in the Greek and Hebrew Textual Traditions: Implications for the Redactional History of the Minor Prophets," in Fuller, "Sequence of Malachi 3," 371–80.

Behold, I will send you Elijah the prophet [אליה הנביא] before the great and terrible day of YHWH comes. And he will turn the hearts of fathers to their children and the hearts of children to their fathers, lest I come and smite the land with a curse. (Mal 4:5–6 [MT 3:23–34])

The job of the messenger is to prepare the way.[3] YHWH himself will execute judgment. In any case, there is no messiah anywhere in Malachi's field of vision and, in this respect, as many interpreters have noted, Malachi is representative of Judean prophets during the Persian period.

In a 1998 essay, Rex Mason compares the prevailing silence the postexilic prophets on the topic of a messiah to the famous exchange in Arthur Conan Doyle's short story *Silver Blaze*, in which Inspector Gregory of Scotland Yard, unable to find a lead in a difficult case, converses with Sherlock Holmes as follows:

"Is there any point to which you would wish to draw my attention?"
"To the curious incident of the dog in the night-time."
"The dog did nothing in the night-time."
"That was the curious incident," remarked Sherlock Holmes.[4]

Explicating the analogy, Mason writes, "The silence of the postexilic prophets other than Haggai and Zechariah [regarding the messiah] . . . is deafening."[5] Deafening because, like Sherlock Holmes with the barking dog, Mason expects to hear something but hears nothing, and he interprets the absence of the expected as a kind of evidence in itself.

In a more recent essay, Joachim Schaper cites Mason's invocation of Sherlock Holmes and undertakes to show that, in effect, the dog did bark in the nighttime, that the silence of Persian-period sources on the messiah is only apparent, not real.[6] In the present chapter, I suggest that Schaper

---

3. See Roberts, "Old Testament's Contribution," 50: "Malachi introduced a prophetic figure into Israel's expectations for God's future intervention . . . though it is not clear in this earlier oracle [Mal 3:1] that the מלאך ('messenger') is even human, much less specifically a prophet."

4. Arthur Conan Doyle, "Silver Blaze," in idem, *Memoirs of Sherlock Holmes* (New York, N.Y.: Burt, 1894), 22.

5. Rex Mason, "The Messiah in the Postexilic Old Testament Literature," in *King and Messiah*, 338–64, here 350, and further at 364: "In summary, then, we have to say how little influence the concept of a renewal of the Davidic line after the exile exercised in the extant post-exilic biblical literature."

6. Joachim Schaper, "Persian Period," 3. Schaper concludes, "Contrary to the claims of many scholars, a lively messianic expectation characterized (the beliefs of at least a significant

116   THE GRAMMAR OF MESSIANISM

is right in his objection to Mason's "dog in the nighttime" interpretation
of messianism in postexilic texts, but wrong in his counterproposal. Both
Mason and Schaper expect the dog to bark. Mason does not hear it and is
perplexed. Schaper listens closely enough to make out the sound of a bark.
My thesis is that the expectation of a bark is itself mistaken. References to
messiahs occur in some early Jewish texts and not in others, and there is
nothing curious, remarkable, or deficient about the texts in which they do
not. It is the expectation on the part of the modern interpreter that creates
the problem.

The Vacuum Hypothesis

Why do modern interpreters come to the primary texts with this expectation?
Although they are, in my view, mistaken to harbor it, at least they come by it
honestly. From the beginning of modern research on the subject, the hypothesis
of a robust messianic hope persisting right through the Second-Temple period
featured prominently in the work of numerous authorities.[7] We find it already in
Heinrich Graetz's mid-nineteenth-century *History of the Jews* under the heading
"The Messianic Hope":

> The most earnest thinkers of that time [the Hellenistic period] had
> long regarded the political condition of the Judaeans since their return
> from the Babylonian exile as a temporary or preparatory state, which
> would only continue until the true prophet arose, and Elijah turned
> the hearts of the fathers to the children, and restored the tribes of
> Jacob.[8]

A generation later, Graetz's Protestant countryman Emil Schürer (cited
here in Vermes's revised edition, which follows the original closely) takes a
similar view: "[Messianic hope] was never entirely lost by the people, even

---

proportion of the adherents of) the YHWH religion throughout the Persian period" ("Persian
Period," 14). In making this case, he follows the precedent of Horbury, *Jewish Messianism and
the Cult of Christ*, 36–63.

7. But not all authorities. Bruno Bauer and the young H. J. Holtzmann (who later changed
his view under the influence of Wilhelm Bousset and Hugo Gressmann) are conspicuous
nineteenth-century exceptions. See the discussion in Horbury, *Messianism among Jews and
Christians*, 1–22.

8. Heinrich Graetz, *History of the Jews*, vol. 2 (ed. and trans. Bella Löwy; Philadelphia,
Pa.: JPS, 1893 [German original, 1853–1876]), 142–43.

though it was not always as vigorous as it became after the Maccabean upris-
ing."[9] And again:

> Did this hope remain constantly alive among the people? In its general
> form as it affected the future for the nation, messianic expectation did
> not die with the disappearance of prophecy. In the last pre-Christian cen-
> turies, and especially in the first century A.D., it became once more very
> lively.[10]

And a generation after Schürer, the Jewish historian Joseph Klausner gives an
account along the same lines:

> [The Apocrypha and Pseudepigrapha] do not show evidence of the
> despair which the Second Destruction put into the hearts of the
> nation's leaders, nor of the Messianic hope and the hope for a life
> after death, of which the nation had such need following the frightful
> catastrophe. But even in the best times for Israel during the period of
> the Second Temple the Messianic idea was not completely forgotten. It
> was not enlarged and developed, nor was it embroidered with strong
> imaginative colors. Yet it was preserved and it endured, even though
> its scope was restricted, and the sages of Israel did not deal with it
> often or in an elaborate fashion, because the time was not ripe for
> doing so.[11]

Perhaps most revealing is Franz Hesse's statement in his article on the χρίω
word group in Gerhard Kittel's *Theologische Wörterbuch zum Neuen Testament.*
Hesse writes:

> It is very difficult, if not impossible, to reconstruct a history of
> the Messianic movement in Israel and post-exilic Judaism from
> these scanty passages, many of which cannot be dated with any
> certainty. There undoubtedly must have been such a movement.
> This is shown by the examples given and it may also be concluded
> from the fact that Messianic emerges into the clear light of his-
> tory in later centuries, not merely as a trend that has just arisen

9. Schürer-Vermes, *History,* 2:492.

10. Schürer-Vermes, *History,* 2:497.

11. Klausner, *Messianic Idea,* 249.

in Judaism, but as a movement with hundreds of years of history
behind it.[12]

It is striking that Hesse acknowledges the paucity of the evidence but reasons that there must have been a vigorous, centuries-long messianic movement to account for even such references as we do find in the sources. Recent
critics have thought, for good reason, that Hesse's claim looks suspiciously
like special pleading.[13] Such, however, was the weight of the received opinion
under which Hesse operated. Nor have latter-day revisionists, among whom
I count myself, completely escaped this weight of received opinion.

Beginning in the mid twentieth century and down to the present, research
in this area has witnessed a groundswell of opinion contradicting the older
hypothesis of a robust, persistent messianic hope from the Babylonian exile
right through the Jewish–Roman wars. This revisionist perspective, which is
now the dominant one, has focused especially on *la longue durée* of the Persian
and Hellenistic periods, especially 500 BCE to 200 BCE, from which centuries
we have very few Jewish messiah texts of any kind. The older scholars were
aware of this feature of the ancient record, of course, but they managed to
interpret it in a manner assimilable to their hypotheses.[14] Scholars writing
after the World War II, however, insisted increasingly that the emperor had no
clothes, that this three hundred-year gap in the historical record must indicate
a three hundred-year gap in messianism itself. We encounter this argument,
for instance, in S. B. Frost's 1952 monograph *Old Testament Apocalyptic*. Frost
writes, "[After ca. 500 BCE,] with the decline of the prophets and the growth
in importance of the priestly school of writers, it [messianism] dropped very
much into the background of Hebrew thought and literature."[15] And again:

After the débâcle of Zerubbabel, the priests sit firmly in the saddle of
the national life and messianism is driven back into the folk-religion of
the people, emerging only in the unfathered oracles of Extra-Isaiah [i.e.,

---

12. Hesse, "χρίω κτλ.," 509.

13. See the apt criticisms of Green, "Messiah in Judaism," 7–8: "To violate ordinary scholarly
principles of evidence and inference with such forced arguments requires powerful external
motivations"; and Collins, *Scepter*, 50: "The emergence of messianism in the first century
BCE does not warrant any inference about a messianic movement at an earlier time."

14. See, for example, Klausner, *Messianic Idea*, 249: "The sages of Israel did not deal with
it [the messianic idea] often or in an elaborate fashion, because the time was not ripe for
doing so."

15. S. B. Frost, *Old Testament Apocalyptic: Its Origins and Growth* (London: Epworth, 1952), 66.

Isa 24–27], Micah 5, and the two references in Deutero-Zechariah. Not until almost the end of our period does the Messiah reappear.[16]

In an important 1977 book, which in other respects is quite old-fashioned in its approach,[17] Joachim Becker coined the term *messianologische Vakuum* for the period 500 BCE to 200 BCE About this long stretch of early Jewish history, Becker writes:

> The theocratic movement expresses its convictions not only positively in terms of the immediate kingship of Yahweh, the transfer of earthly power to foreign rulers, and the collectivization of the idea of the king, but also negatively in messianological silence during the exilic and postexilic period [citing Joel, Obadiah, Malachi, Zephaniah, Third Isaiah, the Priestly writer in the Pentateuch, Psalms, Chronicles, Ben Sira, Daniel, Tobit, Judith, Esther, Baruch, Wisdom of Solomon, 1–4 Maccabees, Book of Watchers, 2 Enoch, Assumption of Moses]. . .. The books of an eschatological cast in particular admit of an argument from silence; in them we should expect to find the figure of a messiah if one had been present in the hopes and expectations of the age.[18]

Looking back at previous research on these Persian- and Hellenistic-period texts, Becker notes, "Scholarship has been concerned to fill this incomprehensible vacuum,"[19] citing Henri Cazelles and L.-B. Gorgulho as examples.[20] As Becker sees it, however, all such efforts are doomed to failure, since "there was not even such a thing as messianic expectation until the last two centuries B.C."[21] Late in the book, Becker manages to rescue the Christian proof from messianic prophecy by means of a dogmatic *deus ex machina*,[22] but his

---

16. Frost, *Old Testament Apocalyptic*, 240. Elsewhere Frost comments, "It would seem that the Messiah owes his reintroduction to Jewish literature [ca. 200 BCE] to much the same influence which secured Fortinbras his place in Shakespeare's Hamlet: he was there in the traditional material and the people would expect to see him" (*Old Testament Apocalyptic*, 67).

17. See the discussion in Chapter 2 in this volume.

18. Becker, *Messianic Expectation*, 79.

19. Becker, *Messianic Expectation*, 79–80.

20. Henri Cazelles, "L'Enfantement de la Sagesse en Prov. VIII," in *Sacra Pagina*, vol. 1 (ed. Joseph Coppens; BETL 12; Gembloux: Duculot, 1959), 511–15; L.-B. Gorgulho, "Ruth et la 'Fille de Sion,' Mère du Messie," *RThom* 63 (1963): 501–14.

21. Becker, *Messianic Expectation*, 93.

22. See Becker, *Messianic Expectation*, 95–96:

enduring contribution to the scholarly discussion of messianism is the notion of a *messianologische Vakuum* in the Second-Temple period. His vivid metaphor has subsequently been cited with approval by the likes of Stefan Schreiber and John Collins,[23] and with disapproval by the likes of William Horbury, Magne Saebo, and Andrew Chester.[24]

This debate about a putative vacuum in the history of messianism ca. 500 BCE to 200 BCE is illustrative of a larger, deeper-seated trend in the literature—namely, a preoccupation with theorizing the absence of messianism in a wide range of primary sources. Rex Mason's comment on the postexilic prophets—that, like Sherlock Holmes's dog in the nighttime, they should have made a noise but did not—is a prime example,[25] and there are many others. James Charlesworth's substantial body of work on messianism amply illustrates this trend.[26] In an important 1979 *ANRW* article on "The Concept of the Messiah in the Pseudepigrapha," he comments, "References to an eschatological Messiah are surprisingly absent in the Apocrypha and understandably missing in Philo and Josephus; but they are present in the Dead Sea Scrolls and Targums."[27] Instructively, for Charlesworth, the cases of Philo and Josephus do not require explanation. They do not mention a messiah, but Charlesworth does not expect them to, so all is well. (Other interpreters have had very different, even opposite, expectations of Philo and Josephus, which just goes to show the profound subjectivity of this way of talking about the sources, as discussed

---

> Above all, we must remember that the messianic interpretation of the Old Testament, arbitrary as it may appear, is nevertheless based on the highest authority. The scriptural interpretation of the early church is not simply a question of the late Jewish mentality; it is carried out with the aid of the Spirit.

23. See Schreiber, *Gesalbter und König*, 154 and n38; Collins, *Scepter*, 50–51 and n120.

24. Horbury, *Messianism among Jews and Christians*, 44:

> The "messianological vacuum" itself is by no means airtight. There is no question of centuries kept clear of any breath of messianic hope. The texts ... from the Apocrypha are contemporary with others in which messianic hope is explicit, including the LXX Pentateuch and Prophets.

Similarly Saebo, "Messianism and Eschatology," 226; Chester, *Messiah and Exaltation*, 276–97; Keith Rosenthal, "Rethinking the Messianological Vacuum: The Prevalence of Jewish Messianism during the Second Temple Period" (Ph.D. diss., Graduate Theological Union, 2006).

25. Mason, "Postexilic Old Testament Literature," 350.

26. See Charlesworth, "Concept of the Messiah in the Pseudepigrapha"; idem, "From Jewish Messianology to Christian Christology"; idem, "From Messianology to Christology"; idem, "Messianic Ideas in Early Judaism"; idem, "Messianology in the Biblical Pseudepigrapha," in *Qumran Messianism*, 21–52.

27. Charlesworth, "Concept of the Messiah in the Pseudepigrapha," 190.

later in this chapter.) The so-called Old Testament Apocrypha, however, pose a problem, because Charlesworth expects to find messiahs in those texts but does not.[28] The same is true of the so-called Old Testament Pseudepigrapha, which—excepting the *Parables of Enoch*, *4 Ezra*, and *2 Baruch*—do not yield the kind of evidence for messianism that Charlesworth expects to find in Jewish texts from this period.[29] Thus, he summarizes:

> The terms "the Messiah," "the Anointed One," and "the Christ" do not appear in the following pseudepigrapha: Ahiqar, the Letter of Aristeas, 3 Maccabees, 4 Maccabees, 2 Enoch, the Testament of Job, the Treatise of Shem, the Lives of the Prophets, the Apocalypse of Abraham, the Apocalypse of Moses, the Hellenistic Synagogal Hymns, the Five Apocryphal Syriac Psalms, the Prayer of Manasseh, the Prayer of Joseph, Joseph and Asenath, the Prayer of Jacob, Pseudo-Phocylides, Pseudo-Philo, the Apocalypse of Adam, the Apocalypse of Ezekiel, Eldad and Modad, the Questions of Ezra, the Apocalypse of Ezra, and the Testament of Solomon . . . . Forty pseudepigrapha, therefore, either do not contain messianic ideas, or employ titles other than "the Messiah" and its derivatives.[30]

This passage is a model of what William Horbury has called the "no hope list," a commonplace in many twentieth-century treatments of ancient messianism. Horbury writes, "The Apocrypha of the English Bible have for long been a centrepiece in a regular manifestation of the study of messianism, which may be called the 'no hope list'—the list of books wherein no messianic hope is to be found."[31] Horbury finds such lists in the work of W. V. Hague, A. F. von Gall, Wilhelm Bousset (as edited by Hugo Gressmann), S. B. Frost, Sigmund Mowinckel, and Joachim Becker, among others,[32] and it would be easy, if perhaps fruitless, to update this list with further examples.

---

28. Similarly Charlesworth, "From Messianology to Christology," 16: "The noun 'Messiah' or 'Christ' does not appear in the thirteen books of the Old Testament Apocrypha. That fact is remarkable."

29. On the use of "apocrypha" and "pseudepigrapha" as labels for these respective corpora, see the apt criticisms of Kraft, "Para-mania"; and Annette Yoshiko Reed, "The Modern Invention of 'Old Testament Pseudepigrapha,'" *JTS* n.s. 60 (2009): 403–36.

30. Charlesworth, "Concept of the Messiah in the Pseudepigrapha," 216, 218.

31. Horbury, *Messianism among Jews and Christians*, 38.

32. See W. V. Hague, "The Eschatology of the Apocryphal Scriptures I: The Messianic Hope," *JTS* 12 (1911): 57–98 at 64; A. F. von Gall, ΒΑΣΙΛΕΙΑ ΤΟΥ ΘΕΟΥ (Heidelberg: Winter, 1926), 376–77; Wilhelm Bousset, *Die Religion des Judentums im späthellenistischen Zeitalter*

Having perceptively diagnosed this curious feature of the secondary literature, Horbury undertakes—like Joachim Schaper in response to Rex Mason—to demonstrate that there is actually hope in these supposedly "no hope" texts. In so doing, however, Horbury misses the opportunity for a more radical and more accurate criticism. A more excellent way, it seems to me, is roundly to reject the terms of the debate altogether.

Morton Smith, in a short article from 1959, actually proposes this very thing, but his insight seems never really to have gained traction.[33] Early in the article in question, Smith compiles his own list of texts *sans* messiah from among the newly published Dead Sea Scrolls and some roughly contemporary Jewish texts. He writes:

> The War [1QM] . . . gives us a detailed account of military goings on so extraordinary that they must be eschatological, but it says nothing whatever of any messiah. Similarly, there is no reference to a messiah in the Hodayot, nor in the Habbakuk commentary, where we should expect one. . . . Many OT prophecies of the coming kingdom or world have no messiah, and there is none in Jubilees (though chap. 23 contains a prophecy of the coming age from which the messiah's absence is conspicuous, and the blessings of Levi and Judah in chap. 31 are on the very verge of messianism), nor in Enoch 1–36 and 91–104, nor in the Assumption of Moses, nor in the Slavic Enoch, nor Sibylline Oracles IV, though all of these contain prophetic passages in which some messiah might reasonably have been expected to make an appearance.[34]

Horbury actually cites this essay of Smith's as an example of the literary form of the "no hope list,"[35] which is understandable but also misses the point. Smith invokes the received notion of "passages in which some messiah might reasonably have been expected to make an appearance" in order to

---

(ed. Hugo Gressmann; 3d ed.; HNT 21; Tübingen: Mohr Siebeck, 1926), 222; Frost, *Old Testament Apocalyptic*, 66–67; Mowinckel, *He That Cometh*, 180.

33. With a few admirable exceptions, for example, Alan Segal, who cites Smith approvingly against Mowinckel's sharp distinction between political messianism and eschatological messianism: "It is much more logical to assume that each community sought legitimation of its historical situation and eschatological aspirations from the text of the Bible" (Alan F. Segal, *Two Powers in Heaven: Early Rabbinic Reports about Christianity and Gnosticism* [Leiden: Brill, 1977], 48n23).

34. Smith, "What Is Implied?" 68.

35. Horbury, *Messianism among Jews and Christians*, 38–39nn.

deconstruct that notion, to show how the primary texts confound interpreters' expectations. Thus, about the quest for messiahs in the Scrolls, he writes, "In a number of instances, to be sure, the concern has proved to be that of the interpreters, rather than the text."[36] In contrast to his bibliographical counterparts, Smith's point about the War Scroll, Hodayot, Habbakuk Pesher, and the rest is emphatically not that they betray a "no hope" perspective, but rather that they express their own hopes in their own terms. Thus Smith concludes, "Just as there are messiahs without Ends, so there are Ends without messiahs."[37]

If this dictum of Smith's is right, as I think it certainly is, then it should have derailed the whole scholarly enterprise of explaining why certain early Jewish texts do not comment on a messiah. And yet, in the last generation of research, from ca. 1980 to the present, that enterprise has positively thrived. Indeed, following through on the logic of the vacuum hypothesis, Jacob Neusner has actually outlined a research agenda around this task. He writes, "What we want to know is where the Messiah-theme matters when it does, and, when that theme proves uninteresting, why, as in the Mishnah's system and in the thought of Philo, the Messiah-theme makes no contribution to the definition and symbolization of a Judaism's teleology."[38] In Neusner's research agenda, it is incumbent on interpreters to explain not only, say, the *Psalms of Solomon*'s conception of a messiah, but equally important, say, Philo's failure to say anything about a messiah. The silence of the latter is taken to be just as heuristically important as the speech of the former. The absence is flagged up and isolated for analysis.

This, it seems to me, is perverse. When we find ourselves devising strategies for analyzing what is not in our primary texts rather than what is in them, it is difficult to avoid the conclusion that a kind of methodological madness has set in. As Benjamin Wright notes in a fine discussion of this issue in the Wisdom of Ben Sira, "It is always somewhat problematic to focus on what is not in a text rather than what is."[39] Problematic, indeed. This methodological madness is not without its reasons, however. It may be perverse, but it

---

36. Smith, "What Is Implied?" 66.

37. Smith, "What Is Implied?" 68. This directly contradicts the roughly contemporary and unfortunately more influential judgment of Sigmund Mowinckel: "An eschatology without a Messiah is conceivable, but not a Messiah apart from a future hope" (Mowinckel, *He That Cometh*, 8).

38. Neusner, "Preface," ix. The contributors to *Judaisms and Their Messiahs* execute this research agenda in their respective essays, and Neusner himself does so for the rabbinic corpus in his *Messiah in Context* (on which see the discussion later in this chapter).

39. Benjamin G. Wright III, "Eschatology without a Messiah in the Wisdom of Ben Sira," in *The Septuagint and Messianism* (ed. M. A. Knibb; BETL 195; Leuven: Peeters, 2006), 323.

is not inexplicable. As Andrew Chester has commented in this connection, "The position of Neusner and Green is entirely understandable as a natural reaction against at least some Christian and New Testament scholarship of past decades (and going back of course much further)."[40] Just so. Neusner's call for an account of why nonmessianic texts are nonmessianic, although bizarre in its own right, is an understandable and perhaps inevitable reaction to the equally bizarre history of research to that point. To put it differently, Neusner's research program looks bizarre to me, but then, I have the benefit of hindsight. Had I been working on the problem during the 1980s, as he was, I might have welcomed his proposal as a dose of relative sanity.[41] But it is sane only relative to the previous history of research.[42] Having benefited a great deal from the reactionary course correction proposed by Neusner and others, we are now, one hopes, in a position to assess the evidence with cooler heads. Cooler heads have indeed prevailed in a number of recent studies,[43] and yet a certain mystery remains around certain supposed gap texts—ones in which messianism is thought to be conspicuously absent—"no hope" texts, to borrow Horbury's turn of phrase. In the balance of this chapter, our task is to revisit several of these texts and, if possible, to dispel some of the mystery.[44]

Philo of Alexandria

One of the figures most often cited in this connection is the great Jewish philosopher of Roman Egypt, Philo of Alexandria (fl. 30s–40s CE).[45] With the

---

40. Chester, *Messiah and Exaltation*, 278.

41. As does, for example, Alan F. Segal, review of *Judaisms and Their Messiahs*, in *Jewish Social Studies* 50 (1988–1992): 117–18: "[Neusner's] assumption is a forceful new way of understanding religious history in the first century.... *Judaisms and Their Messiahs at the Turn of the Christian Era* is itself an impressive work of summation and promise for the future."

42. Thus Segal, review of *Judaisms and Their Messiahs*, 117: "It is worthwhile to review the reasons for [Neusner's] assumption and its felicities over previous ideas.... The problems with this [older] approach are legion."

43. For example, Schäfer, "Diversity and Interaction"; Stuckenbruck, "Messianic Ideas"; Collins, *Scepter*.

44. We might have chosen any of the commonly cited "no hope" texts for treatment, but it is perhaps most efficient to discuss the three most extensive and oft-discussed corpora in this connection—namely, Philo of Alexandria, Flavius Josephus, and the Mishnah.

45. See in particular Erwin Ramsdell Goodenough, *The Politics of Philo Judaeus: Practice and Theory* (New Haven, Conn.: Yale University Press, 1939), especially 21–41, 115–19; Harry Austryn Wolfson, *Philo: Foundations of Religious Philosophy in Judaism, Christianity, and Islam* (2 vols.; Cambridge, Mass.: Harvard University Press, 1947), 2:395–426; J. de Savignac, "Le Messianisme de Philon d'Alexandrie," *NovT* 4 (1960): 319–24; Ray Barraclough, "Philo's

exception of his Judean coethnic Flavius Josephus (who is discussed later in this chapter), Philo is the only Jewish writer from antiquity to have left a non-anonymous literary corpus of any substantial size, and he is by far our most important literary witness to the thriving Jewish community in Egypt.[46] If, per the hypotheses of Schürer, Klausner, and others, hope for the messiah sustained the far-flung Jewish communities in the Mediterranean diaspora,[47] then we might expect some evidence to that effect in Philo's corpus of more than thirty treatises.

Is such evidence forthcoming? Well, as is often the case, it depends what one allows to count as evidence, but even on a generous understanding of evidence for messianism, the results in Philo are meager. Nowhere in his extant works does Philo use the word χριστός, "messiah" or "anointed one." He uses the cognate noun χρῖσμα twice in his *De vita Mosis* (2.146, 152) for the ointment with which Moses anointed the tabernacle furniture and Aaron and his sons (see the same term for the same episode in LXX Exod 29:7; 30:25; 40:9). He also uses the verb χρίω, "to anoint," once in this context (*Mos.* 2.150), as well as in *De fuga et inventione* 110 for the anointing of the high priest, and in *De specialibus legibus* 1.231, 233 for the anointing of the horns of the altar in the protocol for sacrifices. Philo uses the synonymous verb ἀλείφω, too, in some of the same contexts (e.g., *Mos.* 2.146), as the Greek Pentateuch itself sometimes does (e.g., LXX Exod 40:15; Num 3:3).[48]

In short, Philo's use of the lexicon of anointing agrees closely with the usage of the Greek Pentateuch and not at all with the usage of Samuel-Kings and the Psalter. This should come as no surprise. Philo knows and sometimes refers to other Jewish holy books, but he is disproportionately, nay, overwhelmingly concerned with the five books of Moses. In those books, the discourse of ritual anointing applies exclusively to priests and sacra, not to kings. This state of affairs is intuitively obvious, but it comes into sharp relief with a cursory

Politics: Roman Rule and Hellenistic Judaism," *ANRW* II.21.1:417–553; Richard D. Hecht, "Philo and Messiah," in *Judaisms and Their Messiahs*, 139–68; Peder Borgen, "'There Shall Come Forth a Man': Reflections on Messianic Ideas in Philo," in *The Messiah*, 341–61; idem, *Philo of Alexandria: An Exegete for His Time* (NovTSup 86; Leiden: Brill, 1997), 261–81; James Carleton Paget, "Egypt," in *Redemption and Resistance*, 183–97.

46. See Aryeh Kasher, *The Jews in Hellenistic and Roman Egypt* (TSAJ 7; Tübingen: Mohr Siebeck, 1985 [Hebrew original, 1978]); Barclay, *Jews in the Mediterranean Diaspora*, 19–228.

47. For example, Klausner, *Messianic Idea*, 470.

48. For these data, I am dependent on Peder Borgen, Kåre Fuglseth, and Roald Skarsten, *The Philo Index: A Complete Greek Word Index to the Writings of Philo of Alexandria* (Leiden: Brill and Grand Rapids, Mich.: Eerdmans, 2000), for which the base text is Leopold Cohn and Paul Wendland, eds., *Philonis Alexandrini opera quae supersunt* (Berlin: Reimer, 1896–1915).

look at J. W. Earp's scripture index to Philo in vol. 10 of Colson's Loeb edition.[49] In Earp's index, Philo's references to the Pentateuch fill sixty-four pages, while his references to all other Jewish scriptures together make up just shy of seven pages. Each of the five books of Moses has hundreds of references, while none of the other Jewish holy books has more than ten, except for the Psalter, with about twenty-five. This is perfectly intelligible. Philo's literary project is a grand exposition of the law of Moses.[50] Early Jewish messiah discourse, however, takes its literary cues largely (but not exclusively) from Samuel-Kings and the Psalms. If a given writer sets out to expound the Torah, we should not expect to find him waxing messianic. He could do so, of course, but if he does not, there is no reason to allege a non- or antimessianic agenda. We should not think that he has gone out of his way to avoid the topic. The situation is explicable simply in terms of literary genre.

Although, as is universally acknowledged, Philo never speaks of a messiah as such, there is one passage of his that is invoked frequently in connection with messianism—namely, *De praemiis et poenis* 79–172, an extended discussion of the Mosaic blessings and curses in Lev 26 and Deut 27.[51] Under the heading of blessings, Philo discusses Moses's assurance that the righteous will be victorious over their enemies: "Virtue is majestic and august and can unaided and silently allay the onsets of evils however great" (*Praem.* 93). Just here, Philo cites a lemma from the oracle of Balaam in Num 24:

> For *There shall come forth a person* [ἐξελεύσεται γὰρ ἄνθρωπος], says the oracle [φησὶν ὁ χρησμός], and leading his host to war *he will subdue great and populous nations* [ἔθνη μεγάλα καὶ πολυάνθρωπα χειρώσεται], because God has sent to his aid the reinforcement which benefits the godly, that is, dauntless courage of soul and all-powerful strength of body, either of which strikes fear into the enemy, and the two if united are quite irresistible. (*Praem.* 95)

The oracle (χρησμός) cited here is the LXX version of Num 24:7: ἐξελεύσεται ἄνθρωπος ἐκ τοῦ σπέρματος αὐτοῦ καὶ κυριεύσει ἐθνῶν πολλῶν, "There shall

49. J. W. Earp, "Scripture Index to Philo," in *Philo*, vol. 10 (trans. F. H. Colson; LCL; Cambridge, Mass.: Harvard University Press, 1962), 189–268.

50. See Philo, *Opif.* 1.1–2 and everything thereafter. Thus rightly Adam Kamesar, "Biblical Interpretation in Philo," in *The Cambridge Companion to Philo* (ed. Adam Kamesar; Cambridge: Cambridge University Press, 2009), 65–91 at 72: "As far as canon is concerned, Philo's Bible is essentially the Torah, or Pentateuch."

51. On which passage see Alan Mendelson, "Philo's Dialectic of Reward and Punishment," *SPhA* 9 (1997): 104–25.

come forth a person from his [Israel's] seed, and he shall be master over many nations," which differs conspicuously from the Hebrew of the MT and 4QNum^b: יזל־מים מדליו וזרעו במים רבים, "Water shall flow from his buckets, and his seed shall be in many waters."[52] These differences can be explained satisfactorily in terms of a word-for-word approach on the part of the Greek translator, without recourse to the hypothesis of an alternate Hebrew *Vorlage*.[53] Interpreters differ on the question whether the Greek translator's decisions amount to a messianization of the oracle. I think not;[54] but as it concerns Philo's use of Num 24:7 in *Praem.* 95, that debate is rather beside the point, because in any case Philo does not interpret Num 24:7 as a messianic oracle, even in the conventional sense of "messianic." To be sure, *Praem.* 79–172 does envision concrete military success and economic prosperity, but not with special reference to the people Israel, let alone an eschatological Jewish king.

In the immediate context, Philo comments on his citation of the Balaam oracle as follows:

> These are the first blessings which he tells us will fall to the lot of those who follow God and always and everywhere cleave to his commandments and so fasten them to every part of life that no part can go astray into new and unwholesome ways. (*Praem.* 98)

That is to say, "the person who will go forth to rule great and populous nations" (Num 24:7 apud *Praem.* 95) is not a future Jewish king, but the righteous person, the one who follows God.[55] Philo has taken a prophetic oracle

---

52. 4QNum^b is quite fragmentary here, but such text as is extant accords entirely with MT. See Eugene Ulrich, *The Biblical Qumran Scrolls: Transcriptions and Textual Variants* (Leiden: Brill, 2012), 154–55.

53. Thus rightly Johan Lust, "The Greek Version of Balaam's Third and Fourth Oracles: The ΑΝΘΡΩΠΟΣ in Num 24:7 and 17: Messianism and Lexicography," in idem, *Messianism and Septuagint: Collected Essays* (ed. K. Hauspie; BETL 178; Leuven: Peeters, 2004), 69–86; see also Martin Rösel, "Jakob, Bileam und der Messias," in *Septuagint and Messianism*, 151–76.

54. In agreement with Lust, "Greek Version"; *pace* John J. Collins, *Between Athens and Jerusalem: Jewish Identity in the Hellenistic Diaspora* (2d ed.; Grand Rapids, Mich.: Eerdmans, 2000), 137: "In the case of Num. 24:7, the oracle of Balaam used by Philo in *De Praemiis*, the messianic note had already been introduced by the Septuagint translators."

55. Contra Borgen, "There Shall Come Forth a Man," 342:
> [For Philo,] "eschatology" means the realization of the universal aspect of Moses' kingship and of the universal role of the Hebrew nation. This universal realization of Moses' kingship did not take place in Moses' lifetime. It would be accomplished in the future by "a man" who would be commander-in-chief of the Hebrew army and would conquer the enemies and be emperor of many nations.

and made it a gnomic one.[56] Gnomic, but not individual. For Philo, as for Plato
before him, the crown of ethics is politics, and the man who excels in virtue is
the man best suited to rule nations. Philo makes this point both at the beginning and again at the end of *De praemiis et poenis*. In his introduction, a passage reminiscent of the introduction to Aristotle's *Politics*, Philo writes, "The
lessons which he [Moses] gives on privilege, and honour, and on the other
hand on punishments fall under heads arranged in an orderly series: individual men, families, cities, countries and nations, vast regions of the earth"
(*Praem.* 7). From *Praem.* 79 onward, the subject matter is the rewards and
punishments proper to "countries and nations," hence Philo's interpretation
of Num 24:7 as a blessing upon rulers and states who conduct themselves
according to the divine laws. This connection between individual virtue and
national prosperity is also the subject of the closing words of the treatise:

> If in the soul a tiny seed be left of the qualities which promote vir-
> tue, though other things have been stripped away, still from that little
> seed spring forth the fairest and most precious things in human life,
> by which states are constituted manned with good citizens, and nations
> grow into a great population. (*Praem.* 172)

If *De praemiis et poenis* is something of a red herring in the discussion of
messianism, as I think it is, there are nevertheless a few other passages in
Philo that, despite being far less frequently cited in this connection, do shed
some light. Philo does not talk at all about messiahs; but as already hinted
earlier, he does spend considerable time and space discussing the question of
an ideal political order,[57] which is also what many (but not all) messiah texts do
when they talk about their messiahs.[58] When Philo writes political philosophy,
however, he almost always speaks in terms of a pristine past, not a utopian
future.

All-important here is the figure of Moses, who represents for Philo the
quintessence of just rule.[59] He begins his magisterial two-volume *De vita
Mosis* as follows:

---

56. On Philo's manner of interpreting biblical prophecy, see Wolfson, *Philo*, 2:3–72.

57. See Goodenough, *Politics of Philo*, especially 86–120; Wolfson, *Philo*, 2:322–426.

58. On this point, see Chapter 8 in this volume.

59. See Wayne A. Meeks, *The Prophet-King: Moses Traditions and the Johannine Christology* (Leiden: Brill, 1967), 100–131; Louis H. Feldman, *Philo's Portrayal of Moses in the Context of Ancient Judaism* (CJAS 15; South Bend, Ind.: University of Notre Dame Press, 2007), 258–89.

I purpose to write the life of Moses, whom some describe as the legisla-
tor of the Jews, others as the interpreter of the holy laws. I hope to bring
the story of this greatest and most perfect of men [ἀνδρὸς τὰ πάντα
μεγίστου καὶ τελειοτάτου] to the knowledge of such as deserve not to
remain in ignorance of it; for, while the fame of the laws which he left
behind him has travelled throughout the civilized world and reached
the ends of the earth, the man himself as he really was is known to few.
(*Mos.* 1.1–2)

For Philo, the point is not just that Moses promulgated the divine laws at
Sinai, as incomparably excellent as those laws are; it is that Moses himself is
the embodiment of virtue and, consequently, the paradigm of the ideal king.
Thus he writes:

The appointed leader of all these was Moses, invested with this rule and
kingship [τὴν ἀρχὴν καὶ βασιλείαν], not like some of those who thrust
themselves into positions of power by means of arms and engines of
war and strength of infantry, cavalry and navy, but on account of his
goodness and his nobility of conduct and the universal benevolence
[ἀρετῆς ἕνεκα καὶ καλοκἀγαθίας καὶ τῆς πρὸς ἅπαντας εὐνοίας] which he
never failed to show. Further, his office was bestowed upon him by God,
the lover of virtue and nobility, as the reward due to him. (*Mos.* 1.148)[60]

Kings, Philo observes, typically seize power for themselves by this or that
military stratagem, but Moses was granted his kingship by God as a reward
for his unparalleled virtue.

Elsewhere, rather differently and more famously, Philo describes Moses's
kingship as a feature acquired through his uniquely close contact with the
presence of the deity. He writes:

Was not the joy of his partnership with the father and maker of all
magnified also by the honor of being deemed worthy to bear the same
title? For he was named god and king of the whole nation [ὠνομάσθη
γὰρ ὅλου τοῦ ἔθνους θεὸς καὶ βασιλεύς (cf. Deut 33:5; Exod 7:1)], and
entered, we are told, into the darkness where God was [Exod 20:21],
that is into the unseen, invisible, incorporeal and archetypal essence
of existing things [τὴν ἀειδῆ καὶ ἀόρατον καὶ ἀσώματον τῶν ὄντων
παραδειγματικὴν οὐσίαν]. Thus he beheld what is hidden from the sight

---

60. Trans. mod. from Colson in the LCL.

of mortal nature, and, in himself and his life displayed for all to see, he has set before us, like some well-wrought picture, a piece of work beautiful and godlike [πάγκαλον καὶ θεοειδὲς ἔργον], a model for those who are willing to copy it. (*Mos.* 1.158)[61]

According to this passage, Moses was "named god and king" on account of his κοινωνία, "partnership with" or "participation in" God, into whose incorporeal presence no mortal but Moses alone has ever entered. In this *sui generis* encounter, Moses became in certain respects like that which he beheld; his own person was assimilated to aspects of divinity (hence ὠνομάσθη θεός and θεοειδὲς ἔργον).[62]

So it is that Philo can say that Moses fulfills in himself all the essential offices of a rightly ordered state, as at the beginning of book 2 of *De vita Mosis*, where he cites Plato's *Republic* on the ideal of the philosopher king:[63]

It has been said, not without good reason, that states can only make progress in wellbeing if either kings are philosophers or philosophers are kings [Plato, *Rep.* 5.473d]. But Moses will be found to have displayed, and more than displayed, combined in his single person, not only these two faculties—the kingly and the philosophical—but also three others, one of which is concerned with lawgiving, the second with the high priest's office, and the last with prophecy. On these three I have now elected to write, being forced to the conviction that it is fitting that they should be combined in the same person. For Moses, through God's providence, became king and lawgiver and high priest and prophet; and in each function he won the highest place [ἐγένετο γὰρ προνοίᾳ θεοῦ βασιλεύς τε καὶ νομοθέτης καὶ ἀρχιερεὺς καὶ προφήτης καὶ ἐν ἑκάστῳ τὰ πρωτεῖα ἠνέγκατο]. (*Mos.* 2.2–3)

Because he is godlike in his virtue, and because he fulfills all the offices of a rightly ordered state (philosopher, law-giver, king, priest, and prophet),

---

61. Trans. mod. from Colson in the LCL.

62. See further Wayne A. Meeks, "Moses as God and King," in *Religions in Antiquity: Essays in Memory of Erwin Ramsdell Goodenough* (ed. Jacob Neusner; Leiden: Brill, 1968), 354–71; David T. Runia, "God and Man in Philo of Alexandria," *JTS* n.s. 39 (1988): 48–75; Ian W. Scott, "Is Philo's Moses a Divine Man?" *SPhA* 14 (2002): 87–111.

63. On which see Hywel Clifford, "Moses as Philosopher-Sage in Philo," in *Moses in Biblical and Extra-Biblical Traditions* (ed. Axel Graupner and Michael Wolter; Berlin: De Gruyter, 2007), 151–68. On the larger issue of Philo's debt to Plato, see David T. Runia, *Philo of Alexandria and the Timaeus of Plato* (Leiden: Brill, 1986).

Moses is, for Philo, the greatest ruler who has ever lived or will ever live. For just that reason, he is also a paradigm for moral formation and for statecraft, "a piece of work beautiful and godlike, a model for those who are willing to copy it" (*Mos.* 1.158).

This, then, helps makes sense of another curious political passage in Philo. Remarkably similar to his account of ideal kingship in *De vita Mosis* is the passage in the *Legatio ad Gaium* in which he contrasts the gross hubris and impiety of the emperor Gaius (Caligula) with the model virtue and governance of Gaius's dynastic forebear Augustus.[64] In the *Legatio* Philo writes:

> Consider him who in all the virtues transcended human nature [ὁ τὴν ἀνθρωπίνην φύσιν ὑπερβαλὼν ἐν ἀπάσαις ταῖς ἀρεταῖς], who on account of the vastness of his imperial sovereignty as well as nobility of character was the first to bear the name August [ὁ διὰ μέγεθος ἡγεμονίας αὐτοκρατοῦς ὁμοῦ καὶ καλοκαγαθίας πρῶτος ὀνομασθεὶς Σεβαστός], a title received not through lineal succession as a portion of its heritage but because he himself became the source of the veneration which was received also by those who followed him, who from the moment that he had charge of the common weal took in hand the troubled and chaotic condition of affairs. . . . He was also the first and the greatest and the common benefactor in that he displaced the rule of many and committed the ship of the commonwealth to be steered by a single pilot, that is himself, a marvelous master of the science of government [θαυμασίῳ τὴν ἡγεμονικὴν ἐπιστήμην]. For there is justice in the saying, *It is not well that many lords should rule* [*Iliad* 2.204], since multiplicity of suffrages produces multiform evils. (*Leg.* 143, 149)

It is noteworthy that, despite his contempt for Gaius's tenure as emperor, Philo does not despise the imperial office. On the contrary, he cites Homer here in favor of the principle of monarchy,[65] and he holds up Augustus as a model of the institution—a latter-day counterpart to Moses. Augustus is not a Jew, of course, but for Philo the Torah of Moses is the codification of natural law, the ethical standard toward which all humanity should aspire,[66] and Augustus wins praise for achieving it. Not, to be sure, to the unsurpassable

---

64. On this passage, see Gerhard Delling, "Philons Enkomion auf Augustus," *Klio* 54 (1972): 171–92; Maren Niehoff, *Philo on Jewish Identity and Culture* (TSAJ 86; Tübingen: Mohr Siebeck, 2001), 111–36.

65. See Goodenough, *Politics of Philo*, 86–120.

66. See in particular Hindy Najman, "The Law of Nature and the Authority of the Mosaic Law," *SPhA* 11 (1999): 55–73; eadem, "A Written Copy of the Law of Nature: An Unthinkable Paradox," *SPhA* 15 (2003): 54–63.

degree that Moses achieved it, but really and truly, nonetheless.[67] It is instructive that with Augustus, as with Moses, the political ideal belongs to a past
golden age. Moses is a supremely excellent figure from the distant past,
Augustus a relatively excellent figure from the recent past, but both provide
Philo opportunity for saying how he thinks the state ought to be. Messiah discourse is another ancient Jewish way of saying how one thinks the state ought
to be, but it is not Philo's way.[68]

This account of things allows us to cut through the confusing (not to say
confused) secondary literature on messianism in Philo. According to one
influential strand of scholarship, Philo's religious thought was bound to be
non- or even antimessianic. Such an outlook, it is claimed, follows necessarily from Philo's first principles. This view finds classic expression, for
example, in Gressmann's third edition of Bousset's handbook *Die Religion
des Judentums*:

> Die Geschichte des Volkes Israels löst sich ihm auf in eine Psychologie
> des stetig sich gleich bleibenden religiösen Lebens, die Erzväter
> sind die vorbildlichen Gestalten für die einzelnen Lehren dieser
> Psychologie. Alles ist auf einer Fläche aufgetragen, das Nacheinander
> wird ein Nebeneinander. Es geschieht nichts in der Welt als das stän-
> dige Sich-Erheben und Aufsteigen der einzelnen frommen Seelen zu
> dem ewigen Gott.[69]

For Bousset-Gressmann, when Philo interprets the history of Israel as a
symbol of the ascent of the soul to the divine, he cuts the nerve of hope for a
change in the actual political fortunes of the Jews.

---

67. Compare David Dawson, *Allegorical Readers and Cultural Revision in Ancient Alexandria*
(Berkeley, Calif.: University of California Press, 1992), 125:

> Philo's rhetorical encomium of Augustus (and of Tiberius) is thus simply the
> counterpart of his invective of Gaius—neither is ultimately concerned with the
> emperors themselves, for whom Philo had no high regard, but with the presenta-
> tion of an ideal of kingship that might result in a favorable policy toward the Jews.

This lattermost claim is just right; Augustus wins Philo's praise because, in Philo's assessment, he attained to the ideal of kingship. But *pace* Dawson, Philo does hold Augustus in
genuinely high regard, and this because his concern is not to propagandize for the Julio-
Claudians but to articulate a political philosophy.

68. Hence the note of confusion registered, for example, by A. W. van den Hoek, *Clement of
Alexandria and His Use of Philo in the Stromateis* (VCSup 3; Leiden: Brill, 1988), 65: "It is hard
to say ... to what degree messianic elements are present in Philo's description of Moses
since the theme is not developed explicitly."

69. Bousset-Gressmann, *Religion des Judentums*, 443.

Ray Barraclough, in his *ANRW* article on the subject, takes a similar position, arguing that Philo's philosophy entails a profoundly conservative politics. About *Praem.* 169–71, Barraclough writes:

> This seemingly distinct national hope is largely removed to another plane by Philo, because the treatise ends by applying this promise to the budding of the soul to its full virtue. . . . . In the wider compass of his writings the historical denouement is more on the fringe than at the centre of his interest. Messianic expectation features but little in Philo's thought.[70]

And again, "[Philo's] view of the political world around him is plainly one that supports the status quo, based on acceptance of the benefits of Roman rule. His zeal, inspired by philosophy, is not directed toward nationalist aims but the fruits of contemplative world-citizenship."[71]

Other interpreters, however, have argued that Philo's nonmessianism is only apparent, not real. One memorable statement of this position is that of the great American scholar of Hellenistic Judaism, Erwin Ramsdell Goodenough, who writes:

> Philo is usually represented as the complete antitype of the Apocalyptic writers, a man who found his life in metaphysics and mysticism, and who was a total stranger to the hysterical hatred of Rome that looked for a militant Messiah. . . . . He would seem to have had too much political sagacity to sign his name to books in which the Romans were specifically denounced. He was too large minded not to see the value of much in Greek and Roman thought. He was no fanatic, and knew that so long as the Messiah had not yet come, one must get on with the Romans in the most conciliating spirit possible. So Philo kept his Messianism to himself. But one could secretly think, hope and hate. And Philo seems to me to be assuring his Jewish friends that he was passionately doing all three.[72]

Goodenough concurs with the prevailing opinion that one cannot read messianism off the surface of Philo's works, but he suggests that this surface

---

70. Barraclough, "Philo's Politics," 480.

71. Barraclough, "Philo's Politics," 486.

72. Goodenough, *Politics of Philo*, 25.

impression is deceptive, that Philo's messianism is real (and indeed angry) but sublimated, secret, kept to himself. Goodenough's interpretation anticipates the twenty-first-century vogue for discerning hidden transcripts in Jewish texts written under Roman rule.[73] Goodenough's Philo hates the Romans, and assures his countrymen that he does so, but never expresses this sentiment in writing.[74]

Similar but less politically charged is the interpretation of the Belgian scholar J. de Savignac, writing in the mid twentieth century. He comments:

> L'histoire n'est guère pour lui une marche vers quelque grand événement, mais cyclique, et son sens de la vie se réduit trop, comme chez beaucoup de philosophes, à être une attente de la mort. Et pourtant, tenace en espérance comme tout Israélite, il n'a tout de même pas rejeté les attentes de son peuple. Qui pourra dire si Philon, qui n'a jamais renié la religion d'Israël, n'a tout de même pas, tout au fond de lui-même, attendu, dans l'histoire, quelque théophanie merveilleuse, à la fois humaine et divine, qui satisfît non seulement les aspirations de son intelligence à l'Être mais aussi ses aspirations nationales et terrestres consacrées par sa foi?[75]

Savignac's tone is rather more conjectural than Goodenough's (*Qui pourra dire*), but like Goodenough, he acknowledges the prevailing nonmessianism of Philo's outlook and further speculates about what beliefs Philo may have harbored secretly, to himself (*tout au fond de lui-même*). Savignac thinks not that Philo nursed a secret hatred of the Romans, but rather that, despite his cosmopolitan philosophy, Philo's native Jewish piety might have ensured the preservation within him of a spark of nationalist sentiment.

---

73. For which the theoretical model is James C. Scott, *Domination and the Arts of Resistance: Hidden Transcripts* (New Haven, Conn.: Yale University Press, 1992).

74. For an apt criticism of Goodenough's view, see Hecht, "Philo and Messiah," 162–63:

> Philo's neutralization of popular messianism [per Gershom Scholem] means that he was much more conservative than Goodenough understood him to be. . . . Philo does not appear to hide his true feelings while gritting his teeth in hatred of the cursed Romans. This may well be the most distinctive element of Philo's messianism. While other forms of Jewish messianism might have been rejected because of their disastrous results, Philo attempted to accommodate it by transforming its historical and particularistic elements.

Although Hecht's criticism of Goodenough is on target, his appeal to Scholem's rubric of neutralization is not, in my view, adequate for an interpretation of Philo.

75. Savignac, "Messianisme de Philon," 324.

Savignac's account is commendable for its subtlety, but it, too, proceeds by assuming a notion of messianism and pressing Philo to take a position on it. Better in this respect is the comment of Harry Wolfson, who candidly grants a difference between Philo's idiom and that of (what we think of as) mainstream Jewish tradition. Wolfson writes:

> The solution found by Philo for the Jewish problem of his time was the revival of the old prophetic promises of the ultimate disappearance of the diaspora. Without mentioning the term Messiah, he deals in great detail with what is known in Jewish tradition as the Messiah and the Messianic Age.[76]

Wolfson may be mistaken about Philo's view of the diaspora,[77] but his rubric of problem and solution is just right. Philo perceives certain social problems and uses the resources of scripture and philosophy to articulate his own solutions. In this Wolfsonian vein, perhaps the most penetrating comment in the literature on messianism in Philo is one from Yehoshua Amir: "One should not be hard on Philo, therefore, if he expresses opinions here which are in conflict with those we are familiar with elsewhere."[78] Just so. If we come to Philo in search of messianism and find ourselves disappointed, the fault is ours, not his.

Flavius Josephus

Like Philo of Alexandria, the expatriate Judean historian Flavius Josephus managed to leave behind an *oeuvre* of some considerable size with virtually no mention of a messiah. In the case of Josephus, there are actually two puzzles: one to do with the couple of times the word χριστός does appear in his works and another to do with his total nonuse of that word in his account of the Jewish–Roman War. First, as is well known, according to the standard critical Greek text, Josephus uses the word χριστός precisely twice, both times, ironically, with reference to Jesus of Nazareth. One of these is a passing reference

---

76. Wolfson, *Philo*, 2:407.

77. See Erich S. Gruen, *Diaspora: Jews amidst Greeks and Romans* (Cambridge, Mass.: Harvard University Press, 2002), 343–44n51.

78. Yehoshua Amir, "The Messianic Idea in Hellenistic Judaism" (trans. Chanah Arnon), *Immanuel* 2 (1973): 58–60 at 58; Hebrew original "The Messianic Idea in Hellenistic Judaism," *Machanayim* 124 (1970): 54–67; German trans. and abbrev. "Die messianische Idee im hellenistischen Judentum," *Freiburger Rundbrief* 25 (1973): 195–203.

in his brief account of the execution of James the Just under the high priest Ananus:[79]

> He [Ananus] convened the judges of the Sanhedrin and brought before them a man named James, the brother of Jesus who was called messiah [Ἰησοῦ τοῦ λεγομένου χριστοῦ], and certain others. He accused them of having transgressed the law and delivered them up to be stoned. (Josephus, *Ant.* 20.200)[80]

Here χριστός is used as a byname, a means of specifying which Jesus is meant: "Jesus, the one called messiah."[81] This phrase, Ἰησοῦς ὁ λεγόμενος χριστός, is attested roughly contemporaneously in the Gospel of Matthew, both in the narrator's voice (Matt 1:16) and on the lips of Pontius Pilate (Matt 27:17, 22). Like Matthew, Josephus knows that Jesus of Nazareth had come to be known as "messiah"; he was λεγόμενος χριστός.[82]

More problematic is the one other instance of χριστός in Josephus—the famous and endlessly contested *Testimonium Flavianum* at *Ant.* 18.63:[83]

> About this time there lived Jesus, a wise man, if indeed one ought to call him a man. For he was one who wrought surprising feats and was a teacher of such people as accept the truth gladly. He won over many Jews and many of the Greeks. He was the messiah [ὁ χριστὸς οὗτος ἦν]. When Pilate, upon hearing him accused by men of the highest standing amongst us, had condemned him to be crucified, those who had in the first place come to love him did not give up their affection for him. On the third day he appeared to them restored to life, for the prophets of God had prophesied these and countless other marvelous things about him. And the tribe of the Christians [τῶν Χριστιανῶν τὸ φῦλον],

---

79. Compare the parallel account of Hegesippus apud Eusebius, *Hist. eccl.* 2.23.4–18.

80. Greek text ed. Louis Feldman in the LCL; trans. mod.

81. On this conventional use of λεγόμενος, see Elaine Matthews, "Names, personal, Greek," *OCD*³, 1022–24.

82. See the discussions by Paul Winter, "Appendix: Josephus on Jesus and James," in Schürer-Vermes, *History*, 1:428–41, especially 430–32; and Zvi Baras, "The *Testimonium Flavianum* and the Martyrdom of James," in *Josephus, Judaism, and Christianity* (ed. Louis H. Feldman and Gohei Hata; Detroit, Mich.: Wayne State University Press, 1987), 338–48.

83. On the endless contest, see Alice Whealey, *Josephus on Jesus: The Testimonium Flavianum Controversy from Late Antiquity to Modern Times* (Studies in Biblical Literature 36; New York, N.Y.: Peter Lang, 2003).

so called after him, has still to this day not disappeared. (Josephus, *Ant.* 18.63)[84]

Here, conspicuously, Jesus is not "the one called messiah," as in *Ant.* 20.200, but "messiah," full stop, in what looks very much like a confessional formula: ὁ χριστὸς οὗτος ἦν. This, together with several other equally Christian-sounding lines ("if indeed one ought to call him a man," "the prophets of God had prophesied about him"), has raised obvious questions about the authenticity of the passage. To be sure, it is attested unanimously in the Greek manuscript tradition, but that tradition is comprised entirely of Christian manuscripts,[85] so the possibility of interpolation is very real, indeed.[86]

The authenticity of the passage as it stands has been defended by a minority including such lights as F. C. Burkitt and Adolf von Harnack.[87] Most modern critics, however, have seen in the *Testimonium Flavianum* evidence of the hand of a Christian forger, either in whole (thus, for instance, Benedikt Niese, Emil Schürer, and Eduard Norden)[88] or in part (thus, for instance, Paul Winter, David Flusser, and James Carleton Paget).[89] If some or all of the passage was interpolated, this must have happened no later than the fourth century, because the full form of the text is thrice cited by Eusebius of Caesarea (*Dem. ev.* 3.5.125; *Hist. eccl.* 1.11.7–8; *Theoph.* 5.44). In view of these citations, Solomon Zeitlin, writing in the 1920s, suggested that Eusebius was himself

---

84. Greek text ed. Louis Feldman in the LCL; trans. mod.

85. Compare, however, the tenth-century Arabic recension in a manuscript of Agapius's *Kitab al-ʿUnwan*, which lacks the conspicuously Christian clauses (Shlomo Pines, *An Arabic Version of the Testimonium Flavianum and Its Implications* [Jerusalem: Israel Academy of Sciences and Humanities, 1971]).

86. See James R. Davila, *The Provenance of the Pseudepigrapha: Jewish, Christian, or Other?* (JSJSup 105; Leiden: Brill, 2005), 166: "The *Testimonium Flavianum* . . . seems to indicate that Christians were not above tampering with Josephus' text, although, to be fair, the temptation to do so with this passage must have been unbearable."

87. F. C. Burkitt, "Josephus and Christ," *ThT* 47 (1913): 135–44; Adolf von Harnack, "Der jüdische Geschichtsschreiber Josephus und Jesus Christus," *Internationale Monatsschrift für Wissenschaft, Kunst und Technik* 7 (1913), cols. 1037–68.

88. Benedikt Niese, *De Testimonio Christiano quod est apud Iosephum ant. Iud. XVIII, 63 sq. disputatio* (Marburg: Friedrich, 1894); Emil Schürer, "Josephus," *Realenzyklopädie für die protestantische Theologie und Kirche* 9 (1901): 377–86; Eduard Norden, "Josephus und Tacitus über Jesus Christus und eine messianische Prophetie," *NJahrb* 16 (1913): 637–66.

89. Winter, "Josephus on Jesus and James"; David Flusser, "Bericht des Josephus über Jesus," in idem, *Entdeckungen im Neuen Testament*, vol. 1 (Neukirchen-Vluyn: Neukirchener, 1987), 216–25; James Carleton Paget, "Some Observations on Josephus and Christianity," *JTS* n.s. 52 (2001): 539–624, which also includes a very thorough bibliography on the question.

the Christian forger of the *Testimonium Flavianum*.[90] Ken Olson has revived and contended for this view,[91] and it has recently received support from Louis Feldman, as well.[92]

That Eusebius himself was the forger is an intriguing possibility, but against it stands the mid-third-century evidence of Origen, who possibly—but by no means certainly—betrays awareness of an uninterpolated form of the *Testimonium Flavianum* or something like it. Origen erroneously attributes to Josephus the view that the destruction of Jerusalem was a divine punishment upon the Jews for the execution of James the Just,[93] but in making this point, Origen twice says that Josephus "did not accept Jesus as messiah." In his fragmentary *Commentary on Matthew*, Origen writes:

> Flavius Josephus, who wrote the Antiquities of the Jews in twenty books, when wishing to exhibit the cause why the people suffered so great misfortunes that even the temple was razed to the ground, said, that these things happened to them in accordance with the wrath of God in consequence of the things which they had dared to do against James the brother of Jesus who is called messiah. And the wonderful thing is, that, though he did not accept our Jesus as messiah [τὸν Ἰησοῦν ἡμῶν οὐ καταδεξάμενος εἶναι Χριστόν], he yet gave testimony that the righteousness of James was so great. (Origen, *Comm. Matt.* 10.17)[94]

Similarly, in the *Contra Celsum* Origen writes:

> Now this writer [Josephus], although not believing in Jesus as the messiah [καίτοι γε ἀπιστῶν τῷ Ἰησοῦ ὡς Χριστῷ], in seeking after the cause

---

90. Solomon Zeitlin, "The Christ Passage in Josephus," *JQR* 18 (1927–1928): 231–55; also idem, "Josephus on Jesus," *JQR* 21 (1930–1931): 377–417.

91. Ken Olson, "Eusebius and the *Testimonium Flavianum*," *CBQ* 61 (1999): 305–22; idem, "A Eusebian Reading of the *Testimonium Flavianum*," in *Eusebius of Caesarea: Tradition and Innovations* (ed. Aaron Johnson and Jeremy Schott; Hellenic Studies Series 60; Cambridge, Mass.: Harvard University Press, 2013), 97–114.

92. Louis H. Feldman, "On the Authenticity of the *Testimonium Flavianum* Attributed to Josephus," in *New Perspectives on Jewish–Christian Relations* (ed. Elisheva Carlebach and Jacob J. Schechter; BRLJ 33; Leiden: Brill, 2012), 14–30.

93. Perhaps Origen actually had a corrupt text of Josephus that included such a claim or, more economically, perhaps Origen simply attributed this view, which he knew from Hegesippus, to Josephus by accident.

94. Trans. mod. from John Patrick in *ANF*.

of the fall of Jerusalem and the destruction of the temple, . . . says that these disasters happened to the Jews as a punishment for the death of James the Just, who was a brother of Jesus called messiah. (Origen, *Cels.* 1.47)[95]

The question is on what grounds Origen comes to the judgment that Josephus does not accept Jesus as the messiah: whether he simply assumes it, or he infers it from the phrase λεγόμενος χριστός in *Ant.* 20.200, or he infers it from some form of the *Testimonium Flavianum*. The first option is possible but raises the additional question why Origen should assume such a thing; the second is unlikely in view of the commonplace use of λεγόμενος in Greek naming; the third is also possible but necessarily speculative. If the third, then it could not be the extant form of that passage that Origen knows, because there the writer expressly does confess Jesus to be the messiah; it would have to be a more original form *sans* Christian glosses. It is of course possible that neither of the two χριστός texts in Josephus is authentic.[96] On balance, however, I consider it plausible but unverifiable that Origen knew an uninterpolated version of the *Testimonium Flavianum*, one that reported Jesus's famous deeds and messianic reputation and perhaps voiced Josephus's disapproval (thus ἀπιστῶν τῷ Ἰησοῦ ὡς Χριστῷ, per Origen).[97] If so, then it would add a little to what is, in any case, a very small body of messiah discourse in Josephus.

The second puzzle pertaining to messianism in Josephus has to do not with what he says, but with what he does not say—in particular, his total non-use of messiah language in his fulsome accounts of the Jewish insurgents against Roman rule in Palestine. Modern interpreters have not hesitated to identify many of those about whom Josephus writes as messiahs. Thus, to cite one distinguished example, Sigmund Mowinckel: "We may also recall the series of 'false Messiahs' whom Josephus and the Roman authorities characterized as brigands, rioters, and saboteurs."[98] This, however, is to apply an

---

95. Trans. mod. from Frederick Crombie in *ANF*.

96. Thus Tessa Rajak, *Josephus: The Historian and His Society* (London: Duckworth, 1983), 131n73, who suggests that the widespread skepticism about the *Testimonium Flavianum*, which she shares, should have made scholars similarly skeptical about the authenticity of the martyrdom of James passage at *Ant.* 20.200. In this connection, see now Richard Carrier, "Origen, Eusebius, and the Accidental Interpolation in Josephus, *Jewish Antiquities* 20.200," *JECS* 20 (2012): 489–514.

97. With Carleton Paget, "Josephus and Christianity."

98. Mowinckel, *He That Cometh*, 284.

ancient, emic label[99] that Josephus himself could have used but does not,[100] as Marinus de Jonge rightly notes:

> The many insurgents against Herodian and Roman rule mentioned by Josephus are often called "pseudo-Messiahs" by modern scholars. Josephus himself never uses that expression; this may be due to a definite bias on his part, because he had acknowledged Vespasian as the expected ruler and, in consequence, wanted to minimize the connection between some Jewish expectations and the rebellions against Rome, but the fact remains that we do not find a single instance of the use of the word "anointed" in connection with these people.[101]

There are, first of all, several figures mentioned by Josephus who are often invoked in the discussion of messianism but who are not strictly pertinent. These include the Samaritan who led a pilgrimage to Mount Gerizim during the administration of Pontius Pilate (*Ant.* 18.85–87); the self-styled προφήτης ("prophet") Theudas, whom Josephus calls a γόης ("sorcerer"), who in the mid 40s CE led a crowd to the Jordan River promising to part the waters (*Ant.* 20.97–98; cf. Acts 5:36); and the Egyptian ψευδοπροφήτης ("false prophet") who in the 50s CE summoned a crowd on the Mount of Olives promising to make the walls of Jerusalem fall at his command (*War* 2.261–63; *Ant.* 20.169–70; cf. Acts 21:38). These figures are often discussed, especially in connection with the career of Jesus of Nazareth (who is called both προφήτης and χριστός in the sources), under the rubric of "messianic prophets" or "prophet messiahs."[102] Josephus, however, calls some but not all of them prophets, and he calls none of them messiahs. More important still, Josephus maintains a

---

99. I mean χριστός, "messiah," but even ψευδόχριστος, "false messiah" is attested already ca. 70 CE (Mark 13:22; Matt 24:24). On the latter term, see Bousset-Gressmann, *Religion des Judentums*, 223–24.

100. Elsewhere, Josephus makes regular use of the root χρίω, "to anoint": in the nominal sense of "ointment" or "plaster" (*Ant.* 2.221, 300; 4.200; 8.137; 19.239; *Life* 74), with reference to ancient Israelite priestly anointing (*Ant.* 3.197, 198), and with reference to ancient Israelite royal anointing (*Ant.* 6.83, 157, 159; 7.357, 382; 9.106, 149). But he never uses any form of χρίω in connection with the Jewish revolutionaries.

101. De Jonge, "Use of the Word 'Anointed,'" 145.

102. For example, Rudolf Meyer, *Der Prophet aus Galiläa: Studie zum Jesusbild der drei ersten Evangelien* (Darmstadt: Wissenschaftliche Buchgesellschaft, 1970), 82–88; David Hill, "Jesus and Josephus' 'Messianic Prophets,'" in *Text and Interpretation: Studies in the New Testament Presented to Matthew Black* (ed. Ernest Best and R. McL. Wilson; Cambridge: Cambridge University Press, 1979), 143–54; Reinhard Pummer, *The Samaritans in Flavius Josephus* (TSAJ 129; Tübingen: Mohr Siebeck, 2009), 230–43; among many others.

rough but consistent distinction between "prophets" (whom he cynically calls γόητες, "sorcerers") on the one hand and would-be "kings" (whom he cynically calls λῃσταί, "bandits") on the other. In a very few instances—in particular, the case of the Olivet Egyptian—this distinction is blurred, but such instances are exceptions to a clear rule.[103]

Josephus's latter category, the bandit-king, is arguably more relevant to the discussion of messianism. Josephus calls such persons not "messiahs," but rather "graspers of the kingship" and "wearers of the diadem" on the one hand, as well as "bandits" and "tyrants" on the other.[104] Thus, when Herod the Great died in 4 BCE, Josephus says, συχνοὺς βασιλειᾶν ὁ καιρὸς ἀνέπειθεν, "the occasion persuaded many toward the kingship" (*War* 2.55; cf. *Ant.* 2.285). These aspirants to the kingship included one Judah ben Hezekiah, who ζηλώσει βασιλείου τιμῆς, "was zealous for kingly honor" (*Ant.* 17.272). Likewise Simon of Perea, who had been a slave in the household of Herod, διάδημά τε ἐτόλμησε περιθέσθαι, "presumed to put on the diadem," so that αὐτὸς βασιλεὺς ἀναγγελθείς, "he was declared king" by his followers (*Ant.* 17.273–74).[105] Around the same time, a shepherd named Athronges ἐτόλμησεν ἐπὶ βασιλείᾳ, "presumed upon the kingship" (*Ant.* 17.278). Athronges's four brothers served as generals with him, but only he διάδημα περιθέμενος, "put on the diadem," and βασιλεῖ κεκλημένῳ, "was called king" (*Ant.* 17.280–81).

In the course of the Great War with Rome, Josephus reports, another generation of bandits presumed to wear the diadem.[106] He tells how Menahem, son

103. Thus rightly Rebecca Gray, *Prophetic Figures in Late Second Temple Jewish Palestine: The Evidence from Josephus* (New York, N.Y.: Oxford University Press, 1993), 136:

> Movements led by prophetic figures of this sort should be distinguished from other types of popular movements known to us from this period, particularly from those led by figures who claimed to be kings. The distinction between these two quite different types of movements is blurred when the sign prophets are described as "messianic prophets," as they often are.

On Josephus's sorcerer-prophets, see Joseph Blenkinsopp, "Prophecy and Priesthood in Josephus," *JJS* 25 (1974): 239–62; Louis H. Feldman, "Prophets and Prophecy in Josephus," *JTS* n.s. 41 (1990): 386–422; Horsley and Hanson, *Bandits, Prophets, and Messiahs*, 135–89.

104. It is worth noting that, although Josephus does not call these would-be "kings" "anointed ones," in his biblical paraphrases he does speak in terms of the "anointing" of Israelite "kings" Saul, David, Solomon, Jehu, and Jehoash (*Ant.* 6.83, 157, 159; 7.355, 357, 382; 9.106, 149).

105. Compare the report of Tacitus, *Hist.* 5.9: *Post mortem Herodis, nihil expectato Caesare, Simo quidam regium nomen invaserat*, "After the death of Herod, without waiting for Caesar, a certain Simon seized the title of king" (Latin text ed. Moore and Jackson in the LCL; trans. mine).

106. It is striking that John of Gischala, whom Josephus himself had fought in the Galilee (*Life*, passim), is never called a king or a diadem-wearer, although it is said that he μοναρχίας

of Judah the Galilean, after taking Masada for his own armory, οἷα δὴ βασιλεὺς
ἐπάνεισιν εἰς Ἱεροσόλυμα καὶ γενόμενος ἡγεμὼν τῆς στάσεως, "returned to
Jerusalem in the manner of a king and became leader of the revolt" (*War*
2.434). In Josephus's judgment, however, Menahem is a λῃστής, "bandit"
(*War* 2.441), and a τύραννος, "tyrant" (*War* 2.442). Simon bar Giora, one of
the λῃσταί holed up at Masada (*War* 4.504), who is likewise said to τυραννεύω,
"act the tyrant" (*War* 4.508), attains such stature that δημοτικῶν οὐκ ὀλίγων
ὡς πρὸς βασιλέα πειθαρχεῖν, "not a few of the populace obeyed him as a king"
(*War* 4.510). Indeed, Simon's political position was such that, when Jerusalem
finally fell, it was he who was ceremonially executed in the triumph of Titus at
the Capitoline Hill as the leader of the defeated nation (*War* 7.154–55).[107]

In short, it is clear that "grasping for the kingship" and "putting on the
diadem" are Josephan idioms for claims to royal authority.[108] That Josephus
calls those who make such claims "tyrants" and "bandits" is a conspicuous
value judgment on his part.[109] The Jewish freedom fighters will no doubt have
thought of themselves, and been thought of by their followers, in rather more
favorable terms.[110] Josephus's censure of these figures has to do, of course,
with his explanation for the national catastrophe. As he writes in the preface
to the *War*:

That it owed its ruin to civil strife, and that it was the Jewish tyrants [οἱ
Ἰουδαίων τύραννοι] who drew down upon the holy temple the unwilling

---

ἀντιποιούμενος, "set up a monarchy" (*War* 4.390), and τυραννιῶντι, "acted the tyrant"
(*War* 4.389). See Uriel Rappaport, "John of Gischala: From Galilee to Jerusalem," *JJS* 33
(1982): 479–93.

107. On this episode, see Otto Michel, "Studien zu Josephus: Simon bar Giora," *NTS* 14
(1967–1968): 402–8. As in the case of Bar Kokhba, there is at least some numismatic evidence for a messianic movement surrounding Simon bar Giora (see William L. Lane, "Times
of Refreshment: A Study of Eschatological Periodization in Judaism and Christianity"
[Th.D. diss., Harvard Divinity School, 1962]).

108. Elsewhere in Josephus, those who "wear the diadem" include the Pharaohs of Egypt
(*Ant.* 2.233, 235; *Ag. Ap.* 1.98, 100), Darius the Persian (*Ant.* 11.54), Esther (*Ant.* 11.203), the
Seleucid dynasts (*Ant.* 12.360, 389; 13.144, 367, 369), the Ptolemaic dynasts (*Ant.* 13.113), the
Hasmonean dynasts (*War* 1.70; *Ant.* 13.301; 20.241), Herod the Great (*War* 1.387, 390, 393,
451, 483; *Ant.* 15.187, 195; 17.197); Archelaus (*War* 1.671; 2.3, 27; *Ant.* 17.202); Agrippa (*Ant.*
18.237), Monobazus of Adiabene (*Ant.* 20.32), and Artabanus of Parthia (*Ant.* 20.65).

109. Thus rightly Rajak, *Josephus*, 141: "We have certainly seen that when it comes to his
[Josephus's] enemies, his presentation must be deemed somewhat deficient."

110. See Smith, "Robbers, Jurists, Prophets," 46: "[They] took advantage of existent messianic expectations, some of them, no doubt, with complete cynicism, others, probably, with
complete sincerity, finding in these fantastic prophecies and symbolic figures the terms they
needed to explain themselves to themselves."

hands of the Romans and the conflagration, is attested by Titus Caesar himself, who sacked the city. . ... Should, however, any critic censure me for my strictures upon the tyrants or their bands of marauders [τοὺς τυράννους ἢ τὸ λῃστρικὸν αὐτῶν] or for my lamentations over my country's misfortunes, I ask his indulgence for a compassion which falls outside an historian's province. (*War* 1.10–11)[111]

Casting his eye back over the course of the war, Josephus lays the blame for the shoah of 70 CE at the feet of the Jewish leaders of the insurgency.

And yet, although he regards them as tyrants and marauders, Josephus concedes that, by their own lights, these nationalists claimed an indigenous monarchy on the grounds of their interpretation of the Jewish holy books. Thus he writes in a famous passage in book 6 of the *War*:

Reflecting on these things one will find that God has a care for men, and by all kinds of premonitory signs shows his people the way of salvation, while they owe their destruction to folly and calamities of their own choosing. Thus the Jews, after the demolition of Antonia, reduced the temple to a square, although they had it recorded in their oracles [ἀναγεγραμμένον ἐν τοῖς λογίοις] that the city and the sanctuary would be taken when the temple should become foursquare. But what more than all else incited them to the war was an ambiguous oracle, likewise found in their sacred scriptures [χρησμὸς ἀμφίβολος ὁμοίως ἐν τοῖς ἱεροῖς εὑρημένος γράμμασιν], to the effect that at that time one from their country would become ruler of the world [ἀπο τῆς χώρας αυτῶν τις ἄρξει τῆς οἰκουμένης]. This they understood to mean someone of their own race, and many of their wise men went astray in their interpretation of it. The oracle, however, in reality signified the sovereignty [ἡγεμονίαν] of Vespasian, who was proclaimed emperor while in Judaea. (*War* 6.310–13)[112]

The Jewish bandit-kings, Josephus says, justified their royal presumptions on the grounds of a scriptural prophecy about the rise of a Jewish empire. They were pious marauders, religiously motivated bandits.[113] Josephus faults them for interpreting the oracle wrongly; it prophesies, he says, not a Judean

---

111. Greek text ed. H. St. J. Thackeray in the LCL; trans. mod.

112. Greek text ed. H. St. J. Thackeray in the LCL; trans. mod.

113. Rajak, especially, rightly emphasizes the practical, political goals of the insurgents, but she mistakenly and unnecessarily takes this to exclude a religious rationale. See Rajak, *Josephus*, 139:

emperor but an emperor arising from Judea, which, in the event, was how Vespasian came to power at Rome (see Suetonius, *Vesp.* 5.6–8.1). This is—it must be said—an ingenious bit of exegesis, but in any case, Josephus grants that the rebels, too, had an exegesis by which they justified their undertaking.

There is reason to conclude, therefore, that in their native Galilean and Judean contexts, at least some of Josephus's bandit-kings will have been hailed as messiahs, as the Judean bandit-king Shimon bar Kosiba was during the reign of Hadrian.[114] Why, then, does Josephus not say so? Here there is no little disagreement in the secondary literature. It is possible, but I think very unlikely, that Josephus was altogether blind to the world of apocalyptic Judaism in which messianic movements arose, as Arnaldo Momigliano famously suggested.[115] Against this possibility, Tessa Rajak has argued cogently that it is literary style, not ignorance, than constrains Josephus to write the way he does.[116]

Theologically-minded commentators on Josephus (and they are the majority) have read this eschatologically, as referring to the conditions which will arise at the End of Days. Yet even in such circles, more balanced opinion, by taking the actions of the rebels into proper consideration, has allowed that the kind of freedom of which they dreamt—whenever they meant it fully to materialise—must have had as a prominent component the practical liberation of the oppressed. . . . The zealots (in the wide sense) paralleled Josephus in being, for all their piety, political animals.

Here, Rajak is right in what she affirms, but wrong in what she denies.

114. There is at least one case for which we can compare Josephus's Roman-facing account with an inner-Jewish report preserved in the rabbinic midrashim. Eleazar ben Dinai, a mid-first-century CE Judean rebel who was eventually apprehended and extradited to Rome by Antonius Felix, Josephus calls τόν τε ἀρχιληστὴν Ἐλεάζαρον ἔτεσιν εἴκοσι τὴν χώραν λῃσάμενον, "Eleazar the bandit-chief who ravaged the country for twenty years" (*War* 2.253; cf. *War* 2.235–36; *Ant.* 20.121, 161). The late antique *Song of Songs Rabbah*, on the other hand, remembers this same Eleazar—alongside Amram, Shimon bar Kosiba, and Shuthelach ben Ephraim—among "the four generations who tried to hasten the end and came to grief" (*Song Rab.* 2.7.1) (trans. Maurice Simon, *Midrash Rabbah*, vol. 9 [London: Soncino, 1983]). Not a "messiah" in so many words, but a telling illustration of the difference between a native idiom and a translated one.

115. Arnaldo Momigliano, "What Josephus Did Not See" (trans. Joanna Weinberg; Italian original, 1980), in idem, *On Pagans, Jews, and Christians* (Middletown, Conn.: Wesleyan University Press, 1987), 108–19, here 111: "He does not give us any indication of having understood . . . the synagogue. He demonstrates even less understanding of the apocalyptic fervors of the time to which he was antagonistic."

116. Tessa Rajak, "Cio che Flavio Giuseppe Vide: Josephus and the Essenes," in eadem, *Jewish Dialogue with Greece and Rome*, 219–40, here 237:

"What Josephus did not see" should therefore perhaps best be reformulated as "what Josephus did see but could not write about." For there were strong constraints upon him, the constraints not (as is so often suggested) of patronage or of dishonesty, not even just those of his own temperament, but something equally pervasive—the constraints of literary form, the tyranny of text. . . . In the case of

Another, even more influential explanation is that Josephus carefully avoids talk of "messiahs" so as to avoid giving any impression of anti-Roman sympathies. Louis Feldman, in particular, has advanced this argument in a number of venues: "If Josephus suppressed the messianic ideals of the revolutionaries he apparently did so to avoid the wrath of the Romans, who would have recognized that a messiah was a political rebel against Rome."[117]

It is surely the case that Josephus's peculiar political situation will have factored into his writing in a great many important ways, as recent research has rightly emphasized.[118] It is not at all clear, however, that this dynamic explains Josephus's nonuse of the word χριστός. First, one might well ask why narrating anti-Roman insurgency would have suggested subversion on Josephus's own part. In fact, of course, he writes extensively about anti-Roman insurgents, apparently without concern for his coming across as anti-Roman, because he takes for granted that he is functioning as a reporter rather than a Jewish partisan (*War* 1.10–11). And second, in regard to messiah language in particular, why should we think that obscure, culturally Jewish words would incite more suspicion than clear, culturally Roman words would do? If anything, by using readily intelligible Greek terms for what insurrectionists do ("grasping for the kingship," "wearing the diadem"), Josephus makes their activities more clear, not less so, for his Roman patrons.[119] In fact, so far from avoiding mention of insurrection, he effectively translates the rebels' native revolutionary rhetoric ("stars," "scepters," "messiahs") into gentile vernacular ("diadems," "kings," "tyrants"). That is, he translates messiah language into a Roman idiom.[120]

Josephus, it is arguable that the demands of literary form are, all things considered, the largest single determinant in his presentation of Jewish history.

117. Louis H. Feldman, "Introduction," in *Josephus, the Bible, and History* (ed. Louis H. Feldman and Gohei Hata; Leiden: Brill, 1988), 37; similarly idem, "Josephus's Portrait of David," *HUCA* 60 (1989): 129–74; idem, "Josephus's Biblical Paraphrases as a Commentary on Contemporary Issues," in *The Interpretation of Scripture in Early Judaism and Christianity* (ed. Craig A. Evans; SSEJC 7; JSPSup 33; Sheffield: Sheffield Academic, 2000), 124–201.

118. See the essays collected in *Flavius Josephus and Flavian Rome* (ed. Jonathan Edmondson et al.; Oxford: Oxford University Press, 2005), in particular John M. G. Barclay, "The Empire Writes Back: Josephan Rhetoric in Flavian Rome," in ibid., 315–32; and earlier idem, *Jews in the Mediterranean Diaspora*, 346–68.

119. Compare Polybius, *Hist.* 31.11.5, where Polybius urges Demetrius son of Seleucus to τολμᾶν τι βασιλείας ἄξιον, "undertake some bold act worthy of the kingship"; also Polybius, *Hist.* 4.48.11–12, where Achaeus, general under Antiochus III, διάδημα περιθέμενος καὶ βασιλέα προσαγορεύσας αὐτόν, "put on the diadem and took the title of king" (Greek text ed. Theodor Büttner-Wobst, *Polybii historiae* [4 vols.; Leipzig: Teubner, 1893–1905]; trans. mine).

120. See Horsley and Hanson, *Bandits, Prophets, and Messiahs*, 110–11:

[Josephus] studiously avoids the distinctively Palestinian Jewish conceptuality and patterns of thought in favor of Hellenistic–Roman ideas. Thus we have to read

Indeed, this is precisely what Josephus does in his mention of the "ambiguous oracle" that he says especially drove the Jews to revolt (*War* 6.312), noted earlier. He takes what was specifically Jewish, scriptural language and renders it in gentile vernacular.[121] It is widely recognized that this kind of cultural translation is at work in many passages in Josephus, perhaps most famously the accounts of the four Jewish αἱρέσεις, "sects," or φιλοσοφίαι, "philosophies"—Pharisees, Sadducees, Essenes, and militants—which he portrays on the model of the Greco-Roman philosophical schools (*Life* 2.10–12; *War* 2.119–66; *Ant.* 18.11–23).[122] Here and throughout his corpus, Josephus "wrote on the borders of two cultures," to borrow an apt phrase from Momigliano.[123] My point here is that this well-known Josephan tendency, the translation of Jewish idioms into Greek and Roman ones, is quite sufficient to explain why he does not call the insurgents "messiahs." It is not that he fears being perceived as anti-Roman; it is simply that he is carrying out his literary project of cultural translation.[124]

Josephus says in the preface to the *War* that he intends τοῖς κατὰ τὴν Ῥωμαίων ἡγεμονίαν Ἑλλάδι γλώσσῃ μεταβαλὼν ἃ ... τῇ πατρίῳ συντάξας, "to translate in the Greek language, for those living under Roman government, what I composed in my ancestral language" (*War* 1.3).[125] Similarly, he

between the lines, or translate his Hellenistic conceptuality into the apocalyptic idiom current among Palestinian Jews. Thus when Josephus says that a figure "seized the opportunity to seek the throne" or "was proclaimed king" by his followers, we can reasonably surmise that these figures were messianic pretenders.

121. Thus rightly Martin Goodman, "Current Scholarship on the First Revolt," in *The First Jewish Revolt: Archaeology, History, and Ideology* (ed. Andrea M. Berlin and J. Andrew Overman; New York, N.Y.: Routledge, 2002), 15–24 at 19: "The common argument that Josephus suppressed or distorted mention of the messianic hope of the Jews because it was politically dangerous ... is directly contradicted by his explicit statement at *War* 6.312 when discussing the oracles which preceded the war."

122. For example, the "sect of the Pharisees" is said to be παραπλήσιός τῇ παρ' Ἕλλησιν Στωϊκῇ λεγομένῃ, "comparable to that which is called 'Stoic' by the Greeks" (*Life* 1.12).

123. Momigliano, "What Josephus Did Not See," 116.

124. "Cultural translation" is a commonplace in recent postcolonial theory (e.g., Homi K. Bhabha, "How Newness Enters the World: Postmodern Space, Postcolonial Times and the Trials of Cultural Translation," in idem, *The Location of Culture* [2d ed.; London: Routledge, 2004], 303–37), for which reason Josephus himself has been the subject of fruitful postcolonial analysis (e.g., Barclay, "The Empire Writes Back").

125. On the basis of *War* 1.3, Chaim Rabin ("The Translation Process and the Character of the Septuagint," *Textus* 6 [1968]: 1–26) suggests that Josephus may have been familiar with the canons observed by translators of Latin versions of classical works—an interesting but speculative proposal. Gohei Hata ("Is the Greek Version of Josephus' Jewish War a Translation or a Rewriting of the First Version?" *JQR* 66 [1975–1976]: 89–108) argues—unpersuasively, to my mind—that μεταβάλλω in *War* 1.3 refers not to translation but to rewriting in the same language.

describes the *Antiquities* as his effort τηλικαύτην μετενεγκεῖν ὑπόθεσιν εἰς ἀλλοδαπὴν ἡμῖν καὶ ξένην διαλέκτου συνήθειαν, "to translate so great a subject into a custom of language that is alien to us and foreign" (*Ant.* 1.7). In fact, Josephus's whole *oeuvre* can be described as an exercise in μετάληψις or μεταφορά, "translation."[126] In this respect, Rajak is surely right that what constrains Josephus most of all is not patronage or ignorance, but his chosen literary vehicle.[127] As John Barclay comments on the *Antiquities* and *Against Apion*, "These works show us a Diaspora Jew making a supreme—and in fact the last extant—effort to interpret Judaism for non-Jews in the Graeco-Roman world."[128]

This is the most compelling explanation for why Josephus calls the Jewish insurgents "diadem-wearers" and not "messiahs." It is not, as de Jonge and Rajak suggest, that they were not messiahs.[129] In all likelihood, at least some of them were, as Josephus implies in the passage about the "ambiguous oracle" that drove them to war.[130] Nor is it the case that, as Momigliano suggests, Josephus was blithely unaware of Jewish messianism; here again, Josephus gives us reason to think that he does know something about it.[131] Nor, finally, contra Feldman, does Josephus avoid the word "messiah" because he fears that using it would make him sound anti-Roman. On the contrary, Josephus presents himself as a reporter, not a partisan to the revolt, and he makes the insurgents' anti-Romanness more

---

126. Emily Kneebone's comment on the biblical material in the *Antiquities* applies, *mutatis mutandis*, to all of Josephus's work:

> Like all translations, [it] is by its nature a form of cultural mediation, yet Josephus also engages in much more than direct translation, reframing his material and explicitly setting out to explain and celebrate Jewish culture in a manner comprehensible and attractive to a first-century Greco-Roman audience. (Emily Kneebone, "Josephus' Esther and Diaspora Judaism," in *The Romance between Greece and the East* [ed. Tim Whitmarsh and Stuart Thomson; Cambridge: Cambridge University Press, 2013], 165–82 at 165–66).

127. Rajak, "Cio che Flavio Giuseppe Vide."

128. Barclay, *Jews in the Mediterranean Diaspora*, 366.

129. See Tessa Rajak, "Jewish Millenarian Expectations," in *The First Jewish Revolt*, 164–88 at 182: "If we allow that accusations of pretensions to royal grandeur do not amount to claims of messianic status, then no leaders convincingly emerge as would-be messiahs." But in fact, in their own context, many of these pretensions to royal grandeur *do* amount to claims of messianic status.

130. Thus rightly Dahl, "Eschatology and History in Light of the Qumran Texts," 52.

131. In addition to *War* 6.312–13, noted earlier, see *Ant.* 10.210 (on the stone that crushes the kingdoms of the earth in Dan 2); *Ant.* 17.43–45 (on the Pharisees' prophecy of the end of the Herodian dynasty).

clear, not less so, by rendering it in a Roman idiom. The explanation, rather, is that Josephus is constrained by literary convention, by his own chosen project of cultural translation from a Jewish idiom to a Roman one. He calls the insurgents "diadem-wearers" for the same reason that he calls the Pharisees "Stoics": because that is the term by which his audience will understand what he means.

The Mishnah

Another important literary source often cited in defense of *messianologische Vakuum* hypotheses is the Mishnah, the early-third-century CE compendium of rabbinic legal opinion, the textual core upon which the Tosefta and the Talmuds subsequently expanded over the course of late antiquity.[132] As is well known, the Mishnah contains relatively few references to messiahs, and recent interpreters—in a marked departure from older scholarship—have made much of this ostensible silence.[133] Perhaps most influential is the theory of Jacob Neusner, developed in a series of studies from the 1980s, that the Mishnah expresses the worldview of the tannaim without remainder, so that its relative quiet on the subject of messiahs must be understood as a statement of the early rabbis' rejection of messianism *tout court*.[134] Neusner writes:

> The Mishnah's framers constructed a system of Judaism in which the entire teleological dimension reached full exposure while hardly invoking the person or functions of a messianic figure of any kind. Perhaps

---

132. The traditional attribution of the Mishnah to the lone editorial hand of Rabbi Judah the Patriarch is, although not strictly accurate, at least in the right chronological vicinity. See H. L. Strack and Günter Stemberger, *Introduction to the Talmud and Midrash* (trans. Markus Bockmuehl; Minneapolis, Minn.: Fortress, 1996), 108–48; Catherine Hezser, "The Mishnah and Ancient Book Production," in *The Mishnah in Contemporary Perspective, Part One* (ed. Alan J. Avery-Peck and Jacob Neusner; Leiden: Brill, 2002), 167–92.

133. Here, as with Philo and Josephus, previous generations of scholars tended to find evidence of messianism despite the Mishnah's relative quiet. Thus, for example, Klausner, *Messianic Idea*, 393:

> Why has not a single messianic saying of these great Sages [Beit Hillel and Beit Shammai] been preserved? Certainly it is not because these earliest Tannaim rejected the Messianic idea. It is for an entirely different reason: as long as Judea retained a remnant of political autonomy, and the Temple still stood in all its glory, the leaders of the popular party, the foremost Pharisees, did not see the necessity of elaborating further the Messianic ideas of the prophets.

134. See, in particular, Jacob Neusner, *Judaism: The Evidence of the Mishnah* (BJS 129; Atlanta, Ga.: Scholars Press, 1988); idem, *Messiah in Context*; idem, "Mishnah and Messiah," in *Judaisms and Their Messiahs*, 265–82.

in the aftermath of Bar Kokhba's debacle, silence on the subject served to express a clarion judgment. I am inclined to think so.[135]

Of course, both Talmuds, the Yerushalmi in part and the Bavli more fully, add a considerable amount of messianic speculation to the frame provided by the Mishnah. For Neusner, however, these talmudic traditions are, first, foreign impositions on the thought of the Mishnah and, second, not philosophically significant in any case. He writes:

> So far as we examine the original canon of the ancient rabbis, framed over the second through seventh centuries, we find these inherited facts [i.e., messiah traditions] either reformed and reshaped for use in an essentially nonmessianic and ahistorical system, or left like rubble after a building has been completed: stones that might have been used, but were not. So Judaism as we know it presents no well-crafted doctrine of the Messiah, and thus its eschatology is framed within the methods of an essentially ahistorical teleology.[136]

In short, on Neusner's account, "The Mishnah presents us with a kind of Judaism possessed of an eschatology without Messiah, a teleology beyond time."[137]

More recently, Philip Alexander has articulated a similar position, albeit with rather more theoretical subtlety.[138] Alexander allows for a number of pertinent reasons for the Mishnah's relative quiet, but he, too, finally diagnoses a basic philosophical incompatibility between Mishnah and messianism. He writes:

> There is little need, indeed no place, for the Messiah in the Mishnaic world-view. It can be argued that it is hardly surprising that the Mishnah says nothing about the Messiah. After all, it is simply not talking about such matters. But this argument misses the point. The Mishnah is the manifesto of the rabbinic party. It is intended, surely, to

---

135. Neusner, *Messiah in Context*, 74. Similarly Charlesworth, "From Jewish Messianology to Christian Christology," 250: "Josephus and the compilers of the Mishnah may have ignored [messianism] because of the holocaust produced by revolutionary messianic Jews."

136. Neusner, *Messiah in Context*, ix.

137. Neusner, "Mishnah and Messiah," 267.

138. Latterly in the 2012 Sherman Lectures at the University of Manchester, "The Messianic Idea in Judaism Revisited," as yet unpublished.

present a comprehensive religious worldview. The fact, therefore, that the Messiah plays no part in that worldview is highly significant. The Mishnah's dominant perspective is this-worldly. It is concerned with defining and achieving piety and a civic society here and now.[139]

Here Alexander acknowledges the important objection that the Mishnah does not suppress messianism but is simply about other things.[140] He summarily dismisses this objection, however, on the Neusnerian premise that the Mishnah means to speak comprehensively, to give an account of everything that the tannaim consider important ("the manifesto of the rabbinic party," in Alexander's idiom). If so, then all omissions are intentional slights. Thus Alexander writes in a 2007 essay:

> The lack of reference in the earlier texts looks intentional. The authors of those texts saw little role for messianism in their theology. For them the focus was on the present.... They are not interested in history as a grand narrative of salvation stretching from the creation to the consummation.[141]

Alexander differs from Neusner, however, in granting that the baroque messiah traditions in the Bavli and later midrashim do betray a genuinely eschatological outlook akin to that attested in the early-Roman-period apocalypses. About this development, Alexander writes:

> It is a seismic shift, a move away from the essentially timeless Rabbinism of the Tannaitic and early Amoraic periods, to a re-engagement with history. The forward-looking, eschatological Judaism of late Second Temple times, sidelined by the Rabbis during the second and third centuries, thrust its way back into their theology in late Amoraic times.[142]

On this latter issue, the messianism of the amoraic literature, Alexander's assessment seems to me basically right. But regarding the earlier period, his dismissal of the objection that the Mishnah is simply concerned with other matters as "missing the point" deserves closer scrutiny. Several interpreters

---

139. Alexander, "King Messiah in Rabbinic Judaism," 470.

140. Compare my account of Philo earlier in this chapter.

141. Alexander, "Rabbis and Messianism," 235.

142. Alexander, "Rabbis and Messianism," 240.

have raised forms of this objection, which, in fact, cannot be dismissed so easily. The premise stipulated by Neusner and Alexander—that the Mishnah is coextensive with the philosophy of the tannaim—is by no means uncontroversial. As Shaye Cohen has emphasized, "[The Mishnah] lacks a preface; nowhere does the author . . . address his readership or explain the purpose or setting of the work."[143] In a context unrelated to messianism, E. P. Sanders criticizes Neusner sharply on this matter of genre. About Neusner's premise, Sanders writes:

> This would be an extraordinary position to take were the Mishnah actually a *Summa*. Almost everyone knows that even philosophers do not put into their books everything which they think important. All the more is this true of a collection of legal debates and opinions—which is what the Mishnah is.[144]

And again, more tersely: "Neusner wants the Mishnah to be more profound than it is."[145] Craig Evans cites Sanders approvingly on genre and extends the criticism to the issue of messianism, in particular, noting the different distributions of halakhic and haggadic material in the Mishnah and the Talmuds, respectively. Evans writes:

> The difference between the Mishna and the Talmuds is not as complex as Neusner would have us believe. The former contains halakah almost exclusively, while the latter contains large amounts of haggadah. . . . It is within the haggadic traditions that we encounter the messianic components. The Talmuds do not represent a fundamental shift in thinking. . . . [They] represent an encyclopedic widening of focus, a widening from an almost exclusive concern with law to an inclusive interest in everything Jewish—law, lore, eschatology, and all.[146]

---

143. Cohen, *From the Maccabees to the Mishnah*, 206. And further, appropriately cautiously, "The Mishnah is full of legal material but is not a law code. Rather, it is a digest or anthology; indeed, it resembles the *Digest* of Roman law published by the emperor Justinian in 533 CE" (Cohen, *From the Maccabees to the Mishnah*, 207).

144. E. P. Sanders, *Jewish Law from Jesus to the Mishnah: Five Studies* (London: SCM, 1990), 314.

145. Sanders, *Jewish Law*, 317.

146. Craig A. Evans, "Mishna and Messiah 'in Context': Some Comments on Jacob Neusner's Proposals," *JBL* 112 (1993): 267–89 at 281–82.

Martin Goodman has recently made a related point: "The rabbinic movement in the first two centuries C.E. preserved almost no traces of messianic
speculation." But, he adds, "The genre of halakhic compilations such as
Mishnah and Tosefta did not encourage inclusion of theological ideas."[147]
A better point of comparison with amoraic messiah lore would be the tannaitic midrashim, which, Goodman rightly notes, are similarly quiet on
the topic. If one wanted to argue for a messianic vacuum in the tannaitic
period, then this, not the Mishnah, would be the corpus from which to
do so.[148]

When we turn to the Mishnah itself, we find that, in fact, reports of
the silence of the tannaim on messiahs are greatly exaggerated. In fact,
there are scores of references in the Mishnah to משיחים of various kinds.
Morton Smith's generalization about the rabbinic corpus is precisely to the
point: "Even greater variety occurs in rabbinic literature, where a messiah
may be an 'anointed' (high) priest, or another priest anointed for a special
function, or any past or future king of Judah or Israel who has been or is to
be anointed, to say nothing of the other meanings inherited from the OT."[149]
There are, first of all, the two well-known mishnaic uses of "messiah" in
formulaic phrases to signify spans of time in the mythical future. The first
of these occurs in the first chapter of the first tractate of the Mishnah, in a
discussion of the proper time for saying the *berakhah* for the exodus from
Egypt:[150]

It is written: *That you may remember the day when you came forth out of
the land of Egypt all the days of your life* [Deut 16:3]. "The days of your life"
[would mean] the days only; but "all the days of your life" [means] the
nights also. The sages say: "The days of your life" [means] this age only,
but "all the days of your life" is to include the days of the messiah [ימות
המשיח]. (*m. Ber.* 1:5)[151]

---

147. Martin Goodman, "Messianism and Politics in the Land of Israel, 66–135 C.E.," in
Redemption and Resistance, 149–57 at 151.

148. Thus rightly Goodman, "Messianism and Politics," 151; and similarly Lawrence H.
Schiffman, "Messianism and Apocalypticism in Rabbinic Texts," in *CHJ*, 4:1053–72 at 1063.

149. Smith, "What Is Implied?" 67–68.

150. On this unit as a whole, see the recent discussion of Judith Hauptman, *Rereading the
Mishnah: A New Approach to Ancient Jewish Texts* (TSAJ 109; Tübingen: Mohr Siebeck, 2005),
125–42.

151. Trans. mod. from Danby; Hebrew text ed. Philip Blackman, *Mishnayoth* (New York,
N.Y.: Judaica, 2000).

Here ימות המשיח, "the days of the messiah," is a contrast term for העולם הזה, "this age." Thus, in this context, "the days of the messiah" means something very much like העולם הבא, "the age to come," even though elsewhere (e.g., *b. Sanh.* 91b), these latter two phrases signify different periods, respectively.[152]

Second and better known, because it occurs in the context of a gloomy decline-of-civilization narrative reminiscent of some Second Temple-period texts, is the mention of the "footsteps of the messiah" at *m. Sotah* 9:15:

> With the footsteps of the messiah [בעקבות משיחא] presumption shall increase and dearth reach its height; the vine shall yield its fruit but the wine shall be costly; and the empire shall fall into heresy and there shall be none to utter reproof. The council-chamber shall be given to fornication. . . . On whom can we stay ourselves? On our father in heaven. (*m. Sotah* 9:15)

This passage, which comprises the final words of tractate Sotah, concludes a long discussion of an inevitable future descent into impiety (*m. Sotah* 9:9–15), each paragraph of which repeats the refrain "On whom can we stay ourselves? On our father in heaven."[153] In this context, the עקבות משיחא, "footsteps of the messiah," signifies the woes that precede the messianic age. The phrase itself is a clever reuse of a biblical idiom from Ps 89, in which wicked people harass the Judahite king:

> Lord, where is your steadfast love of old, which by your faithfulness you swore to David? Remember, O Lord, how your servant is scorned; how I bear in my bosom the insults of the peoples, with which your enemies taunt, O YHWH, with which they mock the footsteps of your anointed [עקבות משיחך]. Blessed be YHWH for ever! Amen and Amen. (Ps 89:50–53 [ET 89:49–52])

---

152. On this terminological anomaly, see the still valuable discussion of Moore, *Judaism*, 2:378–79.

153. There are redaction-critical questions surrounding this mishnah, noted, for example, by Reeves, *Trajectories*, 106n3: "It is likely that this mishnah represents a later supplemental addition to the tractate drawn from two *baraitot* contained in *b. Sanh.* 97a." See the thorough discussion and complicated source-critical proposal of Klausner, *Messianic Idea*, 442–50, and the dating proposal of Schäfer, *History of the Jews*, 176: "The minor apocalypse in the Mishnah is possibly a later addition and might therefore come from this period [mid fourth century]; the government's turn to 'heresy' would then be the transition to Christian rule."

Thus the psalmist's "footsteps of the anointed" at which the scoffers scoff becomes the "footsteps of the messiah" during which time godliness will ebb low before the end.[154]

One might get the impression from the secondary literature that these are the only two references to messiahs in the Mishnah, but it is not so. Per Morton Smith's observation, cited earlier, "messiah" in the Mishnah is frequently used to signify one or another category of priest.[155] Indeed, Neusner himself makes just this point in another context: "When the framers of the Mishnah spoke of 'the Messiah,' they meant a high priest designated and consecrated to office in a certain way, and not in some other way."[156] Examples of this usage are numerous. One is the important halakhic distinction between "the priest anointed with the oil of unction" (that is, the high priest of the first temple) and "the one dedicated by the many garments" (that is, the high priest of the second temple) because, according to a rabbinic tradition, the Aaronic anointing oil had disappeared at the time of King Josiah and thus was unavailable for anointing high priests in the Second Commonwealth, who were consecrated by their vestments instead (see *t. Soṭah* 13:1; *y. Šeqal.* 6:1; *y. Soṭah* 8:3; *b. Hor.* 12a; *b. Yoma* 52b; *b. Ker.* 5b).[157] Thus Mishnah Megillah: "The priest anointed with the oil of unction [כהן משוח בשמן המשחה] differs from him that is dedicated by the many garments only in the bullock that is offered for [the unwitting transgression of] any of the commandments" (*m. Meg.* 1:9). And similarly Mishnah Horayot:

> And who is the anointed one [המשיח]? He that is anointed with the oil of unction [המשוח בשמן המשחה], but not he that is dedicated by the many garments. The priest anointed with the oil of unction [כהן המשוח בשמן המשחה] differs from him that is dedicated by the many garments only in the bullock offered for [the unwitting transgression of] any of the commandments. (*m. Hor.* 3:4)

---

154. On this feature of *m. Soṭah* 9:15, see Alexander Samely, *Rabbinic Interpretation of Scripture in the Mishnah* (Oxford: Oxford University Press, 2002), 115; Novenson, *Christ among the Messiahs*, 55.

155. Smith, "What Is Implied?" 67–68. On the rabbinic preoccupation with policing the (lapsed) priesthood, see Peter Schäfer, "Rabbis and Priests, or: How to Do Away with the Glorious Past of the Sons of Aaron," in *Antiquity in Antiquity: Jewish and Christian Pasts in the Greco-Roman World* (ed. Gregg Gardner and Kevin L. Osterloh; TSAJ 123; Tübingen: Mohr Siebeck, 2008), 155–72.

156. Neusner, *Messiah in Context*, 74.

157. On this tradition, see Liver, "Doctrine of the Two Messiahs," 152–54; de Vaux, *Ancient Israel*, 387–403.

Joseph Liver argues speculatively but not unreasonably that the Mishnah's "priest anointed with the oil of unction" is close in many respects to the "messiah of Aaron" of the Qumran sectarians:

> In Mishnaic law, only the anointed high priest has full authority, but in view of the absence of the oil of unction there can only be an anointed high priest at the end of days. This Halakhah comes from traditional Judaism, but as it does not in any way run counter to the principles of the [Qumran] Sect, we may reasonably assume that it prevailed among them.[158]

Liver assumes too much. The Mishnah's anointed high priest arguably fits as well in a mythical past or an imaginary present as in an eschatological future.[159] But inasmuch as these are different ways of conceiving an ideal polity, Liver's basic observation holds true: The Mishnah, like 1QS before it, cares that the archetypal high priest be duly anointed with oil in the ancient pattern of the sons of Aaron.

There are, moreover, several mishnaic passages that detail the duties of the priest who delivers the oracle of war to the Israelite troops in Deut 20:1–4. In Deuteronomy, he is simply a כהן, "priest," but in the Mishnah he is called כהן משוח מלחמה, "the priest anointed for battle," or simply משוח מלחמה, "the anointed for battle."[160] Thus Mishnah Sotah:

> These must be said in the holy language: the paragraph of the first-fruits, the words of *halitzah*, the blessings and the cursings, the blessings of the priests, and the blessings of the high priest, the paragraph of the king, the paragraph of the heifer whose neck is to be broken, and [the words of] the anointed for battle [משוח מלחמה] [Deut 20:2–7] when he speaks unto the people. (*m. Sotah* 7:2)

And again:

> When the anointed for battle [משוח מלחמה] speaks unto the people he speaks in the holy language, for it is written: *And it shall be, when you*

---

158. Liver, "Doctrine of the Two Messiahs," 153.

159. On the puzzle of the rabbis legislating for the (nonexistent) temple, see Naftali S. Cohn, *The Memory of the Temple and the Making of the Rabbis* (Philadelphia, Pa.: University of Pennsylvania Press, 2013).

160. On this "war messiah," see Bezalel Bar-Kochva, *Judas Maccabaeus: The Jewish Struggle against the Seleucids* (Cambridge: Cambridge University Press, 1989), 494–99; and Reuven Firestone, *Holy War in Judaism: The Fall and Rise of a Controversial Idea* (New York, N.Y.: Oxford University Press, 2012), 65–138, especially 77–80.

draw near to the battle, that the priest shall approach (this is the priest anointed for the battle [כהן משוח מלחמה]) *and shall speak unto the people* (in the holy language) *and shall say to them, Hear, O Israel, you draw near to battle this day against your enemies* [Deut 20:2–3]. (*m. Sotah* 8:1)

Mishnah Makkot, in a discussion of the law regarding cities of refuge for those who have committed manslaughter (Num 35), collocates this "anointed for battle" with other categories of priest:

R. Jose b. Judah says: . . . [A high priest that dies,] no matter whether he was anointed with the oil of unction [משוח בשמן המשחה] or whether he was dedicated by the many garments or whether he had passed from his high priesthood suffers the manslayer to return [re: Num 35:25]. R. Judah says: Also he that was anointed for battle [משוח מלחמה] [when he dies] suffers the manslayer to return. (*m. Mak.* 2:6)[161]

Yet another usage is attested in the extended discussion in Mishnah Horayot about legal decisions to be rendered either by the court (בית דין) or by the high priest, in which the high priest is consistently called כהן משיח, "the anointed priest," or simply המשיח, "the anointed one." Thus:

If the anointed priest [כהן משיח] made a decision for himself [that transgressed any of the commandments enjoined in the law], and he made it unwittingly and acted [transgressing] unwittingly, he must offer a bullock. . . . The decision of an anointed priest [כהן משיח] made for himself is like the decision given by the court for the congregation. (*m. Hor.* 2:1)

And again: "The court becomes liable only if it gives a decision which in part annuls and in part sustains [what the law enjoins]; so too it is with the anointed one [המשיח]" (*m. Hor.* 2:2). And again: "The court is liable only if it gives a decision that leads to a transgression for which if it is done wantonly the penalty is extirpation and if unwittingly a sin-offering. So too it is with the anointed one [המשיח]" (*m. Hor.* 2:3). And so on.[162]

---

161. On these passages, see further Etienne Nodet, "The Sabbath and War," in idem, *A Search for the Origins of Judaism: From Joshua to the Mishnah* (Sheffield: Sheffield Academic, 1997 [French original, 1992]), 63–92 at 76–84.

162. On the social setting of these mishnaic rules for jurisdiction, see Shaye J. D. Cohen, "The Rabbi in Second-Century Judean Society," in *CHJ*, vol. 3 (ed. William Horbury et al.; New York, N.Y.: Cambridge University Press, 1999), 922–90.

In view of such passages, the commonplace claim that the Mishnah is silent on the topic of messiahs is patently false. The related but more nuanced hypothesis of Neusner and Alexander, that the Mishnah represents a philosophical flight from messianism, rests entirely on a sufficiently narrow definition of messianism. Their hypothesis can be articulated in such a way as to be defensible, but then it leaves us powerless to explain such references to משיחים as we do have in the Mishnah. Better, it seems to me, to theorize messianism in such a way as to account for all the available evidence.[163] Lawrence Schiffman has gone some way toward this goal, invoking Gershom Scholem's classic rubric of types of messianism by way of explaining the usage of the Mishnah.[164] On Schiffman's account:

> Tannaitic Judaism moves away from the utopian aspects of messianism, seeing these as having led to the terrible destructions Israel experienced. It continues to hope for restorative messianism.... The Mishnah speaks as if these institutions [viz. kingship, priesthood, temple] are actually functioning, as if the nation, its tribes, and its sanctuary are still in place, for this is the ideal world. Restorative messianism is everywhere present in the Mishnah.[165]

This lattermost claim seems to me overstated, and I have doubts about the stability of Scholem's restorative–utopian distinction;[166] but these quibbles aside, I find Schiffman's analysis extremely perceptive. In their meticulous legislation for Jewish institutions that were long since defunct, the tannaim express something of the way they think the world ought to be. It is, for the most part, a past-facing rather than a future-facing political statement, but it is a political statement nonetheless. What else are the Mishnah's "anointed

---

163. On this methodological point, see Chapter 1 in this volume.

164. See Scholem, "Messianic Idea," 3 (emphasis mine):

> The *conservative* forces are directed toward the preservation of that which exists and which, in the historical environment of Judaism, was always in danger.... The *restorative* forces are directed to the return and recreation of a past condition which comes to be felt as ideal.... [The *utopian* forces] aim at a state of things which has never yet existed. The problem of Messianism in historical Judaism appears within the field of influence of these forces.

165. Schiffmann, "Messianism and Apocalypticism in Rabbinic Texts," 1063–64. See relatedly Dan Jaffé, "Croyances et conceptions messianiques dans la literature talmudique: entre rationalisme et utopie," in *Aux origines des messianismes juifs*, 173–202.

166. On the one hand, utopian visions cannot avoid using language and imagery from the past to articulate their ideal futures; and on the other, the pasts invoked in restorative visions are always to some extent mythical rather than real. Thus the distinction breaks down.

priest" and the "one anointed with the oil of unction" and the "anointed for battle" but so many messiahs in rabbinic terms?

Problems and Solutions

In modern research on our question, the one crucial thing that these otherwise disparate texts and writers—Philo, Josephus, and the Mishnah—have in common is their utility for the hypothesis of a conspicuous absence in the history of ancient Jewish messianism. These sources have been taken to be significant not for what they say, but for what they do not say (or say in the wrong way). Admittedly, careful attention to silences in texts can sometimes yield valuable interpretive insights,[167] but it is always a methodological gamble, because as often as not a text's silence on a given theme is simply a factor of what the author chose to write about, nothing more. Why does Plato's *Apology* not comment on the theory of forms? Why does Josephus not relate the disputes between Beit Hillel and Beit Shammai? Why does the apostle Paul's Letter to the Romans not mention the eucharistic meal? Why does Lucian's *Parliament of the Gods* not include Poseidon? To many such questions, the sanest answer is simply that the text is about something else.

Significant absences are in the eye of the beholder, and in the case of ancient Jewish messianism, modern interpreters have inherited a jaundiced eye. Having been taught by our disciplinary forebears to expect messianism always and everywhere in ancient Judaism, interpreters either find it by sheer force of will or, marginally better, they admit not finding it and then undertake to theorize its absence. With other, less ideologically fraught topics, however, we generally do not proceed in this way. When we read an ancient Jewish text that happens not to comment on, say, menstrual impurity, or liturgical prayer, or ritual slaughter, we normally do not conclude that such a text demonstrates a waning of or a deficiency in the phenomenon in question. And rightly so, because we normally recognize that ancient Jewish writers, like writers in all times and places, deal with sundry problems in divers manners. My point here is that we should think of messianism as we think of menstrual impurity or liturgical prayer or ritual slaughter in this respect. It is one discourse among many for addressing one social problem among many.[168] If messiah language were, as Klausner and his contemporaries thought, "the summation

---

167. See Günter Figal, "On the Silence of Texts: Toward a Hermeneutic Concept of Interpretation," in idem, *For a Philosophy of Freedom and Strife: Politics, Aesthetics, Metaphysics* (trans. Wayne Klein; Albany, N.Y.: SUNY Press, 1998 [German original, 1994]), 1–11.

168. A point well made by Mack, "Wisdom Makes a Difference."

of the most exalted hopes . . . of our greatest and most venerated dreamers,"[169] then we might well expect to find it everywhere, as they did, and be perplexed when we do not. But it is not that, nor does it need to be. Among ancient Jewish thinkers, talk about an anointed ruler was important for the people for whom it was important, and that is enough.[170]

Just here lies the fundamental problem with Joachim Becker's influential notion, discussed earlier in this chapter, of a *messianologische Vakuum*. The metaphor of a vacuum implies a privation, a lack, an absence of something that should be there but is not. It is an unnatural state of affairs. *Natura abhorret vacuum*, as Aristotle speculated and Rabelais wrote.[171] In Becker's own treatment, that is precisely the point. He articulates a modern form of the very old Christian proof from messianic prophecy: The classical prophets foretold the coming of the messiah, and although in the Second Commonwealth pious hope ebbed low, at the time of Jesus the messianic expectations of the Jewish people were revived.[172] Most scholars have long since abandoned this apologetic narrative as a historical description of ancient Jewish messianism,[173] but many have nonetheless clung to the curious metaphor of a vacuum. The burden of this chapter has been to argue that that metaphor should be abandoned, along with the assumptions that underlie it.

Rather than asking the primary texts to confirm, either by their speech or by their silence, a theory of messianism arrived at on other grounds, we should approach the sources afresh with an eye to the problems they identify

---

169. Klausner, *Messianic Idea*, 6.

170. On this point, I note my gratitude for a valuable conversation with Markus Bockmuehl and Alison Salvesen, whose perceptive comments helped me to clarify my thinking.

171. Aristotle, *Physics*, book 4; François Rabelais, *Gargantua et Pantagruel*, vol. 1 (Paris: Larousse, 1913 [1st ed., 1532]), 47.

172. Becker concedes, "The apologetic proof from prophecy cannot be cited in the naive way it traditionally has been. We must accept facts and refuse to embark on any dubious attempts to rescue the situation" (Becker, *Messianic Expectation*, 95). Nevertheless, he reasons:

> Does this eliminate the traditional picture of messianic expectation? Such a conclusion would contradict one of the most central concerns of the New Testament, which insists with unprecedented frequency, intensity, and unanimity that Christ was proclaimed in advance in the Old Testament. Historical–critical scholarship can never set aside this assertion of the New Testament. We must therefore find an explanation which does justice to both the historical approach and the witness of the New Testament. To appeal to the light of faith for this synthesis is not a schizophrenic act of intellectual violence, for revelation and faith go hand in hand with a manifestation of their rationality. (Becker, *Messianic Expectation*, 93)

173. As does, for example, Green, "Messiah in Judaism," 6: "The model limned by an apologetic use of scripture was accepted by later scholarship as a literary fact and a historical reality, not only of scripture itself, but also of Israelite and Jewish religion."

and the solutions they propose. As Michael Stone has commented perceptively about *4 Ezra*—a text that, of course, does feature a messiah—"The Messiah was not the answer to the questions that Ezra was asking."[174] Or again, we may recall Harry Wolfson's comment on the slim evidence for messianism in Philo: "The solution found by Philo for the Jewish problem of his time was the revival of the old prophetic promises of the ultimate disappearance of the diaspora."[175] Whatever Philo's view of the diaspora, Wolfson's observation that Philo perceived certain problems in contemporary Jewish life and used scripture and philosophy to supply solutions is to the point. As it happens, Philo does not find the scriptural idiom of anointed rulers useful for saying what he wants to say, and there are relatively straightforward literary reasons why this should be the case. With Philo, as with Josephus and the Mishnah, there is no puzzle to be solved, no vacuum to be filled, no deafening silence to be explained.

---

174. Michael Stone, "The Concept of the Messiah in IV Ezra," in *Religions in Antiquity*, 295–312 at 312.

175. Wolfson, *Philo*, 2:407.

5

The Quest for the First Messiah

SOMETIME DURING THE second or first century BCE, in the inhospitable Judean desert near the Dead Sea, a pious Jewish writer composed a poem in the first-person singular, relating the great sorrows and the ultimate apotheosis of his literary speaker. The poem reads, in part:

> ... [for]ever a mighty throne in the congregation of the gods [עז כסא
> אלים בעדת]. None of the ancient kings shall sit in it, and their nobles
> shall not ... shall not be like my glory, and none shall be exalted save
> me, nor shall come against me. For I have taken my seat in his [throne]
> in the heavens and none ... I shall be reckoned with the gods [עם אני
> אתחשב אלים] and established in the holy congregation. I do not desire
> as would a man of flesh ... everything precious to me is in the glory
> of [the gods in the dwelli]ng place. Who has been despised on my
> account? And who can be compared with me in my glory [בכבדי ומיא]?
> ... Who be[ars all] griefs as I do? And who [suff]ers evil like me? ...
> And any teaching will not be equal to [my teaching].... Who will stop
> me from speaking? And who shall measure the flow of my speech, and
> who shall be my equal and be like me in my judgment? For I shall be
> reckoned with the gods [אחשב אלים עם אניא כיא], and my glory with [that
> of] the king's sons. (4Q491 frg. 11)[1]

If the writer gave a name to his hymn, it has not survived in the several manuscript fragments in which the text is preserved,[2] but for the sake of

---

1. Text ed. Esther Eshel, "4Q471b: A Self-Glorification Hymn," *RevQ* 17 (1996): 175–203; trans. mod.

2. Namely, 4Q471b; 4Q491 frg. 11; 1QH^a cols. 26–27; and 4QH^a frg. 7 col. 1 and frg. 12.

convenience interpreters have come to refer to the poem by the not inaccurate name "the Self-Glorification Hymn."[3] It is not at all clear, however, who the glorified self of the poem is, much less who the actual author is. Some interpreters have thought that the former is the latter, that the poem is an autobiographical account of a mystical ascent to heaven, which is admittedly possible but for which our context-less poem provides little in the way of evidence. Among the interpreters who take this view, a subset have identified this translated poet as the messiah of the Qumran sect, a charismatic sectarian who suffers injustice but is vindicated and exalted to the right hand of God. And this—according to this school of thought—explains why Jesus of Nazareth, in turn, was likewise understood as a suffering and exalted messiah. In fact, the Self-Glorification Hymn is just one of a number of ancient texts on which recent interpreters have based claims to have identified the first messiah. This scholarly quest for the first messiah represents an important trend in recent research, but it is, in my view, profoundly misguided. The purpose of this chapter is to explain why this is the case.

Origins of the Quest

There is a strand in modern scholarship on ancient Jewish messianism whose practitioners set for themselves the goal of identifying the first messiah, the one historical figure with whose career certain ancient Judean oracles became associated in such a way as to exercise world-historical influence, the "patient zero"—to borrow an image from epidemiology—to whom later puzzles in the development of messianism can be traced back and thereby explained. Chief among these later puzzles, for most practitioners of this strand of research, is the rise of a messiah movement around the figure of Jesus of Nazareth in the first century CE. As ancient Jewish critics already noted, and modern historical Jesus scholars have corroborated, Jesus would seem, by all accounts, to be a most unlikely messiah: an itinerant teacher and exorcist from the North executed as a troublemaker by the Roman authorities in Jerusalem. How was such a figure ever identified as a messiah at all?[4] Precisely here, say the questers for

---

3. Following Eshel, "Self-Glorification Hymn." There is a considerable body of secondary literature on the poem, much of which is discussed later in this chapter. A brief, lucid overview is provided by Esther Eshel, "Self-Glorification Hymn," in *Eerdmans Dictionary of Early Judaism* (ed. John J. Collins and Daniel C. Harlow; Grand Rapids, Mich.: Eerdmans, 2010), 1215.

4. Among the ancient sources, see Justin Martyr, *Dial.* 39; 48; Origen, *Cels.* 3.1; 4.2. Among the modern, see the classic treatments of William Wrede, *The Messianic Secret* (trans. J. C. G. Greig; Cambridge: Clarke, 1971), especially 209–30; and Bultmann, *Theology of the*

the first messiah, there must be a missing link, a pre-Christian Jewish messiah whose unique circumstances and powerful influence are sufficient to explain the otherwise inexplicable phenomenon of the Jesus messiah movement.

This is, however, a relatively recent development. For most of the history of modern biblical criticism, the prevailing view had been that ancient Jewish messianism was more or less one thing, and that Jesus himself was the cause of a radical conceptual innovation resulting in the rise of Christianity. On this older account, there is no need to posit a missing link, a pre-Christian first messiah. The pertinent developments in the history of ideas can be attributed directly to the influence of the great man. Jesus himself is the first messiah, so to speak. Indeed, there is a considerable weight of nineteenth- and early-twentieth-century opinion in this direction.[5] There are serious problems with this older perspective, which I shall discuss later. In any case, however, this was roughly the *communis opinio* among scholars of messianism throughout the nineteenth and up to the mid twentieth century.

What we may call the quest for the first messiah is related very closely to the discovery and publication of the scrolls from the Judean desert near Qumran,[6] and understandably so. In the Dead Sea Scrolls, we have a literary record of a Jewish sect from the two centuries before the death of Jesus, and in this record we find more than a few mentions of messiahs, as well as references to one or more charismatic individuals from the history of the sect.[7] If

---

New Testament, 1:26–32; and the more recent summary comment of Charlesworth, "From Messianology to Christology," 10: "If Jesus' life and teachings were not parallel to those often or sometimes attributed to the coming of 'the Messiah' or 'the Christ,' then why, how, and when did Jesus' earliest followers contend that he was so clearly the promised Messiah?"

5. See, for example, V. H. Stanton, *The Jewish and the Christian Messiah* (Edinburgh: T. & T. Clark, 1886), 387:

> We have noted the grand effects of the claim of Jesus to be the Messiah, which began to tell from the first, in that the conception of the nature and prerogatives of the Messiah was immeasurably raised, while at the same time a new ideal of human life was presented to men.

See also Mowinckel, *He That Cometh*, 447, 450:

> Jesus understood and fulfilled the thought of the unknown Messiah on earth in a manner entirely different from its presentation in the Jewish legend.... For Jesus, the Jewish Messianic idea was the temptation of Satan, which He had to reject. The new conception of a saviour, which Jesus created, unites in itself the loftiest elements in both the Jewish and the "Aryan" spirit, and fuses them in a true unity, which is realized in Jesus Himself.

6. There is, however, a kind of precursor in the work of Gressmann, *Messias*, 449–78 .

7. The secondary literature on messianism in the Scrolls is vast, but see in particular the seminal study of Van der Woude, *Messianische Vorstellungen*; and the more recent, definitive treatment of Zimmermann, *Messianische Texte*.

there were a missing link to be found, this would presumably be a promising place for scholars to search for it. And search they did, beginning in the early, heady days after the discovery and initial publication of the first manuscript fragments from Qumran. During the 1950s, as the Essene hypothesis for the identification of the Qumran site and scrolls gained ground,[8] there arose an animated discussion of a number of ostensible parallels between Essenism and early Christianity. Perhaps the foremost chronicler of such parallels was the long-time professor of Semitic languages at the Sorbonne, André Dupont-Sommer.[9]

In a series of studies published between 1949 and 1959, Dupont-Sommer revived the famous dictum of his nineteenth-century countryman Ernest Renan: *Le christianisme est un essénisme qui a largement réussi*, "Christianity is an Essenism which was largely successful."[10] More specifically relevant to our purposes, Dupont-Sommer also argued for a direct connection between the messiahship of the Teacher of Righteousness—which he takes to be firmly established—and the messiahship of Jesus of Nazareth.[11] In a 1950 study, Dupont-Sommer writes:

> It is from the womb of this religious ferment [viz. Qumran Essenism] that Christianity, the Christian "New Covenant," emerged. In history there are scarcely any absolute beginnings, and Christianity is no excep-tion to the rule. . . .. Everything in the Jewish New Covenant heralds and prepares the way for the Christian New Covenant. The Galilean Master, as he is presented to us in the writings of the New Testament, appears as an astonishing reincarnation of the Master of Justice [i.e., מורה הצדק, "Teacher of Righteousness"]. . . .. The question at once arises, to which of the two sects, the Jewish or the Christian, does the priority belong?

---

8. Beginning from the remarkably prescient proposal of Eliezer L. Sukenik, *Hidden Scrolls: First Survey* (Jerusalem: Bialik Institute, 1948) (in Hebrew).

9. His earliest comment on the subject is André Dupont-Sommer, "La grotte aux manu-scrits du désert de Juda," *Revue de Paris* (July 1949): 79–90. His major treatments are idem, *Aperçus préliminaires sur les manuscrits de la mer Morte* (Paris: Maisonneuve, 1950); ET *The Dead Sea Scrolls: A Preliminary Survey* (trans. E. Margaret Rowley; Oxford: Blackwell, 1952); and idem, *Les Écrits esséniens découverts près de la mer Morte* (Paris: Payot, 1959); ET *The Essene Writings from Qumran* (trans. Geza Vermes; Oxford: Blackwell, 1961).

10. Ernest Renan, *Histoire du Peuple d'Israël* (5 vols.; Paris: Calmann Lévy, 1887–1893), 5:70.

11. The Teacher of Righteousness, a founding figure in the institutional history of the Qumran sect, is mentioned expressly at CD 1:11 (and cf. CD 6:11); 1QpHab 1:13; 2:2; 5:10; 7:4; 8:3; 9:9–10; 11:5; 1QpMic (=1Q14) frgs. 8–10, line 6; 4QpPs[a] (=4Q171) 1–10 iii 15; 1–10 iii 19; 1–10 iv 8; 1–10 iv 27; 4QpPs[b] (=4Q173) 1:4, 2:2. For basic background, see James C. VanderKam, *The Dead Sea Scrolls Today* (Grand Rapids, Mich.: Eerdmans, 1994), 99–108.

Which of the two was able to influence the other? The reply leaves no room for doubt. ... In every case where the resemblance compels or invites us to think of a borrowing, this was on the part of Christianity.[12]

From the innocuous premise that "in history there are scarcely any absolute beginnings," Dupont-Sommer makes the quite radical inference that the Jesus messiah movement not only borrowed from but actually reincarnated its Qumranite antecedent.

This is also the position taken by the early John Marco Allegro: The unusual messianic career of Jesus of Nazareth was modeled after that of his Qumranite forebear.[13] It was later, in the 1960s, that Allegro came round to the more radical view for which he is better known—namely, that Jesus of Nazareth is an entirely mythical figure whose story, as related in the Gospels, is a thinly veiled retelling of the actual messianic career of the Teacher of Righteousness.[14] But that is a longer, stranger story.[15] Throughout the course of lively debate during the 1950s and early 1960s, the hypotheses of Dupont-Sommer and Allegro failed to gain consensus among Qumran specialists, and the quest for the first messiah effectively lapsed.[16] So it was for about a generation, until the turn of the millennium, when the quest was resuscitated, simultaneously but independently, by Michael Wise in the United States and by Israel Knohl in Israel.[17]

---

12. Dupont-Sommer, *Preliminary Survey*, 98–99.

13. Thus John M. Allegro, *The Dead Sea Scrolls* (Harmondsworth: Penguin, 1956), 148–62.

14. See John M. Allegro, *The Sacred Mushroom and the Cross: A Study of the Nature and Origins of Christianity within the Fertility Cults of the Ancient Near East* (London: Hodder & Stoughton, 1970); and idem, *The Dead Sea Scrolls and the Christian Myth* (Newton Abbot: Westbridge, 1979).

15. A sympathetic account of Allegro's unconventional career is given by his daughter Judith Anne Brown, *John Marco Allegro: The Maverick of the Dead Sea Scrolls* (Grand Rapids, Mich.: Eerdmans, 2005). A briefer, more objective account is given by John J. Collins, *The Dead Sea Scrolls: A Biography* (Princeton, N.J.: Princeton University Press, 2013), 96–138.

16. Writing at about this time, William Brownlee makes the related argument that New Testament messianism is directly dependent upon Qumran messianism but, importantly, not upon a particular historical personage from Qumran (William H. Brownlee, "Messianic Motifs of Qumran and the New Testament," *NTS* 3 [1956]: 12–30). I therefore do not count Brownlee among the questers for the first messiah.

17. Fitzmyer comments about Wise and Knohl, "They have undoubtedly forgotten or been unaware of a similar claim that was made in France shortly after the announcement of the discovery of the Dead Sea Scrolls and the first publication of some of them by no less a scholar than André Dupont-Sommer" (Fitzmyer, *One Who Is to Come*, 115). But in fact, Wise cites Dupont-Sommer approvingly at a number of points (e.g., Wise, *First Messiah*, 310n43, 335n1). Knohl cites neither Dupont-Sommer nor Allegro, but not, I expect, because of ignorance or forgetfulness.

The Quest à la Michael Wise

In his 1999 book *The First Messiah*, Michael Wise argues that the Teacher of Righteousness at Qumran, whose *floruit* Wise dates controversially to the 70s BCE and to whom he gives the personal name Judah, identified himself as a messiah after the pattern of the suffering servant of Deutero-Isaiah and, in so doing, effectively created the messianic idea in Judaism.[18] Wise makes his case chiefly on the evidence of the so-called Teacher Hymns from the Hodayot (1QHᵃ cols. 10–16), whose anonymous first-person speaker Wise takes to be the Teacher of Righteousness. Wise discerns in the Teacher Hymns not, as some interpreters have done, the voice of a liturgist praying on behalf of the pious congregation,[19] but rather the inner monologue of a charismatic coming into awareness of his own messianic identity. (There is an interesting analogy here to the debate among Pauline interpreters about the identity of the first-person speaker in Rom 7:7–25.)[20] Wise writes, "After intense psychological and physical suffering, and one or more journeys to heaven, Judah now stood in possession of a complete vision of himself. . ... By his fifth hymn, Judah saw himself as something momentous and new to recorded history. He was the first messiah."[21]

One especially important text in Wise's argument is 1QHᵃ 11:1–10,[22] which he renders as follows:

---

18. Wise, *First Messiah*. The majority second-century BCE date for the Teacher's career is represented, for example, by Lawrence H. Schiffman, *Reclaiming the Dead Sea Scrolls* (Philadelphia, Pa.: JPS, 1994), 83–95; and VanderKam, *Dead Sea Scrolls Today*, 99–108. For Wise's alternative, first-century BCE date, see Michael O. Wise, "Dating the Teacher of Righteousness and the *Floruit* of His Movement," *JBL* 122 (2003): 53–87; idem, "The Origins and History of the Teacher's Movement," in *The Oxford Handbook of the Dead Sea Scrolls* (ed. Timothy H. Lim and John J. Collins; Oxford: Oxford University Press, 2010), 92–122.

19. See Carol A. Newsom, *The Self as Symbolic Space: Constructing Identity and Community at Qumran* (STDJ 52; Leiden, Brill, 2004), 287–346; and differently Angela Kim Harkins, *Reading with an "I" to the Heavens: Looking at the Qumran Hodayot through the Lens of Visionary Traditions* (Ekstasis 3; Berlin: De Gruyter, 2012), 69–113.

20. On which see the recent treatment of Emma Wasserman, *The Death of the Soul in Romans 7* (WUNT 2.256; Tübingen: Mohr Siebeck, 2008).

21. Wise, *First Messiah*, 122.

22. As part of his speculative chronological arrangement of the Teacher Hymns, Wise also adduces the Self-Glorification Hymn (cited at the beginning of this chapter) as evidence for the Qumran covenanters' interpretation of the Teacher after his death and apotheosis, a poem written in his voice and added to the Hodayot by its redactors. See Wise, *First Messiah*, 222–26, 322–23; idem, "מי כמוני באלים: A Study of 4Q491c, 4Q471b, 4Q427 7, and 1QHᵃ 25:35–26:10," *DSD* 7 (2000): 173–219. The Self-Glorification Hymn is more integral to Israel Knohl's argument than it is to Wise's, so I discuss it later in this chapter in connection with Knohl.

O my God, [you] lit my face with your glory as I received your covenant
. . . . [I have w]alked in eternal glory among all [your holy ones]. . . . [Those
who despise me] have considered me [an object of derision and mock]ing
and I have been rendered as a ship upon the [r]aging sea, like a fortified
city besieged by [her enemies]. I am in distress, like a woman in labor
with her firstborn when her travail begins . . . . Yet through the breakers of
death she delivers a male child, and through hellish agonies bursts forth
from the bearer's womb: a wonderful counselor with his mighty power.
(1QHª 11:1–10)[23]

Here, significantly, Wise interprets the very lacunose lines 3 and 4 as a report
of a mystical ascent to heaven on the part of the author ("You lit my face with
glory . . . . I walked in eternal glory among all your holy ones"). What is more, he
takes line 10 as a figurative but nevertheless explicit declaration of messiahship,
in which the author identifies himself both with the mother in travail—the messianic birth pangs—and with the "wonderful counselor with mighty power" (Isa
9:6; 11:2) emerging from the womb—the coming of the messiah in glory.[24]

That much of the argument is not uncontroversial,[25] but Wise further
suggests that the hymnist's experience established the pattern for all subsequent Jewish messiah texts. (And this is my particular concern in this chapter,
because it has received very little in the way of scrutiny.) Wise writes:

The rise of literary activity and actual movements in the years after him
was no coincidence. The fact of Judah, the reality of the first messiah,
had entered the myth-dream. . . . Judah's movement became—apart
from early Christianity—the most dynamic and enduring crisis cult of
these centuries of Jewish civilization. If similar events happened later
among others who resonated with the Judah-inspired, revised myth-
dream of Israel, it was only to be expected. This is the way the myth-
dream works.[26]

---

23. Trans. Wise, *First Messiah*, 105.

24. Wise, *First Messiah*, 105.

25. For example, Brownlee, "Messianic Motifs," 24–25, comments on this text:

Does the author think of himself being in travail in order to give birth to the
Messiah? Probably in part this is so, but only in so far as he is the corporate head
of the Community. In the last analysis the mother is Zion (or Israel). . . . Yet the
author may have felt that in a peculiar way it would be through his sufferings
(though not without reference to the Community) that the Messiah would be born.

26. Wise, *First Messiah*, 131.

In particular, Wise is concerned to make the point that the messiahship of Jesus of Nazareth is unthinkable apart from the model established by the Teacher of Righteousness. He argues:

> If Judah had not been what he was, had not lived the first messianic life, then the myth-dream of Israel would have been something different—perhaps much different—when a young carpenter from Nazareth began to give it new voice. Had that been the case, then the message of that carpenter could not have invoked the precise combination of elements that it did.[27]

Wise's conception of messianism as a reified "myth-dream" is deeply indebted to the messianic idea trope in nineteenth- and early-twentieth-century scholarship (especially Gershom Scholem), filtered, however, through a late modern anthropological theory of crisis cults (especially Max Weber).[28]

Despite the great learning and ingenious argumentation evidenced in Wise's book, there are several objections that may be raised.[29] For one thing, Wise's arguments for dating the Teacher's career to the first century BCE, although formidable, are to my mind not sufficient to overturn the weight of evidence for the more conventional second-century BCE date.[30] For another, there is the problem of the so-called Teacher Hymns, whose association with the Teacher of Righteousness himself is a plausible conjecture, but a conjecture

---

27. Wise, *First Messiah*, 208.

28. Wise invokes and endorses Gershom Scholem's Idealist account of Jewish messianism (*First Messiah*, 122). For his model of crisis cults (*First Messiah*, 1–36), Wise adduces comparative evidence from the flagellant disciples of Konrad Schmid, the Sabbatian messianists, the Frankist messianists, the Millerites of upstate New York, the Melanesian cargo cults, and the Sioux Ghost Dance of 1890. With respect to anthropological theory, he leans heavily on Max Weber, *On Charisma and Institution Building: Selected Papers* (ed. S. N. Eisenstadt; Chicago, Ill.: University of Chicago Press, 1968); and Kenneth Burridge, *Mambu: A Melanesian Millennium* (London: Methuen, 1960).

29. In this connection, see John J. Collins, "Teacher and Servant," *Revue d'histoire et de philosophie religiuses*, 80 (2000): 37–50.

30. See Devorah Dimant, "The History of the Qumran Community in Light of New Developments," in eadem, *History, Ideology and Bible Interpretation in the Dead Sea Scrolls* (FAT 90; Tübingen: Mohr Siebeck, 2014), 241n98:

> [Wise's] late date ... is not in accordance with the older dating of major sectarian texts (such as the *Rule of the Community* and 1QS, being dated to 100 BCE), or with other data culled from the scrolls. Also notable is the fact that the scrolls contain no historical allusions subsequent to the conquest of the land of Israel by Pompey in 63 BCE (referred to by the *Pesher of Nahum*, 4Q169 3–4 ii).

nonetheless.[31] More significant for our purposes are several difficulties with Wise's account of messianism. Wise classifies the Teacher of Righteousness as a messiah in the sense specified by his Weberian model of crisis cults. At the level of exegesis, however, not only does the first-person voice of the Teacher Hymns not self-identify as a "messiah," in fact none of the Hodayot contains any references to a messiah, even in the third person. Equally importantly, the Teacher of Righteousness is never called a messiah in any of the manuscripts in which he appears. Indeed, in CD, at least, both the Teacher and one or more messiahs appear as demonstrably different characters. One might appeal, as Wise does, to a redaction-critical scenario in which, in the *Urtext* of CD, the Teacher of Righteousness and the messiah were identical, but in a later redaction they were reimagined as two separate figures.[32] There is no textual evidence for such a scenario, however, only speculative reconstruction, which in this instance amounts to special pleading.[33] In short, Wise's identification of the first messiah, although clever and inventive, is finally unconvincing.

The Quest à la Israel Knohl, Part 1

At first contemporaneously with Wise, and then further subsequently, Israel Knohl has made his own case for a "messiah before Jesus," appealing to some of the same and also some other primary texts and identifying a different historical figure. Beginning with his 2000 book *The Messiah before Jesus*, Knohl has argued that a category of "catastrophic messianism" (adapted from Gershom Scholem's taxonomy)[34] emerged in the Jewish revolt following the death of Herod the Great

---

Admittedly, the majority second-century BCE date for the Teacher is not as secure as it used to be, but no alternative date is any more secure. On both of these points, see John J. Collins, "The Time of the Teacher: An Old Debate Renewed," in *Studies in the Hebrew Bible, Qumran, and the Septuagint Presented to Eugene Ulrich* (ed. Peter W. Flint et al.; VTSup 101; Leiden: Brill, 2006), 212–29.

31. Thus rightly Newsom, *Self as Symbolic Space*, 287–346; and Angela Kim Harkins, "Who Is the Teacher of the Teacher Hymns? Re-examining the Teacher Hymns Hypothesis Fifty Years Later," in *A Teacher for All Generations*, 1:449–67.

32. Thus, for example, Philip R. Davies, *The Damascus Covenant: An Interpretation of the "Damascus Document"* (JSOTSup 25; Sheffield: JSOT, 1983); idem, "The Teacher of Righteousness and the End of Days," *RevQ* 13 (1988): 313–17.

33. Thus rightly John J. Collins, review of Philip R. Davies, *The Damascus Covenant*, in *JBL* 104 (1985): 530–33.

34. See Scholem, "Messianic Idea," 7: "Jewish Messianism is in its origins and by its nature—this cannot be sufficiently emphasized—a theory of catastrophe. This theory stresses the revolutionary, cataclysmic element in the transition from every historical present to the Messianic future."

in 4 BCE in connection with the career of Menahem the Essene, whom Knohl identifies as the messiah of the Qumran community.[35] This ideological development, in turn, provided Jesus and the apostles with a ready-made model for interpreting the life and death of Jesus. Knohl states his thesis as follows:

> I propose to show that Jesus really did regard himself as the Messiah and truly expected the Messiah to be rejected, killed, and resurrected after three days, for this is precisely what was believed to have happened to a messianic leader who had lived one generation before Jesus. . . . Thus, for the first time in the history of Judaism, a conception emerged of "catastrophic" messianism in which the humiliation, rejection, and death of the Messiah were regarded as an inseparable part of the redemptive process. The hero of our book, this slain Messiah, is the missing link in our understanding of the way Christianity emerged from Judaism.[36]

Knohl's argument is built on the collocation of a number of ancient texts that might otherwise appear to be unrelated. The centerpiece is the much-discussed Self-Glorification Hymn from Qumran, cited at the beginning of this chapter, whose anonymous first-person speaker Knohl takes to be the messiah of the Qumran community:

> . . . [for]ever a mighty throne in the congregation of the gods [כסא עוז בעדת אלים]. None of the ancient kings shall sit in it, and their nobles shall not . . . be like my glory, and none shall be exalted save me, nor shall come against me. For I have taken my seat in his [throne] in the heavens and none . . . . I shall be reckoned with the gods [אני עם אלים אתחשב] and established in the holy congregation. I do not desire as would a man of flesh . . . everything precious to me is in the glory of [the gods in the dwelli]ng place. Who has been despised on my account? And who can be compared with me in my glory [ומיא בכבדי]? . . . Who be[ars all] griefs as I do? And who [suff]ers evil like me? . . . And any teaching will not be equal to [my teaching] . . . . Who will stop me from speaking? And who shall measure the flow of my speech, and who shall be my equal and be like me in my judgment? For I shall be reckoned with the gods [כיא אניא עם אלים אחשב], and my glory with [that of] the king's sons. (4Q491 frg. 11)[37]

---

35. Knohl, *Messiah before Jesus*.

36. Knohl, *Messiah before Jesus*, 2–3.

37. Text ed. Eshel, "Self-Glorification Hymn"; trans. mod.

Knohl's identification of the first-person speaker is not uncontroversial. Maurice Baillet, who edited the first manuscript of the hymn in 1972, suggested that the speaker is the archangel Michael.[38] Against this hypothesis, Morton Smith famously objected that an archangel would have no reason to boast of his place among the gods, so that the Hymn must represent the point of view of a translated human being.[39] The secondary literature since the 1980s has seen these proposals persist, and others join their ranks, as well. Florentino García Martínez has defended the angel hypothesis against the criticisms of Smith and others,[40] whereas James Davila, like Smith, has interpreted the hymn as a report of a mystical ascent experienced by the anonymous author.[41] Rather differently, Crispin Fletcher-Louis reads the Hymn as an account of apotheosis as experienced by a priest presiding over the community's liturgy.[42] Proposals for fictive speakers, especially, have multiplied. Martin Abegg proposes that the literary "I"—but not the actual author—of the Hymn is the Teacher of Righteousness.[43] Esther Eshel identifies the speaker as the mythical High Priest of Qumran eschatology (1QSb), who is not himself

---

38. Based in part on the clever suggestion that the line מי כמוני באלים, "Who is like me among the gods?" is a midrash on the name מיכאל, "Who is like god?" see Maurice Baillet, "Les manuscrits de la Règle de Guerre de la grotte 4 de Qumrân," *RB* 79 (1972): 217–26; and subsequently idem, *Qumrân Grotte 4:3 (4Q482– 4Q520)* (DJD 7; Oxford: Clarendon, 1982).

39. Morton Smith, "Ascent to the Heavens and Deification in 4QMª," in *Archaeology and History in the Dead Sea Scrolls* (ed. Lawrence H. Schiffman; Sheffield: JSOT Press, 1990), 181–88; idem, "Two Ascended to Heaven: Jesus and the Author of 4Q491," in *Jesus and the Dead Sea Scrolls* (ed. James H. Charlesworth; New York, N.Y.: Doubleday, 1991), 290–301. Smith considers and rejects the hypothesis that the translated human speaker is the Teacher of Righteousness himself, writing, "It is probably better to suppose that the Dead Sea group or groups produced more than one preposterous poet with an exaggerated notion of his own sanctity" ("Two Ascended to Heaven," 298).

40. Florentino García Martínez, "Old Texts and Modern Mirages: The 'I' of Two Qumran Hymns," *ETL* 78 (2002): 321–29; repr. in idem, *Qumranica Minora I: Qumran Origins and Apocalypticism* (ed. Eibert J. C. Tigchelaar; STDJ 63; Leiden: Brill, 2007), 105–25.

41. James R. Davila, "Heavenly Ascents in the Dead Sea Scrolls," in *The Dead Sea Scrolls after Fifty Years: A Comprehensive Assessment* (2 vols.; ed. Peter W. Flint and James C. VanderKam; Leiden: Brill, 1998), 2:461–85.

42. Crispin H. T. Fletcher-Louis, *All the Glory of Adam: Liturgical Anthropology in the Dead Sea Scrolls* (STDJ 42; Leiden: Brill, 2002), 199–216. Similar but more subtle is the interpretation of Philip Alexander, *The Mystical Texts: Songs of the Sabbath Sacrifice and Related Manuscripts* (CQS; London: T. & T. Clark, 2006), 89–91.

43. Martin Abegg, "Who Ascended to Heaven? 4Q491, 4Q427, and the Teacher of Righteousness," in *Eschatology, Messianism, and the Dead Sea Scrolls* (ed. Craig A. Evans and Peter W. Flint; Grand Rapids, Mich.: Eerdmans, 1997), 61–73.

the Teacher of Righteousness but is modeled after him.[44] Eric Miller identifies the speaker of the Hymn as the literary figure of the translated Enoch, a human being who gains a place among the gods in the *Book of the Watchers*.[45] Menahem Kister has recently interpreted the Hymn as a speech on the lips of the personified figure of divine wisdom, such as we find in Prov 8.[46] John Collins, like Eshel, suggests that the speaker is perhaps one of the mythical *dramatis personae* of Qumran eschatology, perhaps the eschatological high priest (1QSb) or the teacher at the end of days (CD 6:11).[47] But Collins also, like Emile Puech before him, concedes the question may finally be unanswerable, at least on the basis of the extant text.[48]

Knohl is not the first to suggest that the speaker of the Self-Glorification Hymn might be a messiah,[49] but he is the first to identify this hypothetical messiah–psalmist further with a particular figure known to us from external history. Highlighting the phrase אני ידיד המלך, "I am a friend of the king" in the Hymn (4Q471b [frgs. 1–2], line 7), Knohl suggests an identification with the first-century BCE Essene leader Menahem, who, according to Josephus, prophesied the accession of Herod the Great (thus "friend of the king"). At the relevant place in *Antiquities* book 15, Josephus relates a story explaining why Herod had a reputation for favoring the Essene sect:

> There was a certain Essene named Menahem, whose virtue was attested in his whole conduct of life and especially in his having from God a foreknowledge of the future. This man had once observed Herod, then still a boy, going to his teacher, and greeted him as "king of the Jews."
> ... At the moment Herod paid very little attention to his words, for he was quite lacking in such hopes, but after gradually being advanced to

---

44. Esther Eshel, "The Identification of the 'Speaker' of the Self-Glorification Hymn," in *The Provo International Conference on the Dead Sea Scrolls: Technological Innovations, New Texts, and Reformulated Issues* (ed. Donald W. Parry and Eugene Ulrich; STDJ 30; Leiden: Brill, 1999), 619–35. Similarly Peter Schäfer, *The Origins of Jewish Mysticism* (Tübingen: Mohr Siebeck, 2009), 146–54.

45. Eric Miller, "The Self-Glorification Hymn Reexamined," *Hen* 31 (2009): 307–24.

46. Menahem Kister, "Divine and Heavenly Figures in the Dead Sea Scrolls," unpublished paper from the Fourteenth International Orion Symposium (Jerusalem, 2013).

47. Collins, *Scepter*, 159.

48. Collins, *Scepter*, 163. Similarly Emile Puech, *La croyance des Esséniens en la vie future: Immortalité, résurrection, vie éternelle?* (EB 21–22; Paris: Gabalda, 1993), 494.

49. For an earlier proposal to the same effect, see Martin Hengel, "'Sit at My Right Hand!' The Enthronement of Christ at the Right Hand of God and Psalm 110:1," in idem, *Studies in Early Christology* (Edinburgh: T. & T. Clark, 1995 [German original, 1993]), 119–225 at 203.

kingship and good fortune, when he was at the height of his power, he sent for Menahem and questioned him about the length of time he would reign. Menahem said nothing at all. In the face of his silence Herod asked further whether he had ten years more to reign, and the other replied that he had twenty or even thirty, but he did not set a limit to the appointed time. Herod, however, was satisfied even with this answer and dismissed Menahem with a friendly gesture. And from that time on he continued to hold all Essenes in honour. (Josephus, *Ant.* 15.373–78)[50]

Knohl then further identifies Josephus's Essene Menahem with Menahem the predecessor of Shammai spoken of in *m. Hag.* 16b: יצא מנחם ונכנס שמאי, "Menahem went forth, and Shammai entered."[51] In other words, Menahem demitted office, and Shammai succeeded him as head of the Beit Din.[52] The gemara in *b. Hag.* 16b inquires about Menahem's going forth:

Where did he go? Abaye said: He went forth into evil courses [לתרבות רעה]. Raba said: He went forth to the king's service [לעבודת המלך]. Thus it is also taught: Menahem went forth to the king's service, and there went forth with him eighty pairs of disciples dressed in silk garments [סירייקון].[53]

It is not clear from the context to what "going forth to the king's service" refers, but Knohl, harmonizing with Josephus, takes the phrase as an oblique reference to the court of Herod the Great.

Abaye's ominous comment about Menahem going out into evil courses finds a parallel in *y. Hag.* 2:2, which comments on the mishnah "Menahem went forth" thusly:

Where did he go? Some say that he went from one set of principles to another. And some say that he turned around and went out; he and

50. Trans. mod. from H. St. J. Thackeray in the LCL.

51. This identification has venerable precedent, for example, in Graetz, *History*, 2:100–1. There is, however, no positive evidence in its favor, as rightly noted by Jacob Neusner, *The Rabbinic Traditions about the Pharisees before 70* (3 vols.; Leiden: Brill, 1971), 1:185:

> Hoenig identifies Menahem [in *m. Hag.* 2:2] with Menahem ben Signai of M. 'Ed. 7:8. Others have found our Menahem in Menahem b. Judah, the Galilean Sicarius, and Menahem the Essene, both mentioned by Josephus. I see no merit in any of these guesses. So far as I can see, the Menahem of M. Hag. 2:2 appears only there. We do not gain much by supplying him with new patronymics and identities.

52. On this succession, see Sidney B. Hoenig, "Menahem, Hillel's First Associate," *Bitzaron* 52 (1964–1965): 87–96 (in Hebrew).

53. Text from and trans. mod. from Soncino.

eighty pairs of rabbinic disciples clad in golden armor [or: garments],[54] with faces black as the side of a pot. For they had said to them: Write on an ox's horn that you have no share in the God of Israel. (*y. Hag.* 2:2)[55]

The end of this passage is an excommunication scene; Menahem and his disciples are ritually cast out of the Jewish community. The Yerushalmi gives no reason for their excommunication, but Knohl points, first, to their armor (תירקי) as an ostensible sign of participation in the revolt of 4 BCE and, second, to the nearby passage in *m. Hag.* 2:1 that forbids expounding on the esoteric doctrines of creation (מעשה בראשית) and the divine presence (מרכבה).[56] Menahem, Knohl concludes, must have declared himself to be the messiah son of God, thereby offending against God's honor, and subsequently died in the revolt while trying to establish his messianic kingdom.

The final layer of Knohl's argument is an appeal to several instances of the name Menahem in later Jewish and Christian legend about the messiah. His earliest piece of evidence comes from the farewell discourse of the Gospel of John, where Jesus promises the disciples, "I will ask of the father, and he will give you another comforter [ἄλλον παράκλητον δώσει ὑμῖν], to be with you forever" (John 14:16). And again, "The comforter [ὁ παράκλητος], the holy spirit, whom the father will send in my name, he will teach you all things, and

---

54. *y. Hag.* 2:2 reads תירקי, "armor"; cf. סיריקון, "silk garments" (a loan-word from Greek σηρικόν), in the parallel passage in *b. Hag.* 16b noted earlier. See the discussion of Taylor, *Essenes*, 192:

> This tradition has been read by Israel Knohl … with a reading of the Hebrew as indicating that the disciples were wearing shining armour, leading him to suppose wrongly that there was a militaristic (even Messianic) interest on the part of Menahem. The Hebrew is, however, very unlikely to mean "shining armour"; instead, there seems to be a disparagement of the disciples of Menahem for wearing extremely fine clothing.

55. Trans mine. This passage has a parallel in the medieval midrash *Midr. Song Zuta* 8:14, which begins, "In the days of Menahem and Hillel, when there was a dispute between them and Menahem went forth…," whence Knohl concludes that Hillel himself excommunicated Menahem for messianic heresy (*Messiah before Jesus*, 62–66). The text of *Midr. Song Zuta* is given in the editions of S. Buber, *Midrasch Suta* (Berlin: Mekize Nirdamim, 1894) and Solomon Schechter, *Agadath Shir HaShirim* (Cambridge: Bell, 1896).

56. *m. Hag.* 2:1:

> The forbidden degrees may not be expounded before three persons, nor the Story of Creation before two, nor [the chapter of] the Chariot before one alone, unless he is a Sage that understands his own knowledge. Whosoever gives his mind to four things it were better for him if he had not come into the world—what is above? what is beneath? what was beforetime? and what will be hereafter? And whosoever takes no thought for the honour of his Maker, it were better for him if he had not come into the world. (trans. Danby)

bring to your remembrance all that I have said to you" (John 14:26).[57] Knohl finds in the semantic equivalency of Hebrew מנחם, "comforter," with Greek παράκλητος, "comforter," the proverbial smoking gun.[58] On his reading, Jesus, a messiah after the pattern of Menahem, promises that when he departs, God will send yet another messiah, another Menahem, to shepherd his people.

This then dovetails, for Knohl, with the several references in the Talmud to Menahem as the name of the messiah who is to come, such as the story in *y. Ber.* 2:4:

> It happened that a certain Jew was plowing when his cow lowed. A certain Arab was passing by and heard its sound. "Oh Jew, oh Jew," he said, "Unharness your cow and disengage your plow, for the temple has been destroyed." It lowed a second time. "Oh Jew, oh Jew," he said, "Harness your cow and engage your plow, for the king messiah has been born." The Jew asked, "What is his name?" "Menahem," he said. "And what is his father's name?" he asked. "Hezekiah," he said. "Where is he from?" he asked. "From the royal city, Bethlehem in Judah," he said. (*y. Ber.* 2:4)[59]

Or again in *b. Sanh.* 98b, where several rabbinic schools debate among themselves what the name of the messiah will be. Some say Shiloh, some say Yinnon, some say Haninah, but some say: "His name is Menahem ben Hezekiah, for it is written, *For a comforter* [מנחם, Menahem] *is far from me, one to revive my courage* [Lam 1:16]" (*b. Sanh.* 98b).[60] On Knohl's account, these talmudic stories, like Jesus's promise of the παράκλητος in John 14, betray the origins of the messianic idea in the brief, glorious career of Menahem the Essene, the messiah of Qumran.[61]

Knohl's argument is admittedly ingenious, but the intertextual connections are simply too many and too tenuous. Josephus's Menahem the Essene is never

---

57. On which passage see Sigmund Mowinckel, "Die Vorstellungen des Spätjudentums vom heiligen Geist als Fürsprecher johanneische Paraklet," *ZNW* 32 (1933): 97–130; Raymond E. Brown, "The Paraclete in the Fourth Gospel," *NTS* 13 (1966–1967): 113–32.

58. Here Knohl was anticipated by Abraham Geiger, "Menachem, der Messias, der Paraklet, der heilige Geist," *JZWL* 8 (1870): 35–43, on which see Susannah Heschel, *Abraham Geiger and the Jewish Jesus* (CSHJ; Chicago, Ill.: University of Chicago Press, 1998), 180–81.

59. Trans. Himmelfarb, "Mother of the Messiah."

60. My trans. On this passage, see Michael Fishbane, "Midrash and Messianism: Some Theologies of Suffering and Salvation," in *Toward the Millennium*, 57–71.

61. Gressmann, *Messias*, 458–62, makes a structurally similar argument, but for him the generative figure is a different Menahem: Menahem b. Judah b. Hezekiah, the Galilean insurgent operative in the mid-first century CE (discussed in Chapter 6 in this volume).

called a messiah,[62] nor is he ever connected in the primary texts with the community at Qumran. As for the Qumran scrolls, neither the first-person speaker of the Self-Glorification Hymn nor the first-person speaker of the Hodayot Teacher Hymns is ever called a messiah. The figure who is called a messiah in the Damascus Document is a character in an eschatological drama, not a member of the community. As for the rabbinic texts, there is no evidence for identifying Menahem the predecessor of Shammai with Josephus's Menahem the Essene, aside from the shared personal name, nor is there any evidence that Menahem's "going out" had anything to do with a messianic heresy. As for the name Menahem in later legend, Knohl's appeal to the παράκλητος in John 14 requires a primitive, Semitic-language Johannine tradition for which there is no positive evidence; and the talmudic trope that the messiah's name is Menahem is more economically understood as a midrash than a historical memory (cf. *b. Sanh.* 98b citing Lam 1:16). The credulity required to connect all these dots is more than can reasonably be asked of a reader.

The Quest à la Israel Knohl, Part 2

The publication in 2007 of an apparently ancient Hebrew text written in ink on a limestone slab provided another layer to Knohl's theory of the origins of catastrophic messianism.[63] The text, called *Hazon Gabriel* or the *Gabriel Revelation* after its fragmentary contents, is unprovenanced and therefore of questionable authenticity.[64] The format of ink on limestone, although not unprecedented, is unusual enough to raise questions pertinent to the authenticity debate. Even so, the initial paleographical assessment of Yardeni and Elizur, a subsequent microarcheological analysis by Yuval Goren, and linguistic analyses of Moshe Bar-Asher and Gary Rendsburg all

---

62. Of course, Josephus never calls anyone a messiah, except perhaps Jesus of Nazareth. On this puzzle, see Chapter 4 in this volume.

63. The *editio princeps* is Ada Yardeni and Binyamin Elizur, "A Prophetic Text on Stone from the First Century BCE: First Publication," *Cathedra* 123 (2007): 155–66 (in Hebrew); ET "A Hebrew Prophetic Text on Stone from the Early Herodian Period: A Preliminary Report," in *Hazon Gabriel: New Readings of the Gabriel Revelation* (ed. Matthias Henze; Atlanta, Ga.: SBL, 2011), 11–29. A more recent edition incorporating a number of improved readings is Elisha Qimron and Alexey Yuditsky, "Notes on the Inscription 'The Vision of Gabriel,'" *Cathedra* 133 (2009): 133–44 (in Hebrew); ET "Notes on the So-Called *Gabriel Vision* Inscription," in *Hazon Gabriel*, 31–38.

64. The owner of the stone, Swiss collector David Jeselsohn, relates the story of its acquisition from Jordanian antiquities dealer Ghassan Rihani in David Jeselsohn, "The Jeselsohn Stone: Discovery and Publication," in *Hazon Gabriel*, 1–9.

agree in dating the stone and its text to the late Second-Temple period, first century BCE or first century CE.[65]

It is hard to make out a flow of thought in the lacunose text, but the language is reminiscent of biblical vision or prophecy (hence the designation *Hazon Gabriel*). Yardeni and Elizur summarize

> The text is very fragmentary, but it seems to be a collection of short prophecies dictated to a scribe, in a manner similar to prophecies appearing in the Hebrew Bible. . . .. The text is written in the first person, possibly by someone calling himself Gabriel [lines 77, 80, 83] . . . and is addressed to someone in the second person singular.[66]

The first legible lines read roughly as follows:

> YHWH you ask me, thus said the Lord of Hosts . . . the house of Israel and I will recount the greatness of Jerusalem. Thus said YHWH the God of Israel: Soon all the nations fight against Jerusalem and . . . One, two, three, four. The prophets and the elders and the pious ones. David, my servant, asked me: Answer me, I ask you for the sign. . . (lines 11–17)

And the several much-discussed lines near the end of the extant text as follows: "Who are you? I am Gabriel . . . you shall save them. A prophet and a shepherd will save you. I ask from you three shepherds, three prophets. In three days the sign will be given. I am Gabriel. . ." (lines 77–80).[67]

In a series of publications from 2007 to the present,[68] Knohl has argued that *Hazon Gabriel* provides additional, independent attestation for the emergence of a catastrophic model of messianism among Palestinian Jews in the

---

65. See Yardeni and Elizur, "Hebrew Prophetic Text"; Yuval Goren, "Micromorphologic Analysis of the Gabriel Revelation Stone," *IEJ* 58 (2008): 220–29; Moshe Bar-Asher, "On the Language of 'The Vision of Gabriel,'" *RevQ* 23 (2008): 491–524; Gary A. Rendsburg, "Linguistic and Stylistic Notes to the Hazon Gabriel Inscription," *DSD* 16 (2009): 107–16.

66. Yardeni and Elizur, "Hebrew Prophetic Text," 17.

67. Trans. mod. from Qimron and Yuditsky, "Notes on the So-Called *Gabriel Vision*."

68. Israel Knohl, "Studies in the Gabriel Revelation," *Tarbiz* 76 (2007): 303–28 (in Hebrew); idem, "'By Three Days, Live': Messiahs, Resurrection, and Ascent to Heaven in Hazon Gabriel," *JR* 88 (2008): 147–58; idem, "The Messiah Son of Joseph: 'Gabriel's Revelation' and the Birth of a New Messianic Model," *BAR* 34 (2008): 58–62, 78; idem, *Messiahs and Resurrection*; idem, "The Apocalyptic and Messianic Dimensions of the Gabriel Revelation in Their Historical Context," in *Hazon Gabriel*, 39–59.

wake of the revolt of 4 BCE.[69] In particular, Knohl argues that the text provides first-century BCE evidence for, first, the idea of a suffering messiah ben Joseph (or messiah ben Ephraim) and, second, the idea of a messiah rising from the dead after three days. The first claim rests on Knohl's transcription of lines 16–17: עבדי דוד בקש מן לפני אפרים וישים האות, "My servant David, ask of Ephraim that he place the sign."[70] Here, according to Knohl, the archangel Gabriel petitions the messiah ben David to ask the messiah ben Joseph to place a sign heralding final redemption. This sign, Knohl suggests, is the messiah ben Joseph's own blood,[71] which becomes the premise for Knohl's second controversial interpretive claim.

In his articles from 2007 to 2009 and in his 2009 monograph, Knohl transcribes line 80 of the stone to read לשלושת ימין חאיה, "By three days, live."[72] This Knohl takes to be an imperative spoken by Gabriel to the messiah ben Joseph, raising him from the dead on the third day by divine fiat. This transcription, however, has met with considerable resistance. In the *editio princeps*, Yardeni and Elizur transcribe the last word in the clause חא.., declaring the initial ח uncertain and the third and fourth characters illegible.[73] In a 2009 article, Ronald Hendel proposes the reading האות ("the sign") in place of Knohl's חאיה ("live");[74] and Qimron and Yuditsky corroborate this reading in their 2009 edition.[75] Notably, in his 2011 essay, Knohl concedes that Hendel and Qimron and Yuditsky may indeed have the better reading: "I now accept the reading האות ('the sign')." But he continues, "I still maintain that the reading חאיה ('live') is

---

69. Knohl, *Messiahs and Resurrection*, xii:

> The rebellion, which originated in Jerusalem and quickly spread throughout the country, was brutally crushed by the Roman Army under the command of Varus, Legate of Syria. . . . Apparently, *The Gabriel Revelation* was composed in response to the Roman army's brutal suppression of the rebellion. Its author, seeking to raise the spirits of the people, announces that redemption is at hand.

70. See Knohl, "Apocalyptic and Messianic Dimensions," 43, 54.

71. Knohl, *Messiahs and Resurrection*, 45:

> The "prince of princes" in *The Gabriel Revelation* is an earthly leader of Israel, probably a messianic leader, who was killed by the enemy. This slain leader conforms to a high degree with the image of biblical Ephraim, a warrior, suffering son of God. If this understanding of "Ephraim" is true, then Ephraim's "sign" can be understood to be his own blood. It is only after the messianic leader is killed and his blood is placed as a sign that the process of redemption can begin.

72. See Knohl, *Messiahs and Resurrection*, 26–27, 97–100.

73. Yardeni and Elizur, "Hebrew Prophetic Stone," 15.

74. Ronald Hendel, "The Messiah Son of Joseph: Simply 'Sign,'" *BAR* 35 (2009): 8.

75. Qimron and Yuditsky, "Notes on the So-Called *Gabriel Vision*," 32, 37.

possible graphically."[76] Knohl may or may not yield on the question of third-day resurrection, but in any case he steadfastly maintains that *Hazon Gabriel* attests the messiah ben Joseph motif already in the first century BCE, early enough to provide the apostles, and indeed Jesus himself, with the model of a suffering messiah.[77]

As with Knohl's earlier argument regarding Menahem the Essene, problems arise. For one thing, it is possible that *Hazon Gabriel* is not even authentic. But, granting for the sake of argument that it is authentic,[78] both of the transcriptions on which Knohl's hypothesis depends—אפרים in line 16 and חאיה in line 80—are at least questionable and, according to all the paleographers who have treated the text, actually mistaken.[79] Moreover, even if Knohl's transcriptions are right, his interpretations do not necessarily follow. This problem is particularly acute with respect to the matter of the identity of Ephraim. Knohl takes Ephraim in *Hazon Gabriel* to be identical with the dying messiah ben Joseph of rabbinic legend, who first appears in *b. Sukkah* 52a:[80]

> *The land shall mourn, each family by itself; the family of the house of David by itself, and their wives by themselves* [Zech 12:12]. . . . What is the cause of the mourning? R. Dosa and the rabbis differ on the point. One explained: The cause is the slaying of messiah ben Joseph. The other explained: The cause is the slaying of the evil inclination. It is well according to him

---

76. Knohl, "Apocalyptic and Messianic Dimensions," 43n12.

77. The majority view is that the messiah ben Joseph myth is a late antique development, perhaps an *ex eventu* interpretation of the Bar Kokhba war (see the discussion in Chapter 6 in this volume). A few scholars have tried in vain to date the myth to the Second-Temple period, although not, as Knohl does, by tying it to a particular historical figure. See especially David C. Mitchell, "Rabbi Dosa and the Rabbis Differ: Messiah ben Joseph in the Babylonian Talmud," *RRJ* 8 (2005): 77–90; idem, "The Fourth Deliverer: A Josephite Messiah in 4Q175," *Bib* 86 (2005): 545–53; idem, "Firstborn *Shor* and *Rem*: A Sacrificial Josephite Messiah in *1 Enoch* 90.37–38 and Deuteronomy 33.17," *JSP* 15 (2006): 211–28; idem, "Messiah bar Ephraim in the Targums," *ArSt* 4 (2006): 221–41; idem, "Messiah ben Joseph: A Sacrifice of Atonement for Israel," *RRJ* 10 (2007): 77–94; idem, "A Dying and Rising Josephite Messiah in 4Q372," *JSP* (2008): 181–205. Boyarin (*Jewish Gospels*, 129–56) argues that the idea that the messiah must suffer—but not the idea of a second, dying Ephraimite messiah—was current already in the Second-Temple period.

78. With John J. Collins, "Gabriel and David: Some Reflections on an Enigmatic Text," in *Hazon Gabriel*, 99–112 at 100: "Since the experts who have examined it are satisfied . . . we must proceed on the assumption that it is authentic until proven otherwise."

79. Regarding Knohl's אפרים in line 16, Yardeni and Elizur declare the second character uncertain, suggesting פ and מ as possibilities, and Qimron and Yuditsky read אמרים, from the verb אמר, "say."

80. On this identification, see further Israel Knohl, "On 'the Son of God,' Armilus, and Messiah Son of Joseph," *Tarbiz* 68 (1998): 13–38 (in Hebrew).

who explains that the cause is the slaying of messiah ben Joseph, since that well agrees with the scripture: *When they look on him whom they have pierced, they shall mourn for him as one mourns for an only child, and weep bitterly over him as one weeps over a firstborn* [Zech 12:10]. (*b. Sukkah 52a*)[81]

This talmudic messiah ben Joseph is indeed slain—but, importantly, not raised from the dead—but he is never called Ephraim.

There is a messiah actually named Ephraim in the ninth-century midrashic collection *Pesikta Rabbati* (at homilies 34, 36, and 37).[82] But, as Michael Fishbane and Peter Schäfer have shown, this Ephraim is the messiah ben David himself, not a different, dying messiah.[83] There is, furthermore, a messiah bar Ephraim mentioned in several late ancient Targumim.[84] (His patronym parallels the talmudic messiah ben Joseph, but, problematically for Knohl's thesis, not the simple name Ephraim in *Hazon Gabriel* or, for that matter, *Pesikta Rabbati*.) This messiah bar Ephraim appears by himself at *Tg. Ps.-J.* Exod 40:11 and alongside the messiah bar David at *Tg. Song* 4:5; 7:4. Unlike the messiah ben Joseph of the Talmud, however, the messiah bar Ephraim of the Targum

---

81. Trans. mod. from Soncino. On this passage, see my discussion in Chapter 6 in this volume.

82. See *Pes. Rab.* 36:1:

> In that hour all princely counterparts of the nations will say to Him: Master of the universe, who is this through whose power we are to be swallowed up? What is his name? What kind of a being is he? The Holy One, blessed be He, will reply: He is the messiah, and his name is Ephraim, my true messiah, who will pull himself up straight and will pull up straight his generation, and who will give light to the eyes of Israel and deliver his people.

Pes. Rab. 36:2:

> It was because of the ordeal of the son of David that David wept, saying, *My strength is dried up like a potsherd* [Ps 22:16]. During the ordeal of the son of David, the Holy One, blessed be He, will say to him: Ephraim, my true messiah, long ago, ever since the six days of creation, you took this ordeal upon yourself.

And *Pes. Rab.* 37:1: "In the month of Nisan the patriarchs will arise and say to the messiah: Ephraim, our true messiah, even though we are your forebears, you are greater than we, because you suffered for the iniquities of our children, and terrible ordeals befell you" (trans. mod. from William G. Braude, *Pesikta Rabbati* [2 vols.; YJS 18; New Haven, Conn.: Yale University Press, 1968]).

83. Fishbane, "Midrash and Messianism," especially 65; Schäfer, *Jewish Jesus*, 236–71, especially 237. Why only here the messiah ben David has the name Ephraim is a puzzle. Nachman Krochmal speculated that there may have been a contemporary messianic claimant, otherwise unknown to us, by the name of Ephraim, whose career lay behind the messianic homilies in *Pesikta Rabbati* (*The Writings of Nachman Krochmal* [ed. Simon Rawidowicz; London: Ararat, 1961], 255 [in Hebrew]).

84. On whom see Levey, *Messiah*, 15–16, 142–44.

does not suffer and die. The one tantalizing exception is a marginal note in Codex Reuchlinianus (Sperber's manuscript F) that purports to give a reading from the lost Targum Yerushalmi on Zech 12:10:

> And I shall cause to rest upon the house of David and upon the inhabitants of Jerusalem the spirit of prophecy and true prayer. And afterwards the messiah son of Ephraim will go out to do battle with Gog, and Gog will kill him in front of the gate of Jerusalem. And they will look to me and will inquire from me why the nations pierced the messiah son of Ephraim. And they will mourn for him just as a father and mother mourn for an only son, and they will lament for him just as they lament for a firstborn.[85]

This targum is obviously extremely close to the interpretation of Zech 12:10 in *b. Sukkah* 52a, but with "messiah son of Ephraim" in place of "messiah son of Joseph," which perhaps gets us almost to the hypothesis of a single Ephraimite–Josephite suffering messiah myth.

There is only one text, as far as I know, that actually attests both names, Ephraim and Joseph, with reference to a messiah—namely, the early seventh-century CE apocalypse *Sefer Zerubbabel*,[86] which reads:

> Concealed there [in Naphtali] as well is a man whose name is Nehemiah ben Hushiel ben Ephraim ben Joseph. . . . The Lord's messiah, Nehemiah ben Hushiel . . . will collect all Israel together as one entity and they will remain for [four] years in Jerusalem, [where] the children of Israel will offer sacrifice, and it will be pleasing to the Lord. . . . [But in the last battle, Armilus] will come against the holy people of the Most High, and with him there will be ten kings wielding great power and force, and he will do battle with the holy ones. He will prevail over them and will kill the messiah of the lineage of Joseph, Nehemiah ben Hushiel, and will also kill sixteen righteous ones alongside him. (*Sefer Zerubbabel*)[87]

Here in *Sefer Zerubbabel*, finally, the several strands of this putative myth seem to come together in a single text (and with many other strands, besides, but

---

85. Trans. Robert P. Gordon, "Messianism in Ancient Bible Translations in Aramaic and Syriac," in *Redemption and Resistance*, 262–73 at 269. Text in Alexander Sperber, ed., *The Bible in Aramaic*, vol. 3: *The Latter Prophets according to Targum Jonathan* (Leiden: Brill, 1962), 495.

86. On which see Chapter 1 in this volume.

87. Trans. Reeves, *Trajectories*, 40–66.

those would take us too far afield.)[88] But this is more than six hundred years after *Hazon Gabriel*, if the latter is authentic, and even on the most charitable reading the parallels are very inexact.

Thus far the problems with the identity of Ephraim, which is the main issue, but there are other problems, as well. Even if חאיה, "live," is the right reading in line 80 (which Knohl himself now doubts), this need not suggest resurrection from the dead, because that interpretation depends on Knohl's thinly supported speculation that the "sign" of line 17 is Ephraim's blood. And in any case, none of the figures in *Hazon Gabriel* is ever called a messiah. (Here, again, I note the too easy slippage between ancient lexeme and modern construct.) In sum, Knohl's argument for a first messiah, a pre-Christian template for the Jesus messiah movement, founders on the same kind of objections that Wise's does. In the end, there is simply too great a gap between the available evidence on the one hand and their respective claims on the other.

A Misguided Quest

Having now looked in some detail at the modern quest for the first messiah, what conclusions can we draw? The first thing to say is that the several "first messiah" hypotheses are not borne out by the particular evidence adduced, as I have tried to show.[89] In this judgment, I am by no means alone. Dupont-Sommer's interpretation of *Pesher Habakkuk* was ably rebutted already by Jean Carmignac in 1960 and by Gert Jeremias in 1963.[90] And in 1998, working with a greatly expanded corpus of scrolls, Johannes Zimmerman argued decisively against the suggestion that the Teacher of Righteousness was himself the messiah of the Qumran community.[91] Since the year 2000, Knohl's and Wise's respective interpretations of the Damascus Document, the Hodayot,

---

88. See further Martha Himmelfarb, "Sefer Zerubbabel," in *Rabbinic Fantasies: Imaginative Narratives from Classical Hebrew Literature* (ed. David Stern and Mark J. Mirsky; New Haven, Conn.: Yale University Press, 1990), 67–90; eadem, "*Sefer Zerubbabel* and Popular Religion," in *A Teacher for All Generations*, 2:621–34.

89. Admittedly, there are some who would disagree with me and declare the quest successful, for example, James D. Tabor, "Are You the One? The Textual Dynamics of Messianic Self-Identity," in *Knowing the End from the Beginning: The Prophetic, the Apocalyptic, and Their Relationships* (ed. Lester L. Grabbe and Robert D. Haak; LSTS 46; London: T. & T. Clark, 2003), 179–90.

90. J. J. Carmignac, "Les citations de l'Ancien Testament et spécialement des Poèmes du Serviteur dans les Hymnes de Qumrân," *RevQ* 2 (1960): 357–94; Gert Jeremias, *Der Lehrer der Gerechtigkeit* (SUNT 2; Göttingen: Vandenhoeck & Ruprecht, 1963), 268–307.

91. Zimmerman, *Messianische Texte*, 455–58.

and (in Knohl's case) *Hazon Gabriel* have also been subjected to criticism along the lines of what I have argued here.[92]

Most such criticism has focused, quite appropriately, on matters of exegesis, on this or that interpretation of this or that primary text. In this connection, critics have rightly insisted that the problem does not lie in any dogmatic concern to protect the uniqueness of Christianity. So John Collins, responding to Knohl and Wise, writes, "There is no a priori reason why there should not have been a messiah before Jesus. The question is not one of a priori possibility, however, but of historical evidence."[93] And Collins, for his part, finds the historical evidence wanting. Similarly, Jörg Frey has suggested, "There is nothing to fear in the idea that Jesus' teaching and the phenomenon of Early Christianity have analogies in biblical and post-biblical Judaism. But the wide-scale analogies initially drawn by Dupont-Sommer were based on some misreadings of the scrolls."[94] And with reference to Wise and Knohl, Frey writes, "The parallels drawn by both authors are over-hypothetical and far-fetched to allow for the assumption of a suffering and at the same time divine messianic figure in the scrolls."[95] Collins's and Frey's criticism, which is along the lines of the criticism I have raised to this point, is that the questers for the first messiah have failed to put forward compelling interpretations of the primary texts. It is not that they could not be right, just that they happen not to be right.

Upon reflection, however, it strikes me that that judgment actually concedes too much. I would like to push the criticism one step further, to suggest that the quest for the first messiah not only happens to have been unsuccessful so far, but is actually fundamentally misguided. It is

---

92. See García Martínez, "Old Texts and Modern Mirages"; James VanderKam and Peter Flint, *The Meaning of the Dead Sea Scrolls* (London: T. & T. Clark, 2002), 267–72; John J. Collins, "A Messiah before Jesus?" in *Christian Beginnings and the Dead Sea Scrolls* (ed. John J. Collins and Craig A. Evans; Grand Rapids, Mich.: Baker, 2006), 15–36; idem, "An Essene Messiah? Comments on Israel Knohl, *The Messiah before Jesus*, in *Christian Beginnings and the Dead Sea Scrolls*, 37–44; idem, *Scepter*, 164–70; Fitzmyer, *One Who Is to Come*, 111–15; Jörg Frey, "Critical Issues in the Investigation of the Scrolls and the New Testament," in *Oxford Handbook of the Dead Sea Scrolls*, 517–45 at 519–21; Adela Yarbro Collins, "Response to Israel Knohl, *Messiahs and Resurrection in The Gabriel Revelation*," in *Hazon Gabriel*, 93–98; Harkins, "Who Is the Teacher of the Teacher Hymns?"; Per Bilde, *The Originality of Jesus: A Critical Discussion and a Comparative Attempt* (Göttingen: Vandenhoeck & Ruprecht, 2013), 183–88.

93. Collins, "Messiah before Jesus," 19.

94. Frey, "Critical Issues," 520–21.

95. Frey, "Critical Issues," 521.

misguided not because it is theologically intolerable,[96] but because it is conceptually unstable. In particular, it presupposes an Idealist model of messianism that is demonstrably incommensurate with the relevant evidence. The questers, following an influential but problematic strand of modern scholarship, conceive of the messianic idea as a *Geist* in the Hegelian sense, a world-historical force that exists quite independently of the ancient texts available to us (a "myth-dream," in Michael Wise's formulation).[97] There are, however, fatal flaws at the very center of this model.[98] As Martin Karrer and Peter Schäfer, among others, have argued, because our actual evidence for messianism in antiquity consists of texts, not suprahistorical ideas, the mode of analysis that best fits the evidence is historical and linguistic, not otherwise.[99] Furthermore, as Gerbern Oegema and Loren Stuckenbruck have shown, all ancient messiah texts, Jewish or Christian, are the product of the reinterpretation of scriptural oracles in the light of the experience of their respective authors.[100] For Christian messiah texts, of course, the experience of the authors will have included exposure to traditions about Jesus of Nazareth, but the same is true, *mutatis mutandis*, of many Jewish messiah texts, as well, with respect to other historical figures.[101] In this crucial respect, Christian messiah texts do not require any special explanation. There is no missing link.

At just this point, ironically, the quest for the first messiah actually reinscribes the very paradigm of Christian uniqueness that the questers

---

96. Thus rightly Collins, "Messiah before Jesus"; and Frey, "Critical Issues." In fact, it is not clear how theologically intolerable the idea of a messiah before Jesus ever was to any actual Christian theologians. On this point, see the sanguine comments of Krister Stendahl, "The Scrolls and the New Testament: An Introduction and a Perspective," in *The Scrolls and the New Testament*, 1–17.

97. See Wise, *First Messiah*, 1–36, 279–84, here 32–33:

> The siren song that draws [crisis cults] along that forward path is the myth-dream. . . . The myth-dream is any particular culture's ideal reality. . . . A myth-dream is the assurance of things hoped for, the conviction of things not seen. And the crisis cult tries to make the myth-dream happen.

98. See my discussion in Chapter 1 in this volume.

99. Karrer, *Gesalbte*; Schäfer, "Diversity and Interaction," especially 17:

> Since the history of religious ideas in Judaism is mediated mainly through literature, the literary analysis of the respective sources is the indispensable prerequisite for any further investigation. However, since literature does not float in a vacuum, literary analysis must always be coupled with historical analysis.

100. Oegema, *Anointed and His People*; Stuckenbruck, "Messianic Ideas."

101. On this point, see Chapter 6 in this volume.

ostensibly, and I presume really, want so much to avoid. It appears radical, prima facie, but in fact it operates on the same problematic assumptions on which older scholars such as Stanton and Mowinckel operated. Most significantly, it assumes that Christian messiah texts alone—but not the messiah texts about Cyrus of Persia or Zerubbabel ben Shealtiel or Shimon bar Kosiba or R. Judah the Patriarch—require an extraordinary historical explanation. For the questers, those other ancient messiah texts are explicable as they stand, but Christian messiah texts require the discovery of a missing link in the history of ideas. In this way, contrary to the rhetoric of the quest, Christian uniqueness is once again underscored, just at one remove.[102]

In any case, given the Idealist model presupposed by the quest, even if—for the sake of argument—the quest were to be successful, the net effect would be to push the problem back by fifty or a hundred years, not to solve it. For if, say, Knohl were right about Menahem the Essene and the Self-Glorification Hymn, then the question would follow: What is the missing link that explains the origin of Qumran messianism? Or, to make the same point from a different angle, if the death of Menahem the Essene can explain the origin of the divine suffering messiah motif, then why can the death of Jesus of Nazareth not explain it? If ever Ockham's razor applied, then surely it does here.[103] It is of course quite possible that an earlier messiah movement influenced the Jesus messiah movement, but there is no need whatsoever to postulate the former in order to explain the latter.

Early Christian messiah texts yield the particular combination of features they do not because they are unique,[104] but because they do, in their particular way, what all ancient messiah texts do—namely, reinterpret scripture in the light of their own historical circumstances.[105] Consequently, even if someone were to succeed where Dupont-Sommer, Allegro, Wise, and Knohl have failed, if someone were to identify incontrovertibly a divine suffering messiah among the persons resident in the Qumran sect, she would not have found the first messiah. She would have found *a* messiah, one in a vast web

---

102. On this obstinate problem, see Smith, *Drudgery Divine*.

103. Kraft, "Para-mania," 22–26 rightly insists that Ockham's razor, as a methodological rule, is less well suited to history than it is to the natural sciences. In this particular instance, however, it seems to me to be immediately relevant.

104. Contra V. H. Stanton and Mowinckel on the one hand and Wise and Knohl on the other.

105. On this point, see especially Stuckenbruck, "Messianic Ideas."

of ancient Jewish and Christian intertexts. This would of course be a tremendous contribution to our knowledge of the period, but it would not be a revolution in the history of ideas. There are the scriptural oracles, and there are ancient Jewish and Christian interpreters,[106] but there is no such thing as the first messiah.

---

106. On this way of characterizing the situation, see James L. Kugel, *The Bible As It Was* (Cambridge, Mass.: Harvard University Press, 1999).

6

The Jewish Messiah–Christian Messiah Distinction

WHEN, IN JUSTIN Martyr's second-century CE *Dialogue with Trypho the Jew*, the characters Justin and Trypho dispute the identity of the messiah, their dispute takes two rather different forms.[1] In the first and perhaps better known form, Justin and Trypho agree on the main lines of the category "messiah," but disagree whether Jesus can be said to fit the category. An example is the well-known passage at *Dial.* 89.1–2:

> Trypho said, "Be assured that our whole tribe also awaits the messiah, and we confess that all the scriptures that you cited speak of him [πᾶν τὸ γένος ἡμῶν τὸν Χριστὸν ἐκδέχεται, καὶ ὅτι πᾶσαι αἱ γραφαί, ἃς ἔφης, εἰς αὐτὸν εἴρηνται, ὁμολογοῦμεν]. What is more, I admit that the name Jesus, by which the son of Nave was called, inclines me toward such a view. We doubt, however, whether the messiah should be dishonorably crucified in this way. For Cursed is he who is crucified [cf. Deut 21:23], it says in the Torah, so that on this point I am very skeptical. It is clear that the scriptures proclaim that the messiah suffers [παθητὸν μὲν τὸν Χριστὸν ὅτι αἱ γραφαὶ κηρύσσουσι, φανερόν ἐστιν], but whether it is through a suffering cursed in the Torah, we want to know whether you can adduce a proof of this." (Justin, *Dial.* 89.1–2)[2]

---

1. On the relevant passages, see A. J. B. Higgins, "Jewish Messianic Belief in Justin Martyr's *Dialogue with Trypho*," *NovT* 9 (1967): 298–305; Timothy J. Horner, *Listening to Trypho: Justin Martyr's Dialogue with Trypho Reconsidered* (CBET 28; Leuven: Peeters, 2001), 155–64.

2. Greek text ed. E. J. Goodspeed, *Die ältesten Apologeten* (Göttingen: Vandenhoeck & Ruprecht, 1915); trans. mine.

In this passage, Trypho objects to the incommensurability of the mode of Jesus's death with an article of Deuteronomic law;[3] but up to that point, he agrees with Justin's explication of the concept "messiah."

In a second, different form of the dispute, however, Trypho suggests that he and Justin actually mean quite different things when they use the word "messiah."[4] At *Dial.* 8, Trypho suggests that the gentile Justin would have done better to remain a Platonist than to become a Christian, because Platonism is at least a noble form of paganism, whereas Christianity is neither good paganism nor good Judaism. About the folly of Christianity, Trypho comments:

> The messiah, if he has indeed come and is somewhere, is incognito; he does not even know himself yet nor does he have any power until Elijah comes and anoints him and makes him manifest to everyone. But you, having accepted a vain report, are reinventing a messiah for yourselves [ὑμεῖς δέ, ματαίαν ἀκοὴν παραδεξάμενοι, Χριστὸν ἑαυτοῖς τινα ἀναπλάσσετε] and are now perishing heedlessly on his account. (Justin, *Dial.* 8.4)

Christians, Trypho says, Χριστὸν ἑαυτοῖς τινα ἀναπλάσσετε, "reinvent a messiah for yourselves." In other words, what Christians mean by "messiah" is not the same thing as what the Jews mean by "messiah." Christians have made up their own meaning for this venerable old Jewish word. Later in the *Dialogue*, Trypho, in a more irenic mood, actually goes so far as to concede that Jesus might in fact be the messiah of the Christians—indeed, even the god of the Christians—but certainly not of the Jews:

> Trypho said, "Let him be known as your lord and messiah and god, you from among the gentiles ["Εστω ὑμῶν, τῶν ἐξ ἐθνῶν, κύριος καὶ Χριστὸς καὶ θεὸς γνωριζόμενος], as the scriptures signify, you who from his name are all called Christians. But we, being worshipers of the God who made this man himself, are not obligated to confess or do obeisance to him. (Justin, *Dial.* 64.1)

---

3. As the apostle Paul does in Gal 3:13. An economical explanation is that Justin gets this idea from Paul, but the matter is complicated by the puzzling fact that Justin never mentions or quotes from the apostle, on which see Paul Foster, "Justin and Paul," in *Paul and the Second Century* (ed. Michael F. Bird and Joseph R. Dodson; LNTS 412; London: T. & T. Clark, 2011), 108–25.

4. Thus rightly Graham Stanton, "Messianism and Christology: Mark, Matthew, Luke, and Acts," in *Redemption and Resistance*, 78–96 at 78–79.

Although Trypho's words are of course supplied by Justin, who proceeds to rebut them in the person of his own character,[5] this is a remarkable concession. Justin acknowledges the possibility of conceiving the Jewish messiah and the Christian messiah as mere homonyms, categorically different things that share a common name. This idea would turn out to have remarkable staying power.

The Jewish Messiah–Christian Messiah Distinction

One of the most reliable commonplaces in modern studies of ancient messianism is the distinction between the Jewish messiah and the Christian messiah. Perhaps the best-known statement of this distinction comes from the opening line of Gershom Scholem's classic 1959 essay "Zum Verständnis der messianischen Idee im Judentum": "Any discussion of the problems relating to Messianism is a delicate matter, for it is here that the essential conflict between Judaism and Christianity has developed and continues to exist."[6] Scholem parses the difference between the respective messiahs in this way:

> Judaism ... has always maintained a concept of redemption as an event which takes place publicly, on the stage of history and within the community.... In contrast, Christianity conceives of redemption as an event in the spiritual and unseen realm, an event which is reflected in the soul, in the private world of each individual, and which effects an inner transformation which need not correspond to anything outside.[7]

---

5. On the artificiality of the character of Trypho, see Tessa Rajak, "Talking at Trypho: Christian Apologetic as Anti-Judaism in Justin's Dialogue with Trypho the Jew," in *Apologetics in the Roman Empire: Pagans, Jews, and Christians* (ed. Mark Edwards et al.; Oxford: Oxford University Press, 1999), 59–80.

6. Scholem, "Messianic Idea," 1; German original: "Zum Verständnis der messianischen Idee im Judentum," *ErJb* 28 (1959): 173–239; repr. in idem, *Judaica*, vol. 1 (Frankfurt: Suhrkamp, 1963), 7–74.

7. Scholem, "Messianic Idea," 1. On the Jewish side, Scholem further subdivides messianism into three now famous types:

> The *conservative* forces are directed toward the preservation of that which exists and which, in the historical environment of Judaism, was always in danger.... The *restorative* forces are directed to the return and recreation of a past condition which comes to be felt as ideal.... There are, in addition, forces which press forward and renew; they are nourished by a vision of the future and receive *utopian* inspiration. ("Messianic Idea," 3; emphasis mine)

THE GRAMMAR OF MESSIANISM

The distinction is much older than Scholem, of course, but it is conspicuous in studies of early Jewish messianism from the nineteenth century to the present. Vincent Henry Stanton took up the distinction as the theme for his Hulsean Lectures for 1879, published as *The Jewish and the Christian Messiah*:

> The Jewish idea of the Messiah, as we are all more or less familiar with it ... is so different from the Christian that we may naturally inquire whether Christians have any right to use the title, whether the meaning they attach to it preserves any part of the original idea.[8]

On Stanton's account, they do, and it does, but only by way of a radical redefinition of a the relevant terms. In particular, "The whole idea of His [the messiah's] work underwent a spiritualizing process. ... For national deliverance from anarchy and oppression we have a deliverance to be apprehended by individuals, one by one, in a purely moral and spiritual manner."[9]

Writing during the early twentieth century, Joseph Klausner articulates a similar rubric. On the one hand: "The Jewish Messiah is a redeemer strong in physical power and in spirit, who in the final days will bring redemption, economic and spiritual, to the Jewish people—and along with this, eternal peace, material prosperity, and ethical perfection to the whole human race."[10] On the other hand:

> By contrast, the Christian Messiah: Christianity is based wholly on the personality of the Messiah. ... [Because Jesus] was not successful in the political sense, having failed to redeem his people Israel ... [for Christianity] the Messiah did not come to redeem from political oppression and economic wrong, but to redeem from spiritual evil alone.[11]

Klausner's younger contemporary Sigmund Mowinckel, writing during World War II, locates the origin of the Jewish messiah–Christian messiah distinction in the Gospel narratives, which he takes to reflect Jesus's own self-understanding:

---

8. Stanton, *Jewish and Christian Messiah*, 146.

9. Stanton, *Jewish and Christian Messiah*, 150.

10. Klausner, *Messianic Idea*, 519. Stinespring's ET is based on the third Hebrew edition (1949), but the section quoted here originally appeared in Hebrew as an essay in *Sefer Magnes* (Jerusalem: Hebrew University Press, 1938).

11. Klausner, *Messianic Idea*, 525–26.

The very fact that Jesus related His teaching both positively and nega-tively to the Messianic ideas prevalent in later Judaism shows that He did not adopt them just as they were. The Gospels depict him as con-stantly in conflict with certain aspects of the Jewish Messianic ideal which was in the minds of His disciples.[12]

On Mowinckel's account, Jesus partly accepted and partly rejected the pre-vailing Jewish model of the messiah, and this idiosyncrasy on his part accounts for what we call the Christian understanding of the messiah.

Scholarly fashions come and go, but the Jewish messiah–Christian mes-siah distinction has scarcely waned in influence since the mid twentieth century. John Collins, for instance, cites Scholem's version of the distinction with qualified approval: "To be sure, the contrast is overdrawn. . . . As a broad generalization, however, the contrast has merit, in underlining a dominant characteristic of each religion."[13] And Dan Cohn-Sherbok takes it over with unqualified approval: "[The Jewish] objection to Jesus concerns his otherworld-liness. The rabbis sought to provide adequate social legislation, but Jesus had a different view from theirs. . . . The vision of messianic redemption brought about by Jesus is therefore at odds with traditional Judaism."[14] Similarly, James Charlesworth argues that, although early Christian writers inherit the concept "messiah" from their Jewish heritage, they decisively "remint" it to correspond to the life, death, and resurrection of Jesus. He concludes, "Suffice it to be stated now that Jewish messianology does not flow majestically into Christian christology."[15]

As recently as 2007, Magnus Zetterholm has commented:

A concept of a Messiah exists both within Judaism, where it originated, and in Christianity, where perhaps it underwent its most profound transformation. But . . . messianism scarcely constitutes a common ground for Jews and Christians. . . . [On the contrary,] "the Messiah" has been the most important concept that distinguishes Christianity from Judaism.[16]

---

12. Mowinckel, *He That Cometh*, 9.

13. Collins, *Scepter*, 1. Compare Collins, *Scepter*, 237, however, for a rather more critical assessment of the distinction.

14. Cohn-Sherbok, *Jewish Messiah*, 77, 79.

15. Charlesworth, "From Jewish Messianology to Christian Christology," 255.

16. Magnus Zetterholm, "Introduction," in *The Messiah in Early Judaism and Christianity* (ed. Magnus Zetterholm; Minneapolis, Minn.: Fortress, 2007), xxiv.

And in his own 2007 study, Joseph Fitzmyer expressly endorses and restates Joseph Klausner's version of the distinction. Fitzmyer's Jewish messiah is "a human kingly figure who was (and is) to bring deliverance, at once political, economic, and spiritual, to the Jewish people, and through them peace, prosperity, and righteousness to all humanity."[17] Fitzmyer's Christian messiah, on the other hand,

> has already come . . . [and is] identified with Jesus of Nazareth. . . . His mission differed, too, because it was no longer deliverance in a political or economic sense, but solely in a spiritual sense; and because it was aimed directly at all human beings, it no longer was considered as coming through a chosen people.[18]

As these examples show, the Jewish messiah–Christian messiah distinction has been drawn in different ways by its modern proponents, but certain common themes appear again and again. The contrast "Jewish messiah" versus "Christian messiah," we are told, corresponds to the contrasts political versus spiritual, outward versus inward, public versus private, national versus universal, corporate versus individual, natural versus supernatural, and earthly versus heavenly. As Peter Schäfer has observed, all such binaries are broad stereotypes.[19] And in fact, they are compromised by numerous counterexamples from ancient Jewish and Christian texts. The Jewish messiah of the *Parables of Enoch* is a preexistent heavenly figure (1 En. 48), whereas the Christian messiah of the Gospel of Mark is a human teacher and exorcist (Mark 1). The Jewish messiah of 2 Baruch exercises universal rule over all the nations of the earth (2 Bar. 72), whereas the Christian messiah of the Epistle of James is lord of the twelve tribes of Israel in the diaspora (Jas 1:1). The Jewish messiah of *Targum Jonathan* to Isaiah secures forgiveness of sins (*Tg.* Isa 53:4–12), whereas the Christian messiah of Irenaeus's *Against Heresies* establishes an imperial capital in Jerusalem (Irenaeus, *Haer.* 5.31–36). And so on. In short,

---

17. Fitzmyer, *One Who Is to Come*, 182.

18. Fitzmyer, *One Who Is to Come*, 183.

19. Schäfer, commenting on the old debate about whether the Bar Kokhba revolt should be classified as messianic, writes:

> I do not quite understand the trend in much of the relevant scholarship to distinguish neatly between merely a "down-to-earth" military leader/warrior on the one hand and a utopian figure with "divine and supernatural qualities" on the other. . . . It seems to me that the distinction between the "religious" and the "political" is here misguided. (Schäfer, "Bar Kokhba and the Rabbis," 17)

the oft-cited stereotypes of the Jewish messiah and his Christian counterpart are as inaccurate as they are oft-cited.

A more sophisticated version of the Jewish messiah–Christian messiah distinction is based not on any a priori binary, but on the problem posed by the figure of Jesus himself.[20] Such a version goes roughly as follows: In Jewish usage the word "messiah" signifies a future, ideal figure whose characteristics (whether Davidic ancestry, Aaronic ancestry, ritual purity, just rule, or otherwise) are drawn from the biblical tradition, whereas in Christian usage "messiah" simply signifies the person Jesus, full stop, so that whatever Jesus is remembered to have done is what the messiah is meant to do. Nils Dahl, for example, comments on the meaning of "messiah" or "Christ" in the Pauline Epistles: "The name 'Christ' does not receive its content through a previously fixed conception of messiahship but rather from the person and work of Jesus Christ. An *interpretatio christiana* is carried out completely."[21] Similarly George MacRae: "To the extent that the title *Christos* became progressively more central to early Christian proclamation, to that same extent it departed further from the Jewish understanding of the Messiah."[22] According to this version of the distinction, the Jewish messiah is a product of mythical tradition, while the Christian messiah is a product of empirical circumstance. This more nuanced form of the distinction is a force to be reckoned with, and the balance of this chapter comprises an effort to reckon with it.

Although it is a commonplace in modern scholarship, as Justin Martyr illustrates, the Jewish messiah–Christian messiah is not a modern invention. In fact, it has roots in our earliest extant Christian texts. It became plausible, as an idea, as soon as early Christians began to claim scriptural necessity for the circumstances of Jesus's life—that is, to claim that the tradition said the messiah had to undergo certain things that, according to the story, Jesus had undergone. Perhaps the most notorious example is the Gospel of Matthew, who says of a dizzying number of events—the slaughter of the innocents by Herod, the flight of the holy family to Egypt, Jesus's entry into Jerusalem on the back of a donkey and a colt, and so on—that it happened in such and such a way in order to fulfill the scripture that said it had to happen in just that way.[23] Summarizing this literary phenomenon, William Scott Green comments:

---

20. A point well made already by Klausner, *Messianic Idea*, 525–26.

21. Dahl, "Messiahship of Jesus in Paul," 17.

22. MacRae, "Messiah and Gospel," 174.

23. See Matt 1:22–23; 2:4–6, 16–18, 23; 3:1–3; 4:12–16; 8:16–17; 11:2–6; 12:15–21; 13:34–35; 17:9–13; 21:1–5; 26:24, 31, 51–56; 27:3–10. On this motif, see Krister Stendahl, *The School of St. Matthew and Its Use of the Old Testament* (Lund: Gleerup, 1954); Graham N. Stanton, *A Gospel*

New Testament authors, particularly of the gospels of Matthew and
Luke, made the Hebrew scriptures into a harbinger of his [Jesus's]
career, suffering, and death. The "promise-fulfillment" motif, which
casts Jesus as a foreseen figure, is perhaps the major achievement
of New Testament apologetics.... The fulfillment formulas and their
attached verses are strategic devices, the result of *post facto* choice,
rather than remnants of an exegetical heritage.[24]

Other early Christian writers do not claim scriptural necessity for nearly
as many circumstances as Matthew does, but many agree in invoking scriptural necessity for one circumstance in particular—namely, Jesus's death.[25]
As in Matthew, when Peter attempts by violence to prevent Jesus's arrest, and
Jesus scolds him and asks, "How then would the scriptures be fulfilled, that
it must be so [πῶς οὖν πληρωθῶσιν αἱ γραφαὶ ὅτι οὕτως δεῖ γενέσθαι]?" (Matt
26:54). So, too, in the Gospel of Luke, when the risen Jesus surprises two
confused disciples on the road, he asks them, "Was it not necessary for the
messiah to suffer these things [οὐχὶ ταῦτα ἔδει παθεῖν τὸν χριστόν] and enter
into his glory?" (Luke 24:26). Again, in the Acts of the Apostles, Paul spends
three sabbaths in the synagogue in Thessalonica "explaining and demonstrat-
ing that it was necessary for the messiah to suffer and to rise from the dead
[τὸν χριστὸν ἔδει παθεῖν καὶ ἀναστῆναι ἐκ νεκρῶν]" (Acts 17:3). Similarly, the
apostle Paul writes to his gentile congregation in Corinth, "The messiah died
for our sins according to the scriptures [κατὰ τὰς γραφάς], he was buried, and
he was raised on the third day according to the scriptures [κατὰ τὰς γραφάς]"
(1 Cor 15:3). Jesus had suffered and risen; those were the circumstances. For
these early Christian authors, then, the tradition must have said that it had to
be so.[26]

From the perspective of many contemporary Jews, of course, the tradition said no such thing. Indeed, this is a leitmotif in the replies of Trypho in
Justin's *Dialogue*, with which this chapter began. Justin marshals argument
after argument from scripture proving, to his own satisfaction, that Jesus is

---

for a New People: Studies in Matthew (Edinburgh: T. & T. Clark, 1992), 346–63; and Ulrich
Luz, *Matthew 1–7: A Commentary* (trans. James E. Crouch; ed. Helmut Koester; Hermeneia;
Minneapolis, Minn.: Fortress, 2007), 125–32.

24. Green, "Messiah in Judaism," 4–5.

25. Thus rightly Luz, *Matthew 1–7*, 132: "The fulfillment quotations [in Matthew] are not a
completely new phenomenon in the history of early Christian theology. They are merely the
intensified and principled expression of a conviction that all of early Christianity shares."

26. On this early Christian logic, see Juel, *Messianic Exegesis*, 1–29.

the messiah, but at every turn, Trypho replies that Justin has simply misunderstood the scriptures.[27] Over the course of their exchange, a gap emerges between Trypho's conventional Jewish interpretation of scripture and Justin's novel, Christian interpretation.[28] This gap is apparent already in at least some first-century sources. So it is in John 12:34, where the crowd quarrels with Jesus, "We have heard from the Torah that the messiah remains for ever [ἡμεῖς ἠκούσαμεν ἐκ τοῦ νόμου ὅτι ὁ χριστὸς μένει εἰς τὸν αἰῶνα]. How then can you say that the son of man must be lifted up [δεῖ ὑψωθῆναι τὸν υἱὸν τοῦ ἀνθρώπου]?" Or again in John 20:9, where Peter and the beloved disciple look in the tomb for Jesus's body "because they had not yet understood the scripture that he must rise from the dead [οὐδέπω γὰρ ᾔδεισαν τὴν γραφὴν ὅτι δεῖ αὐτὸν ἐκ νεκρῶν ἀναστῆναι]." As these passages illustrate, some early Christian authors were well aware of the contestability of their claim that scripture said the messiah had to do what Jesus had done. They knew that the necessity of the messiah's death and resurrection was not equally obvious to all readers of the scriptures. It was this contestability, this lack of obviousness, that gave rise to the Jewish messiah–Christian messiah distinction.

Nowadays, the distinction is cited so often and with such confidence in the secondary literature that it enjoys the appearance of self-evidentness. It is the kind of scholarly trope that is always cited, never defended. From time to time, however, interpreters have questioned whether the rubric really is adequate to describe what it purports to describe. Jacob Taubes, for instance, challenges Scholem's famous formulation in this way:

> Scholem's method of dividing the Messianic cake seems to me not to derive from historical analysis.... Such a static opposition between Jewish and Christian notions of redemption obfuscates the dynamics inherent in the Messianic idea itself.... Interiorization is not a dividing

---

27. For example, "Trypho said, 'All the words of prophecy that you cite, sir, are ambiguous and have no force to prove what you want to prove'" (*Dial.* 51.1); "Trypho said, 'We do not draw this conclusion from the words cited above'" (*Dial.* 60.1); "Trypho answered, 'Scripture does not say, *Behold, the virgin* [παρθένος] *shall conceive and bear a son*, but rather, *Behold, the young woman* [νεᾶνις] *shall conceive and bear a son* [Isa 7:14], and so on, as you quoted. And the whole prophecy is spoken with reference to Hezekiah'" (*Dial.* 67.1); "Trypho said ... 'Concerning this psalm that you just cited from among the words of David [viz. Ps 96], it does not seem to me to speak of anyone other than the father, the maker of heaven and earth'" (*Dial.* 74.1).

28. It is broadly true that, as Marc Hirshman argues, the literary purpose of the character Trypho is simply to set up Justin's proofs (Hirshman, *Rivalry of Genius*, 31–41). But as the passages just cited illustrate, it is also the case that Trypho's replies reflect a coherent hermeneutic in their own right (thus rightly Horner, *Listening to Trypho*, 147–65).

line between "Judaism" and "Christianity"; it signifies a crisis within Jewish eschatology itself.[29]

Moshe Idel objects to Scholem's Jewish messiah–Christian messiah distinction for similar reasons.[30] More recently, Loren Stuckenbruck, writing in a different context, has made a related point: "If we allow for such diversity in both early Christian and Jewish communities, there is no reason to suppose that, beyond the reconciliation of 'Messiah' by Christians to the experiences of Jesus, Jewish and Christian ideas were necessarily very distinct from one another."[31] In other words, perhaps the only significant difference between the Jewish messiah and the Christian messiah in ancient texts is the reconciliation by early Christian writers of scriptural traditions to the life of Jesus. Just here, I want to suggest that this rather innocuous-sounding observation is, in fact, not innocuous at all. Building on Taubes, Idel, and Stuckenbruck, I propose that Jewish messianism—of which Christian messianism can be thought of as just an extraordinarily well-documented example—always and everywhere involves the interplay of biblical tradition and empirical circumstance. In this crucial respect, there is no difference whatsoever between the Jewish messiah and the Christian messiah.

Against the Jewish Side of the Distinction

The claim that certain early Christian messiah texts invoke scriptural necessity where, on the surface of it, there appears to be no such necessity, that they bend scriptural tradition to fit empirical circumstance, has been much

---

29. Jacob Taubes, "The Price of Messianism," *JJS* 33 (1982): 595–600 at 596. Similar, but not concerned directly with Scholem, is the comment of David Flusser, "Jewish Messianism Reflected in the Early Church," in idem, *Judaism of the Second Temple Period*, 2:258–88 at 288:

> Scholarship on ancient Jewish messianism has maintained a dichotomous view, with Jewish messianism understood as grounded and realistic, while Christian messianism is suffused with supernatural hopes. This dichotomy is buttressed by a single-mindedly political interpretation of Jewish messianism and a stilted sociological approach.

30. Idel, *Messianic Mystics*, 30:

> In his attempt to differentiate Jewish eschatology from the Christian one, Scholem went too far by emphasizing the national and historical elements, above all apocalypticism, in the constellation of ideas that constitutes Jewish messianism, at the expense of the spiritual ones, while reducing Christian views of redemption to solely one stand, the spiritual one. In fact, both Judaism and Christianity have shown a great variety of responses to this vital issue, and the comparisons between the two must be made in a much more complex and sensitive manner.

31. Stuckenbruck, "Messianic Ideas," 113n44.

discussed and, indeed, theorized with considerable sophistication.[32] But one also finds in the secondary literature a corollary claim, frequently adduced but rarely explicated—namely, the claim that Jewish messiah texts are innocent of such special pleading because they, unlike their Christian counterparts, are products of more or less pure tradition. Thus influentially Scholem:

> Unlike Christian or Shiite Messianism, no memories of a real person are at work here which, though they might arouse the imagination and attract old images of expectation, nonetheless are always bound to something deeply personal. Jesus or the Hidden Imam, who once existed as persons, possess the unmistakable and unforgettable qualities of a person. This is just what the Jewish image of the Messiah, by its nature, cannot have since it can picture everything personal only in completely abstract fashion, having as yet no living experience on which to base it.[33]

This corollary claim warrants a great deal more scrutiny than it has received.[34] In point of fact, contrary to stereotype, there are numerous Jewish messiah texts from the Babylonian exile through the amoraic period (and down to the present, for that matter) that attest the same literary phenomenon that one finds in the early Christian texts just cited—namely, the bending of messianic tradition to fit historical circumstances.

An excellent example is provided by the extant records of the ill-fated Bar Kokhba revolt of 132 to 136 CE. Like Jesus of Nazareth, who was executed by the Roman provincial authorities on a charge of sedition before the first Jewish–Roman war, Shimon bar Kosiba was a charismatic leader of a Judean populist movement whose followers hailed him as the messiah.[35] Hence the onomastic wordplay Bar Kokhba, בר כוכבא, "son of the star," after the "star from Jacob" oracle in Num 24:17: דרך כוכב מיעקב וקם שבט מישראל, "A star [כוכב] goes forth from Jacob, a scepter rises from Israel." The actual name Bar Kokhba is attested

---

32. For example, Dahl, "Crucified Messiah"; Kugel and Greer, *Ancient Biblical Interpretation*; Juel, *Messianic Exegesis*; Marcus, *Way of the Lord*; Richard B. Hays, *The Conversion of the Imagination: Paul as Interpreter of Israel's Scripture* (Grand Rapids, Mich.: Eerdmans, 2005).

33. Scholem, "Messianic Idea," 17–18.

34. A commendable exception, however, is Oegema, *Anointed and His People*. I take issue with some of Oegema's particular conclusions, but his case for the importance of the historical circumstances of the writers of Jewish messiah texts is foundational for my argument in this chapter.

35. On the archeological evidence for the movement, see Yadin, *Bar Kokhba*.

only in ancient Christian sources;[36] but the messianic acclamation and the exegesis of Num 24:17 are preserved in the Talmud and midrash.[37] Unlike Jesus, Bar Kosiba got a remarkably successful armed revolt up and running for a period of several years, so successful that Dio Cassius records heavy losses sustained by the Roman army;[38] and material remains from Palestine in this period include thousands of Bar Kokhba coins inscribed, for instance, שנת אחת לגאולת ישראל, "year one of the redemption of Israel," or ש[נת] ב לחירות ישראל, "year two of the freedom of Israel."[39] The Yerushalmi preserves the tradition that R. Akiba, the greatest sage of that generation, himself acclaimed Bar Kosiba as the messiah. There are reasons for questioning this particular literary tradition,[40] but the case for an early second-century CE messiah movement surrounding Shimon bar Kosiba is quite secure.

This second Jewish–Roman war ended with the death of Bar Kosiba in battle at Betar and the reestablishment of Jerusalem as the Roman city Aelia

---

36. See Justin Martyr, *1 Apol.* 31.6: ἐν τῷ νῦν γεγενημένῳ Ἰουδαϊκῷ πολέμῳ Βαρχωχέβας ὁ τῆς Ἰουδαίων ἀποστάσεως ἀρχηγέτης, "In the present Jewish war, Barchochebas the leader of the rebellion of the Jews"; Eusebius, *Hist. eccl.* 4.6.2: ἐστρατήγει δὲ τότε Ἰουδαίων Βαρχωχεβας ὄνομα, ὃ δὴ ἀστέρα δηλοῖ, "The commander of the Jews at that time was a man by the name of Barchochebas, which means 'star'" (Greek text ed. G. Bardy, *Eusèbe de Césarée. Histoire ecclésiastique* [3 vols.; SC 31, 41, 55.; Paris: Cerf, 1952–1958]); Eusebius, *Chron.* Hadrian year 17, apud Jerome, *Chron. ad loc.*: *Barcochebas dux factionis Judaeorum*, "Barchochebas, leader of the sect of the Jews" (PL 27:619–20).

37. See y. *Ta'an.* 4:8 (68d):

> R. Shimon b. Yohai taught, "My teacher Akiba used to expound, *A star* [כוכב] *goes forth from Jacob* [Num 24:17]: Koziba [כוזבא] goes forth from Jacob." When R. Akiba saw Bar Koziba, he said, "This is the king messiah." R. Yohanan b. Torta said to him, "Akiba, grass will come up between your cheeks and still the son of David will not have come" (and compare the parallels at *Lam. Rab.* 2:2 §4; *Lam. Rab.*, ed. Buber, p. 101).

38. Dio Cassius, *Roman History* 69.12–15, here §14:

> Many Romans, moreover, perished in this war. Therefore Hadrian in writing to the senate did not employ the opening phrase commonly affected by the emperors, "If you and our children are in health, it is well; I and the legions are in health." (trans. Earnest Cary in Dio Cassius, *Roman History* [LCL; Cambridge, Mass.: Harvard University Press, 1914–1927])

See further Glen W. Bowersock, "A Roman Perspective on the Bar Kokhba War," in *Approaches to Ancient Judaism*, vol. 2, 131–41; Werner Eck, "The Bar Kokhba Revolt: The Roman Point of View," *JRS* 89 (1999): 76–89.

39. Transcriptions per A. Reifenberg, *Ancient Jewish Coins* (3d ed.; Jerusalem: Rubin Mass, 1963), 60–66. On the Bar Kokhba coins, see further Mildenberg, *Coinage of the Bar Kokhba War*; and the plates in Ya'akov Meshorer, *A Treasury of Jewish Coins from the Persian Period to Bar Kokhba* (Jerusalem: Yad Ben-Zvi, 2001).

40. See Schäfer, *Bar Kokhba-Aufstand*, 168–69; idem, "Bar Kokhba and the Rabbis"; Novenson, "Why Does R. Akiba."

Capitolina under Hadrian.[41] In view of this outcome, the rabbinic literature, which postdates the revolt, is understandably ambivalent about Bar Kosiba. For the most part, the rabbis are strongly inclined to denounce him as a false messiah. So, for one thing, the only name ever used for him in the Talmud is yet another wordplay on his patronym: "Bar Koziba" from the root כזב, so "son of lies" or "liar."[42] For another, there is the fanciful story in *b. Sanh.* 93b in which a rabbinic court tries and executes Bar Kosiba for his false messianic claim.[43] And yet, to many of his contemporaries, perhaps including some of the rabbis' own forebears, it had seemed certain that he was the messiah, and therefore the rabbis also have an interest in accounting for this embarrassing circumstance. For them, Bar Kosiba has to have been a false but still plausible messiah.

This is the ideological context for the curious passage in the early midrash *Lamentations Rabbah* that purports to explain why R. Akiba said that Bar Kosiba was the messiah, since from the rabbis' perspective he obviously had not been. The midrash reads: "What did Ben Koziba used to do? He used to catch the missiles from the enemy's catapults on one of his legs and throw them back, killing many men. For this reason R. Akiba said what he said [viz. that Bar Kokhba was the messiah]" (*Lam. Rab.* 2:2 §4).[44] Interpreters have sometimes noted the apparent arbitrariness of this passage, because superhuman strength such as that attributed here to Bar Kosiba is not a standard feature of the messianic tradition of this period. It would seem strange, therefore, to appeal to it as a reason for R. Akiba's opinion.[45] But that is precisely the point. This text is not a literary reflection on the tradition; it is a means of

---

41. On this period, see Jodi Magness, *The Archaeology of the Holy Land: From the Destruction of Solomon's Temple to the Muslim Conquest* (New York, N.Y.: Cambridge University Press, 2012), 256–85.

42. Pre-World War II scholarship entertained the possibility that the name as given in the Talmud, Bar Koziba, was authentic and derived from a biblical place name, either Chezib (כזיב in Gen 38:5) or Chozeba (כזבא in 1 Chr 4:22). But the documents from the revolt excavated in the Judean desert by Yadin during the early 1960s unanimously attest the personal name as Ben or Bar Kosiba (with ס or שׂ, but not ז), making it likely that the talmudic variant is a scornful wordplay (thus rightly Schäfer, *Bar Kokhba-Aufstand*, 51–55).

43. *b. Sanh.* 93b:

> Bar Koziba reigned two and a half years. He said to the rabbis, "I am the messiah." They said to him, "Of the messiah it is written, *He smells and judges* [Isa 11:3–4]. Let us see whether he smells and judges." When they saw that he was unable to smell and judge, they killed him. (text from Soncino; trans. mine)

44. Text ed. Mosheh Mirkin, *Midrash Rabbah* (11 vols.; Tel Aviv: Yavneh, 1977); trans. mine.

45. On this aspect of this text, see Reinhartz, "Rabbinic Perceptions," 185–86; Novenson, "Why Does R. Akiba," 552.

reckoning with an obstinate historical circumstance—namely, the memory of
R. Akiba's mistaken assessment of Bar Kosiba. The midrash bends the tradition to fit the circumstance.

More interesting still, this very ancient association of Shimon bar Kosiba
with the office of messiah exerted an influence on the tradition for centuries
thereafter. So Maimonides, the great Sephardi philosopher of the twelfth century CE, in an account of the messiah in his *Mishneh Torah*, reasons as follows:

> Do not think that King Messiah will have to perform signs and wonders,
> bring anything new into being, revive the dead, or do similar things. It
> is not so. Rabbi Akiba was a great sage, a teacher of the Mishnah, yet
> he was also the armor-bearer of Ben Kozba. He affirmed that the latter
> was King Messiah; he and all the wise men of his generation shared
> this belief until Ben Kozba was slain in (his) iniquity, when it became
> known that he was not (the Messiah). Yet the Rabbis had not asked him
> for a sign or token. (Maimonides, *Mishneh Torah* 14.11.3)[46]

Maimonides stands broadly in the main stream of medieval Judaism in
anticipating the future coming of the messiah.[47] His point here, against certain of his contemporaries, is that the messiah, when he comes, will not be
a miracle-worker. How does Maimonides know this? Because, he explains,
Bar Kosiba was not a miracle-worker. Of course Maimonides, like the amoraim before him, knows full well that Bar Kosiba was not the messiah. But
Maimonides also knows that R. Akiba thought that he was, and R. Akiba,
being one of the great sages of the Mishnah, cannot have been grossly mistaken.[48] So the messiah, who is yet to come, must necessarily share certain
attributes with Bar Kosiba, because Bar Kosiba must have been close enough
to the real thing for R. Akiba to have been warranted in holding the opinion
he did. As a result, remarkably, Maimonides' formulation of the messianic

---

46. Trans. Abraham M. Hershman, *The Code of Maimonides: Book 14: The Book of Judges* (YJS 3; New Haven, Conn.: Yale University Press, 1949).

47. On Maimonides's account of the messiah, see further David Novak, "Maimonides' Concept of the Messiah," *JRelS* 9 (1982): 42–50; Joel L. Kraemer, "On Maimonides' Messianic Posture," in *Studies in Medieval Jewish History and Literature*, vol. 2 (ed. Isadore Twersky; Cambridge, Mass.: Harvard University Press, 1984), 109–42; Yehuda Liebes, "Appendix: Messianism in Maimonides," in idem, *Studies in Jewish Myth and Jewish Mysticism* (trans. Batya Stein; Albany, N.Y.: SUNY Press, 1993), 61–64.

48. Interestingly, Maimonides makes the additional claim that all the sages of R. Akiba's generation shared his opinion about Bar Kosiba. This claim contradicts the rabbinic accounts, in
which R. Akiba's colleagues rebuke him for taking the view that he does. This latter picture,
although earlier and closer to the events in question, is not necessarily more accurate.

tradition is constrained to a great extent by the circumstances of Bar Kosiba's career a millennium earlier.[49]

It is also possible that the rabbinic myth of the messiah ben Joseph—the warrior messiah who dies in the eschatological battle with Gog before the final victory of the messiah ben David—represents an accommodation of scriptural tradition to the empirical circumstances of the Bar Kokhba revolt.[50] The origin of the Josephite messiah has long been and remains a puzzle in the study of Jewish messianism.[51] Instructively, the puzzle has to do precisely with the degrees of causal power accorded to biblical tradition and historical circumstance, respectively. Many interpreters, emphasizing the influence of the former, have tried to explain the Josephite messiah as a product of the mysterious alchemy of ancient exegesis. Representative of this approach is Charles Cutler Torrey, who reasons thusly:

---

49. On the enduring significance of Bar Kosiba, see Marks, *Image of Bar Kokhba*.

50. The most important early reference to the messiah ben Joseph is *b. Sukkah* 52a:

> *The land shall mourn, each family by itself; the family of the house of David by itself, and their wives by themselves* [Zech 12:12]. . . . What is the cause of the mourning? R. Dosa and the rabbis differ on the point. One explained: The cause is the slaying of messiah ben Joseph. The other explained: The cause is the slaying of the evil inclination. It is well according to him who explains that the cause is the slaying of messiah ben Joseph, since that well agrees with the scripture: *When they look on him whom they have pierced, they shall mourn for him as one mourns for an only child, and weep bitterly over him as one weeps over a firstborn* [Zech 12:10]. (*b. Sukkah* 52a)

The earlier parallel at *y. Sukkah* 5:2 (55b) mentions the messiah, but without any patronym: "[Interpreting Zech 12:12 there were] two amoraim. One said, 'This refers to a lament for the messiah.' The other said, 'This refers to a lament for the evil impulse.'" Other key primary texts on the Josephite messiah include *b. Sukkah* 52a–b; *Tg. Ps.-J.* Exod 40:11; *Tg. Yer.* Zech 12:10; *Tg. Song* 4:5; 7:4; *Gen. Rab.* 75:6; 99:2; *Num. Rab.* 14:1.

51. Castelli, *Il messia secondo*, cautions that it is "a matter which has led astray wiser men that I" (cited at Klausner, *Messianic Idea*, 483). The most important studies include Gustaf Dalman, *Der leidende und sterbende Messias der Synagoge im ersten nachchristlichen Jahrtausend* (Schriften des Institutum Judaicum in Berlin 4; Berlin: Reuther, 1888), especially 1–26; Klausner, *Messianic Idea*, 483–501; and Joseph Heinemann, "The Messiah of Ephraim and the Premature Exodus of the Tribe of Ephraim," *HTR* 68 (1975): 1–15; Hebrew original in *Tarbiz* 40 (1970–1971): 450–61. In recent research, David Mitchell has undertaken to revive the view that the Josephite messiah was a widespread, pretannaitic article of faith. See Mitchell, "Rabbi Dosa and the Rabbis Differ"; idem, "Fourth Deliverer"; idem, "Firstborn *Shor* and *Rem*"; idem, "Messiah bar Ephraim in the Targums"; idem, "Sacrifice of Atonement for Israel"; idem, "Josephite Messiah in 4Q372." But the evidence that Mitchell adduces is either ambiguous or of questionable date or both, and I therefore remain unconvinced. Rather differently, Robert Kraft has mounted a speculative but plausible argument for a pre-Christian Jewish messiah–Joshua tradition that could conceivably have provided fodder both for Christian reflection on a messiah Jesus and for the rabbinic myth of an Ephraimite messiah (Robert A. Kraft, "Was There a Messiah–Joshua Tradition at the Turn of the Era?" IOUDAIOS, 1992).

Some biblical passage or picture, indeed, is to be looked for as the source of this remarkable feature of Jewish eschatology. It would seem to be beyond question that a tenet of such importance, well established in the Talmud, Targum, and Midrash, must have its proof texts in canonical Hebrew scripture.[52]

Among interpreters who accept this premise, however, there is no consensus on the question where exactly in the Jewish scriptures the messiah ben Joseph originated. Torrey, following a suggestion of Ferdinand Weber, identifies the anonymous afflicted figure of Isa 53 as the scriptural source.[53] August Wünsche, James Drummond, and Gustaf Dalman argue that the Josephite messiah was originally an interpretation of "the one whom they have pierced" in Zech 12:10, a view that finds some support in the Talmud and Targums.[54] Dalman also adduces a secondary scriptural source in Moses's blessing upon the tribe of Joseph in Deut 33:17: "His [Joseph's] horns are the horns of a wild ox; with them he shall gore the peoples, all of them, even the ends of the earth."[55] Billerbeck, for his part, makes this passage from Deuteronomy the primary source of the myth.[56] G. H. Dix traces the Josephite messiah, by way of some moderate textual emendation, to a different Pentateuchal testament: the deathbed speech of Jacob in Genesis 49, in the phrases "until he comes to Shiloh" (Gen 49:10), "the archers fiercely attacked him" (Gen 49:23), and "the shepherd, the rock of Israel" (Gen 49:25).[57] George Foot Moore suggests an origin for the myth in an oracle of Obadiah: "The house of Jacob shall be a fire, and the house of Joseph a flame, and the house of Esau stubble; they shall burn them and consume them" (Obad 18).[58] And examples might

---

52. Charles C. Torrey, "The Messiah Son of Ephraim," *JBL* 66 (1947): 253–77 at 257.

53. Torrey, "Messiah Son of Ephraim," 256–59; and compare Ferdinand Weber, *Jüdische Theologie* (2d ed.; Leipzig: Dörffling & Franke, 1897), 362–64.

54. August Wünsche, *Die Leiden des Messias* (Leipzig: Fues, 1870), 109–10; Drummond, *Jewish Messiah*, 357; Dalman, *Der leidende und der sterbende Messias*, 17–18. The Josephite messiah is connected directly with this verse at *b. Sukkah* 52a; *Tg. Yer.* Zech 12:10. The hypothesis of a midrashic origin in this verse is a second, more speculative step.

55. Dalman, *Der leidende und der sterbende Messias*, 19–20. This connection, too, has some direct support in the ancient sources, as in *Gen. Rab.* 75:6, where Deut 33:17 is interpreted as referring to the מלחמה משוח, "anointed for war" or "war messiah."

56. Hermann L. Strack and Paul Billerbeck, *Kommentar zum Neuen Testament aus Talmud und Midrasch* (3 vols.; Munich: Becksche, 1924), 2:292–99, especially 293.

57. G. H. Dix, "The Messiah ben Joseph," *JTS* 27 (1926): 130–43.

58. Moore, *Judaism*, 2:371.

be multiplied further. It is no doubt the case that the messiah ben Joseph has roots in the Bible, but identifying a point of origin in one scriptural oracle rather than another turns out to be a complicated task.

For this reason, other interpreters have insisted that ancient exegesis alone is not a sufficient explanans, that the messiah ben Joseph myth must have arisen as a means of reckoning with some traumatic historical development. Thus Klausner writes, "The fashioning of the Jewish Messianic idea is inevitably influenced by the outstanding historical events of the time."[59] And again, "A passage of Scripture (unless it indicates a certain fact with complete clarity) does not create a new idea; but the new idea, which is already emerging, finds proof and support in the Scriptural passage."[60] Likewise Mowinckel:

> This idea can hardly have arisen simply by exegesis of the Scripture passages referred to. There was no reason for interpreting the one "whom they have pierced" in Zech. xii,10 as a national, warlike Messiah, if the idea of his death was not already taken for granted on other grounds.[61]

But what other grounds? Here lies the possible connection to the Bar Kokhba revolt.

Among those who have explained the Josephite messiah with reference to external history, the most successful hypothesis to date is that the myth arose as a post hoc interpretation of the ill-fated Jewish revolt under Hadrian.[62] This

---

59. Klausner, *Messianic Idea*, 401.

60. Klausner, *Messianic Idea*, 485.

61. Mowinckel, *He That Cometh*, 291.

62. An alternative, minority view is that the messiah ben Joseph myth was originally a rabbinic response to early Christianity, as suggested already by Graetz, "Stages," 164. This view has recently been championed by Israel Jacob Yuval, *Two Nations in Your Womb: Perceptions of Jews and Christians in Late Antiquity and the Middle Ages* (Berkeley, Calif.: University of California Press, 2006), 35–38; Holger M. Zellentin, "Rabbinizing Jesus, Christianizing the Son of David: The Bavli's Approach to the Secondary Messiah Traditions," in *Discussing Cultural Influences: Text, Context, and Non-Text in Rabbinic Judaism* (ed. Rivka Ulmer; Lanham, Md.: University Press of America, 2007), 99–127; and most fully and forcefully Martha Himmelfarb, "The Messiah Son of Joseph in Ancient Judaism," in *Envisioning Judaism: Studies in Honor of Peter Schäfer* (ed. Raʿanan S. Boustan et al.; 2 vols.; Tübingen: Mohr Siebeck, 2013), 2:771–90, here 788: "The choice of Joseph as ancestor may well reflect the impact of the Christian messiah and his human father"; and 790: "The weight of the evidence suggests that the figure of the messiah son of Joseph developed as a popular Jewish response to the Christian narrative, an attempt to provide Jews with a dying and rising savior of their own." This is an intriguing possibility, but the moniker "son of Joseph" seems to me an unlikely point for Jewish counterhaggadah to seize upon, given its relative unimportance in early Christian tradition (compare the much more important "son of Mary" and "son of God").

view goes back at least as far as the late nineteenth-century talmudic dictionaries of Jacob Levy and Jacob Hamburger.[63] In Levy's influential formulation, the function of the Josephite messiah myth is to heroize the unhappy fate of the Bar Kosiba partisans, to reinterpret a national disaster as a necessary step in the drama of redemption. And this because of a profound sense of devotion not to Bar Kosiba himself, but rather to his patron R. Akiba. The death of the Josephite messiah in the battle with Gog is then a kind of *homage* to the death of Bar Kosiba in the battle with Rome. This explanation, in its main lines, at least, has won many adherents. Among twentieth-century interpreters, a messiah ben Joseph-Bar Kokhba connection is maintained by Klausner, Billerbeck, Hurwitz, Heinemann, Vermes, and Levey, to single out just a few leading lights.[64]

In the last generation of research, the most important voice in favor of this connection is Joseph Heinemann, whose reasoning parallels Levy's in the 1880s:

> The Rabbis of the post-Hadrianic generation, who were all, to some extent, disciples of R. Akivah, would hardly have imputed such a gigantic fraud to their master after his martyrdom. On the contrary, this generation must have attempted, by hook or by crook, to achieve the impossible: to uphold Bar Kokhba's messianity in spite of his failure. This paradoxical position could find no more suitable expression than in the highly ambivalent legend of the militant Messiah who is doomed to fall in battle, and yet remains a genuine redeemer.[65]

Furthermore, Heinemann marshals an impressive argument for a two-stage myth: a pre-Hadrianic stage in which the Josephite messiah slays Gog, and a post-Hadrianic stage in which he is slain by Gog.[66] Heinemann's study has proved compelling to many, and recent interpreters have tended to favor

---

63. Jacob Levy, *Neuhebräisches und chaldäisches Wörterbuch über die Talmudim und Midraschim*, vol. 3 (Leipzig: Brockhaus, 1883), 271, s.v. משח. Similarly Jacob Hamburger, *Real-Encyclopädie des Judentums* (3d ed.; 3 vols.; Strelitz, 1905 [1st ed. Koehler, 1896]), 2:767–70, especially 768, s. v. "Messias Sohn Joseph."

64. Klausner, *Messianic Idea*, 489–96 (but with caveats); Strack-Billerbeck, *Kommentar*, 2:294; Siegmund Hurwitz, *Die Gestalt des sterbenden Messias* (Studien aus dem C. G. Jung-Institut 8; Zurich: Rascher, 1958), 178–80; Heinemann, "Messiah of Ephraim"; Geza Vermes, *Jesus the Jew: A Historian's Reading of the Gospels* (London: Collins, 1973), 140; Levey, *Messiah*, 16.

65. Heinemann, "Messiah of Ephraim," 9.

66. See Heinemann, "Messiah of Ephraim," 6–10. Both variations of the story are indeed attested in the rabbinic sources, and Heinemann suggests plausibly that the former would

the hypothesis accordingly. Thus John Collins writes, "While the origin of this figure is obscure, he most probably reflects in some way the defeat and death of Bar Kokhba, whom Rabbi Akiba had hailed as messiah."[67] Similarly Oskar Skarsaune:

> It is difficult to prove, but it remains a fascinating possibility that the portrait of the Messiah of Ephraim who fights for Israel but ends up being killed, thus preparing the way for the Messiah of David, may be an attempt to invest the fate of Bar Kokhba with some meaning.[68]

In view of the relative success of the messiah ben Joseph–Bar Kokhba hypothesis, which admittedly has much to commend it, it is instructive to compare an alternative, parallel hypothesis that exercised considerable influence in the first half of the twentieth century. Hugo Gressmann argued that the dying Josephite messiah was a concession not to the hero of the second Jewish–Roman war but to a hero of the first—that is, not to Shimon bar Kosiba but to Menahem b. Judah (Josephus, *War* 2.433–48). This hypothesis is part of Gressmann's reconstruction from the reports of Josephus in *Ant.* 14.159; 17.271–72 and *War* 1.204; 2.118, 433–48 of a dynasty of Galilean messiahs spanning four generations from the reign of Augustus to the reign of Nero.[69] Sigmund Mowinckel, in turn, commended and developed Gressmann's theory. He,

---

never have arisen at all if the latter were already standard. If the latter indeed arose in the wake of the revolt under Hadrian, then the former must have been current before that event.

67. Collins, *Scepter*, 148. Collins further suggests, "The association of the dying messiah with Ephraim or Joseph remains obscure. Perhaps it harkens back to the old division between northern Israel (Ephraim) and Judah" (Collins, *Scepter*, 148n150). This possibility is much discussed in the older literature, as well. For example, Castelli, *Il messia secondo*, 234–36, makes a similar suggestion, which is dismissed hastily by Klausner, *Messianic Idea*, 485. But in the absence of one obvious scriptural source for the myth, a very ancient, widely attested motif like the two kingdoms may be more the sort of thing that would constitute a solution to the puzzle.

68. Oskar Skarsaune, "Jews and Christians in the Holy Land, 135–325 C.E.," in *Redemption and Resistance*, 158–70 at 161.

69. Namely, Hezekiah "the bandit chief" (*Ant.* 14.159; *War* 1.204), Judah b. Hezekiah "the Galilean" (*Ant.* 17.271–72; 18.23; *War* 2.118), Menahem b. Judah b. Hezekiah (*War* 2.433–48); and Eleazar b. Yair b. Judah (*War* 7.252–58, 320–401). See Gressmann, *Messias*, 449–78, especially 458–62. On this family, see further Martin Hengel, *The Zealots* (trans. David Smith; Edinburgh: T. & T. Clark, 1989 [German original, 1961]) 290–302. Elsewhere, alternatively, Gressmann speculates that the messiah ben Joseph myth might reflect the death by suicide of the Tobiad Hyrcanus ben Joseph, in view of their shared patronym (Josephus, *Ant.* 12.186–236; cf. 2 Macc 3:11) (Hugo Gressmann, "Die ammonitischen Tobiaden," *SPAW* 39 [1921]: 663–71).

Mowinckel, writes, "The explanation is very attractive; the more so since it is explicitly stated that the Messiah ben Joseph will appear in Upper Galilee"—that is, in the ancient northern kingdom.[70] And again, "They all [Hezekiah, Judah, and Menahem] fell in the conflict with the ungodly Rome, and Rome was at that time regarded as the fulfillment of the prophecy about Gog and Magog, or as Edom."[71]

Gressmann and Mowinckel agree with Levy and Heinemann that the Josephite messiah is a concession to the empirical circumstances of the Jewish conflict with Rome, but they disagree on the question which empirical circumstances in particular: which revolt and which messiah. In my view, the Bar Kokhba hypothesis is the more compelling of the two, in particular because the rabbinic sources genuinely puzzle over the question of his messiahship, whereas they never even expressly mention Hezekiah the bandit chief and his descendants.[72] Even so, the Gressmann–Mowinckel hypothesis—and likewise the Graetz–Himmelfarb account of the messiah ben Joseph in relation to Christianity—demonstrates the difficulty of identifying the particular historical circumstances behind the haggadah, even when there are good reasons for thinking that there must be some such circumstances.[73]

The messiah texts about Shimon bar Kosiba make an excellent case study, but one could establish the same point by looking backward from the second century to Hezekiah ben Ahaz, Cyrus of Persia, or Zerubbabel ben Shealtiel; or forward from the second century to R. Judah the Patriarch, Sabbatai Zevi, or Menahem Mendel Schneerson.[74] For as long as there have been Jewish

70. Mowinckel, *He That Cometh*, 291.

71. Mowinckel, *He That Cometh*, 291; and relatedly Mowinckel, *He That Cometh*, 284.

72. The principal rabbinic discussions of the messiahship of Bar Kosiba are at *y. Ta'an.* 4:8 (68d); *Lam. Rab.* 2:2 §4; *Lam. Rab.* ed. Buber, p. 101; and *b. Sanh.* 93b. The rabbis never mention the Galilean bandits Hezekiah, Judah, and Menahem, but Gressmann (*Der Messias*, 458–62) adduces several talmudic passages in which the names Hezekiah and Menahem appear in connection with the messiah—in particular, *y. Ber.* 2:4 (5a) and *b. Sanh.* 98b. In these passages, however, the names are drawn from scripture (2 Kgs 18–20; Lam 1:16), without any sign of connection to particular first-century CE persons. Admittedly, such a connection is not impossible, but it remains entirely speculative, and the talmudic texts are quite intelligible without it. On this issue, see further my discussion of Knohl, *Messiah before Jesus*, in Chapter 5 in this volume.

73. Oegema, *Anointed and His People*, has rightly demonstrated the likelihood of such circumstantial influence in a wide range of ancient messiah texts, although in my view not all the particular influences he proposes are borne out by the evidence.

74. On Cyrus, Zerubbabel, and R. Judah the Patriarch, see Chapters 2 and 3 in this volume. On this aspect of the messiah texts about Sabbatai Zevi, see W. D. Davies, "From Schweitzer to Scholem: Reflections on Sabbatai Svi," *JBL* 95 (1976): 529–58; and Taubes, "Price of Messianism." On this aspect of the messiah movement surrounding the

messiah texts, those texts have been characterized by the necessity of negotiating mythical tradition on the one hand and empirical circumstance on the
other, the biblical and parabiblical reflections on what a messiah would be like
when he came, and the obstinate facts of the lives of actual messiahs and their
followers. Morton Smith's observation about messianic movements during
the Second-Temple period is precisely to the point:

> When trying to decide whether or not a man was a messiah, his con-
> temporaries would find that he matched their favorite picture in some
> points, but not in others. Insofar as the messianic pretender won fol-
> lowers, or those determined to be followers found a figure they could
> identify as a messiah, the meaning of the term "messiah" was changed
> to accommodate these new phenomena.[75]

Just so. A would-be messiah acts out the traditional script, so to speak, but he
also inevitably rewrites parts of the script along the way.[76] If what scholars have
called "Christian messianism" is indeed an ingenious, even desperate assimila-
tion of scriptural tradition to the circumstances of a particular messiah's life,
then it is not at all something separate from or other than Jewish messianism.
On the contrary, it is just an exceptionally well-documented instance of the latter.

Against the Christian Side of the Distinction

If there are many ancient Jewish messiah texts in which—contrary to
stereotype—the language of the biblical tradition is assimilated to the circumstances of historical figures or events, there are also many ancient Christian
messiah texts in which—contrary to stereotype—utopian biblical traditions

---

Lubavitcher Rebbe, see Joel Marcus, "The Once and Future Messiah in Early Christianity
and Chabad," *NTS* 47 (2001): 381–401; and more exhaustively Elliot R. Wolfson, *Open
Secret: Postmessianic Messianism and the Mystical Revision of Menahem Mendel Schneerson*
(New York, N.Y.: Columbia University Press, 2009).

75. Smith, "Robbers, Jurists, Prophets," 41–42. Similarly Dahl, "Eschatology and History in
Light of the Qumran Texts," 56:

> [There is a] correlation between the sociological structure and history of the com-
> munities and their eschatological interpretation of Scripture and messianic doc-
> trine. Events and persons are understood in light of eschatological prophecies, and
> transmitted texts and concepts receive new explanations from events.

76. Compare Collins, *Scepter*, 215–37, who describes the popular royal movements in 4 BCE
and 66 to 70 CE as "messianic dreams in action," a phrase that captures nicely the former
dynamic but not the latter.

are ingeniously maintained despite their apparent nonfulfillment in the events of Jesus's career. In other words, the Jewish messiah–Christian messiah distinction is undermined by counterexamples on the one side as well as the other. The predominant early Christian mechanism for maintaining biblical messiah traditions in the face of the suboptimal circumstances of Jesus's life is the belief in the parousia of Jesus. At the parousia, which is more or less future, according to different early Christian texts, Jesus will discharge a range of messianic duties that he did not discharge during the course of his ministry:[77] He will judge the wicked (Jas 5:7), gather the elect and raise the dead (1 Thess 2:19; 3:13; 4:15; 5:23), slay the great and final enemy of God (2 Thess 2:1–12), subdue all evil powers and hand over the kingdom to God (1 Cor 15:20–28), put an end to the present age and usher in the age to come (2 Pet 3:1–10), and so on. As Paula Fredriksen, writing in a different context, has put it, "Early Christian descriptions of the Parousia, both in Paul's letters and in the later gospels, are the measure of the strength of this Jewish tradition. Jesus' classically messianic performance at his Second Coming was to offset his untraditional earthly ministry."[78]

This early Christian trope is attested already in our earliest extant Christian text, 1 Thessalonians.[79] There, the apostle Paul praises his Macedonian gentiles-in-Christ, who

> turned to God from idols, to serve a living and true God, and to wait for his son from heaven [ἀναμένειν τὸν υἱὸν αὐτοῦ ἐκ τῶν οὐρανῶν], whom

---

77. See Philipp Vielhauer and Georg Strecker, "Introduction: Apocalyptic in Early Christianity," in *New Testament Apocrypha* (rev. ed.; 2 vols.; ed. Edgar Hennecke and Wilhelm Schneemelcher; trans. R. McL. Wilson; Cambridge: Clarke, 1992), 2:571: "In place of the expectation of the reign of God there now appears the expectation of the Parousia of Christ, and at this point the momentous influx of apocalyptic ideas takes place." But Vielhauer's distinction between the kingdom of God and the parousia of Christ is overdrawn. A critical retrospective on Vielhauer's essay is given by William Adler, "Introduction," in *The Jewish Apocalyptic Heritage in Early Christianity* (ed. James C. VanderKam and William Adler; CRINT 3.4; Assen: Van Gorcum, 1996), 1–31, especially 1–8. See further Joost Holleman, *Resurrection and Parousia: A Tradition–Historical Study of Paul's Eschatology in 1 Corinthians 15* (NovTSup 84; Leiden: Brill, 1996), 95–122.

78. Paula Fredriksen, *From Jesus to Christ* (2d ed.; New Haven, Conn.: Yale University Press, 2000), 168. See also Flusser, "Jewish Messianism Reflected in the Early Church," 276–77:

> The Christian faithful yearned for a speedy and successful conclusion to the messianic drama. The belief in Christ's advent parallels the Jewish messianic hopes, and it is clear that Christian thought on this topic, throughout history, was influenced by corresponding Jewish thought with regard to messianic biblical interpretation and other matters.

79. See Hogeterp, *Expectations of the End*, 207–13.

he raised from the dead, Jesus who delivers us from the wrath to come [Ἰησοῦν τὸν ῥυόμενον ἡμᾶς ἐκ τῆς ὀργῆς τῆς ἐρχομένης]. (1 Thess 1:9–10)

For Paul, Jesus's messiahship certainly includes the fate that befell him in Judea some twenty years before (1 Thess 2:15), but those circumstances do not displace his traditional messianic role as eschatological judge. The same messiah Jesus who died and rose (1 Thess 4:14, 16) will come again soon as avenger and deliverer: "Let no one transgress and wrong his brother in this matter, because the Lord is an avenger in all these things [διότι ἔκδικος κύριος περὶ πάντων τούτων], as we solemnly forewarned you" (1 Thess 4:6). Hence Paul's prayer "that God may establish your hearts blameless in holiness before our God and Father, at the coming of our Lord Jesus with all his holy ones [ἐν τῇ παρουσίᾳ τοῦ κυρίου ἡμῶν Ἰησοῦ μετὰ πάντων τῶν ἁγίων αὐτοῦ]" (1 Thess 3:13). In short, the pastness of the messiah does not displace his still-future coming in glory. Paul does not redefine *messiah* to mean just "he who died for our sins."[80] Rather, he expands the conventional motif of a victorious messiah ben David to include the latter idea, as well.[81]

Paul writes in the 50s CE, just two decades after the death of Jesus, but an analogous perspective on the messiahship of Jesus and the parousia is attested a generation later in Luke-Acts. Luke, like Paul, sees the death and resurrection of Jesus as a necessity of his messianic office. He tells a story of Paul reasoning with a group of Jews in Thessalonica, "explaining and proving that it was necessary for the messiah to suffer and to rise from the dead [τὸν χριστὸν ἔδει παθεῖν καὶ ἀναστῆναι ἐκ νεκρῶν]" (Acts 17:3). Nevertheless, for Luke as for Paul, it still remains for the messiah Jesus to discharge his office in full. So Luke has Peter say in his speech in the Jerusalem temple complex in Acts 3:

Repent therefore, and turn again, that your sins may be blotted out, that times of refreshing may come from the presence of the Lord, and

---

80. *Pace* Dahl, "Messiahship of Jesus in Paul," 17: "An *interpretatio christiana* is carried out completely." Compare the more accurate statement of Dahl, "Messiahship of Jesus in Paul," 22:

> For Paul the parousia is somehow tied to Jerusalem: "The Deliverer will come from Zion, he will banish ungodliness from Jacob." This nonspiritualized, Old Testament messianic expectation cannot be regarded as an isolated and inconsequential rudiment in the Son of God and kyrios Christology. On the contrary, this confirms that Jesus' messiahship actually had a fundamental significance for the total structure of Paul's Christology.

81. See Novenson, *Christ among the Messiahs*, 143–46, 156–60, 174–78; also Joel Willitts, "Davidic Messiahship in Galatians: Clearing the Deck for a Study of the Theme in Galatians," *JSPL* 2 (2012): 143–62; and Matthew V. Novenson, "The Messiah ben Abraham in Galatians: A Response to Joel Willitts," *JSPL* 2 (2012): 163–70.

that he may send the messiah appointed for you, Jesus [ἀποστείλῃ τὸν προκεχειρισμένον ὑμῖν χριστὸν Ἰησοῦν], whom heaven must receive until the time for establishing [ὃν δεῖ οὐρανὸν μὲν δέξασθαι ἄχρι χρόνων ἀποκαταστάσεως] all that God spoke by the mouth of his holy prophets from of old. (Acts 3:19–21)[82]

It is not the case that Luke rejects a messiah who restores the kingdom in favor of a messiah who suffers on behalf of his people; it is just that heaven must hold him until the time comes for the restoration.[83]

The Apocalypse of John, probably written or at least redacted into its current form during the 90s CE, is perhaps the clearest early Christian statement of the ideal, still-future messiahship of Jesus.[84] John of Patmos, like his predecessors, reconciles biblical messiah traditions to the unhappy circumstances of Jesus's death:

One of the elders said to me, "Do not weep. See, the lion of the tribe of Judah, the root of David, has conquered [ἐνίκησεν ὁ λέων ὁ ἐκ τῆς φυλῆς Ἰούδα, ἡ ῥίζα Δαυίδ], so that he can open the scroll and its seven seals." And between the throne and the four living creatures and among the elders, I saw a lamb standing, as though it had been slain [ἀρνίον ἑστηκὸς ὡς ἐσφαγμένον]. (Rev 5:5–6)[85]

This slaughtered-lamb-messiah motif notwithstanding, however, the Apocalypse is stridently triumphalist in its portrayal of the parousia of Jesus.[86] "Behold, he is coming with the clouds, and every eye will see him, every one who pierced him; and all tribes of the earth will wail on account of him" (Rev 1:7). And again:

The seventh angel blew his trumpet, and there were loud voices in heaven, saying, "The kingdom of the world has become the kingdom

---

82. On this verse, see my discussion later in this chapter.

83. Thus rightly Richard H. Hiers, "The Problem of the Delay of the Parousia in Luke-Acts," *NTS* 20 (1974): 145–55, in response to Hans Conzelmann, *The Theology of St. Luke* (New York, N.Y.: Harper & Row, 1960 [German original, 1953]). See further Strauss, *Davidic Messiah in Luke-Acts*, 261–336; Arie W. Zwiep, *The Ascension of the Messiah in Lukan Christology* (NovTSup 87; Leiden: Brill, 1997), 175–82

84. On this point, see Richard Bauckham, *The Climax of Prophecy: Studies on the Book of Revelation* (London: T. & T. Clark, 1993), 38–91, 92–117.

85. On the slaughtered lamb messiah in Revelation, see Brian K. Blount, *Revelation: A Commentary* (NTL; Louisville, Ky.: WJK, 2009), 116–18.

86. Thus rightly Adela Yarbro Collins, *Crisis and Catharsis: The Power of the Apocalypse* (Philadelphia, Pa.: Westminster, 1984), 141–44.

of our lord and of his messiah [ἡ βασιλεία τοῦ κόσμου τοῦ κυρίου ἡμῶν καὶ τοῦ χριστοῦ αὐτοῦ], and he shall reign for ever and ever [βασιλεύσει εἰς τοὺς αἰῶνας τῶν αἰώνων]." (Rev 11:15)

In short, although the messianism of the Apocalypse is demonstrably shaped by the circumstances of Jesus's death, it does not for that reason interiorize, spiritualize, or otherwise do away with the triumphalist messiah ben David tradition. John accommodates the former to the latter, apparently unaware of any incompatibility of the sort identified by proponents of the Jewish messiah–Christian messiah distinction.[87] This is to cite a few examples from the first Christian century, but the same function of the doctrine of the parousia is evident in the chiliasm of certain ecclesiastical writers of the second and third centuries.[88] The classically messianic functions are not abandoned or reinterpreted; they are just postponed until the proper time.[89]

Indeed, so striking is this tendency among the parousia texts that a number of major twentieth-century writers on early Christology—in particular, John A. T. Robinson in Britain, Ferdinand Hahn in Germany, and R. H. Fuller in the United States—took the view that the title "messiah" only became attached to Jesus in connection with the early Christian hope for the parousia.[90] From there, the argument goes, the title gradually became associated in early Christian usage with other aspects of Jesus's career—healing the sick, dying for sins, rising on the third day, and so on—but from the beginning it was not so. In the earliest layer, "the most primitive Christology of all," to use

---

87. On this twofold Christology in the Apocalypse, see Matthias Reinhard Hoffmann, *The Destroyer and the Lamb: The Relationship between Angelomorphic and Lamb Christology in the Book of Revelation* (WUNT 2.203; Tübingen: Mohr Siebeck, 2005).

88. See Chapter 7 in this volume.

89. Contra Neusner, *Messiah in Context*, 229:

> Insofar as the apocalyptic expectations were not realized—indeed, could not have been realized—the Messiah had to become something other than what people originally expected. True, he will still be called Christ. But he will be what the Church needs him to be: anything but the terminus of a world history that—up to now—refuses to come to an end.

90. See J. A. T. Robinson, "The Most Primitive Christology of All?" *JTS* n.s. 7 (1956): 177–89; idem, *Jesus and His Coming: The Emergence of a Doctrine* (London: SCM, 1957), 140–59; Ferdinand Hahn, *Christologische Hoheitstitel: Ihre Geschichte im frühen Christentum* (FRLANT 83; Göttingen: Vandenhoeck & Ruprecht, 1963); ET *The Titles of Jesus in Christology: Their History in Early Christianity* (trans. Harold Knight and George Ogg; London: Lutterworth, 1969), 136–239, especially 161–68; R. H. Fuller, *The Foundations of New Testament Christology* (New York, N.Y.: Scribner, 1965), 158–60.

Robinson's phrase, Jesus was only *messias designatus*, not *messias constitutus*. The most important text in support of this hypothesis is the fragment of Peter's speech in Acts 3: "Repent therefore, and turn again . . . that the Lord may send the messiah appointed for you, Jesus [ἀποστείλη τὸν προκεχειρισμένον ὑμῖν χριστὸν Ἰησοῦν]" (Acts 3:19–20). On one possible interpretation of this text, "the messiah appointed for you" designates an office that Jesus does not yet hold, not even after the resurrection, much less in his itinerant ministry.[91] Hahn reasons along these lines:

> The messianic concept was exclusively applied to the ultimate activity of Jesus, to His coming again, and to the hope of salvation connected with this. The messianic status of Jesus was therefore not at first confessed in view of his resurrection and exaltation, but relatively to His authoritative action at the coming parousia.[92]

And again, "Jewish messianism furnished no possibility of including the earthly work of Jesus under a title of exaltation. If the theory could be applied at all, it had to be exclusively in regard to the eschatological work of Jesus."[93] On this account, in other words, the very earliest Christian messianism was every bit as future-oriented as its Jewish counterpart.

In point of fact, this *messias designatus* hypothesis is a bridge too far. As Nils Dahl pointed out, the notion of the messiahship of Jesus is too thoroughly attested in the Gospel tradition, and elsewhere in too many contexts entirely unrelated to the parousia.[94] What is more, the parousia passages actually use the titles "lord" and "son of man" far more than they do "messiah," so that the respective terms appear in the wrong contexts relative to the theory.[95] These criticisms notwithstanding, Hahn and like-minded interpreters are quite right

---

91. Compare the earlier view of William Wrede, who pushed the origin of the messiahship of Jesus from his ministry to the resurrection, but not as far as the parousia: "In his earthly life, to be sure, Jesus lacks only one thing in order to be the messiah: namely the sovereign dignity and power. But this one thing is the whole thing. It is precisely what makes the concept of messiah what it is" (Wrede, *Messianic Secret*, 216).

92. Hahn, *Titles of Jesus*, 162.

93. Hahn, *Titles of Jesus*, 189.

94. Dahl, "Crucified Messiah." Albert Schweitzer had argued along similar lines in response to Wrede (Albert Schweitzer, *The Quest of the Historical Jesus: A Critical Study of Its Progress from Reimarus to Wrede* [trans. W. Montgomery; New York, N.Y.: Macmillan, 1961 (German original, 1906)], 330–97).

95. On this point, see Nils A. Dahl, "Messianic Ideas and the Crucifixion of Jesus," in *The Messiah*, 382–403 at 395–96; Graham N. Stanton, "The Gospel Traditions and Early

to insist that early Christian messianism does not simply redefine *messiah* to reflect its memories of Jesus; its messiah remains idealized and still future, at least in large part. The early Christian belief in the parousia of Jesus had a kind of compensatory function, enabling the preservation of certain utopian aspects of the messiah myth alongside the many concessions to the circumstances of Jesus's life.[96]

Upon reflection, then, the one side of the Jewish messiah–Christian messiah distinction turns out to be as problematic as the other. The scholarly stereotype is that early Christian messiah texts redefine *messiah* to fit the circumstances of the life of Jesus, whereas early Jewish messiah texts project biblical tradition into an ideal future. But in fact, on both sides of the putative distinction, the counterexamples pile up. Many early Jewish messiah texts are shaped by particular historical persons and events, and many early Christian messiah texts maintain ideal biblical traditions despite their nonfulfillment in the life of Jesus. When the counterexamples begin to outnumber the examples, one wonders whether the time has come to abandon the rubric altogether. In fact, it is simpler and more accurate to say that all ancient messiah texts, Jewish as well as Christian, find themselves having to manage ideal biblical traditions on the one hand and empirical historical circumstances on the other. In this respect, messianism is just another instance of the vast ancient Jewish and Christian enterprise of biblical interpretation.[97]

Cui Bono

If the Jewish messiah–Christian messiah distinction is indeed liable to the criticisms that I have leveled here, it is worth considering, finally, why it has been such a dominant motif in modern scholarship. On this question, although it is impossible to divine the motives of any particular interpreter, it is possible to get an idea of the rhetorical uses to which the distinction has been put by its proponents, Jewish, Christian, and otherwise.[98] And rhetorically useful it

---

Christological Reflection," in *Christ, Faith, and History: Cambridge Studies in Christology* (ed. S. W. Sykes and J. P. Clayton; Cambridge: Cambridge University Press, 1972), 191–204 at 202.

96. On this point, see further John G. Gager, *Kingdom and Community: The Social World of Early Christianity* (Englewood Cliffs, N.J.: Prentice-Hall, 1975), 37–49.

97. On which see Kugel, *The Bible As It Was*, 1–50.

98. For a model of this kind of analysis, see Dale B. Martin, "Paul and the Judaism/Hellenism Dichotomy: Toward a Social History of the Question," in *Paul beyond the Judaism/Hellenism Divide* (ed. Troels Engberg-Pedersen; Louisville, Ky.: WJK, 2001), 29–61.

has certainly been.[99] Several such uses, at least, are readily apparent in the secondary literature. To a certain supersessionist Christian line of reasoning, less
popular now than a generation ago but by no means obsolete, the Christian
messiah is so different from the Jewish messiah as to be morally or religiously
superior to it. On such a view, the early Jewish concept "messiah" suffers
from some perceived deficiency (e.g., carnality or this-worldliness or ethno-
centrism or a tendency to violence), but Jesus purges, spiritualizes, redefines,
or revolutionizes the concept. Mowinckel, for instance, writes about Jesus's
Selbstverständnis:

> The Jewish Messianic concept is thereby transformed, and lifted up to a
> wholly other plane. In fact, the Jewish Messiah, as originally conceived,
> and as most of Jesus' contemporaries thought of him, was pushed aside
> and replaced by a new redeemer and mediator of salvation. . ... For Jesus,
> the Jewish Messianic idea was the temptation of Satan, which He had
> to reject. The new conception of a saviour, which Jesus created, unites
> in itself the loftiest elements in both the Jewish and the "Aryan" spirit,
> and fuses them in a true unity, which is realized in Jesus Himself.[100]

Contrariwise, to a certain apologetic Jewish line of reasoning, the Christian
messiah is so different from the Jewish messiah as to be, well, not a messiah at
all. On such a view, Christian talk about a spiritual messiah is really so much
wishful thinking. To resort to the idea of a spiritual messiah is, effectively,
to concede that the person in question is simply not a messiah. As R. J. Zwi
Werblowsky has commented:

> Jewish apologists tended to view Christian accusations of a "carnal"
> understanding of messianic deliverance as a compliment. To them it
> seemed that a certain type of spirituality was merely an escape into
> a realm where one was safe from the challenges of historical reality
> whose tests one evaded.[101]

Such a view is represented, for example, in the well-known comment of
Martin Buber:

---

99. Thus rightly Reed, "Messianism between Judaism and Christianity," 23: "Christianity's
origins in Jewish messianism has [sic] served as a potent site for reflection on religious
identity—not just in the first century, but in Late Antiquity and modernity as well."

100. Mowinckel, *He That Cometh*, 449–50.

101. Werblowsky, "Messianism in Jewish History," 44.

In the perspective of my faith, the word spoken to Jesus by Peter at Caesarea Philippi—"You are the Messiah"—was sincere but nevertheless untrue; and its repetition over the centuries has not brought it any closer to the truth. According to my faith, the Messiah has not appeared in a definite moment of history, but rather his appearance can only mark the end of history. In the perspective of my faith, the redemption of the world did not happen nineteen centuries ago. On the contrary, we still live in an unredeemed world.[102]

Very differently and more recently, to a certain ecumenical line of reasoning, the Jewish messiah–Christian messiah distinction is invoked as warrant for the welcome mutual noninterference of the two religions. On such a view, if the Christian messiah is simply not the same thing as the Jewish messiah, then the two can be construed as nonoverlapping magisteria, so to speak, and any christological grounds for interreligious criticism or proselytization dissolves altogether. John Gager, for instance, cites with approval Lloyd Gaston's claim that "for Paul, Jesus is neither a new Moses nor the Messiah, he is not the climax of the history of God's dealing with Israel, but he is the fulfillment of God's promises concerning the Gentiles";[103] whence Gager infers: "If we remove this apocalyptic mystery [from Pauline theology] altogether . . . we are left with two basic affirmations: one, God's unshakable commitment to Israel and to the holiness of the law (=Judaism); and, two, the redemption of the Gentiles through Jesus Christ (=Christianity)."[104]

These several interpretations of the Jewish messiah–Christian messiah distinction have been variously influential according as their respective proponents and audiences have found them useful. The salient point, however, is that they are religious value judgments, not historical descriptions. More

---

102. As cited in translation by J. Louis Martyn, *Theological Issues in the Letters of Paul* (London: T. & T. Clark, 2005 [1997]), 279. The quote comes from a letter written by Buber in 1926 and recorded in Franz von Hammerstein, *Das Messiasproblem bei Martin Buber* (Stuttgart: Kohlhammer, 1958), 49. Reinhold Niebuhr records a similar statement from a speech of Buber to a conference of Dutch ministers: "To the Christian the Jew is the stubborn fellow who in a redeemed world is still waiting for the Messiah. For the Jew the Christian is a heedless fellow who in an unredeemed world affirms that somehow or other redemption has taken place" (Reinhold Niebuhr, "Martin Buber: 1878–1965," *Christianity and Crisis* 25 [12 July 1965]: 146). Buber's version of the Jewish messiah–Christian messiah distinction is developed in his *Two Types of Faith* (trans. Norman P. Goldhawk; New York, N.Y.: Macmillan, 1951).

103. Lloyd Gaston, *Paul and the Torah* (Vancouver: UBC Press, 1987), 33; cited in John G. Gager, *Reinventing Paul* (New York, N.Y.: Oxford University Press, 2000),142.

104. Gager, *Reinventing Paul*, 152.

specifically, they are attempts to cope with precisely that feature of the early Jewish and Christian texts that has been the burden of this chapter—namely, the use by those texts of the very same cluster of discursive resources.[105] In fact, the Jewish messiah–Christian messiah distinction does not recognize a difference; it creates one. It inscribes a convenient notional boundary where there is otherwise uncomfortable contested territory. Scholem is quite right in observing that the modern discussion of messianism remains a delicate affair, still today as in the mid twentieth century when he was writing. Ironically, however, the delicacy of the subject matter has to do not so much with a putative ideological chasm between Judaism and Christianity as with their awkward proximity to one another.

---

105. Thus rightly Reed, "Messianism between Judaism and Christianity," 23: "It may be a truism that belief in Jesus as messiah is what differentiates 'Christian' from 'Jew,' but this point of differentiation is predicated on the entanglement of their histories." On this point, see further José Costa, "Le Messie judéo-chrétien et les rabbins," in *Aux origines des messianismes juifs*, 203–27.

7

The Fate of Messiah Christology in Early Christianity

SOMETIME IN THE early the second century CE, probably in Alexandria in Egypt, an anonymous Christian author who later tradents identified with Barnabas the companion of the apostle Paul (Gal 2:1, 9, 13; 1 Cor 9:6; cf. Acts 11–15) wrote an elaborate supersessionist tractate claiming a list of venerable ancient Israelite institutions for the Christians and denying them to the Jews.[1] The *Epistle of Barnabas* warns his readers to give no quarter to the fleshly children of Abraham: "Watch yourselves now, and do not be like some people, piling up your sins by saying that the covenant is both theirs and ours. It is ours" (*Barn.* 4.6–7).[2] In due course, the author comes to the topic of the messiah, who according to the Jews is the son of David but according to *Barnabas* is the son of God. Our author writes:

> See again Jesus, not son of man, but son of God, manifested in a type in the flesh. Since then they are going to say that the messiah is the son of David ['Επεὶ οὖν μέλλουσιν λέγειν ὅτι ὁ χριστὸς υἱός ἐστιν Δαυίδ], David himself prophesies, fearing and understanding the error of the sinners: *The lord said to my lord* [Εἶπεν κύριος τῷ κυρίῳ μου]: *Sit at my right hand until I make your enemies a footstool for your feet* [Ps 110:1 (OG Ps 109:1)]. And again Isaiah speaks thus: *The lord said to the messiah my lord* [Εἶπεν κύριος τῷ χριστῷ μου κυρίῳ], *whose right hand I held, that the nations should obey before him, and I will shatter the strength of*

---

1. On issues of critical introduction, see Jay Curry Treat, "Barnabas, Epistle of," *ABD* 1:611–14.

2. Greek text ed. Pierre Prigent and Robert A. Kraft, *Épître de Barnabé* (SC 172; Paris: Cerf, 1971); trans. mine.

kings [Isa 45:1]. See how David calls him "lord" and does not say "son."
(*Barn.* 12.10–11)

Not for nothing has *Barnabas* been called a stridently anti-Jewish text.[3] But whereas the anti-Judaism of, say, Marcion of Sinope expresses itself in a contempt for the Jewish scriptures, the anti-Judaism of *Barnabas* expresses itself in a zealous appropriation of those scriptures. In this short passage we have a hermeneutical *tour de force* and an excellent illustration of the curious fate of messiah Christology in early Christianity.[4]

The *Epistle of Barnabas* would seem to have virtually no interest in maintaining a messiah Christology. Only here (*Barn.* 12.10–11) and at one other place (*Barn.* 2.6) does he call Jesus χριστός, "messiah" or "Christ," otherwise consistently preferring "Jesus" and "lord."[5] And yet, he raises the messiah issue at *Barn.* 12.10 for polemical reasons. "They are going to say that the messiah is the son of David," but *Barnabas* has a stake in a son of God Christology, which he takes to exclude the Jewish—and, for that matter, Christian—tradition of the Davidic ancestry of the messiah. (*Barnabas* will not cede the word "messiah" to the Jews, even if he has little use for it himself.) He engages, therefore, in a bit of messianic exegesis, invoking two scriptural oracles that also feature prominently in a number of other early Jewish and Christian messiah texts. His use of the first oracle, Ps 110:1 (OG Ps 109:1), is almost identical to the use of that text in the famous *Davidssohnfrage* episode in the Synoptic Gospels.[6] The Synoptists (certainly Matthew and Luke, and probably Mark, too) regard Jesus's Davidic ancestry as quite compatible with his divine sonship. Not

---

3. For example, S. Lowy, "The Confutation of Judaism in the Epistle of Barnabas," *JJS* 11 (1960): 1–33; Martin B. Shukster and Peter Richardson, "Temple and *Bet Ha-midrash* in the Epistle of Barnabas," in *Anti-Judaism in Early Christianity*, vol. 2 (ed. Stephen G. Wilson; ESCJ 3; Waterloo, Ont.: Wilfrid Laurier University Press, 1986), 17–32.

4. On this passage, see in particular Robert A. Kraft, "Barnabas' Isaiah Text and the 'Testimony Book' Hypothesis," *JBL* 79 (1960): 336–50, especially 341–42; idem, "The Epistle of Barnabas: Its Quotations and Their Sources" (Ph.D. diss., Harvard University, 1961), 242–45; James Carleton Paget, *The Epistle of Barnabas: Outlook and Background* (WUNT 2.64; Tübingen: Mohr Siebeck, 1994), 154–62.

5. *Barn.* 2.6: ὁ καινὸς νόμος τοῦ κυρίου ἡμῶν Ἰησοῦ Χριστοῦ, "the new law of our lord Jesus Christ."

6. Mark 12:35–37:

> [Jesus] said, "How can the scribes say that the messiah is the son of David? David himself, inspired by the holy spirit, said, *The lord said to my lord: Sit at my right hand, until I put your enemies under your feet.* David himself calls him lord; so how is he his son?"

so *Barnabas*. For the latter, the Davidic ancestry of the messiah is ruled out by the psalm.[7]

Barnabas then quotes a second oracle in support of this same point. Isaiah, he says, writes, "The lord said to the messiah my lord [Εἶπεν κύριος τῷ χριστῷ μου κυρίῳ], whose right hand I held," and so on. Perhaps our author was attracted to the close verbal parallel between his text of Isa 45:1 (Εἶπεν κύριος τῷ χριστῷ μου κυρίῳ) and his text of Ps 110:1 (Εἶπεν κύριος τῷ κυρίῳ μου), but there are two conspicuous problems here: one logical and the other text-critical. First, although David's calling the messiah "lord" might seem to preclude the messiah's Davidic ancestry, Isaiah's calling the messiah "lord" does no such thing; the Isaiah citation is not to the point. Second, Isaiah does not in fact call the messiah "lord," at least, not in any known text of Isaiah prior to *Barnabas*.[8] Isaiah calls the messiah "Cyrus" (Greek κύρῳ, transliterating Hebrew כורש), not "lord" (Greek κυρίῳ).[9] Admittedly, the difference is only a single iota; but without that iota, *Barnabas*'s whole point is undone. We should not be too hard on him, however. Deutero-Isaiah's reference to the Achaemenid Persian king Cyrus II as the messiah of YHWH (Isa 45:1) proved a challenge to other ancient exegetes far abler than *Barnabas*.[10] Whether he found his Isaiah text already corrupted or made the change himself, *Barnabas* uses Isa 45:1 as an occasion to wade into the morass of early Jewish and Christian messiah discourse. Never mind that *Barnabas* has no ideological commitment to messiah

---

Compare the parallel passages at Matt 22:41–46 and Luke 20:41–44, and see the discussion in Chapter 3 in this volume.

7. On the question of a literary relation between *Barnabas* and the Synoptic Gospels, see Helmut Koester, *Synoptische Überlieferung bei den Apostolischen Vätern* (TUGAL 65; Berlin: Akademie-Verlag, 1957), 124–58.

8. The reading κυρίῳ is not attested in any manuscripts of OG Isaiah, but after *Barnabas*, it is attested in Christian writers including Irenaeus, Tertullian, Cyprian, Novatian, Lactantius, Tyconius, Evagrius, and Jerome. See the discussion by Kraft, "Barnabas' Isaiah Text," 342, who notes, "This testimony from Isa 45 1 apparently had gained a revered spot in the apologetic of early Christianity."

9. Compare MT Isa 45:1: כה־אמר יהוה למשיחו לכורש; OG Isa 45:1: Οὕτως λέγει κύριος ὁ θεὸς τῷ χριστῷ μου Κύρῳ; Isa 45:1 *apud* Barn. 12.11: Εἶπεν κύριος τῷ χριστῷ μου κυρίῳ.

10. See the ingenious repunctuation of the oracle given in *b. Meg.* 21a:

R. Nahman b. R. Hisda gave the following exposition: What is the meaning of the verse, *Thus says YHWH to his messiah, to Cyrus* [כה־אמר יהוה למשיחו לכורש], *whose right hand I have grasped* [Isa 45:1]? Now, was Cyrus the messiah? Rather, what it means is: The Holy One, blessed be He, said to the messiah: I have a complaint for you against Cyrus [א"ל הקב"ה למשיח קובל אני על כורש]. I said, *He shall build my city and send forth my exiles* [Isa 45:13], but he said, *Whoever is among you of all his people, let him go up* [Ezra 1:3=2 Chr 36:23]. (text from and trans. mod. from Soncino)

On this passage, see my discussion in Chapter 2 in this volume.

Christology. The word "messiah" was attached to Jesus by dint of tradition, and the Jews had a counterclaim on the word, so *Barnabas* undertakes a messianic exegesis to claim it for the Christians.[11] For him, as for many early Christian writers of diverse perspectives, messianism continued to present a kind of discursive puzzle.

The End of Messiah Christology?

Although, as I argued in Chapter 6, the messianic movement around Jesus of Nazareth was not generically different from other Roman-period Jewish messianic movements, the *Nachleben* of the Jesus movement did of course prove different, inasmuch as it yielded late antique Christianity. By the turn of the second century, several factors in particular—the delay of the parousia of Jesus, the destruction of the Jerusalem temple, and the demographic shift within the sect to a Greek-speaking, gentile majority—contributed to significant changes in messiah discourse in early Christianity. In fact, according to many leading lights, messiah discourse effectively disappeared from early Christianity by the turn of the second century. Thus, for instance, Jacob Neusner writes:

> Insofar as the apocalyptic expectations were not realized—indeed, could not have been realized—the Messiah had to become something other than what people originally expected. True, he will still be called Christ. But he will be what the Church needs him to be: anything but the terminus of a world history that—up to now—refuses to come to an end.[12]

On Neusner's account, the name "Christ" in early Christianity is a relic of the movement's origins in Jewish messianism, nothing more. The category "messiah" ceased to be meaningful to Christians in late antiquity, for which reason Christian texts—despite their conspicuous use of the relevant words—contribute nothing to an understanding of ancient messianism.

Harris Lenowitz has made a related argument from the perspective of the sociology of religion. He writes:

> Christianity achieved its power and endurance largely by abandoning the goals and society of Jesus and his disciples following his death. Within Judaism, Jesus is not regarded as a fulfilled messiah, and the

---

11. For this point, I am indebted to a valuable conversation with David Lincicum.

12. Neusner, *Messiah in Context*, 229; and compare idem, "Mishnah and Messiah," 280.

Jesus Christ of Christianity is generally thought of as the retrospective application of a name to a host of sociohistorical events and identities that neither he nor his immediate following had much to do with. Christianity in fact ceased to be a messianic movement and became instead a revitalization movement.[13]

On Lenowitz's social-science model, Jewish messianic movements, by definition, do not last longer than a generation. They cannot, because each messianic movement performs the script of the thrilling rise and inevitable fall of the messiah figure.[14] Lenowitz grants that Jesus of Nazareth and his circle constituted a messianic movement, but what came after Jesus's death was something else entirely, a revitalization movement. To speak of messiah Christology in early Christian texts is, therefore, a category mistake.

The assessments of Neusner and Lenowitz find confirmation in a number of treatments of early Christian Christology, in which messianism is said to figure little or not at all. Thus George MacRae argues that, already in the first century CE and *a fortiori* thereafter, Christian writers betray a preoccupation with the man Jesus rather than messiah traditions and with Greek categories rather than Jewish ones. He writes:

> Messianism is essentially a product of Jewish religion, with its roots, if not its most explicit articulation, deeply embedded in the literature of Israel. Our general question must involve this inquiry: How do we recognize the older messianic aspirations in the literature of a movement [viz. Christianity] that expresses itself almost exclusively in Greek and more often than not in Greek categories of thought?[15]

In point of fact, MacRae concludes, we do not, by and large, recognize the older messianic aspirations therein. Early Christian Christology is about other things.[16] A similar note is struck by Aloys Grillmeier in his history of Christology from the first to the fifth century. Grillmeier writes:

> The second century introduced the great task of the patristic period, that of achieving a better grasp of the data of revelation with the help

---

13. Lenowitz, *Jewish Messiahs,* 7.

14. See Lenowitz, *Jewish Messiahs,* 3–22, especially 5–9.

15. MacRae, "Messiah and Gospel," 169.

16. See MacRae, "Messiah and Gospel," 184: "One may be surprised to observe, not how central the messianic idea is to the gospel, but how it is in a sense peripheral."

of pagan philosophy. This proved to be a powerful driving force to theological progress and a favourite starting point for heresies. It had important consequences for christology: the dynamic presentation of the mission of Christ in the economy of salvation was impregnated more and more with a static-ontological awareness of the reality of Christ as God and man.[17]

On Grillmeier's account, to the extent that the ecclesiastical writers were concerned with "a static-ontological awareness of the reality of Christ as God and man"—which is to say, to a very great extent—the biblical category "messiah" fell out of currency in late antique Christology.

There is more than a little truth in this prevailing scholarly opinion. It is certainly the case that Christian writers of the second through the fifth centuries expended enormous energy on christological questions (e.g., the problem of the passibility of Christ) that never entered the minds of their first-century forebears. And relatedly, many of the questions that preoccupied the first and second generations (e.g., the necessity of proselyte circumcision for admission to the messianic kingdom) began to fade from view under changed circumstances.[18] And yet. In many instances, questions raised and discourses adopted during the apostolic period set the terms for discussion for centuries to come, even as those questions and discourses were thoroughly revised, reformulated, and supplemented. Messiah Christology, I mean to argue in this chapter, is one such instance. Even as other, quite different christological questions came to the fore in late antiquity, the deeply ingrained habit of speaking of Jesus as "Christ" or "messiah" endured as a possibility and a puzzle for early Christian writers.

Just here, I take a cue from David Flusser, who, in a perceptive essay titled "Jewish Messianism Reflected in the Early Church," makes this methodological point: "Christianity was originally a Jewish messianic movement. Even when it separated from Judaism, changed its structure and became an independent religion, the Jewish messianic ideas within it continued their independent life within the church, sometimes with their original nature essentially unchanged."[19] I find different instances of this phenomenon than Flusser does, and I see rather more creativity and change in the texts than he

---

17. Aloys Grillmeier, *Christ in Christian Tradition*, vol. 1 (trans. J. S. Bowden; London: Mowbray, 1965), 40.

18. A point well made by Paula Fredriksen, "How Later Contexts Affect Pauline Content, or: Retrospect is the Mother of Anachronism," in *Jews and Christians in the First and Second Centuries: How to Write Their History* (ed. Peter J. Tomson and Joshua Schwartz; CRINT 13; Leiden: Brill, 2014), 17–51.

19. Flusser, "Jewish Messianism Reflected in the Early Church," 258.

allows, but I take his fundamental point as a welcome insight: The Jewish messiah discourse that is so prominent in texts from the first and second generations of the Jesus movement does not just disappear at the turn of the second century. There is more to the story. There are traces of messiah discourse, albeit in sometimes surprising permutations, here and there throughout late antique Christianity, in heterodox circles as well as orthodox.

There is some support for an argument of this kind in the secondary literature on patristic Christology, as well. J. N. D. Kelly, for instance, comments:

> Until the middle of the second century, when Hellenistic ideas began to come to the fore, Christian theology was taking shape in predominantly Judaistic moulds, and the categories of thought used by almost all Christian writers before the Apologists were largely Jewish. This explains why the teaching of the Apostolic Father[s], for example, while not strictly unorthodox, often strikes a strange note when judged by later standards. And it is certain that this "Judaeo-Christian" theology continued to exercise a powerful influence well beyond the second century.[20]

Kelly, more so than Grillmeier, entertains the possibility that certain Jewish discourses from the earliest days of the Jesus movement may have echoed on in the history of doctrine, not only in the early second century, and not only in so-called "Jewish Christian" circles, but in the main stream of early Christian theology. In the case of messiah Christology, at least, Kelly's claim can indeed be borne out. In the balance of this chapter, I will show, by means of several interesting examples, how this is so.[21]

---

20. J. N. D. Kelly, *Early Christian Doctrines* (5th ed.; London: Continuum, 2006 [1st ed., 1958]), 6.

21. In keeping with the aim of this book, my focus in this chapter is the fate of the name "messiah" or "Christ" itself as an object of reflection in early Christian discourse. Relatedly but differently, some modern critics have argued for an enduring early Christian messianism in the form of chiliasm, especially the notion of an earthly, interim kingdom of Christ headquartered in Jerusalem. For this line of argument, see, for example, Robert L. Wilken, "Early Christian Chiliasm, Jewish Messianism, and the Idea of the Holy Land," *HTR* 79 (1986): 298–307; William Horbury, "Messianism among Jews and Christians in the Second Century," *Aug* 28 (1988): 71–88; repr. in idem, *Messianism among Jews and Christians*, 275–88; Charles E. Hill, *Regnum Caelorum: Patterns of Millennial Thought in Early Christianity* (2d ed.; Grand Rapids, Mich.: Eerdmans, 2001); Jan-Eric Steppa, "The Reception of Messianism and the Worship of Christ in the Post-Apostolic Church," in *Messiah in Early Judaism and Christianity*, 79–116; Brian E. Daley, "'Faithful and True': Early Christian Apocalyptic and the Person of Christ," in *Apocalyptic Thought in Early Christianity* (ed. Robert J. Daly; Grand Rapids, Mich.: Baker, 2009), 106–26.

Christ in Translation

In his late fourth-century *Onomasticon*, Jerome includes the following terse but accurate entry: *Messias unctus, id est Christus.*[22] Jerome gives three Latin lexemes as mutual equivalencies: one, *messias*, a transliteration from Hebrew; the second, *unctus*, a proper translation from Hebrew or Greek or both; and the third, *Christus*, a transliteration from Greek. He thereby illustrates the complications involved in rendering "Christ" in early Christian polyglot.[23] In modern Anglophone convention, we commonly use the Hebrew-to-English transliteration "messiah" to refer to the exalted figure of Jewish tradition, in contradistinction to the Greek-to-English transliteration "Christ," which we reserve to refer to Jesus of Nazareth.[24] This convention ostensibly means to reflect an ancient distinction between Jewish sources and traditions on the one hand and Christian ones on the other.[25] Significantly, however, the ancient sources themselves do not make this distinction. There is an apparent parallel to our modern usage in the rare attestation of Greek μεσσίας alongside χριστός. Ironically, however, μεσσίας occurs only in Christian, not Jewish, texts, and it is used not as a contrast term for χριστός, but as an equivalency for it. So it is, in Latin, in Jerome (as mentioned previously), and also as early as the turn-of-the-second-century CE Greek idiom of the Gospel of John: "[Andrew] first found his brother Simon and said to him, 'We have found the messiah,' which is translated 'anointed' [εὑρήκαμεν τὸν μεσσίαν, ὅ ἐστιν μεθερμηνευόμενον χριστός]" (John 1:41). And again, several chapters later: "The [Samaritan] woman said to him [Jesus], 'I know that the messiah, who is called 'anointed,' is coming [μεσσίας ἔρχεται ὁ λεγόμενος χριστός]; when he comes, he will tell us everything" (John 4:25).[26] Thereafter, μεσσίας is attested in a number of patristic

---

22. Paul de Lagarde, ed., *Onomastica Sacra* (Göttingen, 1870), 66. This entry is recorded also in an old Latin glossary in Codex Sangallensis 912, an edition of which is given by Minton Warren, "On Latin Glossaries, with Especial Reference to the Codex Sangallensis 912," *TAPA* 15 (1884): 124–28 at 168.

23. On the ideological issues at stake in early Christian translation decisions, see Catherine M. Chin, *Grammar and Christianity in the Late Roman World* (Philadelphia, Pa.: University of Pennsylvania Press, 2008), 72–109.

24. See *OED*, s.v. "messiah" and "Christ," respectively; compare the analogous use of *Messias* and *Christus* in German-language scholarship and *messie* and *Christ* in French. In the scholarly literature, see, for example, Charlesworth, "From Jewish Messianology to Christian Christology."

25. See BDAG, s.v. χριστός, glosses 1 and 2, respectively, for precisely this distinction. But compare LSJ, s.v. χριστός, which successfully avoids it.

26. On which see, inter alia, S. Sabugal, "El título Messias-Christos en el contexto del relato sobre l'actividad de Jesús in Samaría," *Aug* 12 (1972): 79–105.

commentaries on the Gospel of John, but it does not otherwise gain currency.[27] It is an apparent analogy to the modern usage of "messiah" opposite "Christ," but it turns out not to be a real analogy after all. In antiquity, as a rule, there are not different words for the Jewish "messiah" and the Christian "Christ."[28]

The establishment of Greek χριστός as the accepted equivalency for משיח provided occasion for one interesting development in early Christian idiom: the occasional use, via itacism, of Greek χρηστός, "good, excellent," for χριστός, "anointed" (and, consequent upon a standard transliteration, Latin *chrestus* for *christus*, as well). This has often been commented on, especially in connection with Suetonius's famous account of the expulsion of the Jews from Rome under Claudius (*Claud.* 25: *Judaeos impulsore Chresto assidue tumultuantes Roma expulit*), as a result of simple misunderstanding, the confused substitution of a familiar name for an unfamiliar one.[29] And in some instances, this is doubtless the case. Thus Tertullian, in his *Ad nationes*, mocks certain pagans for their ignorance in pronouncing *Christiani* as *Chrestiani*[30]:

> The name Christian, however, so far as its meaning goes, bears the sense of anointing [*Christianum vero nomen, quantum significatio est, de unctione interpretatur*]. Even when by a faulty pronunciation you call us Chrestians [*etiam cum corrupte a vobis Chrestiani pronuntiamur*] (for you are not certain about even the sound of this noted name), you in fact lisp out the sense of pleasantness and goodness [*suavitate vel bonitate*]. You are therefore vilifying in harmless men even the harmless name we bear. (Tertullian, *Ad. nat.* 1.3.8–10)[31]

---

27. It does not even merit an entry in Lampe's *PGL*.

28. A partial exception is Aquila's Greek translation of the Jewish scriptures, in which, according to Origen, Aquila avoided the old LXX gloss χριστός on account of its use among Christians and instead used the synonym ἠλειμμένος ("anointed, smeared") for משיח. Origen's report is borne out by the extant fragments of Aquila at 1 Sam 2:35; 2 Sam 1:21; Pss 2:2; 84:10; 89:39; Dan 9:26.

29. For example, Schürer-Vermes, *History*, 3.1:77–78. It is possible, however, that this Suetonius passage is not a confused reference to Christ, but rather an accurate reference to an otherwise unknown Chrestus who had nothing to do with the Jesus sect (thus H. Dixon Slingerland, "Chrestus: Christus?" in *New Perspectives on Ancient Judaism*, vol. 4: *The Literature of Early Rabbinic Judaism* [ed. Alan J. Avery-Peck; Lanham, Md.: University Press of America, 1989], 133–44).

30. On Tertullian's posture of shaming his pagan audience in this passage, see David E. Wilhite, *Tertullian the African: An Anthropological Reading of Tertullian's Context and Identities* (Berlin: De Gruyter, 2007), 63–65.

31. Latin text ed. J. W. P. Borleffs, *Tertulliani Ad Nationes, libri duo* (Leiden: Brill, 1929); trans. Holmes in *ANF*.

Tertullian notes that, in fact, the name *Christiani* comes from a word for anointing (*de unctione*) but that pagans often say it *Chrestiani*, suggesting pleasantness or goodness (Greek χρηστότης; Latin *suavitas, bonitas*). Tertullian is happy to take the unintended compliment, and he claims that Christians are indeed pleasant, good, and harmless.

This latter move is, in fact, a common one. Among early Christian writers (especially apologists), there is a venerable tradition of knowingly exploiting the homophony of χριστός with χρηστός to rhetorical and sometimes theological ends. The earliest example is the mid-second-century *Apology* of Justin Martyr, who writes:

> By the mere application of a name, nothing is decided, either good or evil, apart from the actions implied in the name; and indeed, so far at least as one may judge from the name we are accused of, we are most excellent [χρηστότατοι] people. . . . Those among yourselves who are accused you do not punish before they are convicted; but in our case you receive the name as proof against us, and this although, so far as the name goes, you ought rather to punish our accusers. For we are accused of being Christians [Χριστιανοί], and to hate what is excellent [χρηστόν] is unjust. (Justin, *1 Apol.* 1.4)[32]

A prominent theme throughout Justin's *Apology* is the legal distinction between censure for the deeds a person does, which is just, and censure for the name a person bears, which is unjust.[33] It is in this connection that he raises the issue of the name Χριστιανοί. Having raised it, Justin leverages the homophony with χρηστόν to score a rhetorical point: So far from being wicked, the Christians are, in fact, *chreston*, excellent.

Writing in Egypt at the beginning of the third century, Clement of Alexandria also appeals to the phonetic relation of χρηστός to χριστός. In book 2 of his *Stromata*, Clement writes:

> Now those who have believed in Christ [Χριστόν] both are and are called excellent [χρηστοί], as those who are cared for by the true king are kingly. For as the wise are wise by their wisdom, and those observant of law are so by the law; so also those who belong to Christ the king are

32. Greek text ed. Goodspeed, *Apologeten*; trans. Marcus Dods and George Reith in *ANF*.

33. See the discussion of Laura Salah Nasrallah, *Christian Responses to Roman Art and Architecture: The Second-Century Church amid the Spaces of Empire* (New York, N.Y.: Cambridge University Press, 2010), 130–53.

kings [οἱ Χριστῷ βασιλεῖ βασιλεῖς], and those that are Christ's Christians [οἱ Χριστοῦ Χριστιανοί]. (Clement, *Strom.* 2.4.18)[34]

Clement here invokes the philosophical distinction between the thing and the name, being something and being called something.[35] Under optimal circumstances, the name corresponds to the thing, and so it is in Clement's examples. He argues that people who pursue certain ends become, and take the names of, the objects pursued. Those who study wisdom are, and are called, wise. Those who obey the laws are, and are called, lawful. For those who follow Christ, however, Clement gives two names corresponding to the object of their devotion. They are, and are called, Χριστιανοί, "Christians," and also χρηστοί, "excellent persons." Here the context is not apologetic, as in the Justin and Tertullian texts cited earlier, but rather philosophical. Clement is establishing the claim that the Christians meet the exacting standard set by Plato in the *Statesman*: "The knowledge of the true king is kingly; and he who possesses it, whether a prince or private person, shall by all means, in consequence of this act, be rightly styled royal" (Clement, *Strom.* 2.4 citing Plato, *Stat.* 259b).[36] Perhaps unsurprisingly, this happy accident of pronunciation— χρηστός for χριστός—continues to turn up here and there in fourth-century and later Christian writers, as well.[37] It does not displace the accurate Greek etymology, as Tertullian's comment in *Ad nationes* illustrates, but it is such low-hanging fruit that its popularity hardly needs explaining.[38]

Even as Greek remained a *lingua franca* for Christians in all corners of the Mediterranean world, late antiquity saw the growth of multiple Christian vernaculars: Latin, Syriac, and Coptic, especially, as well as Ethopic, Arabic, Slavonic, and more.[39] In connection with this development, the third-century

---

34. Greek text ed. L. Früchtel, O. Stählin, and U. Treu, *Clemens Alexandrinus* (GCS; Berlin: Akademie Verlag, 1960–1970); trans. William Wilson in *ANF*.

35. The seminal ancient discussion is Plato's *Cratylus*.

36. But in the *Statesman*, it is the anonymous stranger, not Socrates, who makes this claim.

37. For example, Lactantius, *Div. Inst.* 4.7.5: *Sed exponenda huius nominis ratio est propter ignorantium errorem, qui eum immutata littera Chrestum solent dicere*, "But the meaning of this name must be set forth, on account of the error of the ignorant, who by the change of a letter are accustomed to call him *Chrestus*" (Latin text PL 6:464; trans. William Fletcher in *ANF*).

38. See further the learned but overly speculative discussion of J. B. Mitchell, *Chrestos: A Religious Epithet, Its Import and Influence* (London: Williams & Norgate, 1880).

39. On these developments, see the relevant essays in *Übersetzung, Translation, Traduction*, vol. 2 (ed. Harald Kittel et al.; Berlin: De Gruyter, 2007), especially the sections "Übersetzung in und zwischen den Kulturen: Die Antike Welt" (pp. 1109–70) and "Übersetzung in und zwischen den Kulturen: Der Vordere Orient im Altertum und Mittelalter" (pp. 1171–1249).

CE *Gospel of Philip* provides another important testimony. In its particular eso-teric idiom, *Gospel of Philip* confirms what a lexical survey of the pertinent Jewish and Christian texts from the period also suggests. The author writes:

> "Jesus" is a hidden name, "Christ" is a revealed name. For this reason "Jesus" is not particular to any language; rather he is always called by the name "Jesus." While as for "Christ," in Syriac it is "Messiah," in Greek it is "Christ." Certainly all the others have it according to their own language. "The Nazarene" is he who reveals what is hidden. (*Gos. Phil.* 56.3–15)[40]

The *Gospel of Philip* knows that the name "Christ" is not simply identical with the name "Jesus." The author's explanation for this phenomenon has to do with a speculative distinction between hidden and revealed names,[41] but he is also reporting on prevailing translation practices. "Jesus," the author reports, "is not particular to any language." That is, it is transliterated across languages, as we would expect for a proper name (ישוע, Ἰησοῦς, *Iesus*, and so on). As for "Christ," however, "all the others have it according to their own language." That is, it is customarily translated with a meaningful equivalency in each target language.[42]

  Gospel of Philip's rule does not hold in the case of Latin, where Greek χριστός overwhelmingly comes over as a transliteration (*Christus*) rather than a translation (*unctus*).[43] Unlike Greek χριστός, Latin *Christus* was not an existing word in the target language, and so has all the appearance of a transliterated proper name, the more so when we take into account itacism for the relatively

---

40. Trans. Isenberg in *NHL*.

41. On which see Elliot R. Wolfson, "Becoming Invisible: Rending the Veil and the Hermeneutic of Secrecy in the *Gospel of Philip*," in *Practicing Gnosis: Essays in Honor of Birger A. Pearson* (ed. April DeConick et al.; NHMS 85; Leiden: Brill, 2013), 124:

> The unexpected reversal of identifying Jesus as the hidden name and Christ as the revealed name partakes of the same hermeneutical axiom but from the inverted perspective: the mundane nature of the historical Jesus is, as it were, the open secret that reveals the divine nature of the primeval Christ.

42. The author only mentions Greek and Syriac. Our text of the *Gospel of Philip* itself is Coptic, but this is probably a translation of a Greek *Vorlage*. Its interest in Syriac etymolo-gies (e.g., *Gos. Phil.* 56.7–9; 62.6–17; 63.21–23) has often been taken to suggest a Syrian provenance, as, for example, by Eric Segelberg, "The Antiochene Background of the Gospel of Philip," *BSAC* 18 (1965–1966): 205–23; idem, "The Antiochene Origin of the Gospel of Philip," *BSAC* 19 (1967–1968): 207–10. But compare the contrary view of Bas van Os, "Was the *Gospel of Philip* Written in Syria?" *Apocrypha* 17 (2006): 87–94.

43. See Lewis and Short, s.v. *Christus* and *unctus*, respectively.

common Roman name *Chrestus* (from Greek Χρηστός).[44] A naif from the Latin West could be forgiven for thinking that Christus was simply the name of the cult deity of the Christians.[45] From time to time, however, Latin Christian writers have occasion to recall that this is not the case. Tertullian, for example, argues against the monarchian views of Praxeas—the latter, Tertullian complains, "makes Christ the father" [*Christum facis patrem*]—by appealing to the etymology of *Christus*. Tertullian writes:

> And so, most foolish heretic, you make Christ to be the Father without once considering the actual force of this name, if indeed Christ is a name and not rather a surname or designation [*apellatio*], for it signifies "anointed" [*unctus*]. But "anointed" [*unctus*] is no more a proper name [*nomen*] than "clothed" [*vestitus*] or "shod" [*calceatus*]; it is only an accessory to a name. . . . Whether it be the name Jesus which occurs alone, Christ is also understood, because Jesus is the anointed one [*unctus*], or if the name Christ is the only one given, then Jesus is identified with him, because the anointed one [*unctus*] is Jesus. Now of these two names Jesus Christ, the former is the proper one [*proprium*] which was given to him by the angel, and the latter is only an adjunct [*accidens*] predicable of him from his anointing, thus suggesting the proviso that Christ must be the Son, not the Father. (Tertullian, *Adv. Prax.* 28.1, 8)[46]

On this account, *Iesus* is the *nomen proprium* of the son of God, whereas *Christus* is an *apellatio* and an *accidens*. It is an equivalency for Latin *unctus*, "anointed," Tertullian explains, but Jesus has his anointing from God the father, so that the father cannot be simply identical with the son, else the anointing would have to come from outside the Godhead, which is a theological absurdity. Q. E. D. The memory of the meaning of the transliteration *Christus* secures, for Tertullian, the metaphysical distinction between the father and the son.[47]

---

44. The latter is amply attested in *Thesaurus Linguae Latinae: Onomasticon*, vol. 2 (Leipzig: Teubner, 1907–1913).

45. See M. David Litwa, *Iesus Deus: The Early Christian Depiction of Jesus as a Mediterranean God* (Minneapolis, Minn.: Fortress, 2014).

46. Latin text ed. Ernest Evans, *Tertullian's Treatise against Praxeas* (London: SPCK, 1948); trans. mod. from Holmes in *ANF*.

47. On this passage, see Eric Osborn, *Tertullian: First Theologian of the West* (Cambridge: Cambridge University Press, 1997), 120–21. On the problem of the identity of

If the Latin rendering of "Christ" leads it further linguistically from its biblical roots, the Syriac rendering leads it closer. In Christian Syriac, significantly, Christ is not "Christ" but rather "messiah," *mšiḥa*, a retrotranslation to the Aramaic root (משיחא) of which χριστός itself was a very early Christian translation.[48] As Sebastian Brock has pointed out, one consequence of this translation convention is that there is considerable linguistic overlap between Syriac Christian texts and contemporary Aramaic Jewish texts in regard to the set phrase, which is quite common in both corpora, *malka mšiḥa*, "king messiah."[49] Significantly, however, this is not the case with the cognate terms "Christian" and "Christianity," which mostly come over to Syriac, as they do to Latin, as transliterations of Greek χριστιανός and χριστιανισμός.[50] As a result, the connection between "Christ" (*mšiḥa*) and "Christian" (*krisṭyānā*) is not immediately clear in Syriac.

Perhaps for this reason, several early Christian writers make the connection clear. The second-century Syrian teacher Bardaisan of Edessa, for example, is reported by his student Philip in the *Book of the Laws of Countries* to have said:

> What shall we say of the new people of us Christians, whom the messiah has caused to arise in every place and in all climates by his coming?

Praxeas, see Allen Brent, *Hippolytus and the Roman Church in the Third Century* (Leiden: Brill, 1995), 525–29.

48. On patterns of Greek-to-Syriac translation in antiquity, see Anton Schall, *Studien über griechische Fremdwörter im Syrischen* (Darmstadt: Wissenschaftliche Buchgesellschaft, 1960); Sebastian Brock, "Greek and Syriac in Late Antique Syria," in idem, *From Ephrem to Romanos: Interactions between Syriac and Greek in Late Antiquity* (Aldershot, UK: Ashgate, 1999), 149–60; idem, "Greek Words in Syriac: Some General Features," in *From Ephrem to Romanos*, 251–62.

49. Sebastian Brock, "Syria and Mesopotamia: The Shared Term *Malka Mshiḥa*," in *Redemption and Resistance*, 171–82, here 182:

> There can be little doubt that the Syriac use of the term *malka mshiḥa* had its origin in the Jewish Palestinian Aramaic milieu out of which the Palestinian Targums also emerged, thus providing yet another clear example of the influence of the Jewish roots of at least one strand of early Syriac Christianity.

50. Thus rightly Stephen Gero, "With Walter Bauer on the Tigris: Encratite Orthodoxy and Libertine Heresy in Syro-Mesopotamian Christianity," in *Nag Hammadi, Gnosticism, and Early Christianity* (ed. Charles W. Hendrick and Robert Hodgson; Cascade, Ore.: Wipf & Stock, 2005), 289:

> The precise import of the various eastern Syriac designations for "Christian" is still not quite clear; but it is likely that the loanword *krisṭyānā* was introduced by Greek-speaking immigrants from the Byzantine provinces at a relatively early date, and this later became the most common self-designation.

For behold, we all, wherever we may be, are called Christians [*krisṭyānā*] after the one name of the messiah [*mšiḥa*].[51]

Bardaisan was classed posthumously as a heretic (most influentially by Ephrem in his fourth-century *Hymns against Heresies*), but his actual views remain rather opaque to modern interpreters, and there is nothing theologically deviant about this statement, at least.[52] It is, in fact, an accurate summary of the Syrian adoption of the Greek name of the Christians.

In one fascinating story in the *History of the Marvellous and Divine Struggles* of Mar Aba I, the sixth-century patriarch of the East, the use of the name *mšiḥa* in the Syrian churches is invoked as a point of difference with the Marcionites, who call themselves "Christians" but do not worship the "messiah." I cite the story as related by Walter Bauer, *Orthodoxy and Heresy*, and translated into English by Robert Kraft:

Mar Aba, originally a fanatical pagan, during an attempt to cross the Tigris was brought to see the light through a miracle and an ensuing conversation with a Christian ascetic Joseph, whose surname was Moses. He was struck by the strangeness of Joseph's clothing, and wishing to know whether Joseph might be an orthodox, a Marcionite or a Jew, he asked: "Are you a Jew?" The answer was "Yes." Then comes a second question: "Are you a Christian?" To this comes also an affirmative response. Finally: "Do you worship the Messiah?" Again agreement is expressed. Then Mar Aba becomes enraged and says: "How can you be a Jew, a Christian, and a worshipper of the Messiah all at the same time?" Here the narrator inserts by way of explanation: "Following the local custom he used the word Christian to designate a Marcionite." Joseph himself then gives his irate companion the following explanation: "I am a Jew secretly; I still pray to the living God ... and abhor the worship of idols. I am a Christian truly, not as the Marcionites, who

---

51. Bardaisan, *The Book of the Laws of Countries* (ed. and trans. H. J. W. Drijvers; Semitic Texts with Translations III; Assen: van Gorcum, 1965), 59–61. I am grateful to William Adler for pointing me to this reference. The same explanation for the relation between "messiah" and "Christian" in Syriac is given by Aphrahat, *Dem.* 20.10.

52. On Bardaisan's Christology, see the appropriately cautious comment of Nicola Denzey, "Bardaisan of Edessa," in *A Companion to Second-Century Christian 'Heretics'* (ed. Antti Marjanen and Petri Luomanen; Leiden: Brill, 2008), 159–84 at 172: "Whether or not Bardaisan understood the Logos of Thought as having incarnated into the body of Jesus of Nazareth—in other words, whether or not Bardaisan thought that Jesus Christ was the

falsely call themselves Christians. For Christian is a Greek word, which in Syriac means Messiah-worshipper. And if you ask me 'Do you worship the Messiah?', I worship him truly."[53]

Bauer takes this episode from the life of Mar Aba as an important piece of evidence for his thesis that so-called heresy actually antedated orthodoxy in many quarters during the first Christian centuries.[54] The smoking gun, for Bauer, is that narrator's claim that "following the local custom he [Mar Aba] used the word Christian to designate a Marcionite." In this context, Bauer reckons, Marcionism is not a deviant sect; it is just mainstream Christianity.[55] For our purposes, the relevant feature of the story is the way Joseph the monk explains his religious affiliation: "I am a Christian truly, not as the Marcionites, who falsely call themselves Christians. For Christian is a Greek word, which in Syriac means messianist." With this explanation, Joseph supplies the missing middle term, proving to Mar Aba that Syriac kristyānā ("Christian") actually means mšiḥāyā ("messianist"), partisan of mšiḥa. The fact that Joseph is a Jew also illustrates Sebastian Brock's point, noted earlier, about the overlap between Jewish Aramaic and Christian Syriac during this period.[56] In short, like Bardaisan before him, the hagiographer of Mar Aba gives an account of "Christ" in Syriac translation.

Messiah—remains for us an unanswered question." See also, more generally, H. J. W. Drijvers, *Bardaisan of Edessa* (SSN 6; Assen: Van Gorcum, 1966).

53. Walter Bauer, *Orthodoxy and Heresy in Earliest Christianity* (trans. Robert A. Kraft et al.; Minneapolis, Minn.: Fortress, 1971), 23; German original *Rechtgläubigkeit und Ketzerei im ältesten Christentum* (Tübingen: Mohr Siebeck, 1934), 28. The Syriac text of this episode is given by Paul Bedjan, ed., *Histoire de Mar-Jabalaha, de trois autres patriarches, d'un prêtre et de deux laiques, nestoriens* (Paris: Harrassowitz, 1895), 211–14.

54. Bauer's study is a landmark in the modern study of orthodoxy and heresy, although many of his particular historical judgments have been overturned by subsequent research. See the retrospects provided by Daniel Harrington, "The Reception of Walter Bauer's *Orthodoxy and Heresy in Earliest Christianity* in the Last Decade," *HTR* 73 (1980): 289–98; and Lewis Ayres, "The Question of Orthodoxy," *JECS* 14 (2006): 395–98.

55. See Bauer, *Orthdoxy and Heresy*, 24:

> This story reveals that even at a relatively late date, Marcionites designated themselves as *the* Christians—much to the offence of the orthodox, who must be content with misleading alternatives such as "Messiah-worshippers." Is it not reasonable to suggest that something similar was true with respect to the beginnings of Christianity in Edessa?

For an assessment of Bauer's interpretation, see Gero, "Bauer on the Tigris," 289–92.

56. See Gero, "Bauer on the Tigris," 290n9: "The juxtaposition of mšiḥāyā with the (supposedly 'secret') confession of Judaism by the monk who bears the very Hebraic name of 'Joseph who was called Moses' should be noted."

Christ in Etymology

Not a few early Christian texts, rightly perceiving the relation of the name χριστός to the verb χρίω, set about supplying back-stories for this etymology, accounts of the actual anointing of Christ—the agent who anointed him, the unguent with which he was anointed, the time at which it happened, and so on. We have no such accounts from the apostolic period. Neither the apostle Paul (50s) nor the Gospel of Mark (ca. 70), for instance, says anything about the chrismation of Christ; both presuppose the archaic figurative use of χριστός as a royal epithet. The anonymous Epistle to the Hebrews (late first century CE) is the first Christian text to speculate in this way. Like his predecessors, Hebrews presupposes a scriptural, royal sense of χριστός,[57] so that he can cite several royal psalms and oracles as if they are about Jesus (e.g., OG Ps 2:7 in Heb 1:5; 2 Kgdms 7:14 in Heb 1:5; OG Ps 109:1 in Heb 1:13).[58] In this context, though, Hebrews cites one royal psalm in particular that speaks of the anointing of the sitting king:

> [God] says about his son, *Your throne, O god, is forever and ever; the scepter of your kingship is an upright scepter; you love righteousness and hate lawlessness; therefore God, your God, anointed you with the oil of gladness* [ἔχρισέν σε ὁ θεὸς ὁ θεός σου ἔλαιον ἀγαλλιάσεως] *beyond your peers.* (Heb 1:8–9 citing OG Ps 44:7)

Hebrews uses this psalm citation to specify one way in which Christ is greater than his peers (μέτοχοι), here probably the angels[59]—namely, that he alone was anointed (ἔχρισέν) by God with the oil of gladness. By virtue of this chrismation, he is the Christ (χριστός).[60]

Writing around the turn of the second century, the anonymous author of Luke-Acts also undertakes to explain the chrismation of Christ. In a uniquely Lukan scene in the Gospel, the author has Jesus himself explain his anointing by citing an oracle from Second Isaiah. One sabbath day, in the synagogue in

---

57. See Flusser, "Messianology and Christology in the Epistle to the Hebrews."

58. See Susan E. Docherty, *The Use of the Old Testament in Hebrews: A Case Study in Early Jewish Bible Interpretation* (WUNT 2.260; Tübingen: Mohr Siebeck, 2009), 144–81.

59. Although compare the counterargument of David M. Moffitt, *Atonement and the Logic of Resurrection in the Epistle to the Hebrews* (NovTSup 141; Leiden: Brill, 2011), 47–53.

60. See Harold W. Attridge, *The Epistle to the Hebrews* (Hermeneia; Minneapolis, Minn.: Fortress, 1989), 60: "In applying the psalm to Christ ('the anointed one') the tradition and the author both thought no doubt of the exaltation, since no traditions record any formal anointing of Jesus."

his hometown of Nazareth in Galilee, Jesus gives the reading from the book of the prophet: "The spirit of the Lord is upon me, because he has anointed me to preach good news to the poor [ἔχρισέν με εὐαγγελίσασθαι πτωχοῖς]. He has sent me to proclaim release to the captives and recovering of sight to the blind," and so on (Luke 4:18 citing Isa 61:1).[61] Upon finishing the reading, Jesus says to those gathered there, "Today this scripture has been fulfilled in your hearing" (Luke 4:21). He, Jesus, whom Luke calls "the anointed one" (χριστός in Luke 4:41 and passim), has been anointed (ἔχρισέν) by God to preach good news to the poor, as prophesied by Isaiah.[62]

In his second volume, Luke has the apostles articulate this account of the chrismation of Christ. Thus in Acts 4, Peter and John, having been arrested and then released by the Jerusalem council, pray with the other disciples, citing Psalm 2:

> The kings of the earth establish themselves, and the rulers are gathered together, against the Lord and against his anointed one [κατὰ τοῦ κυρίου καὶ κατὰ τοῦ χριστοῦ αὐτοῦ] [OG Ps 2:1–2]—for truly in this city they were gathered together against your holy servant Jesus whom you anointed [τὸν ἅγιον παῖδά σου Ἰησοῦν ὃν ἔχρισας], both Herod and Pontius Pilate, with the gentiles and the peoples of Israel. (Acts 4:26–27)

Luke here identifies Jesus with the anointed one of the royal psalm, and he glosses the psalm citation with a comment to the effect that God anointed Jesus.[63] He does not, in this instance, specify the medium or the purpose of the unction. Then in Acts 10, Peter, speaking to a pious Roman named Cornelius, gives a *precis* of Jesus's remarkable career, recounting "how God anointed Jesus of Nazareth with the holy spirit and with power [Ἰησοῦν τὸν

---

61. On the oracle in its original setting in Third Isaiah, see Williamson, *Variations on a Theme*, 174–88, here 187: "[The speaker] takes to himself the task of proclaiming the future fulfilment of all the as yet unrealized tasks entrusted to a variety of figures in Deutero-Isaiah: Cyrus, the servant, the herald of good news, God's ministers in the heavenly court and the prophet himself."

62. See Francois Bovon, *Luke 1: A Commentary on the Gospel of Luke 1:1–9:50* (trans. Christine M. Thomas; Hermeneia; Minneapolis, Minn.: Fortress, 2002), 154: "Anointing with the Spirit justifies the title 'Messiah.' . . . But Luke does not advocate a narrow royal messianism. His Christ is the son of David but also bears prophetic characteristics; much in the citation alludes to his message."

63. See Kirsopp Lake and H. J. Cadbury, *The Beginnings of Christianity: The Acts of the Apostles*, vol. 4 (London: Macmillan, 1933), 47: "ἔχρισας refers to the meaning of χριστός, and it must be translated 'make Messiah' if χριστός be rendered 'Messiah.' When was Jesus made Messiah? Unfortunately Acts gives no clear clue to the author's opinion."

ἀπὸ Ναζαρέθ, ὡς ἔχρισεν αὐτὸν ὁ θεὸς πνεύματι ἀγίῳ καὶ δυνάμει], and how he went about doing good and healing all that were oppressed by the devil, for God was with him" (Acts 10:38). Again it is said that God anointed Jesus, and here Luke specifies the twofold medium of the anointing—namely, holy spirit and power—which recalls Jesus's recitation of Isa 61 in Luke 4: "The spirit of the Lord is upon me, because he has anointed me to preach good news to the poor," and so on.[64] For Luke, then, Jesus the anointed one was anointed by God not with oil, but with holy spirit and power to the end that he might preach good news to the poor.

Relatedly, some gnostic (or demiurgical) Christian texts[65] attribute the anointing of Christ either to the highest god or to one of his emanations. In particular, there is a well-attested Sethian myth in which Christ is anointed by Barbelo, the first and greatest emanation from the "invisible spirit" or "parent of the entirety."[66] The *Apocryphon of John* (a second-century Greek text preserved in several fourth-century Coptic manuscripts), according to the long recension attested in Nag Hammadi Codices II and IV, narrates the begetting and anointing of Christ as follows:

> It [the invisible spirit] gazed at the Barbelo, (who was) in the uncontaminated light around the invisible spirit and (in) its radiation. And the Barbelo conceived by it, and it begot a luminous spark consisting of light in an image that was blessed, though not equal to its parent's magnitude. This was the only-begotten offspring of the mother-father, which appeared, and the mother-father's only begetting; (it was) the only-begotten of the parent, the uncontaminated light. And the invisible virgin spirit rejoiced at the light that had come to exist and that had been shown forth out of the first power of the spirit's forethought, who is the Barbelo. And the spirit anointed [from Greek χρίω] it (the spark) with its own kindness [from Greek χρηστότης] until it became perfect, needing no further kindness [χρηστότης] since it had been anointed [χρίω] with the kindness [χρηστότης] of the invisible spirit. And it stood at rest in the presence of the spirit, which was pouring upon it. And the

---

64. A connection rightly noted by Lake and Cadbury, *Beginnings of Christianity*, 4:120.

65. On the terminological problem, see Michael Allen Williams, *Rethinking 'Gnosticism': An Argument for Dismantling a Dubious Category* (Princeton, N.J.: Princeton University Press, 1996), who suggests replacing "gnosticism" with the more precise "biblical demiurgical traditions."

66. On Sethian cosmology, see John D. Turner, *Sethian Gnosticism and the Platonic Tradition* (Leuven: Peeters, 2001), 57–92.

moment that it received from the spirit it glorified the holy spirit and perfect forethought, because of which it had become disclosed. And it made a request that it be given a coactor, namely intellect. And the spirit consented . . .. And while the invisible spirit was consenting, intellect was disclosed. And it stood at rest along with the anointed (Christ) [from Greek χριστός], glorifying the spirit and the Barbelo. (*Ap. John* 6.10–7.3)[67]

In this account, Barbelo begets a spark, and the invisible spirit anoints the spark with its own kindness. Thus for the *Apocryphon of John*, Christ is, as his name suggests, "the anointed one," anointed with the kindness (from Greek χρηστότης, an aural wordplay on χριστός) of the invisible spirit at the moment of his, Christ's, begetting by Barbelo before all worlds.[68]

Another Sethian Christian text from Nag Hammadi, *Trimorphic Protennoia* (attested in a single fourth-century Coptic manuscript, but probably a second-century Greek composition), attributes the anointing of Christ to Barbelo herself. Early in the text, Barbelo speaks in the first person:

The sound that has derived from my thinking exists as three compartments: Father, Mother, Son—a voice existing perceptibly. It contains within it a verbal expression (or Word), which possesses all glory, and which possesses three masculinities and three powers and three names: all three are thus □□□,[69] quadrangles, secretly in the silence of the ineffable: [the] only-begotten, who [is the anointed (Christ)], whom I myself anointed with glory. (*Trim. Prot.* 37)[70]

There are partial lacunae in the manuscript here, but it seems clear that Barbelo claims to have anointed, with the unguent of glory, the only-begotten one (from Greek μονογενής), who is, as a result of this anointing, called Christ, as in the parallel in *Apocryphon of John*.

Among some early Christian writers, there is a related convention of connecting the anointing of Christ with the anointing of Christians. Already in the

---

67. Ed. and trans. Bentley Layton, *The Gnostic Scriptures: A New Translation with Annotations and Introductions* (ABRL; New York, N.Y.: Doubleday, 1995).

68. See further Sasagu Arai, "Zur Christologie des Apokryphons des Johannes," *NTS* 15 (1968): 302–18.

69. A diagram of the three quadrangles appears at this point in the manuscript.

70. Trans. Layton, *Gnostic Scriptures*, following the Coptic text of Y. Janssens, ed., *La Protennoia Trimorphe* (Bibliothèque copte de Nag Hammadi; Textes vol. 4; Leuven: Peeters, 1978).

mid first century, the apostle Paul speaks of Christ-followers being figuratively "anointed" (χρίω) by God: "It is God who establishes us with you into Christ [εἰς Χριστὸν] and has anointed us [χρίσας ἡμᾶς]" (2 Cor 1:21).[71] Paul supplies no evidence for an actual ritual of unction in the Christ-assemblies, although the first-century Epistle of James does: "If any one of you is sick, let him summon the elders of the assembly, and let them anoint him with oil [ἀλείψαντες αὐτὸν ἐλαίῳ] in the name of the lord and pray over him" (Jas 5:14). Significantly, however, James uses the verb ἀλείφω, not χρίω, and he has in view a medical ritual, not a sectarian initiation.[72]

From the beginning and middle of the second century, we have several texts that speak of the anointing of Christian adepts at least in a figurative sense and possibly also in a ritual sense. Thus the First Epistle of John contrasts the many ἀντίχριστοι, "opponents of Christ," who have apostasized from the sect with the faithful insiders who have the χρῖσμα, "anointing," from God. "[The antichrists] went out from us, for they were not of us. ... But as for you, you have the anointing from the Holy One, and you all know" (1 John 2:19–20). And again, "As for you, the anointing which you received from him remains in you, and you do not have need that anyone should teach you" (1 John 2:27). Here the χρῖσμα, which is cleverly coordinated with references to χριστός and ἀντίχριστός, signifies the divine guarantee of knowledge of the sect's doctrines among the adepts.[73]

The *Gospel of Truth* from Nag Hammadi Codex I, which is probably— although not certainly—the same *Gospel of Truth* known to Irenaeus (*Haer.* 3.11.9), but in a Coptic version translated from the second-century Greek original,[74] connects the anointing of Christ and the anointing of Christians in a way very much like the Johannine Epistles do. *Gospel of Truth* comments:

> Because of the coming of Christ it was said publicly: Seek, and those that are disturbed will receive restoration, and he will anoint them with

---

71. On this passage, see Novenson, *Christ among the Messiahs*, 146–49; Karl Olav Sandnes, "Seal and Baptism in Early Christianity," in *Ablution, Initiation, and Baptism: Late Antiquity, Early Judaism, and Early Christianity* (ed. David Hellholm et al.; 3 vols.; BZNW 176; Berlin: De Gruyter, 2011), 2:1441–81 at 1446–50.

72. See Owsei Temkin, *Hippocrates in a World of Pagans and Christians* (Baltimore, Md.: Johns Hopkins University Press, 1991), 109–25, especially 111–12.

73. See Judith Lieu, *The Theology of the Johannine Epistles* (Cambridge: Cambridge University Press, 1991), 27–31; Udo Schnelle, "Salbung, Geist, und Taufe im 1. Johannesbrief," in *Ablution, Initiation, and Baptism*, 1:629–54.

74. See J. Helderman, "Das Evangelium Veritatis in der neueren Forschung," *ANRW* II.25.5:4054–4106.

ointment. The ointment is the mercy of the father, who will be merci-
ful to them; and those whom he has anointed are the perfected. (*Gos. Truth* 36)[75]

For *Gospel of Truth*, as for 1 John, Jesus is the Christ, the anointed one, and the
members of the Christ sect themselves are anointed by God. For *Gospel of Truth*,
the medium of this anointing is "the mercy of the father," probably reflecting a
wordplay in the Greek *Vorlage* of ἔλεος, "mercy," for ἔλαιον, "oil."[76]

Figurative talk of the anointing of Christian adepts with knowledge (as in 1
John) or mercy (as in *Gospel of Truth*) may or may not presuppose an initiatory
oil ritual. But other early Christian sources certainly attest the latter.[77] Tertullian
reports that in his North African, proto-orthodox circles, a Christian's water baptism is accompanied by anointing with oil as a matter of course.[78] He writes:

> Then, after exiting from the [baptismal] font, we are anointed all over
> with a blessed anointing, from the old discipline whereby they used to
> be anointed in the priesthood with oil from a horn, ever since Aaron
> was anointed by Moses. Whence he [Aaron] is called "Christ" [*unde
> Christus dicitur*], from the "chrism," that is, the anointing [*a chrismate
> quod est unctio*], which, made spiritual, adapted a name for the Lord,
> because he was "anointed" with the Spirit by God the Father [*quia spir-
> itu unctus est a Deo Patre*]. (Tertullian, *Bapt.* 7)[79]

This is an interesting passage. Rather than reasoning from the anointing
of Christ to the anointing of Christians, Tertullian begins by simply reporting
that Christian baptism includes an oil ritual, then points to the precedent of
the biblical anointing of Aaron as high priest, which, he says, also gave the
Lord the name "Christ."

Taking this logic still further, the late second-century Syrian
bishop Theophilus of Antioch, in his apology addressed to the pagan

---

75. Trans. mod. from Layton, *Gnostic Scriptures*.

76. See Einar Thomassen, "Baptism among the Valentinians," in *Ablution, Initiation, and
Baptism*, 2:895–915 at 901–2.

77. See Charles Munier, "Initiation chrétienne et rites d'onction (IIe–IIIe siècles)," *RSR* 64
(1990): 115–25.

78. On Tertullian's *De Baptismo*, see Øyvind Norderval, "Simplicity and Power: Tertullian's
De Baptismo," in *Ablution, Initiation, and Baptism*, 2:947–72.

79. Latin text ed. Ernest Evans, *Tertullian's Homily on Baptism* (London: SPCK, 1964).

Autolycus,[80] makes anointing with oil the sole necessary and sufficient ritual of Christian initiation.[81] Theophilus writes:

> And about your laughing at me and calling me Christian, you know not what you are saying. First, because that which is anointed is sweet and serviceable, and far from contemptible. For what ship can be serviceable and seaworthy, unless it be first anointed? Or what castle or house is beautiful and serviceable when it has not been anointed? And what man, when he enters into this life or into the gymnasium, is not anointed with oil? And what work has either ornament or beauty unless it be anointed and burnished? Then the air and all that is under heaven is in a certain sort anointed by light and spirit. And are you unwilling to be anointed with the oil of God? Wherefore we are called Christians on this account, because we are anointed with the oil of God [τοιγαροῦν ἡμεῖς τούτου εἵνεκεν καλούμεθα χριστιανοὶ ὅτι χριόμεθα ἔλαιον θεοῦ]. (Theophilus of Antioch, *Autol.* 1.12)[82]

Not only, in contrast to Tertullian, does water baptism not figure in Theophilus's account; Christ himself is altogether absent. For this reason, J. Bentivegna has argued that Theophilus's system of doctrine is more accurately termed a Christianology than a Christology, because Theophilus does not include Christ as a middle term. What makes a person a Christian is the rite of "being anointed with the oil of God."[83] Along the same lines, Robert Grant comments:

> While Theophilus refers to himself as a Christian, he explains the name as "being anointed with the oil of God," without reference to Jesus as the Christ (1.12). Being "anointed" would make one a christos, not a Christian, as both Luke [Luke 4:18; Acts 10:38] and Justin [*Apol.* 2.6.3] indicate; indeed, the Gnostic Gospel of Philip says precisely that one

---

80. On which see Robert M. Grant, "Theophilus of Antioch to Autolycus," *HTR* 40 (1947): 227–56; and more generally idem, "The Problem of Theophilus," *HTR* 43 (1950): 180–96.

81. On the Syrian context for Theophilus's position, see Alastair H. B. Logan, "Post-Baptismal Chrismation in Syria: The Evidence of Ignatius, the *Didache*, and the *Apostolic Constitutions*," *JTS* n.s. 49 (1998): 92–108.

82. Greek text ed. Robert M. Grant, *Theophilus of Antioch. Ad Autolycum* (Oxford: Clarendon, 1970); trans. mod. from Marcus Dods in *ANF*.

83. J. Bentivegna, "A Christianity without Christ by Theophilus of Antioch," *Studia patristica* 13 (1975): 107–30, especially 128–30.

who receives chrism is "no longer a Christian but a Christ." Theophilus also provides rhetorical praise for the oil of chrismation, just as Melito praises the water of baptism.[84]

Grant here cites the *Gospel of Philip* as a parallel to Theophilus's interpretation of anointing, which is partly accurate. The relevant passage from *Gospel of Philip* reads:

> Not only must those who produce the names of father, son, and holy spirit do so, but also [those who] have acquired these. If someone does not acquire them, the name too will be taken from that person. But if one gets them in the chrism of … the force of the cross, which the apostles called right and left. For this person is no longer a Christian but rather a Christ. (*Gos. Phil.* 67)[85]

As Grant notes, the *Gospel of Philip* rightly perceives that "Christ" means "anointed one," "one who has undergone anointing," so that, taken literally, it should apply to initiates themselves. The rite of anointing with oil is a key part of *Gospel of Philip*'s sacramental liturgy.[86] Consequently, it comes up for discussion at a number of points in the Gospel, receiving several quite different explanations.

Another of these explanations is conspicuously different from that of Theophilus. *Gospel of Philip* 74 reads:

> Chrism has more authority than baptism. For because of chrism we are called Christians, not because of baptism. And Christ was named for chrism, for the father anointed the son; and the son anointed the apostles, and the apostles anointed us. Whoever has been anointed has everything: resurrection, light, cross, holy spirit; the father has given it to that person in the bridal chamber, and the person has received (it). (*Gos. Phil.* 74)[87]

---

84. Grant, *Jesus after the Gospels*, 69–70.

85. Trans. mod. from Layton, *Gnostic Scriptures*.

86. See Bas van Os, "Baptism in the Bridal Chamber: The Gospel of Philip as a Valentinian Baptismal Instruction" (Ph.D. diss., University of Groningen, 2007); Eduard Iricinschi, "If You Got It, Flaunt It: Religious Advertising in the *Gospel of Philip*," in *Heresy and Identity in Late Antiquity* (ed. Eduard Iricinschi and Holger M. Zellentin; TSAJ 119; Tübingen: Mohr Siebeck, 2008), 253–72 at 270: "Chrism could have been the distinctive mark of senior members in the 'Philip' group, since chrism is the specific ritual that builds in-group identity, through the linguistic connection between the names 'Christian' and 'Christ,' and the oil of anointment."

87. Trans. mod. from Layton, *Gnostic Scriptures*.

Here (oil) chrism is mentioned in parallel with (water) baptism, although our author pleads for the superiority of the former. It is superior, first, because it accounts for the name of the Christians and, second, because it accounts for the name of Christ himself. There is a proper order, however: The father anoints the son (who is therefore "Christ"), the son anoints the apostles, and the apostles anoint the *Philip* sectarians. This is actually a much more proto-orthodox account than that of Theophilus. As Elaine Pagels comments:

> [In the ritual of chrism,] Christ's paradigm is fulfilled in the initiate.... What matters to Philip is less to delineate the action of each sacrament than to show that the initiate first reenacts Jesus' divine birth, then his resurrection, and, finally, his reunion with his *syzygos*.[88]

There is, finally, a minority strand of early Christian speculation on the etymology of "Christ" that bypasses the lexicon of anointing entirely. This, too, is most clearly attested in the *Gospel of Philip*. The relevant passage reads:

> The apostles who were before us had these names for him: "Jesus, the Nazorean, Messiah," that is, "Jesus, the Nazorean, the Christ." The last name is "Christ," the first is "Jesus," that in the middle is "the Nazarene." "Messiah" has two meanings, both "the Christ" and "the measured." "Jesus" in Hebrew is "the redemption." "Nazara" is "the truth." "The Nazarene," then, is "the truth." "Christ" ... been measured. It is "the Nazarene" and "Jesus" who have been measured. (*Gos. Phil.* 62)[89]

Gospel of Philip says that "messiah" has two different meanings, "anointed" and "measured," which is actually true, or at least defensible, although no other text explicates it in this way. The Semitic root משׁח (whether Hebrew or Syriac) commonly means "to anoint," following classical biblical usage, but in late antiquity this same root also has the second sense "to measure."[90] *Gospel of Philip* knows both senses and makes the christological inference that Jesus the messiah is "the measured one."

---

88. Elaine Pagels, "Ritual in the Gospel of Philip," in *The Nag Hammadi Library after Fifty Years* (ed. John D. Turner and Anne McGuire; NHMS 44; Leiden: Brill, 1997), 280–91 at 286.

89. Trans. Isenberg in *NHL*.

90. See BDB, s.v. משׁח; Marcus Jastrow, *A Dictionary of the Targumim, the Talmud Babli and Yerushalmi, and the Midrashic Literature* (New York, N.Y.: Putnam's, 1903), s.v. משׁח.

Not long after the Nag Hammadi manuscript of the *Gospel of Philip* was first published in the mid twentieth century, W. C. van Unnik perceptively commented on this passage:

> It is a well-known fact that the title "Christ" puzzled the Greek-speaking Christians, since there was no corresponding figure to the Hebrew Messiah in Greek and Roman religion; often they replaced it by "Chrestos" which had the same pronunciation. It may be that some ingenious man discovered the possibility of the double translation. If this is correct we must infer that this wordplay or double translation was already current in Christian circles ca. 130 and that it came up in a bilingual community of Syria (Antioch?), where the Hebrew and Aramaic languages were known, but where a translation for Greek was desirable.[91]

Van Unnik traces this novel etymology—"messiah" meaning "measured"—to second-century Syria because, although *Gospel of Philip* is the clearest witness to the idea, there are earlier witnesses. Especially important for van Unnik is an otherwise obscure passage in book 4 of Irenaeus's late second-century *Adversus Haereses*, in which Irenaeus reports a christological opinion of an anonymous someone, perhaps "the presbyter" whose views he cites elsewhere:[92]

> For God does all things by measure and in order; nothing is unmeasured with him, because nothing is out of order. Well spoke he, who said that the unmeasurable father was himself subjected to measure in the son [*et bene qui dixit ipsum immensum patrem in filio mensuratum*]; for the son is the measure of the father, since he also comprehends him [μέτρον γὰρ τοῦ πατρὸς ὁ υἱός, ἐπεὶ καὶ χωρεῖ αὐτόν, *mensura enim patrem filius, quoniam et capit eum*]. (Irenaeus, *Haer.* 4.4.2)[93]

---

91. W. C. van Unnik, "Three Notes on the Gospel of Philip," *NTS* 10 (1964): 465–69 at 466–67.

92. See H. G. Sobosan, "The Role of the Presbyter: An Investigation into the *Adv. Haer.* of St. Irenaeus," *SJT* 27 (1974): 129–46; W. C. van Unnik, "The Authority of the Presbyters in Irenaeus' Works," in *God's Christ and His People: Studies in Honour of Nils Alstrup Dahl* (ed. Jacob Jervell and Wayne A. Meeks; Oslo: Universitetsforlaget, 1978), 248–60; C. E. Hill, *From the Lost Teaching of Polycarp* (WUNT 186; Tübingen: Mohr Siebeck, 2006), 7–31.

93. Greek and Latin text ed. Adelin Rousseau et al., *Irénée de Lyon, Contre Les Hérésies, Livre IV* (SC 100.1–2; Paris: Cerf, 1965); trans. Roberts and Rambaut in *ANF*.

There is nothing here about "messiah" or "Christ" as such, but significantly, the son is described as the measure of the father (μέτρον τοῦ πατρὸς ὁ υἱός, *mensura patrem filius*), the one in whom the father is subjected to measure (*patrem in filio mensuratum*). Van Unnik reasons, speculatively but not implausibly, that "messiah" is the missing middle term connecting "son" to "measure." Subsequently, Guy Stroumsa, building on van Unnik, comments on this passage:

> The mythologoumenon reported in *Gos. Phil.* is indeed the same as that reinterpreted by Irenaeus: being infinite, and including all things, God cannot in any way be known, or measured. Only his Hypostasis, the Son, can be measured. The Son is, therefore, the μέτρον of the Father.[94]

And this christological curio, Stroumsa argues further, has roots in Jewish mystical speculation about the *shi'ur qomah*, the measurements of the heavenly body of God.[95]

Van Unnik traces the Christ-"measured" etymology as far back as second-century CE Syria, but there is at least a possibility that it goes further still. Michael Fishbane, commenting on *Gos. Phil.* 62, makes a connection to the deutero-Pauline Epistle to the Ephesians (late first century CE). The author of Ephesians says that God purposes

> the building up the body of the messiah [οἰκοδομὴν τοῦ σώματος τοῦ χριστοῦ], until we all attain to the oneness of faith and of the knowledge

---

94. Gedaliahu G. Stroumsa, "Form(s) of God: Some Notes on Metatron and Christ," *HTR* 76 (1983): 269–88 at 286.

95. Stroumsa, "Forms of God," 285:

> It is difficult to make sense of this word-play if we do not suppose that its inventor(s) knew Jewish traditions about the figure of the divine hypostasis which was, in contradistinction to God himself, measurable and which had, in other words, a *shi'ur qomah*. These Jewish–Christians seem to have applied to Christ conceptions previously attributed to Yahoel.

On this Jewish tradition, see Peter Schäfer, *The Hidden and Manifest God: Some Major Themes in Early Jewish Mysticism* (trans. Aubrey Pomerance; Albany, N.Y.: SUNY Press, 1992), 162:

> The decisive statement of *Shi'ur Qomah* is that God does, on the one hand, look like a human being; but, on the other hand, he exceeds all human measurements. God's hidden being expresses itself in dimensions that surpass all human categories and, paradoxically, is conceivable in its imperceptibility.

The classical *shi'ur qomah* texts from the Hekhalot corpus are collected in Martin Samuel Cohen, *The Shi'ur Qomah: Texts and Recensions* (TSAJ 9; Tübingen: Mohr Siebeck, 1985).

of the son of God, to mature manhood, to the measure of the stature of the fulness of the messiah [μέτρον ἡλικίας τοῦ πληρώματος τοῦ χριστοῦ]. (Eph 4:12–13)[96]

Fishbane, analogously to Stroumsa, sees in this talk of adepts participating in "the body of the messiah" and "the measure [μέτρον] of the full stature of the messiah" a very early Christian version of *shiʿur qomah* speculation.[97] He concludes:

> The pun in *The Gospel According to Philip* only makes sense in light of an older Christological tradition which linked the Redeemer to the measure or figure of divine Glory on high. That is to say: for the Jewish–Christian circles behind this Gnostic gospel, as well as for the disciples of the apostle Paul, the ancient anthropomorphic figure in heaven was identified as the Christ. Put otherwise, the "measured One" was believed to be none other than the "messiah" himself.[98]

It is not certain that the Ephesians and Irenaeus references attest the same alternate etymology for "messiah" that *Gospel of Philip* does, but the most economical explanation is that they do. If so, then we have very early evidence for Christian speculation on hidden meanings of the *nomen sacrum* "messiah." In this connection, Richard Longenecker comments:

> Under gnostic influence Jesus as the revealer of truth received exclusive emphasis. But the *Gospel of Philip*, rooted as it is in a Jewish subsoil and probably independent of the canonical Gospels, still preserves the memory of what χριστός originally meant—even though it does it in a very garbled fashion and even though it prefers to use it as a name and present for it a decidedly secondary etymology.[99]

---

96. And, possibly related, Eph 1:23, where the assembly of the holy ones "is the body of the messiah, the fulness of him who fills all in all [ἐστὶν τὸ σῶμα αὐτοῦ, τὸ πλήρωμα τοῦ τὰ πάντα ἐν πᾶσιν πληρουμένου]."

97. See also Markus Bockmuehl, "'The Form of God' (Phil 2:6): Variations on a Theme of Jewish Mysticism," *JTS* n.s. 48 (1997): 1–23, who makes a related argument for the authentically Pauline Epistle to the Philippians, where Paul says that the messiah "exists in the form of God [ἐν μορφῇ θεοῦ ὑπάρχων]" (Phil 2:6) and "has a body of glory [τῷ σώματι τῆς δόξης αὐτοῦ]" (Phil 3:21), but without reference to the messiah-"measured" etymology.

98. Michael Fishbane, "The 'Measures' of God's Glory in the Ancient Midrash," in *Messiah and Christos*, 53–74 at 72.

99. Richard N. Longenecker, *The Christology of Early Jewish Christianity* (London: SCM, 1970), 82.

This comment is helpful but also a bit unfair to *Gospel of Philip*. Yes, "measured" is a secondary etymology for "messiah," but *Gospel of Philip* attests the primary etymology, too, and he distinguishes the two quite clearly, so his presentation is not garbled. Rather, *Gospel of Philip*, like Ephesians before him, takes the morphological ambiguity of the word "messiah" as an occasion for christological improvisation.

Christ and the Jews

To this point we have been describing how ancient Christian writers explained "Christ" to themselves via the linguistic work of translation and etymologizing. But messiah Christology also played a particular role in Christian self-definition vis-à-vis proximate outsiders, especially Jews and *sogenannte* heretics.[100] First, the Jews.[101] If, as noted earlier, there were not in antiquity different words for the Jewish "messiah" and the Christian "Christ," then one might expect to encounter some contention regarding Jewish and Christian claims on the same word. And this is indeed what we find, albeit much more on the one side than the other. Although it is the case that, for most early Christian writers, the title "Christ" was attached axiomatically to Jesus, that title also remained, for many of these same writers, the standard term for the messiah of the Jews, which is a major theme in early Christian *contra Iudaeos* literature.[102]

Thus the character of Trypho the Jew, in Justin Martyr's *Dialogue with Trypho*, makes a number of claims about Jewish beliefs about the messiah, always using the word χριστός.[103] Trypho says:

> Be assured that all our nation waits for the messiah [πᾶν τὸ γένος ἡμῶν τὸν χριστὸν ἐκδέχεται]; and we admit that all the scriptures which you

100. Indeed, it is largely because of their common status as proximate outsiders that Jews and heretics are not infrequently conflated by ancient Christian writers. See Averil Cameron, "Jews and Heretics—A Category Error?" in *Ways That Never Parted*, 345–60.

101. Among the vast secondary literature, see in particular Judith Lieu, "History and Theology in Christian Views of Judaism," in *The Jews among Pagans and Christians in the Roman Empire* (ed. Judith Lieu et al.; New York, N.Y.: Routledge, 1992), 79–96.

102. On the genre, see A. Lukyn Williams, *Adversus Judaeos: A Bird's-Eye View of Christian Apologiae until the Renaissance* (Cambridge: Cambridge University Press, 1935); Ora Limor and Guy G. Stroumsa, eds., *Contra Iudaeos: Ancient and Medieval Polemics between Christians and Jews* (TSMEMJ 10; Tübingen: Mohr Siebeck, 1996).

103. On Justin's knowledge of Judaism, see David Rokeah, *Justin Martyr and the Jews* (JCP 5; Leiden: Brill, 2002). The *Dialogue* is a literary creation, not a transcription of an event, and

have quoted refer to him. . . .. But whether the messiah [χριστόν] should be so shamefully crucified, this we are in doubt about. (*Dial.* 89.1–2)

And elsewhere:

If this man [Jesus] should appear to be the messiah [ἐὰν δὲ οὗτος φαίνηται ὢν ὁ χριστός], he must certainly be known as a man of men; but from the fact that Elijah has not yet come, I infer that this man [Jesus] is not he [the messiah]. (*Dial.* 49)

Meanwhile, the Christian Justin refers consistently to Jesus as χριστός, and sometimes, because of his and Trypho's disagreement over the applicability of the term, ὁ ἡμέτερος χριστός, "our messiah" (*Dial.* 36.5; 43.7; 49.5; 66.4; 70.4). In the *Dialogue*, there is not a Jewish "messiah" and a Christian "Christ"; there is just "our messiah" and "your messiah."[104]

We find a similar dynamic in Hippolytus. The author of the fragmentary *Treatise against the Jews*, whether Hippolytus himself or an imitator, cites several biblical psalms in support of his claim that the Jews are guilty for rejecting Jesus.[105] Then he comments, "What do you say to this, O Jew? It is neither Matthew nor Paul who says these things, but David, your messiah [Δαυιδ ὁ σὸς χριστός], who awards and declares these terrible sentences on account of the messiah [διὰ χριστόν]" (*Adv. Jud.* 8).[106] King David of old, here in his role as psalmist, is "your messiah," the messiah of the Jews, who by his oracles condemns the Jews on behalf of the messiah Jesus. Elsewhere, in his account of Jewish doctrine in the *Refutation of All Heresies*, Hippolytus claims that belief in the future coming of the messiah is held in common by all sects of Jews. "They all likewise await the messiah [οἱ δὲ πάντες ὁμοίως χριστὸν προσδέχονται]. For the law and the prophets announced beforehand that he would come, but the Jews did not recognize the time of his coming" (Hippolytus, *Haer.* 9.30.5). And again, "They say that the messiah who was sent by God [τὸν ἀποσταλέντα

Trypho is a character, not a person (thus rightly Rajak, "Talking at Trypho"), but it remains contested how much of the character of Trypho may have been taken from life (see Horner, *Listening to Trypo*).

104. See further Higgins, "Jewish Messianic Belief"; Oskar Skarsaune, *The Proof from Prophecy: A Study in Justin Martyr's Proof-Text Tradition* (Leiden: Brill, 1987), especially 191–225.

105. On the vexed questions of authorship and provenance of the Hippolytan corpus, see Brent, *Hippolytus and the Roman Church*; J. A. Cerrato, *Hippolytus between East and West* (OTM; Oxford: Oxford University Press, 2002), especially 3–123.

106. Greek text ed. Eduard Schwartz, "Zwei Predigten Hippolyts," *SBAW* 3 (1936): 19–23.

ὑπὸ τοῦ θεοῦ χριστὸν] is not him, but that another will come, who does not yet exist" (Hippolytus, *Haer.* 9.30.6).[107] For Hippolytus, as for Justin, Jesus is the messiah who was in fact sent by God, but the Jews mistakenly await another messiah.

Even in the Latin West, where, as far as we know, there is no pre-Christian Jewish use of the transliteration *Christus*,[108] that word is used by early Christian writers to refer not just to Jesus, but also to the messiah of Jewish legend. Tertullian writes in his treatise *Against the Jews*,[109] "For that the messiah was to come [*venturum enim Christum*], we know that even the Jews do not attempt to disprove, inasmuch as it is to his advent that they are directing their hope" (Tertullian, *Adv. Jud.* 7).[110] And again, "Therefore, since the Jews still contend that their messiah has not yet come [*igitur quoniam adhuc contendunt Judaei necdum venisse Christum eorum*], whom we have in so many ways proved to have come, let the Jews recognise their own fate" (Tertullian, *Adv. Jud.* 13). Here, again, there is one word for "messiah"; the only question is whether or not he has come.

Many early Christian writers put the matter thusly, but their Jewish contemporaries generally do not. Indeed, as is well known, Jewish sources from the centuries before the rise of Islam tend not to mention Christianity explicitly at all. Andrew Jacobs summarizes:

> Rabbinic texts do not treat Christianity with the same obsessiveness as Christians speak of Judaism. . . . . When Christianity appears in the rabbinic writings, or in poetical or apocalyptic texts, it is thickly veiled and coded, or lumped together with the panoply of "heresies" (*minim*) that serve for the theoretical and rhetorical construction of rabbinism.[111]

And if ancient Jewish sources say little about Christianity, they certainly do not single out the identity of messiah as the dividing line between Jews and

---

107. Greek text ed. M. Marcovich, *Hippolytus. Refutatio omnium haeresium* (Patristische Texte und Studien 25; Berlin: De Gruyter, 1986).

108. See Lewis and Short, s.v. *Christus*. Evidence for Jewish Latin is extremely sparse in any case, but see the indirect evidence adduced by D. S. Blondheim, *Les parlers judéo-romans et la Vetus Latina* (Cambridge: Cambridge University Press, 2013 [1925]).

109. On which see Geoffrey D. Dunn, *Tertullian's Adversus Ioudaeos: A Rhetorical Analysis* (PMS 19; Washington, D.C.: Catholic University of America Press, 2008).

110. Latin text ed. Hermann Tränkle, *Q. S. F. Tertulliani Adversus Iudaeos* (Wiesbaden: Steiner, 1964).

111. Andrew S. Jacobs, "Jews and Christians," in *The Oxford Handbook of Early Christian Studies* (ed. Susan Ashbrook Harvey and David C. Hunter; Oxford: Oxford University Press,

Christians. Which is not to say that these Jewish sources do not have their own versions of a messiah myth; many do. But they do not single it out as constitutive of religious identity, as Annette Reed has rightly argued:

> There is a striking lack of firsthand evidence for ancient Jewish counterparts to such [Christian] assertions; if anything, we glimpse rabbinic resistance to Christian claims about the power of messianic and other beliefs to produce "religion" and difference. Ancient Christian sources often insist that Jews concur with Christians on everything about the Messiah except his advent and identity, and modern scholars often take such claims at face value. Ancient Jewish sources, however, model quite different approaches to mapping identity.[112]

One-sided though it was, this discursive conflict over Jewish and Christian claims to the word "messiah" sometimes came, under certain social circumstances, to more serious, nondiscursive expression. For instance, some early Christian sources on the second Jewish–Roman (Bar Kokhba) War of the 130s CE interpret Bar Kosiba's brief *regnum* in terms of a conflict between Jewish messianism and Christian messianism in the land of Israel. Writing within a generation of the events, Justin Martyr reports:

> In the Jewish war which lately raged, Barcochebas, the leader of the revolt of the Jews, gave orders that Christians alone should be led away to cruel punishments, unless they should deny that Jesus is the messiah and blaspheme [εἰ μὴ ἀρνοῖντο Ἰησοῦν τὸν Χριστὸν καὶ βλασφημοῖεν]. (Justin, *1 Apol.* 31.5–6)[113]

Eusebius preserves a less detailed report of the same: "Cochebas, prince of the Jewish sect, killed the Christians with all kinds of persecutions, [when]

2008), 169–85 at 173. But although the rabbis do not speak obsessively about the Christians, there is good reason to suspect Christian influence on rabbinic thinking at numerous points, as rightly noted by Yuval, *Two Nations in Your Womb*; Schäfer, *Jewish Jesus*; and Holger M. Zellentin, *Rabbinic Parodies of Jewish and Christian Literature* (TSAJ 139; Tübingen: Mohr Siebeck, 2011).

112. Reed, "Messianism between Judaism and Christianity," 24.

113. Greek text ed. Goodspeed, *Apologeten*; trans. mine. It is striking to note how nearly identical are 1 John's job description for antichrists on the one hand—ἀρνούμενος ὅτι Ἰησοῦς οὐκ ἔστιν ὁ Χριστός, "denying that Jesus is the messiah"—and Justin's report of Bar Kokhba's mandate for Levantine Christians on the other—ἀρνοῖντο Ἰησοῦν τὸν Χριστὸν, "denying that Jesus is the messiah."

they refused to help him against the Roman troops" (Eusebius, *Chron.* Hadrian Year 17).[114]

We know from the documentary remains left by the Bar Kokhba partisans that their leader exercised *de facto* despotic authority in the land of Israel for the three years of the conflict.[115] He was in a position, in other words, to persecute Christians in the homeland, although no non-Christian source corroborates the claim that he, in fact, did so. Non-Christian sources do, however, attest the tradition that Bar Kokhba was regarded by his followers as the messiah. In the extant papyrus letters, he refers to himself as נשיא ישראל, "prince of Israel," although not as messiah.[116] Multiple rabbinic texts, all of which postdate the war, associate Bar Kokhba with the title messiah in particular, and most of these texts take pains to contest his claim to that title (especially *y. Ta'an.* 4:8 [68d]; *b. Sanh.* 93b).[117] Famously, the Yerushalmi preserves the tradition that R. Akiba himself acclaimed Bar Kokhba as messiah and conferred his honorific name by means of an ingenious interpretation of Num 24:17: "Kokhab ["a star"] goes out from Jacob" means "Kosiba goes out from Jacob" (*y. Ta'an.* 4:8 [68d]; cf. *Lam. Rab.* 2:2 §4), thus Bar Kosiba, "son of Kosiba," became Bar Kokhba, "son of the star." This passage has been much contested, of course. I have argued elsewhere that that the R. Akiba connection is historically suspect, but that the story is a literary expression of a real messianic movement surrounding Bar Kosiba during his own lifetime.[118]

If there was indeed such a movement, then the reports in Justin and Eusebius of persecution of Christians at the hands of Bar Kosiba become both more intelligible and more plausible. According to Eusebius, the putative offense for which Christians were punished was failure to aid the revolt against the Romans. But why would some Levantine Christians not have joined with their countrymen in throwing off the Roman yoke? Justin's account implies a reason. According to Justin, Bar Kosiba's policy was to punish Christians unless they would "deny that Jesus is the messiah and blaspheme." In other

---

114. See the polyglot edition of Alfred Schoene and H. Petermann, eds., *Eusebi Chronicorum Libri Duo* (2 vols.; Berlin: Weidmann, 1866–1875).

115. See Schäfer, *Bar Kokhba-Aufstand*; Hannah M. Cotton, "The Bar Kokhba Revolt and the Documents from the Judaean Desert," in *Bar Kokhba War Reconsidered*, 133–52; William Horbury, *Jewish War under Trajan and Hadrian* (Cambridge: Cambridge University Press, 2014).

116. See Oppenheimer, "Leadership and Messianism."

117. On the Bar Kokhba messiah texts, see Chapters 3 and 6 in this volume.

118. See Novenson, "Why Does R. Akiba"; and relatedly Schäfer, "R. Aqiba and Bar Kokhba"; idem, "Bar Kokhba and the Rabbis."

words, confessing Jesus as the messiah was the offense. This might seem strange were it not for the widespread tradition that Bar Kosiba himself was regarded as the messiah. Perhaps what we have, then, is a case of competing messiahs, aggravated by the fact that one of them happens to be in power.[119] Under other political circumstances, different messianic groups could coexist peaceably enough in the land of Israel. During the 60s CE, for example, there were Qumran covenanters, disciples of Jesus, and partisans of Simon bar Giora all living in the vicinity of Jerusalem, apparently without ever coming into conflict with one another.[120] When Bar Kosiba the messiah came to be in a position to compel obedience, however, then followers of Jesus the messiah were put in a difficult position, because participation in Bar Kosiba's revolt might have amounted, for some at least, to blasphemy. In this case, at least, the curious Christian fixation on the messiah as a marker of religious difference came at a price.

Christ and the Heretics

If some early Christian writers interpret "messiah" in such a way as to differentiate themselves from Jews, others (or, indeed, some of the selfsame writers) interpret "messiah" in such a way as to differentiate themselves from what they consider the wrong kind of Christians—that is, heretics. In particular, there is literary evidence for a dispute among certain early Christians about the use of the word "messiah" or "Christ" to signify the divine nature, essence, part, or aspect (depending on the metaphysics of the writer in question) of Jesus. Whereas some early Christian writers use the word "Christ" virtually interchangeably with "Jesus," others are reported to have used it in an opposite way, precisely as a contrast term for "Jesus," to name the divine being that possessed or inhabited Jesus. Modern interpreters sometimes call this latter group separationists, because they assert the separability of the human Jesus from the divine Christ.[121] Separationism can and should be distinguished from docetism—the teaching that Jesus suffered only in appearance, not in

119. See Horbury, "Messianism among Jews and Christians in the Second Century"; Goodman, "Messianism and Politics"; Skarsaune, "Jews and Christians in the Holy Land."

120. But compare the conflict between the partisans of Simon bar Giora and those of John of Gischala when both groups were vying for control of Jerusalem (Josephus, *War* book 5). On this phase of the war, see Steve Mason, *A History of the Jewish War, A.D. 66–74* (Cambridge: Cambridge University Press, 2016), 402–513.

121. Or alternatively possessionists, because they are said to teach that the human Jesus was possessed for a time by the divine Christ (see Michael Goulder, *St. Paul versus St. Peter: A Tale*

reality—despite the concern, common to both, to maintain divine impassibility.[122] Put simply, docetists maintain divine impassibility by distinguishing appearance from reality, while separationists maintain divine impassibility by distinguishing the human part of Jesus from the divine part.

It is not clear exactly when this putative separationist usage—"Jesus" meaning the human being from Nazareth, "Christ" meaning the divine spirit that possessed him—is first attested, but one possibility is around the turn of the second century in the Johannine Epistles. As is well known, the secessionist "antichrists" mentioned in 1 John and 2 John (1 John 2:18, 22; 4:3; 2 John 7) are accused by the author or authors of denying several essential articles of faith—namely, "that Jesus is the Christ" (1 John 1:22), "that Jesus is the son of God" (1 John 4:15), and "that Jesus Christ has come in the flesh" (1 John 4:2; 2 John 7). According to one plausible interpretation, the secessionists denied that Jesus Christ has come in the flesh for reasons having to do with their doctrine of flesh—in particular, that it is a mode of being not worthy of God. Proponents of this interpretation then explicate the parallel clause, which is likewise denied by secessionists, "that Jesus is the Christ," in an analogous way, as meaning that the human Jesus is identical with the divine Christ.[123] If this reading is right, then we would have here secondhand evidence of the separationist parsing of "Jesus" and "Christ."

The principal alternative is the view that the Johannine secessionists are not separationists but simply Jews, ones who deny that Jesus is the messiah who is to come.[124] This minority view has in its favor a prima facie fit with certain features of the Gospel of John, in particular the notion—widely and rightly accepted since J. Louis Martyn's 1968 *History and Theology in the Fourth Gospel*—of a late first-century schism between the Johannine sect and the mainstream

---

of Two Missions [Louisville, Ky.: WJK, 1995], 107–34). For our purposes, the concepts of separationism and possessionism are, effectively, two sides of the same coin, so in what follows I consistently use the former term for the sake of simplicity.

122. On the distinction between separationism and docetism, see Norbert Brox, "'Doketismus'—eine Problemanzeige," *ZKG* 95 (1984): 301–14; Bart D. Ehrman, *The Orthodox Corruption of Scripture* (New York, N.Y.: Oxford University Press, 1993), 119–80.

123. Thus, for example, Raymond E. Brown, *The Community of the Beloved Disciple* (New York, N.Y.: Paulist, 1979), 109–23; idem, *The Epistles of John* (AB; New York, N.Y.: Doubleday, 1982), 68–115; Pamela E. Kinlaw, *The Christ Is Jesus: Metamorphosis, Possession, and Johannine Christology* (Atlanta, Ga.: SBL, 2005); Tuomas Rasimus, *Paradise Reconsidered in Gnostic Mythmaking* (NHMS 68; Brill, 2009), 255–77.

124. Thus, for example, Terry Griffith, *Keep Yourselves from Idols: A New Look at 1 John* (JSNTSup 233; Sheffield: Sheffield Academic, 2002).

synagogue over the messiahship of Jesus.[125] The minority view has a difficult time, however, accounting for the peculiar emphasis in the Epistles of John on the tangibility of the word of life (1 John 1:1) and the fleshly mode of Jesus's coming (2 John 7). (Indeed, reasoning in an opposite direction, Georg Strecker and Udo Schnelle have argued that not only the Epistles but the Gospel, too, is concerned entirely with Christian docetism and not at all with Jewish messianism.)[126] In my view, the majority interpretation is the more likely correct of the two.[127] The Epistles of John inherit from the Gospel of John the crucial confession that Jesus is the Christ, but they use that confession to reckon with a rather different theological controversy than the Gospel knew.[128] As Raymond Brown comments, "The author had to remain faithful to the formulas that had come down in Johannine tradition even if they were not originally intended to solve the problem he was now facing. To use them as arguments against his opponents he had to reinterpret them."[129] Just so. Even on this interpretation, however, it does not follow that the secessionists were separationists. And even if they were separationists, it does not follow that they distinguished the human Jesus from the divine Christ. Perhaps 1 John understands that to be the shape of their Christology, but this might be a misunderstanding on his part.

Regardless of whether a separationist Christology is attested in the Johannine Epistles, it is attested in Irenaeus's accounts of Valentinian Christology and the Christology of Cerinthus.[130] Irenaeus writes about the Valentinians:

> There are some who say that Jesus was merely a receptacle of Christ, upon whom Christ, as a dove, descended from above [*Iesum quidem receptaculum Christi fuisse, in quem desuper quasi columbam descendisse*

---

125. See Martyn, *History and Theology*; and Marcus, "Birkat Ha-Minim Revisited."

126. And, furthermore, that the Epistles actually antedate and provide the theological context for the Gospel. See Georg Strecker, *The Johannine Letters* (trans. Linda Maloney; Hermeneia; Minneapolis, Min..: Fortress, 1996); Udo Schnelle, *Antidocetic Christology in the Gospel of John* (trans. Linda Maloney; Minneapolis, Minn.: Fortress, 1992).

127. For a fine discussion of the merits and demerits of the different hypotheses, see Judith Lieu, "Messiah and Resistance in the Gospel and Epistles of John," in *Redemption and Resistance*, 97–108.

128. Although there are perhaps signs already in the Gospel, as suggested by Marinus de Jonge, "Variety and Development in Johannine Christology," in idem, *Jesus, Stranger from Heaven and Son of God* (SBLSBS 11; Missoula, Mont.: Scholars Press, 1977), 193–222 at 210: "What is a major christological issue in the First and Second Epistles is a minor one in the Gospel, but the necessity of 'anti-docetic emphasis' is (already) there."

129. Brown, *Community of the Beloved Disciple*, 111n217.

130. For basic background, see Robert M. Grant, *Irenaeus of Lyons* (London: Routledge, 1997).

Christum] ... and that Jesus was the son, but Christ was the father, and the father of Christ, God; while others say that he merely suffered in outward appearance, being naturally impassible. (Irenaeus, *Haer.* 3.16.1)[131]

Irenaeus here distinguishes between docetism proper, the view that "he merely suffered in outward appearance," and separationism, the view that "Jesus was merely a receptacle of Christ" (*Iesum quidem receptaculum Christi fuisse*). "Jesus," according to the latter view, is the human being from Nazareth, "Christ" the impassible divine being that indwelt Jesus.

But the Valentinians are not the only sect whom Irenaeus accuses of teaching that Jesus is a receptacle of Christ. In particular, he attributes almost exactly the same view to Cerinthus, who taught in Asia Minor at the turn of the second century:[132]

[Cerinthus] represented Jesus as having not been born of a virgin, but as being the son of Joseph and Mary according to the ordinary course of human generation, while he nevertheless was more righteous, prudent, and wise than other men. Moreover, after his baptism, Christ descended upon him in the form of a dove [κατελθεῖν εἰς αὐτὸν ... τὸν Χριστὸν ἐν εἴδει περιστερᾶς, *descendisse in eum ... Christum figura columbae*] from the Supreme Ruler, and that then he proclaimed the unknown Father, and performed miracles. But at last Christ departed from Jesus [ἀποπτῆναι τὸν Χριστὸν ἀπὸ τοῦ Ἰησοῦ, *autem reuolasse iterum Christum de Iesu*], and that then Jesus suffered and rose again, while Christ remained impassible, inasmuch as he was a spiritual being [τὸν δὲ Χριστὸν ἀπαθῆ διαμεμενηκέναι πνευματικὸν ὑπάρχοντα, *Christum autem impassibilem perseuerasse exsistentem spiritalem*]. (Irenaeus, *Haer.* 1.26.1)[133]

Irenaeus treats Cerinthus alongside the Ebionites because, he says, their "opinions with respect to the Lord are similar."[134] This similarity is clear in

131. Latin text ed. Adelin Rousseau and Louis Doutreleau, *Irénée de Lyon, Contre Les Hérésies, Livre III* (SC 211; Paris: Cerf, 1974); trans. Roberts and Rambaut in *ANF*. On Irenaeus and the Valentinians more generally, see Geoffrey S. Smith, *Guilt by Association: Heresy Catalogues in Early Christianity* (New York, N.Y.: Oxford University Press, 2014), 131–72.

132. It is notoriously difficult to reconstruct an accurate portrait of Cerinthus from the sources, but see Brown, *Epistles of John*, 766–71 for a fine bare-bones treatment.

133. Greek and Latin text ed. Adelin Rousseau and Louis Doutreleau, *Irénée de Lyon, Contre Les Hérésies, Livre I* (SC 264; Paris: Cerf, 1979); trans. Roberts and Rambaut in *ANF*.

134. On the Ebionites, see Richard Bauckham, "The Origin of the Ebionites," in *The Image of the Judaeo-Christians in Ancient Jewish and Christian Literature* (ed. Peter J. Tomson and Doris

the first part of the quotation, regarding Jesus's natural generation from two human parents. It is less clear in the second part, regarding the divine Christ inhabiting Jesus between his baptism and crucifixion, because this is a view that Irenaeus actually attributes not to the Ebionites, but to the Valentinians. For this reason, Cerinthus has been a puzzle for early Christian prosopography. Is he a gnostic, or a Jewish Christian, or both, or something else altogether?[135]

A Jewish Christian connection in the case of Cerinthus, if accurate, would be remarkable for the purposes of this study, because it is precisely Christian inter-pretation of the archaic Jewish term "messiah" that is the matter before us.[136] If it were a Jewish Christian teacher or group that took the word "messiah" to mean an impassible divine being that temporarily possessed Jesus, this would be a striking piece of evidence for the range of contemporary Jewish views on the subject of the messiah. I suspect, however, that this is not the case. The details of Cerinthus's views are controverted in recent scholarship, but there is good reason to follow the assessment of Klijn and Reininck that he functions in patristic literature as a kind of all-purpose heretic, a cipher for a wide variety of views that Irenaeus and later heresiologists find objectionable.[137] If so, then Cerinthus is not admissible as evidence for a Valentinian-esque separationist Christology among Jewish Christians at the turn of the second century.

More interesting still is the question whether the Valentinians themselves count as evidence for the Valentinian separationist Christology described by

---

Lambers-Petry; WUNT 158; Tübingen: Mohr Siebeck, 2003), 162–81; Joseph Verheyden, "Epiphanius on the Ebionites," in *Image of the Judaeo-Christians*, 182–208; Sakari Häkkinen, "Ebionites," in *Companion to Second-Century Christian Heretics*, 247–78.

135. On this question, see Christoph Markschies, "Kerinth: Wer war er und was lehrte er?" *JAC* 41 (1998): 48–76; C. E. Hill, "Cerinthus, Gnostic or Chiliast? A New Solution to an Old Problem," *JECS* 8 (2000): 135–72; Matti Myllykoski, "Cerinthus," in *Companion to Second-Century Christian Heretics*, 213–46.

136. On the obstinate problems with the term "Jewish Christian," see Matt Jackson-McCabe, "What's in a Name? The Problem of 'Jewish Christianity,'" in *Jewish Christianity Reconsidered: Rethinking Ancient Groups and Texts* (ed. Matt Jackson-McCabe; Minneapolis, Minn.: Fortress, 2007), 7–38; James Carleton Paget, "The Definition of the Term 'Jewish Christian'/'Jewish Christianity' in the History of Research," in idem, *Jews, Christians, and Jewish Christians in Antiquity* (WUNT 251; Tübingen: Mohr Siebeck, 2010), 289–324.

137. See A. F. J. Klijn and G. J. Reininck, *Patristic Evidence for Jewish-Christian Sects* (Leiden: Brill, 1973), 19:

No [ancient] author knows of any other historical traditions about Cerinthus, apart from those which describe him as a heretic living in Asia during the Apostolic period. The idea that he was a "Judaistic-Millenarian-Gnostic," and any conclusion drawn from this supposition regarding the origin or development of Gnosticism, has no historical value. These notions about Cerinthus are the inventions of early Christian authors.

Irenaeus. That is to say, if we bracket the secondhand accounts of the heresi-ologists, what firsthand evidence is there for an early Christian distinction between the human Jesus and the divine Christ? The earliest source said to be associated with a separationist Christology, the Gospel of Mark, certainly does not parse the terms "Jesus" and "Christ" in this way. In Mark's account of the baptism of Jesus, "the spirit came down into him [τὸ πνεῦμα . . . καταβαῖνον εἰς αὐτόν] like a dove" (Mark 1:10). Subsequently, at the crucifixion, Jesus cries out, "Eloi, Eloi, lema sabachthani? which is translated, 'My God, my God, why have you left me [ὁ θεός μου ὁ θεός μου, εἰς τί ἐγκατέλιπές με]?'" (Mark 15:34) Even if we give both verses a separationist translation, as I have done here—with the spirit coming into Jesus and God leaving him—in neither case is it Christ who enters or leaves Jesus. It is the spirit in the one instance and God in the other.[138] This is not to say that Mark cannot be read along separationist lines; it obviously can be. The point is that a Markan separationist would distinguish between Jesus and God, not between Jesus and Christ.[139]

As for later, more explicitly separationist Christian texts, it is not at all clear that they are any closer to Irenaeus's terminological distinction between the human Jesus and the divine Christ. The second-century *Gospel of Peter* is sometimes adduced as a witness to separationist Christology.[140] There the cry of dereliction is related in different terms: "The Lord screamed out, say-ing: 'My power, O power, you have left me!' And having said this, he was taken up" (*Gos. Pet.* 19).[141] Here, that which "forsakes" or "leaves" Jesus is not the divine Christ, but rather the "power." The word "Christ" actually does not appear at all in the *Gospel of Peter*. Moreover, in light of *Gos. Pet.* 10—"They brought two wrongdoers and crucified the Lord in the middle of them. But he was silent, as having no pain"—it may be that the viewpoint of the text is bet-ter described as docetist than as separationist.[142] A more clearly separationist

---

138. The same is true of the *Gospel of the Ebionites*, preserved in part by Epiphanius, from which we have no crucifixion scene but in whose baptism scene the holy spirit descends and enters into Jesus (Epiphanius, *Pan.* 30.13.7), just as in Mark 1:10.

139. For interpretations of Mark along these lines, see Hahn, *Titles of Jesus*, 337–41; Edward P. Dixon, "Descending Spirit and Descending Gods: A 'Greek' Interpretation of the Spirit's 'Descent as a Dove' in Mark 1:10," *JBL* 128 (2009): 759–80.

140. In antiquity Eusebius, *Hist. eccl.* 6.12; and among modern critics Ehrman, *Orthodox Corruption*, 144, 175n126. On the *Gospel of Peter*, see the definitive treatment of Paul Foster, *The Gospel of Peter: Introduction, Critical Edition, and Commentary* (TENTS 4; Leiden: Brill, 2010).

141. Trans. Raymond E. Brown, *The Death of the Messiah* (2 vols.; New York, N.Y.: Doubleday, 1994), 2:1318–21.

142. Or perhaps neither docetist or separationist, as suggested by J. W. McCant, "The Gospel of Peter: Docetism Reconsidered," *NTS* 30 (1984): 258–73; and Peter M. Head, "On the Christology of the Gospel of Peter," *VC* 46 (1992): 209–24.

account of the crucifixion is related in the *Gospel of Philip*, where Jesus's cry on the cross reads, "My God, my God, why, O Lord, have you forsaken me?" and the author comments, "It was on the cross that he said these words, for he had departed from that place" (*Gos. Phil.* 68).[143] Even here, however, the divine being that leaves Jesus on the cross is called "God" and "lord," not "Christ."[144]

The Coptic *Apocalypse of Peter* from Nag Hammadi is another possible first-hand witness to separationist Christology during this period.[145] It is likewise concerned with making a distinction between the passible and the impassible parts of Jesus:

> When he [the Savior] had said those things, I saw him seemingly being seized by them. And I said, "What do I see, O Lord, that it is you your-self whom they take, and that you are grasping me? Or who is this one, glad and laughing on the tree? And is it another one whose feet and hands they are striking?" The Savior said to me, "He whom you saw on the tree, glad and laughing, this is the living Jesus. But this one into whose hands and feet they drive the nails in his fleshly part, which is the substitute being put to shame, the one who came into being in his likeness. But look at him and me." (*Apoc. Pet.* 81)[146]

Here, the impassible being, the one portrayed as "glad and laughing" throughout the course of the crucifixion, is "the living Jesus," which is ironic in light of Irenaeus's claim that for the gnostics, "Jesus" means the passible human being.[147] For this text, the passible being, the one whose hands and feet receive the wounds is called "the fleshly part" and "the substitute." Once again, "Christ" is nowhere to be seen.

In short, for all that Irenaeus makes of the gnostics distinguishing the human Jesus from the divine Christ, there are precious few, if indeed any,

---

143. Trans. Isenberg in *NHL*.

144. See further Einar Thomassen, "How Valentinian Is the *Gospel of Philip*?" in *Nag Hammadi Library after Fifty Years*, 251–79.

145. On the Christology of the Coptic *Apocalypse of Peter*, see Henriette W. Havelaar, *The Coptic Apocalypse of Peter (Nag Hammadi Codex VII,3)* (TUGAL 144; Berlin: Akademie Verlag, 1999), 171–92.

146. Trans. James Brashler and Roger A. Bullard in *NHL*.

147. See Gerard P. Luttikhuizen, "The Suffering Jesus and the Invulnerable Christ in the Gnostic *Apocalypse of Peter*," in *The Apocalypse of Peter* (ed. Jan. N. Bremmer and Istvan Czachesz; SECA 7; Leuven: Peeters, 2003), 187–99, who, like Irenaeus before him, gets the ideas right but the terms "Jesus" and "Christ" wrong.

primary sources in which an early Christian writer claims that view, in those terms, for him- or herself. This raises the hoary old methodological question of the reliability of the heresiologists as sources for the views of their opponents. Perhaps in Irenaeus's account of separationist Christology we have an instance of so-called heretical views being refracted through the prism of proto-orthodox vocabulary.[148] That is, to Irenaeus's way of thinking, the heretics distinguish between the human "Jesus" and the divine "Christ," but for their own part they actually distinguish between the passible "Jesus" and the impassible "God," or between the passible "substitute" and the impassible "living Jesus." If so, then perhaps "Christ" never did mean "the divine being that inhabited Jesus" for any particular early Christian writer. The specter of such a view, however, helped writers such as 1 John and Irenaeus to clarify precisely what they themselves meant when they affirmed that Jesus is the Christ.

Whither Messiah Christology?

There is a fascinating fourth-century text that manages to bring together in a single passage many of the diverse strands of christological speculation that we have considered in this chapter. The *Pseudo-Clementine Recognitions*, which, together with its companion volume the *Homilies*, purports to be an account by a certain Clement (variously identified with Clement bishop of Rome, or Clement the nephew of Vespasian, or both) of his own travels with and of the teachings of the apostle Peter,[149] includes a fulsome explication of the meaning of "Christ." In the midst of a large block of Petrine teaching in *Recognitions* book 1, Clement says to Peter, "I have already learned from your instruction that this true prophet is the Christ, but I should wish to learn what 'the Christ' means, or why he is so called, so that a matter of such great importance may

---

148. On this problem, see Frederik Wisse, "The Nag Hammadi Library and the Heresiologists," *VC* 25 (1971): 205–23, here 219:

> The fact that few if any Nag Hammadi tractates fit into the heresiological categories has now found an explanation. The claim for the existence of sects and the distinction between them appears to be mainly due to the historical accident of what piece of Gnostic writing or information was available to the Church Fathers.

149. On relevant issues of critical introduction, see Johannes Irmscher and Georg Strecker, "The Pseudo-Clementines," in Hennecke-Schneemelcher, *New Testament Apocrypha*, 2:483–541; and now Nicole Kelley, *Knowledge and Religious Authority in the Pseudo-Clementines: Situating the Recognitions in Fourth-Century Syria* (WUNT 2.213; Tübingen: Mohr Siebeck, 2006); also more generally Annette Yoshiko Reed, "'Jewish Christianity' after the 'Parting of the Ways': Approaches to Historiography and Self-Definition in the Pseudo-Clementine Literature," in *Ways That Never Parted*, 188–231.

not be vague and uncertain to me" (*Ps.-Clem. Rec.* 1.44).[150] Clement starts from the confession that the true prophet—a most important christological category in the Pseudo-Clementines[151]—is the Christ, but he admits his ignorance about the latter term, which Peter therefore explains as follows:

> When God had made the world, as lord of the universe, he appointed chiefs over the several creatures. . . .. an angel as chief over the angels, a spirit over the spirits, a star over the stars, a demon over the demons, a bird over the birds, a beast over the beasts, a serpent over the serpents, a fish over the fishes, a man over men, who is Christ Jesus. But he is called Christ by a certain excellent rite of religion [*Christus autem dicitur eximio quodam religionis ritu*]. For as there are certain names common to kings, such as Arsaces among the Persians, Caesar among the Romans, Pharaoh among the Egyptians, so among the Jews a king is called Christ [*nam sicut regum sunt quaedam communia nomina, ut apud Persas Arsaces, apud Romanos Caesar, apud Aegyptios Pharao, ita apud Iudaeos Christus communi nomine rex appellatur*]. And the reason of this appellation is this: Although indeed he was the son of God and the beginning of all things, he became man. Him first God anointed with oil which was taken from the wood of [the tree of] life. From that anointing therefore he is called Christ [*hunc primum pater oleo perunxit, quod ex ligno vitae fuerat sumptum. Ex illo unguento Christus apellatur*]. Thence, moreover, he himself also, according to the appointment of his father, anoints with similar oil every one of the pious when they come to his kingdom, for their refreshment after their labors. (*Ps.-Clem. Rec.* 1.45)[152]

There is a lot going on in this passage. The first claim is that Christ is the divinely appointed chief of human beings, just as, for each species (birds, fish, angels, demons, and so on), God appointed one of its own kind to be chief over the others. Christ is thus a member of the human species, even if he is also chief over it. Second, the author explains the name "Christ" as the standard equivalency for "king" (*rex*) in the Jewish dialect. Each *natio*, he says, has its

---

150. Trans. mod. from Thomas Smith in *ANF*.

151. See H. J. W. Drijvers, "Adam and the True Prophet in the Pseudo-Clementines," in *Loyalitätskonflikte in der Religionsgeschichte* (ed. Christoph Elsas and Hans Kippenberg; Würzburg: Königshausen & Neumann, 1990), 314–23.

152. Latin text ed. Bernhard Rehm and Georg Strecker, *Die Pseudoklementinen II: Rekognitionen in Rufins Übersetzung* (GCS; Berlin: Akademie Verlag, 1994); trans. mod. from Thomas Smith in *ANF*.

own word for *rex*: the Persians say Arsaces, the Romans Caesar, the Egyptians Pharaoh, and the Jews Christ. This explanation appeals not to etymology, but to ethnic (N.B. Jewish, not Christian) usage: Just as "Pharaoh" does not strictly mean anything in Greek or Latin, but is just what Egyptians call their kings, so too "Christ" among the Jews. Third, however, the author does in fact supply an etymology for Christ that rightly traces Greek χριστός back to the verb χρίω.[153] "For he is called Christ by a certain excellent rite of religion"—namely, ritual anointing. But by whom and with what unguent? For Pseudo-Clement, as for Hebrews, Luke-Acts, and other early Christian writers, it is God who anointed Jesus. Unlike these other writers, however, Pseudo-Clement says that God anointed Jesus not with a metaphorical unguent such as power or spirit but rather with oil from the *lignum vitae*, the wood of the tree of life (cf. Gen 2:9; 3:22, 24).[154] Here Pseudo-Clement brings together the myth of the quest for oil from the tree of life (often associated with Adam's son Seth, as in *Life of Adam and Eve* 36.1–44.3)[155] with the oil of anointing of Judahite kings: God anoints Jesus as messiah—that is, *rex* or king—with the paradisal oil. Fourth and finally, the *Recognitions* attest the idea, discussed earlier, that the pious themselves also receive a divine anointing. In Pseudo-Clement's telling, Christ, acting on God's behalf, anoints the pious with the same paradisal oil upon their entry into to the messianic kingdom.

In this way, Pseudo-Clement draws together a number of diverse strands of early Christian messiah Christology: "Christ" the Jewish word for "king," ancient Israelite oil rituals, the anointing of Christ by God, and the anointing of the righteous by God, among other mythologoumena. Critics of a certain disposition might be tempted to dismiss this as a preoccupation of a fringe Jewish–Christian apocryphon, not representative of normative early Christology. But to do so, quite apart from the problem of imposing a notion of normativity, would be to miss the mass of evidence adduced in this chapter for messiah speculation in all corners of early Christianity: Jewish and gentile, orthodox and heterdox, East and West, Greek, Latin, Syriac, Coptic, and other

---

153. We have the *Recognitions* only in Rufinus's Latin translation and some Syriac fragments, but behind these translation lay a Greek *Vorlage*, no longer extant.

154. Of this passage and a parallel mention of "the oil of the tree of life" in *5 Ezra* 2:12, Michael Stone plausibly suggests, "It is possible that the combination of anointing without ablution and the expression 'oil of life' or 'oil of the tree of life' indicates the origin of this material in early Christian sectarian circles" (Michael E. Stone, "The Angelic Prediction in the Primary Adam Books," in *Literature on Adam and Eve: Collected Essays* [ed. Gary Anderson et al.; SVTP 15; Leiden: Brill, 2000], 127n40).

155. On which see Esther C. Quinn, *The Quest of Seth for the Oil of Life* (Chicago, Ill.: University of Chicago Press, 1962); Barbara Baert, *A Heritage of Holy Wood* (CBT 22; Leiden: Brill, 2005), 310–33.

tongues. We can grasp this point if we compare fourth-century Syrian Pseudo-Clement with, say, Isidore of Seville, catholic archbishop of Iberia at the turn of the seventh century. In his monumental *Etymologies*,[156] Isidore explains "Christ" as follows:

> He is named "Christ" [*Christus*] from "chrism" [*chrisma*], that is, "anointed one," for it was a precept among the Jews that they would confect a sacred ointment by which those who were called to the priesthood or the kingship might be anointed. Just as nowadays for kings to be clothed in the purple is the mark of royal dignity, so for them anointing with sacred ointment would confer the royal title and power. Hence they are called "anointed ones" [*Christus*] from chrism, which is unction, for the Greek chrisma is "unction" [*unctio*] in Latin. When this anointing was done spiritually, it accommodated the name "Christ" to the Lord, because he was anointed by the Spirit from God the Father, as in Acts [4:27]: *For there assembled together in this holy city against thy holy child . . . whom thou hast anointed*—by no means with visible oil, but with the gift of grace, for which visible ointment is a sign. "Christ" is not, however, a proper name of the Savior, but a common-noun designation of his power. . . . The name of Christ never occurred at all elsewhere in any nation except in that kingdom alone where Christ was prophesied, and whence he was to come. Again, in Hebrew he is called "Messiah" [*Messias*], in Greek "Christ," in Latin "the anointed" [*unctus*]. (Isidore of Seville, *Etymologies* 7.2.2–6)[157]

In Isidore we find an Iberian, catholic, scholastic expression of a similar kind of messiah Christology to that attested in the Clementina (indeed, featuring many of the same particular motifs). The lesson here is that the roots of messiah discourse in early Christianity go very deep, indeed. As Annette Reed comments:

> Despite emergent notions of "Christianity" as the opposite of "Judaism," something of Christianity's Jewish messianic origins still persisted.

---

156. On which see Mark E. Amsler, *Etymology and Grammatical Discourse in Late Antiquity and the Early Middle Ages* (Philadelphia, Pa.: Benjamins, 1989), 133–72; Andy Merrills, "Isidore's *Etymologies*: On Words and Things," in *Encyclopaedism from Antiquity to the Renaissance* (ed. Jason König and Greg Woolf; Cambridge: Cambridge University Press, 2013), 301–24.

157. Text and trans. Stephen A. Barney et al., eds., *The Etymologies of Isidore of Seville* (Cambridge: Cambridge University Press, 2006). Some of this account of the meaning of *Christus* Isidore takes from Lactantius, *Div. Inst.* 4.7.

These origins remained inscribed in its very name (Acts 11:26). They were embedded in the scope of its canonical scriptures, as perennially a nexus for anxieties about Jewish origins, a potential source for Jewish influence, an inspiration for "Judaizing," and a temptation to exegetical exchange. Accordingly, it perhaps makes sense that messianism qua Christology would form the focus for the delineation of the center and boundaries of the imperial church as well.[158]

In a characteristically erudite essay first published in 1988, William Horbury covers some of the same conceptual ground that I have covered in this chapter.[159] Focusing on Christian sources from the second century (in particular, Justin Martyr, Tertullian, and parts of the Clementina), Horbury proposes that "the concepts of Christ current among second-century Christians have often been discussed with reference to the history of doctrine; but perhaps it is also proper to speak of them as evidences of a messianism."[160] This is very nearly right. Certainly, messianism abides as a theological issue for some of these Christian writers, and for others, too, even long after the second century, as we have seen. Horbury interpret such texts as "evidences of a messianism," because he is invested in proving the existence of such an -ism, but it would be simpler and more accurate to say that these texts show how messiah language persisted as a puzzle and an opportunity for christological speculation among diverse early Christian writers.

At the end of his essay, Horbury concludes, even more ambitiously, "It remains possible, at least to the time of the compilation of the Mishnah, to speak of *one* messianism of the Jews and of the Christians."[161] This claim is more problematic. It is not altogether indefensible, but it rests entirely on a sufficiently broad definition of messianism, which Horbury, for his part, is happy to supply,[162] but which presents significant difficulties. In the nature of the case, the broader the definition, the less precise an analytical tool it can

---

158. Reed, "Messianism between Judaism and Christianity," 33.

159. Horbury, "Messianism among Jews and Christians in the Second Century," in idem, *Messianism among Jews and Christians*, 275–88.

160. Horbury, "Messianism among Jews and Christians in the Second Century," 277.

161. Horbury, "Messianism among Jews and Christians in the Second Century," 288; emphasis original.

162. For example, Horbury, *Jewish Messianism and the Cult of Christ*, 6–7: "Messianism is taken in the broad sense of the expectation of a coming pre-eminent ruler—coming, whether at the end, as strictly implied by the word 'eschatology,' or simply at some time in the future."

be.[163] To his credit, Horbury improves upon the received wisdom (e.g., the treatments by Grillmeier and Neusner discussed at the beginning of this chapter) according to which messiah Christology vanishes from early Christianity almost as soon as it appears. With Horbury, we owe an account of the kind of christological discourse represented in the texts discussed here. *Pace* Horbury, however, there is neither need nor reason to stipulate a single -ism by way of explanation. It is enough to recognize the many scripturally funded discourses inherited by Jews and Christians in late antiquity, of which messiah discourse is one, and to describe its particular twists and turns. The fate of messiah Christology in early Christianity is no simple matter. It did not remain what it had been at the beginning, but neither did it vanish altogether. The ghost of the messianic movement surrounding Jesus of Nazareth haunted early Christian Christology, both orthodox and heterodox, for centuries to follow.

---

163. Thus rightly Meeks, review of Horbury, *Messianism among Jews and Christians*, 340:

> Whereas other scholars speak of a vast variety among eschatological beliefs held by various Jews in the period of the Roman Empire, only some of which involve an *anointed* figure . . . , Horbury sweeps aside the distinction and lumps together under the umbrella "messianic" not only all eschatological beliefs but even non-eschatological uses of texts that are sometimes used eschatologically. This is surely a recipe for confusion.

8

The Grammar of Messianism

AT THE END of the book of Exodus, which finds the Israelites encamped in the wilderness of Sinai, after the tabernacle and all its furniture have been built according to plan, YHWH gives Moses final instructions for erecting and consecrating the holy place, the last step of which is an elaborate oil ritual:

> Then you shall take the anointing oil [שמן המשחה], and anoint the tabernacle [ומשחת את־המשכן] and all that is in it, and consecrate it and all its furniture; and it shall become holy. You shall also anoint the altar of burnt offering [ומשחת את־מזבח העלה] and all its utensils, and consecrate the altar; and the altar shall be most holy. You shall also anoint the laver and its base [ומשחת את־הכיר ואת־כנו], and consecrate it. (Exod 40:9–11)

Thus the priestly writer in the Pentateuch.[1]

When, sometime in late antiquity or the early Middle Ages,[2] an anonymous Aramaic translator in Palestine undertook to render this oracle in the vernacular for popular Jewish use, he came up with the following:

> Then you shall take the anointing oil and anoint the tabernacle and all that is in it, and consecrate it for the crown of the kingdom of the house

---

1. On this episode, see Frank Moore Cross, "The Priestly Tabernacle in the Light of Recent Research," in *Temples and High Places in Biblical Times* (ed. Avraham Biran; Jerusalem: Hebrew Union College, 1981), 169–80; Helmut Utzschneider, "Tabernacle," in *The Book of Exodus: Composition, Reception, and Interpretation* (ed. Thomas B. Dozeman et al.; VTSup 164; Leiden: Brill, 2014), 267–301.

2. The date of Targum Pseudo-Jonathan remains contested, with Robert Hayward, for instance, arguing for an early Byzantine date (C. T. R. Hayward, "The Date of Targum Pseudo-Jonathan: Some Comments," *JJS* 40 [1989]: 7–30) and Avigdor Shinan, for instance, putting it in the Islamic period (Avigdor Shinan, "Dating Targum Pseudo-Jonathan: Some More Comments," *JJS* 41 [1990]: 57–61). On the methodological problem, see A. D. York, "The Dating of Targumic Literature," *JSJ* 5 (1974): 49–62.

of Judah and the king messiah [דמלכותא דבית יהודה ומלכא משיחא], who is
destined to redeem Israel at the end of days. And you shall anoint the
sacrificial altar and all its vessels, and consecrate it as an altar of the
Holy of Holies, for the crown of the priesthood of Aaron and his sons,
and of Elijah the high priest, who is to be sent at the end of the disper-
sions. And you shall anoint the laver and its base, and consecrate it for
Joshua your servant, chief of the Sanhedrin of his people, by whose
hand the land of Israel is to be divided, and from whom is to descend
the messiah son of Ephraim [ומשיחא בר אפרים דנפיק מיניה], by whose hand
the house of Israel is to vanquish Gog and his confederates at the end
of days. (*Tg. Ps.-J.* Exod 40:9–11)[3]

In this expansive paraphrase, the meturgeman seizes upon the language of
"anointing," which in Exod 40 pertains to the sacra in the tabernacle, and uses it
to introduce into the context several anointed persons ("messiahs") from Jewish
legend. Samson Levey has commented aptly on this passage:

The threefold use of the expression "and you shall anoint," and the objects
to be anointed, indicate the three central personalities of the Messianic
drama. The tabernacle represents the Davidic line, builders of the Temple;
the altar represents priesthood, identified as Elijah; the laver and base
represent the more menial, the servant Joshua, the Ephraimite, and his
descendant, the Messiah son of Ephraim.[4]

There is nothing in Exod 40:9–11 itself to suggest the theme of eschatological salvation, only the evocative keyword משח, "to anoint." But of course,
in a different strand in the Jewish scriptures, "anointing" applies to persons
(especially kings and priests), from which usage, more or less directly, comes
virtually all ancient Jewish messiah discourse. Our Aramaic translator has
used the one as an opportunity for talking about the other. He reads Moses's
"anointing" of the holy paraphernalia at Sinai as a figure for the mythological "anointed ones" who will arise in the last days.[5] In so doing, the Targum

---

3. Aramaic text ed. Ernest G. Clarke et al., *Targum Pseudo-Jonathan of the Pentateuch: Text and Concordance* (New York, N.Y.: Ktav, 1984); trans. mod. from Levey, *Messiah*, 15. Compare the more recent translation of Michael Maher, *Targum Pseudo-Jonathan: Exodus Translated with Notes* (ArBib 2; Collegeville, Minn.: Liturgical, 1994).

4. Levey, *Messiah*, 15.

5. On this move as a part of Pseudo-Jonathan's hermeneutical program, see Beverly P. Mortensen, "Pseudo-Jonathan's Temple, Symbol of Judaism," in *Targum and Scripture: Studies*

illustrates nicely the exegetical dynamics at work in ancient messiah texts in general. They invoke the biblical past by way of justifying their real presents and their ideal futures. To say so might seem banal, but in fact it is a quite particular, even controversial, claim relative to the recent history of scholarship.

Jewish Oil, Roman Rods

Depending how one measures importance, a case can be made that the most important book on messianism in the last generation is Martin Karrer's 1989 Erlangen *Habilitationsschrift*, mentioned at a number of points in the previous chapters.[6] With respect to influence and consensus-making, pride of place almost certainly goes to John Collins's definitive *The Scepter and the Star*, but for radical critical reassessment, one can hardly do better than Karrer's *Der Gesalbte*.[7] Laying an ax at the root of hundreds of years of research on messianism, Karrer argues that, by the Roman period, Jewish (and other Greco-Roman) talk of ritual anointing pertained to holy artifacts and signified consecration to the deity, nothing else. When, therefore, early Jewish and Christian texts speak of persons (e.g., Enoch, Jesus of Nazareth, Shimon bar Kosiba) as "anointed," they mean not that such a person fits a mythical job description ("messiah"), but simply that he is "heilig, Gott nah, Gott übergeben."[8] If it is right, Karrer's thesis changes everything. The question is whether it is right.[9]

With all due respect to an ingenious argument, I think that it is not, and *Tg. Ps-J.* to Exod 40:9–11 illustrates why. Karrer's hypothesis, which is prima facie quite sensible, is that early Jewish "anointing" language tracks with contemporary anointing practices. Thus, early Roman-period texts that call persons "anointed" cannot mean the term in the old biblical royal sense, because royal anointing had long since fallen out of practice. They must, so

---

in *Aramaic Translation and Interpretation in Memory of Ernest G. Clarke* (ed. Paul V. M. Flesher; Leiden: Brill, 2002), 129–37.

6. Karrer, *Gesalbte*.

7. Thus rightly Miller, "The Anointed Jesus," in *Redescribing Christian Origins*, 392: "Karrer . . . has inquired into the bases for the significance of the term christos in early Christianity from a perspective that has not been seriously explored, namely, the range of cultural uses of anointing in the Mediterranean world."

8. Karrer, *Gesalbte*, 211.

9. The merits and demerits of Karrer's study are assessed by a number of the contributors to *JBTh* 8 (1993)—in particular, Peter Stuhlmacher, "Der messianische Gottesknecht," 131–54; Dieter Zeller, "Zur Transformation des χριστός bei Paulus," 155–67; and Karl-Wilhelm Niebuhr, "Jesus Christus und die vielfältigen messianischen Erwartungen Israels: Ein Forschungsbericht," 337–46.

the argument goes, mean it in the late-Second-Temple cultic sense of the consecration of artifacts to the deity.[10] But *Tg. Ps-J.* to Exod 40:9–11 reasons in exactly the opposite direction: not from royal anointing to cultic but vice versa, not forward but backward, not contemporizing but archaizing.[11] And in fact, this is the way ancient messiah texts normally work, as when *Ps. Sol.* 17 uses the idiom of 2 Sam 7, or Rom 15 does Isa 11, or Mark 12 does Ps 110, or *4 Ezra* 12 does Dan 7, or *b. Sanh.* 93b does Isa 11, or any one of scores of other such cases.[12] Contra Karrer, as a rule, early Jewish "anointing" language does not track with contemporary anointing practices, but rather adopts the outdated idiom of the scriptures. It is deliberately archaic; that is the point. It uses the language of the past to talk about the present or the future.[13] It is, in other words, an exegetical enterprise. In this respect, messiah discourse is altogether typical of most of the Jewish literature that has come down to us from antiquity.[14] As Wayne Meeks, among others, has noted in this connection:

> If one looks for some central connective tissue in the complex web of beliefs that we call "Judaism," it is most likely to be found in the text of

---

10. See Karrer, *Gesalbte*, 406:

> Denn bei Prägung der Formel ist seit über einem halben Jahrtausend kein König, seit 200 Jahren kein Priester Israels mehr gesalbt worden. Der Kult und das Allerheiligste des Tempels in Jerusalem, wo Gott nah und wirksam ist wie sonst nirgends, sind zum Zentrum der Salbungsvollzüge und zum Maßstab für die Salbungsaussagen Israels geworden; das Allerheiligste gilt aller Wahrscheinlichkeit nach als "das Gesalbte."

11. Of course, for Targum Pseudo-Jonathan, both types of oil rituals, royal and cultic, lay in the distant past, but this only further confirms my main point.

12. Here see, in particular, Oegema, *Anointed*, 290–306.

13. See, for example, Rajak, "Hasmonean Kingship," 44:

> The new supremacy of the high priesthood [in the Hellenistic period] was expressed, then, in the emergence of an appropriate ceremonial [viz. anointing].... This imaging, as we can see from Ben Sira, had been generated out of memories of the first Temple, to suit the requirements of the second.

14. On this point, see Michael Fishbane, "Inner-Biblical Exegesis: Types and Strategies," in idem, *Garments of Torah*, 16:

> In this exegetical anthology [viz. Chronicles], as in others from the period, older textual boundaries collapse before the pressure of an appropriating voice, and the complex intertextuality of the culture is brought to view. Here, all significant speech is scriptural or scripturally-oriented speech. The voices of Israel's teachers will struggle to speak anew in traditions and words handed down from the past.

And more recently, Najman, "Vitality of Scripture."

the Hebrew Bible and in the centuries-long tradition of trying to make sense of it in varying circumstances.[15]

If so, then, contrary to a prominent motif in the history of research, there is nothing at all special about messianism. It is just a part—a very interesting part, to be sure, but no different in kind—of the vast interpretive project of ancient Judaism.[16] Thus, ironically, it is only by recognizing how thoroughly conventional ancient messiah language is that we can hope to understand it in its context.

It may be possible to unpick some of our conceptual difficulties with messiah language by means of an analogy to another ancient political term with a complicated *Nachleben*: the Roman fasces.[17] It was the Etruscan occupants of central Italy during the first half of the first millennium BCE who apparently originated the custom of binding together birch rods for use as an icon of civic authority. The Romans, in turn, famously adopted this institution, to which they gave the name *fasces*, "bundles," probably during the monarchy and, at any rate, by the early Republic.[18] Livy describes the transition from monarchy to Republic in this way:

> The new liberty enjoyed by the Roman people, their achievements in peace and war, annual magistracies, and laws superior in authority to men will henceforth be my theme. . . . All the rights of the kings and all their insignia were possessed by the earliest consuls; only one thing was guarded against—that the terror they inspired should not be doubled by permitting both [consuls] to have the fasces [*si ambo fasces haberent, duplicatus terror videretur*]. Brutus was the first to have them, with his colleague's consent, and he proved as

---

15. Meeks, review of Horbury, *Messianism among Jews and Christians,* 338.

16. On this point, see Juel, *Messianic Exegesis,* 31–57.

17. The Jewish messiahs and Roman fasces are usually not discussed together, but an interesting exception is Alison Salvesen, "The Trappings of Royalty in Ancient Hebrew," in *King and Messiah,* 119–41 at 136–37, on Hebrew שבט and Aramaic שרביט ("scepter") and the question whether they could be related to a Persian precursor to the fasces.

18. See Andrew Drummond, "Fasces," *OCD*³, 587–88; Loretana de Libero, "Fasces," in *Brill's New Pauly* (ed. Hubert Cancik et al.; 22 vols.; Leiden: Brill, 2011), 5:359. Relevant discussions include K.-H. Vogel, "Imperium und Fasces," *ZRG* 67 (1950): 62–111; E. S. Staveley, "The Fasces and Imperium Maius," *Historia* 12 (1963): 458–84; Burkhard Gladigow, "Die sakralen Funktionen der Liktoren: Zum Problem von institutioneller Macht und sakraler Präsentation," *ANRW* I.2:295–314; Anthony J. Marshall, "Symbols and Showmanship in Roman Public Life: The Fasces," *Phoenix* 38 (1984): 120–41.

determined in guarding liberty as he had been in asserting it. (Livy,
Ab urbe condita 2.1, 8)[19]

According to Livy, the consuls took over from the ancient kings the institution of the fasces, but they tempered its unsubtle autocratic overtones by
permitting only one consul out of two to have tenure of the fasces at any
given time.

The fasces of Republican Rome were a bundle of birch or elm rods (six,
twelve, or twenty-four of them, depending on the office), roughly 1.5 meters
in length, bound with red cords, with a single-headed ax enclosed in the
middle—except in the pomerium, where traditionally it was not permitted to
carry the ax. An entourage of lictors carried the fasces in procession ahead of
a magistrate who had tenure thereof. In sources from and about the Republic,
and on into the Empire as well, the fasces appear frequently as a symbol of
Roman imperium. And not only a symbol, but a practical instrument, too. As
Christopher Fuhrmann notes, "Livy and other antiquarians invented chilling
scenes of Roman magistrates commanding their lictors to unbind their fasces,
to deliver corporal or (given the ax) capital punishment."[20] Such literary scenes
were based apparently on the actual use of the fasces during the Republican
period. About this use, Anthony Marshall writes:

> The fasces were not merely decorative or symbolic devices carried
> before magistrates in a parade of idle formalism. Rather, they consti-
> tuted a portable kit for flogging and decapitation.... Roman society
> was therefore unusual in that its central magisterial regalia remained
> directly functional; the fasces continued as both symbol and instru-
> ment of executive power. Thus powerful emotions of pride and fear
> could focus on them, and their symbolic political significance was
> accordingly intensified by their aura of latent violence.[21]

---

19. Text from and trans. mod. from B. O. Foster in the LCL.

20. Christopher J. Fuhrmann, *Policing the Roman Empire: Soldiers, Administration, and Public Order* (New York, N.Y.: Oxford University Press, 2012), 63.

21. Marshall, "Symbols and Showmanship," 130. This same point has been emphasized recently by Giorgio Agamben, *The Power and the Glory: For a Theological Genealogy of Economy and Government* (trans. Lorenzo Chiesa; Stanford, Calif.: Stanford University Press, 2011), 182:

> To define the fasces as the "symbol of imperium," as has sometimes been the case, tells us nothing about their nature or their specific function. So little does the word symbol characterize them that they in fact served to actually inflict capital punish-ment in its two forms.

By the late Republic, the lictors no longer exercised a police role, but the fasces remained a potent representation of Roman order. As Marietta Horster comments, "In republican times, the fasces . . . had a sacral function on their own. From late republican times the lictors no longer had the right to punish. The fasces were reduced to symbols of power."[22] But "reduced" may not be the right word, because what the fasces lost in practical utility they more than made up for in iconic significance. Cicero, for instance, in his eleventh Philippic against Mark Antony, says about Octavian that, when the necessity of war bestowed on him imperium, the senate granted him the fasces accordingly:

> Members of the senate, you would have snatched military authority away from Gaius Caesar if you had not granted it. The veteran soldiers who, following his authority, command, and name, had taken up arms on behalf of the Republic wished to be commanded by him; the Martian Legion and the Fourth Legion had given their support to the authority of the senate and the dignity of the Republic, but at the same time they demanded Gaius Caesar as their general and leader. The necessity of war gave Gaius Caesar the command, the senate gave him the fasces [*Imperium C. Caesari belli necessitas, fascis senatus dedit*]. (Cicero, Phil. 11.20)[23]

Like Jewish unction, the Roman fasces appear in the sources as a shorthand for the glorious rulers of the past and their latter-day counterparts. An apt example is Horace, *Odes* 1.12, a hymn to gods and heroes down to Augustus, during whose principate Horace wrote.[24] The poem begins by praising the Olympian deities, then turns to give due honor to a number of godlike Romans: "After them I hesitate whether to sing of Romulus, or Pompilius' quiet reign, or Tarquin's arrogant fasces [*memorem an superbos Tarquini fascis*], or Cato's illustrious death" (*Odes* 1.12.33–36). Here, in the distinguished company of Romulus and Numa Pompilius, Tarquinius Superbus, the last of the legendary Roman monarchs, is signified by the fasces. This lineage of royal

---

22. Marietta Horster, "Living on Religion: Professionals and Personnel," in *A Companion to Roman Religion* (ed. Jörg Rüpke; Oxford: Blackwell, 2011), 331–41 at 334.

23. Text from and trans. mod. from D. R. Shackleton Bailey in the LCL.

24. Text from and trans. mod. from Niall Rudd in the LCL. On the poem and its context, see G. Williams, "Horace, Odes 1.12 and the Succession to Augustus," *Herm* 118 (1974): 147–55; Michèle Lowrie, "Horace and Augustus," in *The Cambridge Companion to Horace* (ed. Stephen Harrison; Cambridge: Cambridge University Press, 2007), 77–90.

heroes leads, finally and inexorably, to Augustus: "Among them all the Julian star shines out like the moon among the lesser lights [*micat inter omnis Iulium sidus velut inter ignis luna minores*]" (*Odes* 1.12.46–48). The *sidus Iulium*, Julian star, a reference to the comet that was thought to mark Julius Caesar's apotheosis in 44 BCE (Suetonius, *Jul.* 88), here represents Caesar's son, Horace's patron, Augustus the *divi filius*. The poet concludes by entreating Jupiter that Augustus should rule at his right hand:

> Father and protector of the human race, O son of Saturn, you have been entrusted by fate with the care of mighty Caesar; may you have Caesar as vice-regent of your kingdom [*tu secundo Caesare regnes*]. Whether it be the Parthians (now a threat to Latium) that he conquers and leads in a justified triumph, or the Chinese and Indians who live close to the region of the rising sun, he will rule in fairness over a happy world, so long as he is subordinate to you. (*Odes* 1.12.49–57)

In this Roman counterpart to ancient Jewish messiah texts, the fasces appear, alongside pan-Mediterranean language of kingship, divine sonship, and astral immortality, as a culturally specific Roman idiom for royal authority.[25]

Just as the ancient Jewish messiah yielded the modern -ism "messianism" during the mid nineteenth century (French *messianisme* and German *Messianismus* from the 1830s, English "messianism" from the 1860s),[26] so, too, the ancient Roman fasces yielded modern "fascism" around 1920 via the World War I-era *fasci* in Italian party politics.[27] Benito Mussolini famously claimed both the ancient symbol and the modern -ism for his movement, writing, for instance, in his *Dottrina del Fascismo* of 1932:

> [Fascism] wants to remake not only the forms of human life, but the content, man, character, faith. To this end it requires discipline, and an authority that would impress the spirits and dominate them fully. Its

---

25. On the analogy between Jewish and Roman reuses of archaic native traditions, see Rajak, "Hasmonean Kingship," 50:

> Rediscovered tradition, as we know so well from the age of Augustus at Rome, is generally a patchwork: sometimes the old and important is resuscitated, but equally some minor antique observance may grow into a major new practice or ceremony, or else an outmoded one may be given a wholly new look.

26. See *OED*, s.v. "messianism."

27. See *OED*, s.v. "fascism."

sign is thus the *fascio littorio* [lictor's fasces], symbol of unity, force and justice.[28]

Like the Jewish oil of unction, the Roman fasces have proved remarkably polysemous, representing, as in Mussolini's vision, statist domination, but also, as in a great deal of American civic iconography, the union of citizens in a constitutional democracy.[29]

When, however, we want to understand the fasces as an institution of Republican Rome, we do not start from modern Italian fascism and work backward, because to do so would be to put things the wrong way around. We do not debate whether, say, Fabius Maximus, or Julius Caesar, or Hadrian was "fascist in the strict sense," because we do not use the concept "fascist in the strict sense" as an analytical tool for ancient history. We recognize that fascism, although it owes its etymology to the Roman fasces, is a category of modern political philosophy, not applicable to antiquity except perhaps by analogy.[30] Roman historians can and do, however, study the ancient use of and discourse about the fasces, both as a piece of material culture and as a symbol of state power. This is just how we should—but, currently, generally do not—conceive of messiahs and messianism. "Messiah" is a well-attested ancient Jewish and subsequently also Christian way of speaking about political authority, and it can be analyzed productively as such, just as the fasces can be in a Roman context. The ancient term "messiah" is, of course, related etymologically to the very complicated modern construct "messianism," but we can and should abstain from stipulating our own notions of "messianism in the strict sense" and then wielding them as analytical tools for use with the primary texts.

The Stuff Messiah Texts Are Made Of

The fasces analogy brings us around again to the methodological point raised by Jonathan Z. Smith, Burton Mack, and Merrill Miller noted in

---

28. Benito Mussolini, *Scritti e discorsi* 8.73, as cited in translation by Simonetta Falasca-Zamponi, *Fascist Spectacle: The Aesthetics of Power in Mussolini's Italy* (Berkeley, Calif.: University of California Press, 1997), 96.

29. Thus rightly de Libero, "Fasces," 359: "In the modern period, the *fasces* primarily play a role as political symbol of republican freedom and constitution, state unity and continuity, but also as a symbol for unrestricted authoritarian force."

30. In this connection, see the classic study of Ronald Syme, *The Roman Revolution* (Oxford; Clarendon, 1939); and the discussion by H. Galsterer, "A Man, a Book, and a Method: Sir Ronald Syme's *Roman Revolution* after Fifty Years," in *Between Republic and Empire: Interpretations of Augustus and His Principate* (ed. Kurt A. Raaflaub and Mark Toher; Berkeley, Calif.: University of California Press, 1990), 1–20.

Chapter 1—that "messiah," because of its aura of religious uniqueness, is not an analyzable concept and that only a broader comparative taxon (e.g., Mack's "ideal figures of high office") will do.[31] In Chapter 1, I criticized this line of reasoning for foreclosing unnecessarily one worthwhile analytical project (which I have illustrated in the intervening chapters), but just here we can see the important element of truth that it contains: Messiah language is, for the most part, a regional–ethnic subset of ancient Mediterranean political discourse. It is a species of that genus. It is a particularly Jewish and Christian way of talking about a basic social problem—determining who is and who should be in charge[32]—about which Persians, Greeks, Romans, and others had their own ways of talking.[33] As Pseudo-Clement observes, *nam sicut regum sunt quaedam communia nomina, ut apud Persas Arsaces, apud Romanos Caesar, apud Aegyptios Pharao, ita apud Iudaeos Christus communi nomine rex appellatur,* "For as there are certain names common to kings, such as Arsaces among the Persians, Caesar among the Romans, Pharaoh among the Egyptians, so among the Jews a king is called Christ" (*Ps.-Clem. Rec.* 1.45).[34] Of course, there were also ample transcultural ways of talking about these matters (e.g., "kings," like "gods," are attested almost everywhere in antiquity), but even in the wake of the globalization wrought by Alexander, regional cultures preserved their respective idioms, as well: the Persian diadem, Roman fasces, Jewish unction, and so on.[35]

---

31. See Smith, *Drudgery Divine*, 36–53; Mack, "Wisdom Makes a Difference"; Miller, "The Anointed Jesus."

32. On this point, see Oppenheimer, "Leadership and Messianism"; also Goodblatt, *Monarchic Principle*, here 57:

> Predictions of the eschaton are likely to reflect notions of the ideal or proper form of government for Israel. So whether the passages to be discussed refer to eschatological figures, to ideal types of the pre-eschatological era, or to historical figures, they all can contribute to our understanding of [Jewish political philosophy].

And Dan, "Armilus," 73: "Antichrist, like the Messiah, is essentially a historical concept, concerned with the role of leadership. The language of messianism is the language of history, dealing with the impact of leadership—usually conceived as being of divine origin—on the history of the universe."

33. In this connection, see Christian Habicht, "Messianic Elements in the Pre-Christian Greco-Roman World," in *Toward the Millennium*, 47–56 at 47:

> A Messiah in the full sense of the word is not to be found in the Greco-Roman world. For one, ointment, an important (maybe even essential) feature of the Messiah, is never mentioned. [But] we do find saviors and "messianic figures," that is to say: real persons reported as having inaugurated a new and better order, or ideal persons expected to come and do so in the future."

34. Text ed. Rehm and Strecker in GCS; trans. mod. from Smith in *ANF*.

35. See Rajak, "Hasmonean Kingship," 44, on the ritual for installing Jewish high priests in the Hellenistic period: "Such restated 'native' traditions would be more powerful than

In the case of Jewish unction (as, *mutatis mutandis*, for its counterparts in neighboring cultures), that particular ritual also had other traditional applications, especially cultic ones, and a correspondingly wide range of signification. This means that not all ancient Jewish anointing language is political, but also that, because of the polysemy of the term, political and nonpolitical uses could be and sometimes were joined up by imaginative interpreters such as *Targ. Ps.-J.* on Exod 40:9–11. Ancient Jewish writers were not obligated to talk about politics (e.g., *Prayer of Manasseh*), and when they did choose to talk about politics, they were not obligated to use the idiom of anointing (e.g., Philo, *Embassy to Gaius*). Meanwhile, what is more, they could use the idiom of anointing in other, nonpolitical senses (e.g., *m. Šeb.* 8:2). When we grasp this linguistic state of affairs, then we are in a position to make sense of our extant messiah texts in their respective contexts.[36] Mack is quite right that the word "messiah" has inherited a deeply problematic aura of religious uniqueness.[37] But the most sensible solution, at least as far as historical understanding is concerned, is not to abandon the term (which is, after all, a valuable historical artifact in its own right), but rather to retain it and to explicate it, dispelling the aura of uniqueness by means of description and comparison.

Nevertheless, it is a curious feature of the past half-century of secondary literature on messianism that scholars from each of the relevant subfields have, by their analyses, effectively recused themselves from the discussion. Thus, the Hebrew Bible scholars insist that there are no "messiahs" in that corpus, only "anointed ones" upon whom ancient interpreters built mythological castles in the air. But then, scholars of the literature of Second-Temple period—the so-called Apocrypha and Pseudepigrapha and the Qumran scrolls—say that, no, the presence of messiahs in their texts has been much exaggerated. Surely, one thinks, the New Testament scholars, of all people, will be able to explain what messianism is really all about, but then they say that in their texts the idea of the messiah has already undergone a complete *interpretatio Christiana*. The same is true, still more so, of the patrists. Meanwhile, the rabbinicists report that the tannaitic literature has nothing at all to say about messianism and the amoraic literature only slightly more than nothing. Only

---

any external influences in shaping the way in which Hasmonean rulers could present themselves."

36. In this connection, see Talmon, "Concept of *Masiah*," 84: "The diversity which we encounter in the later configurations of messianism can be explained, in part, as being inspired by different literary strata of the Hebrew Canon that in turn served them all as a shared seminal resource."

37. Mack, "Wisdom Makes a Difference."

when we come to scholars of medieval Judaica—the late Hebrew apocalypses, Saadia Gaon, Maimonides, and so on—do we find a straightforward willingness to talk about messianism in the sources, but by this point we have passed over more than a millennium's worth of evidence. (In characterizing the scholarly discussion in this way, I exaggerate, but not by much.) It is as if no one wants to claim responsibility for the idea. The only explanation I can see for this phenomenon is a reactionary impulse, an understandable desire to distance oneself and one's area of expertise from the grand old syntheses of Graetz, Schürer, and the rest. This impulse is commendable, but it cedes completely the terms of the discussion to those nineteenth-century giants, with whose accounts we all now disagree, anyway. Why, then, do we continue to discuss the issue on their terms, only now negatively instead of positively? If, as it turns out, precious few ancient texts attest messianism in the strict sense against which we have been taught to measure messiah texts, then surely the sensible way forward is to part with these received notions and to devise a newer, better approach.[38]

In fact, the seeds of a newer, better approach are scattered here and there in the secondary literature. Even Gershom Scholem, who bears no little responsibility for perpetuating the messianic idea hypothesis in twentieth-century scholarship, sometimes sees through the construct to the details of the primary texts. He writes about the medieval Jewish apocalypses:

> Exegesis becomes a weapon in constructing and destroying apocalypses. The apocalyptists can never get enough of biblical sayings which they can relate to the Last Days: to their dawning and their content. They draw upon everything: not just texts which manifestly deal with the Last Days, but a great deal else, and the more the better.[39]

Just so. Exegesis, we might say, is the stuff messiah texts are made of.[40] Around the same time, Nils Dahl, in a seminal essay on the Qumran messiah

---

38. Thus rightly Richard A. Horsley, "Messianic Figures and Movements in First-Century Palestine," in *The Messiah*, 276–95 at 277: "To carry out any sort of serious historical analysis, therefore, we must cut through (if not simply abandon) the inherited composite concepts of 'Messiah' and 'messianic.'"

39. Scholem, "Messianic Idea," 32.

40. Even Graetz already recognized this, at least in part:

> [By the Roman period,] the idea of the Messiah no longer lived in the breasts of those who yearned for it in its original, naive form. They immersed themselves much more in the Bible and searched collectively for the traits which the future messianic king would manifest. Reflective and synthetic interpretation replaced spontaneous creativity, Aggada replaced prophecy. (Graetz, "Stages," 160)

texts, writes, "I am principally interested ... in what is illustrated by the details, namely, the correlation between the sociological structure and history of the communities and their eschatological interpretation of Scripture and messianic doctrine."[41] Here, Dahl puts a sharper point on Scholem's observation: The messianism of an ancient text lies at the point where that text's interpretation of scripture intersects with its own concrete *Sitz im Leben*. Writing more recently and in a different context, Martin Hengel makes a related, programmatic point: "We ought, therefore, no longer to speak of a 'Messiah dogmatic' or 'Messiah idea,' but of Messiah conceptions, or even better, of messianic Haggada."[42] This, again, is just right. There is no messianic idea in the old Idealist sense, but there is messiah haggadah, a mass of legend spun from scriptural source material by ancient Jewish and Christian authors in their various historical contexts. And more recently still, Wayne Meeks, in a conversation with William Horbury cited earlier in the present chapter, highlights the same phenomenon:

> [Horbury] does readers a service by stressing that the whole family of eschatological beliefs in early Judaism and early Christianity is, at its heart, an interpretative enterprise. If one looks for some central connective tissue in the complex web of beliefs that we call "Judaism," it is most likely to be found in the text of the Hebrew Bible and in the centuries-long tradition of trying to make sense of it in varying circumstances.[43]

"Biblical exegesis." "Interpretation of scripture." "Haggadah." "An interpretative enterprise." My point in this book is that these comments are not just apt descriptions of ancient messiah texts; they amount to a research program. To date, they have not been adopted as such. With a few praiseworthy exceptions, research on messianism has, in general, followed the same well-worn tracks we inherited from our nineteenth-century forebears, even as our differences with those forebears have become ever clearer and greater with the passage of time. We could do otherwise, however. We could move beyond the accurate but tedious refrain that our primary texts do not bear out the received rubrics of "messianism in the strict sense," and give a new, positive account of

---

41. Dahl, "Eschatology and History in Light of the Qumran Texts," 56.

42. Martin Hengel, "Jesus, the Messiah of Israel," in idem, *Studies in Early Christology*, 1–72 at 33.

43. Meeks, review of Horbury, *Messianism among Jews and Christians*, 338.

what it is that the primary texts do, on their own terms. I have tried, in the preceding chapters, to contribute something to this project. When Shakespeare had Richard II say, in the passage comprising the epigraph to this book, "Not all the water in the rough rude sea/Can wash the balm off from an anointed king" (*Richard II*, act 3, scene 2), he summarized unwittingly the situation of messiah language in antiquity. The use of lexicon of unction to talk about affairs of state—king and priest, dynasty and *coup d'état*, past and future, real and ideal—persisted for centuries after the lapse of the Israelite institution whence it originated, becoming a fixture in the literature of ancient Jews and Christians. The future of the study of messianism lies not in vain attempts to measure the vigor of the phenomenon, nor in pedantic quarrels over the definition of "messiah," nor in lightly revised taxonomies of redeemer figures, but rather in fresh expeditions into the primary sources to trace the way the words run, in the exploration, that is, of the grammar of messianism.

Bibliography

PRIMARY SOURCES

Adler, Ada, ed. *Suidae Lexicon*. Leipzig: Teubner, 1931.

Aland, Kurt, Barbara Aland, Johannes Karavidopoulos, Carlo M. Martini, and Bruce M. Metzger, eds. *Novum Testamentum Graece*. 27th ed. Stuttgart: Deutsche Bibelgesellschaft, 1999.

Baillet, Maurice. *Qumrân Grotte 4:3 (4Q482–4Q520)*. Discoveries in the Judaean Desert 7. Oxford: Clarendon, 1982.

Bardaisan. *The Book of the Laws of Countries*. Edited and translated by H. J. W. Drijvers. Semitic Texts with Translations 111. Assen: van Gorcum, 1965.

Bardy, G., ed. *Eusèbe de Césarée: Histoire ecclésiastique*. 3 vols. Sources chrétiennes 31, 41, 55. Paris: Cerf, 1952–1958.

Barney, Stephen A., W. J. Lewis, J. A. Beach, and Oliver Berghof, eds. *The Etymologies of Isidore of Seville*. Cambridge: Cambridge University Press, 2006.

Barthélemy, D., and J. T. Milik, eds. *Qumran Cave I*. Discoveries in the Judaean Desert 1. Oxford: Clarendon, 1955.

Bedjan, Paul, ed. *Histoire de Mar-Jabalaha, de trois autres patriarches, d'un prêtre et de deux laiques, nestoriens*. Paris: Harrassowitz, 1895.

Blackman, Philip, ed. and trans. *Mishnayoth*. New York: Judaica, 2000.

Borgen, Peder, Kåre Fuglseth, and Roald Skarsten. *The Philo Index: A Complete Greek Word Index to the Writings of Philo of Alexandria*. Leiden: Brill, 2000.

Borleffs, J. W. P., ed. *Tertulliani Ad Nationes, libri duo*. Leiden: Brill, 1929.

Braude, William G., trans. *Pesikta Rabbati*. 2 vols. Yale Judaic Studies 18. New Haven: Yale University Press, 1968.

Buber, S., ed. *Lamentations Rabbah*. Vilna: Romm, 1899.

———, ed. *Midrasch Suta*, Berlin: Mekize Nirdamim, 1894.

Büttner-Wobst, Theodor. *Polybii historiae*. 4 vols. Leipzig: Teubner, 1893–1905.

Charlesworth, James H, ed. *Old Testament Pseudepigrapha*. 2 vols. New York: Doubleday, 1983–1985.

Clarke, Ernest G., ed. *Targum Pseudo-Jonathan of the Pentateuch: Text and Concordance.* New York: Ktav, 1984.

Cohen, Martin Samuel. *The Shi'ur Qomah: Texts and Recensions.* Texte und Studien zum antiken Judentum 9. Tübingen: Mohr Siebeck, 1985.

Cohn, Leopold, and Paul Wendland, eds. *Philonis Alexandrini opera quae supersunt.* Berlin: Reimer, 1896–1915.

Colson, F. H., et al., trans. *Philo.* 12 vols. Loeb Classical Library. Cambridge, Mass.: Harvard University Press, 1929–1962.

Cotton, Hannah M., et al., eds. *Corpus Inscriptionum Iudaeae/Palestinae,* vol. 1, part 1. Berlin: De Gruyter, 2010.

Danby, Herbert, trans. *The Mishnah.* Oxford: Clarenson, 1933.

de Lagarde, Paul, ed. *Onomastica Sacra.* Göttingen, 1870.

Dietrich, M., O. Loretz, and J. Sanmartin, eds. *Die keilalphabetischen Texte aus Ugarit.* AOAT 24/1. Neukirchen-Vluyn: Neukirchener Verlag, 1976.

Dio Cassius. *Roman History.* Translated by Earnest Cary. Loeb Classical Library. Cambridge, Mass.: Harvard University Press, 1914–1927.

Earp, J. W. "Scripture Index to Philo." Pages 189–268 in vol. 10 of *Philo.* Translated by F. H. Colson. Loeb Classical Library. Cambridge, Mass.: Harvard University Press, 1962.

Elliger, K., and W. Rudolph, eds. *Biblia Hebraica Stuttgartensia.* Stuttgart: Deutsche Bibelgesellschaft, 1983.

Eshel, Esther. "4Q471b: A Self-Glorification Hymn." *Revue de Qumran* 17 (1996): 175–203.

Evans, Ernest, ed. *Tertullian's Homily on Baptism.* London: SPCK, 1964.

———, ed. *Tertullian's Treatise against Praxeas.* London: SPCK, 1948.

Evetts, B., ed. *History of the Patriarchs of the Coptic Church in Alexandria.* Patrologia Orientalis 1, 5, 10. Paris: Firmin-Didot, 1904–1915.

Foster, Paul. *The Gospel of Peter: Introduction, Critical Edition, and Commentary.* Texts and Editions for New Testament Study 4. Leiden: Brill, 2010.

Freedman, H., and Maurice Simon, eds. *Midrash Rabbah.* 10 vols. London: Soncino, 1939.

Früchtel, L., O. Stählin, and U. Treu, eds. *Clemens Alexandrinus.* Die griechischen christlichen Schriftsteller der ersten Jahrhunderte. Berlin: Akademie Verlag, 1960–1970.

Goodspeed, E. J., ed. *Die ältesten Apologeten.* Göttingen: Vandenhoeck & Ruprecht, 1915.

Grant, R. M., ed. *Theophilus of Antioch: Ad Autolycum.* Oxford: Clarendon, 1970.

Hallo, William W., ed. *The Context of Scripture: Canonical Compositions, Monumental Inscriptions and Archival Documents from the Biblical World.* 3 vols. Leiden: Brill, 2003.

Havelaar, Henriette W., ed. *The Coptic Apocalypse of Peter (Nag Hammadi Codex VII,3).* Texte und Untersuchungen zur Geschichte der altchristlichen Literatur 144. Berlin: Akademie Verlag, 1999.

Hershman, Abraham M., trans. *The Code of Maimonides: Book 14: The Book of Judges.* Yale Judaic Studies 3. New Haven: Yale University Press, 1949.

Himmelfarb, Martha, trans. "Sefer Zerubbabel." Pages 67–90 in *Rabbinic Fantasies: Imaginative Narratives from Classical Hebrew Literature.* Edited by David Stern and Mark J. Mirsky. New Haven: Yale University Press, 1990.

Horace. *Odes* and *Epodes.* Translated by Niall Rudd. Loeb Classical Library. Cambridge, Mass.: Harvard University Press, 2004.

Janssens, Y., ed. *La Protennoia Trimorphe.* Bibliothèque copte de Nag Hammadi, Textes vol. 4. Leuven: Peeters, 1978.

Layton, Bentley, trans. *The Gnostic Scriptures: A New Translation with Annotations and Introductions.* Anchor Bible Reference Library. New York: Doubleday, 1995.

Lévi, Israël. "L'apocalypse de Zorobabel et le roi de Perse Siroès." *Revue des Études Juives* 68 (1914): 131–44.

Maher, Michael, trans. *Targum Pseudo-Jonathan: Exodus Translated with Notes.* Aramaic Bible 2. Collegeville, Minn.: Liturgical Press, 1994.

Marcovich, M., ed. *Hippolytus: Refutatio omnium haeresium.* Patristische Texte und Studien 25. Berlin: De Gruyter, 1986.

Margulies, M., ed. *Leviticus Rabbah.* 5 vols. Jerusalem: American Academy for Jewish Research, 1953–1960.

Meshorer, Ya'akov. *A Treasury of Jewish Coins from the Persian Period to Bar Kokhba.* Jerusalem: Yad Ben-Zvi, 2001.

Migne, J.-P., ed. *Patrologia graeca.* 162 vols. Paris: Imprimerie Catholique, 1857–1886.

———, ed. *Patrologia latina.* 217 vols. Paris: Imprimerie Catholique, 1844–1864.

Mirkin, Mosheh, ed. *Midrash Rabbah.* 11 vols. Tel Aviv: Yavneh, 1977.

Moran, William L., ed. and trans. *The Amarna Letters.* Baltimore: Johns Hopkins University Press, 1992.

Neusner, Jacob, ed. and trans. *The Talmud of the Land of Israel.* 35 vols. Chicago: University of Chicago Press, 1982–1993.

Nickelsburg, George W. E., and James C. VanderKam, trans. *1 Enoch: A New Translation.* Minneapolis: Fortress, 2004.

Pines, Shlomo. *An Arabic Version of the Testimonium Flavianum and Its Implications.* Jerusalem: Israel Academy of Sciences and Humanities, 1971.

Prigent, Pierre, and Robert A. Kraft, eds. *Épître de Barnabé.* Sources chrétiennes 172. Paris: Cerf, 1971.

Pritchard, James B. *Ancient Near Eastern Texts Relating to the Old Testament.* 3d ed. Princeton: Princeton University Press, 1969.

Qimron, Elisha, and Alexey Yuditsky. "Notes on the So-Called Gabriel Vision Inscription." Pages 31–38 in *Hazon Gabriel: New Readings of the Gabriel Revelation.* Edited by Matthias Henze. Atlanta: SBL, 2011. [Translation of "Notes on the Inscription 'The Vision of Gabriel,'" *Cathedra* 133 (2009): 133–44 (in Hebrew).]

Rabelais, François. *Gargantua et Pantagruel,* vol. 1. Paris: Larousse, 1913. (First pub. 1532.)

Rahlfs, Alfred. *Septuaginta.* 2 vols. Stuttgart: Deutsche Bibelgesellschaft, 1979.

Reeves, John C. *Trajectories in Near Eastern Apocalyptic: A Postrabbinic Jewish Apocalypse Reader*. Atlanta: Society of Biblical Literature, 2005.

Rehm, Bernhard, and Georg Strecker, eds. *Die Pseudoklementinen II: Rekognitionen in Rufins Übersetzung*. Die griechischen christlichen Schriftsteller der ersten Jahrhunderte 51. Berlin: Akademie Verlag, 1994.

Reifenberg, A. *Ancient Jewish Coins*. 3d ed. Jerusalem: Rubin Mass, 1963.

Roberts, Alexander, and James Donaldson, eds. *The Ante-Nicene Fathers*. 10 vols. Edinburgh: T. & T. Clark, 1885–1887.

Robinson, James M., ed. *Nag Hammadi Library in English*. 4th rev. ed. Leiden: Brill, 1996.

Rousseau, Adelin, ed. *Irénée de Lyon, Contre Les Hérésies, Livre IV*. Sources chrétiennes 100.1–2. Paris: Cerf, 1965.

Rousseau, Adelin, and Louis Doutreleau, eds. *Irénée de Lyon, Contre Les Hérésies, Livre I*. Sources chrétiennes 264. Paris: Cerf, 1979.

———, eds. *Irénée de Lyon, Contre Les Hérésies, Livre III*. Sources chrétiennes 211. Paris: Cerf, 1974.

Schäfer, Peter, and Hans-Jürgen Becker, eds. *Synopse zum Talmud Yerushalmi*. 7 vols. Tübingen: Mohr Siebeck, 1991–2001.

Schaff, Philip, and Henry Wace, eds. *The Nicene and Post-Nicene Fathers*. 14 vols. Edinburgh: T. & T. Clark, 1886–1889.

Schechter, Solomon, ed. *Agadath Shir HaShirim*. Cambridge: Bell, 1896.

Schoene, Alfred, and H. Petermann, eds. *Eusebi Chronicorum Libri Duo*. 2 vols. Berlin: Weidmann, 1866–1875.

Schwartz, Eduard. "Zwei Predigten Hippolyts." *Sitzungsberichte der bayerischen Akademie der Wissenschaften* 3 (1936): 19–23.

Sperber, Alexander, ed. *The Bible in Aramaic*, vol. 3: *The Latter Prophets According to Targum Jonathan*. Leiden: Brill, 1962.

Tacitus. The *Histories* and the *Annals*. Translated by Clifford H. Moore and John Jacson. 5 vols. Loeb Classical Library. Cambridge, Mass.: Harvard University Press, 1914–1937.

Thackeray, H. St. J., et al., trans. *Josephus*. 10 vols. Loeb Classical Library. Cambridge, Mass.: Harvard University Press, 1926–1965.

Thesaurus Linguae Latinae: Onomasticon. Leipzig: Teubner, 1907–1913.

Tränkle, Hermann, ed. *Q. S. F. Tertulliani Adversus Iudaeos*. Wiesbaden: Steiner, 1964.

Ulrich, Eugene. *The Biblical Qumran Scrolls: Transcriptions and Textual Variants*. Vetus Testamentum Supplements 134. Leiden: Brill, 2012.

Vassiliev, A., ed. *Analecta Graeco-Byzantina*. Moscow: Imperial University, 1893.

Vermes, Geza, trans. *The Complete Dead Sea Scrolls in English*. 7th ed. London: Penguin, 2011.

Yadin, Yigael, Jonas C. Greenfield, Ada Yardeni, and Baruch Levine, eds. *The Documents from the Bar Kokhba Period in the Cave of Letters*. Jerusalem: Israel Exploration Society, 2002.

Yardeni, Ada, and Binyamin Elizur. "A Hebrew Prophetic Text on Stone from the Early Herodian Period: A Preliminary Report." Pages 11–29 in *Hazon Gabriel: New Readings of the Gabriel Revelation*. Edited by Matthias Henze. Atlanta: SBL, 2011. [Translation of "A Prophetic Text on Stone from the First Century BCE: First Publication," *Cathedra* 123 (2007): 155–66 (in Hebrew).]

SECONDARY SOURCES

Abegg, Martin. "The Messiah at Qumran: Are We Still Seeing Double?" *Dead Sea Discoveries* 2 (1995): 125–44.

———. "Who Ascended to Heaven? 4Q491, 4Q427, and the Teacher of Righteousness." Pages 61–73 in *Eschatology, Messianism, and the Dead Sea Scrolls*. Edited by Craig A. Evans and Peter W. Flint. Grand Rapids: Eerdmans, 1997.

Adler, William. "Christians and the Public Archive." Pages 917–38 in vol. 1 of *A Teacher for All Generations: Essays in Honor of James C. VanderKam*. Edited by Eric F. Mason. 2 vols. *Journal for the Study of Judaism Supplements* 153. Leiden: Brill, 2012.

———. "Introduction." Pages 1–31 in *The Jewish Apocalyptic Heritage in Early Christianity*. Edited by James C. VanderKam and William Adler. Compendia rerum iudaicarum ad Novum Testamentum 3.4. Assen: Van Gorcum, 1996.

———. "The Suda and the 'Priesthood of Jesus.'" Pages 1–12 in *For a Later Generation: The Transformation of Tradition in Israel, Early Judaism, and Early Christianity*. Edited by Randal A. Argall, Beverly Bow, and Rodney A. Werline. Harrisburg, Pa.: Trinity, 2000.

Ådna, Jostein. *Jesu Stellung zum Tempel*. Wissenschaftliche Untersuchungen zum Neuen Testament 2.119. Tübingen: Mohr Siebeck, 2000.

Agamben, Giorgio. *The Power and the Glory: For a Theological Genealogy of Economy and Government*. Translated by Lorenzo Chiesa. Stanford: Stanford University Press, 2011.

Aleksandrov, G. S. "The Role of Aqiba in the Bar Kokhba Rebellion." Translated by Sam Driver. Pages 422–36 in vol. 2 of *Eliezer ben Hyrcanus*. Edited by Jacob Neusner. Leiden: Brill, 1973.

Alexander, Philip. "Jesus and His Mother in the Jewish Anti-Gospel (the Toledot Yeshu)." Pages 588–616 in *Infancy Gospels: Stories and Identities*. Edited by Claire Clivaz, Andreas Dettwiler, Luc Devillers, and Enrico Norelli. Wissenschaftliche Untersuchungen zum Neuen Testament 281. Tübingen: Mohr Siebeck, 2011.

———. "The King Messiah in Rabbinic Judaism." Pages 456–73 in *King and Messiah in Israel and the Ancient Near East*. Edited by John Day. London: T. & T. Clark, 2013. [First pub. Sheffield: Sheffield Academic, 1998.]

———. *The Mystical Texts: Songs of the Sabbath Sacrifice and Related Manuscripts*. Library of Second Temple Studies 21. Companion to the Qumran Scrolls 7. London: T. & T. Clark, 2006.

———. "The Rabbis and Messianism." Pages 227–44 in *Redemption and Resistance: The Messianic Hopes of Jews and Christians in Antiquity*. Edited by Markus Bockmuehl and James Carleton Paget. London: T. & T. Clark, 2007.

Allegro, John M. *The Dead Sea Scrolls*. Harmondsworth: Penguin, 1956.

———. *The Dead Sea Scrolls and the Christian Myth*. Newton Abbot: Westbridge, 1979.

———. *The Sacred Mushroom and the Cross: A Study of the Nature and Origins of Christianity within the Fertility Cults of the Ancient Near East*. London: Hodder & Stoughton, 1970.

Alt, Albrecht. "The Monarchy in the Kingdoms of Israel and Judah." Pages 239–59, 311–35 in *Essays in Old Testament History and Religion*. Translated by R. A. Wilson. New York: Doubleday, 1967.

Alter, Robert. *Canon and Creativity: Modern Writing and the Authority of Scripture*. New Haven: Yale University Press, 2000.

Amir, Yehoshua. "The Messianic Idea in Hellenistic Judaism." Translated by Chanah Arnon. *Immanuel* 2 (1973): 58–60. [Hebrew original in *Machanayim* 124 (1970): 54–67. Abridged German translation "Die messianische Idee im hellenistischen Judentum." *Freiburger Rundbrief* 25 (1973): 195–203.]

Ammon, Christoph Friedrich. *Entwurf einer Christologie des Alten Testaments*. Erlangen: Palm, 1794.

Amsler, Mark E. *Etymology and Grammatical Discourse in Late Antiquity and the Early Middle Ages*. Philadelphia: Benjamins, 1989.

Andersen, Francis I. *Habakkuk*. Anchor Bible. New York: Doubleday, 2001.

Anderson, Hugh. "Jewish Antecedents of the Christology in Hebrews." Pages 512–35 in *The Messiah: Developments in Earliest Judaism and Christianity*. Edited by James H. Charlesworth. Minneapolis: Fortress, 1992.

Appelbaum, Alan. *The Dynasty of the Jewish Patriarchs*. Texte und Studien zum antiken Judentum 156. Tübingen: Mohr Siebeck, 2013.

Ap-Thomas, D. R. "An Appreciation of Sigmund Mowinckel's Contribution to Biblical Studies." *Journal of Biblical Literature* 85 (1966): 315–25.

Arai, Sasagu. "Zur Christologie des Apokryphons des Johannes." *New Testament Studies* 15 (1968): 302–18.

Atkinson, Kenneth. "Herod the Great, Sosius, and the Siege of Jerusalem (37 B.C.E.) in Psalm of Solomon 17." *Novum Testamentum* 38 (1996): 313–22.

———. *I Cried to the Lord: A Study of the Psalms of Solomon's Historical Background and Social Setting*. Journal for the Study of Judaism Supplements 84. Leiden: Brill, 2003.

Attridge, Harold W. *The Epistle to the Hebrews*. Hermeneia. Minneapolis: Fortress, 1989.

———. "Giving Voice to Jesus: Use of the Psalms in the New Testament." Pages 320–30 in *Essays on John and Hebrews*. Wissenschaftliche Untersuchungen zum Neuen Testament 264. Tübingen: Mohr Siebeck, 2010.

Ayres, Lewis. "The Question of Orthodoxy." *Journal of Early Christian Studies* 14 (2006): 395–98.

Baert, Barbara. *A Heritage of Holy Wood.* Cultures, Beliefs, and Traditions 22. Leiden: Brill, 2005.

Baillet, Maurice. "Les manuscrits de la Règle de Guerre de la grotte 4 de Qumrân." *Revue Biblique* 79 (1972): 217–26.

Bar-Asher, Moshe. "On the Language of 'The Vision of Gabriel.'" *Revue de Qumran* 23 (2008): 491–524.

Bar-Kochva, Bezalel. *Judas Maccabaeus: The Jewish Struggle against the Seleucids.* Cambridge: Cambridge University Press, 1989.

Baras, Zvi. "The Testimonium Flavianum and the Martyrdom of James." Pages 338–48 in *Josephus, Judaism, and Christianity.* Edited by Louis H. Feldman and Gohei Hata. Detroit: Wayne State University Press, 1987.

Barclay, John M. G. *Jews in the Mediterranean Diaspora.* Edinburgh: T. & T. Clark, 1996.

———. "The Empire Writes Back: Josephan Rhetoric in Flavian Rome." Pages 315–32 in *Flavius Josephus and Flavian Rome.* Edited by Jonathan Edmondson, Steve Mason, and James Rives. Oxford: Oxford University Press, 2005.

Barraclough, Ray. "Philo's Politics: Roman Rule and Hellenistic Judaism." *ANRW* 21.1:417–553. Part 2, *Principat,* 21.1. Edited by H. Temporini and W. Haase. Berlin: De Gruyter, 1984.

Barrett, Anthony A. "Herod, Augustus, and the Special Relationship: The Significance of the Procuratorship." Pages 281–302 in *Herod and Augustus.* Edited by David Jacobson and Niko Kokkinos. IJS Studies in Judaica 6. Leiden: Brill, 2009.

Barrett, C. K. "The Christology of Hebrews." Pages 110–27 in *Who Do You Say That I Am? Essays on Christology.* Edited by Mark Allen Powell and David R. Bauer. Louisville, Ky.: Westminster John Knox, 1999.

Barton, John. "The Messiah in Old Testament Theology." Pages 365–79 in *King and Messiah in Israel and the Ancient Near East.* Edited by John Day. London: T. & T. Clark, 2013. [First pub. Sheffield: Sheffield Academic, 1998.]

———. *Oracles of God: Perceptions of Ancient Prophecy in Israel after the Exile.* London: Darton, Longman & Todd, 1986.

Bauckham, Richard. *Jude and the Relatives of Jesus in the Early Church.* Edinburgh: T. & T. Clark, 1990.

———. *The Climax of Prophecy: Studies on the Book of Revelation.* London: T. & T. Clark, 1993.

———. "The Origin of the Ebionites." Pages 162–81 in *The Image of the Judaeo-Christians in Ancient Jewish and Christian Literature.* Edited by Peter J. Tomson and Doris Lambers-Petry. Wissenschaftliche Untersuchungen zum Neuen Testament 158. Tübingen: Mohr Siebeck, 2003.

———. *The Theology of the Book of Revelation.* Cambridge: Cambridge University Press, 1993.

Bauer, Walter. *Orthodoxy and Heresy in Earliest Christianity.* Translated by Robert A. Kraft and Gerhard Kroedel. Philadelphia: Fortress, 1971. [Translation of *Rechtgläubigkeit und Ketzerei im ältesten Christentum*. Tübingen: Mohr Siebeck, 1934.]

Baumgarten, Albert. "On the Legitimacy of Herod and His Sons as Kings of Israel." Pages 31–37 in *Jews and Judaism in the Second Temple, Mishnah, and Talmud Period*. Edited by Isaiah Gafni, Aharon Oppenheimer, and Menahem Stern. Jerusalem: Yad Ben-Zvi, 1993 (in Hebrew).

Baur, F. C. *Paul the Apostle of Jesus Christ*. Translated by A. Menzies. 2 vols. London: Williams & Norgate, 1873–1875. [Translation of *Paulus, der Apostel Jesu Christi*. Stuttgart: Becher & Müller, 1845.]

Becker, Adam H., and Annette Yoshiko Reed, eds. *The Ways That Never Parted*. Texte und Studien zum antiken Judentum 95. Tübingen: Mohr Siebeck, 2003.

Becker, Joachim. *Messianic Expectation in the Old Testament*. Translated by David E. Green. Philadelphia: Fortress, 1980. [Translation of *Messiaserwartung im Alten Testament*. Stuttgart: Katholisches Bibelwerk, 1977.]

Bentivegna, J. "A Christianity without Christ by Theophilus of Antioch." *Studia patristica* 13 (1975): 107–30.

Bentzen, Aage. *King and Messiah*. Translated by G. W. Anderson. London: Lutterworth, 1955. [Translation of *Messias-Moses redivivus-Menschenson*. Abhandlungen zur Theologie des Alten und Neuen Testaments 17. Zurich: Zwingli Verlag, 1948.]

Beuken, Wim, Sean Freyne, and Antonius G. Weiler, eds. *Messianism through History*. London: SCM, 1993.

Bhabha, Homi K. "How Newness Enters the World: Postmodern Space, Postcolonial Times and the Trials of Cultural Translation." Pages 303–37 in *The Location of Culture*. 2d ed. London: Routledge, 2004.

Biale, David. *Gershom Scholem: Kabbalah and Counter-History*. 2d ed. Cambridge, Mass.: Harvard University Press, 1982.

———. *Power and Powerlessness in Jewish History*. New York: Schocken, 1986.

Bickerman, Elias. "Sur la version vieux-russe de Flavius Josephe." Pages 172–95 in *Studies in Jewish and Christian History, Part 1*. Arbeiten zur Geschichte des antiken Judentums und des Urchristentums 9. Leiden: Brill, 1976.

Bilde, Per. *The Originality of Jesus: A Critical Discussion and a Comparative Attempt*. Göttingen: Vandenhoeck & Ruprecht, 2013.

Blenkinsopp, Joseph. "An Assessment of the Alleged Pre-exilic Date of the Priestly Material in the Pentateuch." *Zeitschrift für die alttestamentliche Wissenschaft* 108 (1996): 495–518.

———. *Isaiah 40–55*. Anchor Bible. New Haven: Yale University Press, 2006.

———. "Prophecy and Priesthood in Josephus." *Journal of Jewish Studies* 25 (1974): 239–62.

Blondheim, D. S. *Les parlers judéo-romans et la Vetus Latina*. Cambridge: Cambridge University Press, 2013. [First pub. 1925.]

Blount, Brian K. *Revelation: A Commentary*. New Testament Library. Louisville, Ky.: Westminster John Knox, 2009.

Bockmuehl, Markus. "'The Form of God' (Phil 2:6): Variations on a Theme of Jewish Mysticism." *Journal of Theological Studies* n.s. 48 (1997): 1–23.

———. "The Son of David and His Mother." *Journal of Theological Studies* n.s. 62 (2011): 476–93.

Bons, Eberhard, and Patrick Pouchelle, eds. *The Psalms of Solomon: Language, History, Theology.* Early Judaism and Its Literature 40. Atlanta: Society of Biblical Literature, 2015.

Borgen, Peder. *Philo of Alexandria: An Exegete for His Time.* Novum Testamentum Supplements 86. Leiden: Brill, 1997.

———. "'There Shall Come Forth a Man': Reflections on Messianic Ideas in Philo." Pages 341–61 in *The Messiah: Developments in Earliest Judaism and Christianity.* Edited by James H. Charlesworth. Minneapolis: Fortress, 1992.

Bousset, Wilhelm. *Die Religion des Judentums im späthellenistischen Zeitalter.* Edited by Hugo Gressmann. 3d ed. Handbuch zum Neuen Testament 21. Tübingen: Mohr Siebeck, 1926.

Bovon, Francois. *Luke 1: A Commentary on the Gospel of Luke 1:1–9:50.* Translated by Christine M. Thomas. Hermeneia. Minneapolis: Fortress, 2002.

Bowersock, Glen W. "A Roman Perspective on the Bar Kokhba War." Pages 131–41 in vol. 2 of *Approaches to Ancient Judaism.* Edited by William S. Green. Chico, Calif.: Scholars Press, 1980.

Boyarin, Daniel. *Border Lines: The Partition of Judaeo-Christianity.* Philadelphia: University of Pennsylvania Press, 2004.

———. *The Jewish Gospels: The Story of the Jewish Christ.* New York: New Press, 2012.

Brent, Allen. *Hippolytus and the Roman Church in the Third Century.* Leiden: Brill, 1995.

Briggs, Charles Augustus. *Messianic Prophecy: The Prediction of the Fulfillment of Redemption through the Messiah: A Critical Study of the Messianic Passages of the Old Testament in the Order of Their Development.* New York: Scribner, 1886.

Brock, Sebastian. "Greek and Syriac in Late Antique Syria." Pages 149–60 in *From Ephrem to Romanos: Interactions between Syriac and Greek in Late Antiquity.* Aldershot, UK: Ashgate, 1999.

———. "Greek Words in Syriac: Some General Features." Pages 251–62 in *From Ephrem to Romanos: Interactions between Syriac and Greek in Late Antiquity.* Aldershot, UK: Ashgate, 1999.

———. "Syria and Mesopotamia: The Shared Term Malka Mshiḥa." Pages 171–82 in *Redemption and Resistance: The Messianic Hopes of Jews and Christians in Antiquity.* Edited by Markus Bockmuehl and James Carleton Paget. London: T. & T. Clark, 2007.

Brown, F., S. R. Driver, and C. A. Briggs. *A Hebrew and English Lexicon of the Old Testament.* Oxford: Clarendon, 1907.

Brown, Judith Anne. *John Marco Allegro: The Maverick of the Dead Sea Scrolls.* Grand Rapids: Eerdmans, 2005.

Brown, Peter. *The World of Late Antiquity.* London: Thames and Hudson, 1971.

Brown, Raymond E. *The Birth of the Messiah: A Commentary on the Infancy Narratives in the Gospels of Matthew and Luke*. Rev. ed. London: Chapman, 1993.

———. *The Community of the Beloved Disciple*. New York: Paulist, 1979.

———. *The Death of the Messiah: A Commentary on the Passion Narratives in the Four Gospels*. 2 vols. New York: Doubleday, 1994.

———. *The Epistles of John*. Anchor Bible. New York: Doubleday, 1982.

———. "The Paraclete in the Fourth Gospel." *New Testament Studies* 13 (1966–1967): 113–32.

Brownlee, William H. "Messianic Motifs of Qumran and the New Testament." *New Testament Studies* 3 (1956): 12–30.

Brox, Norbert. "'Doketismus'—eine Problemanzeige." *Zeitschrift für Kirchengeschichte* 95 (1984): 301–14.

Bruce, F. F. *The Gospel of John*. Grand Rapids: Eerdmans, 1983.

Brutti, Maria. *The Development of the High Priesthood During the Pre-Hasmonean Period*. Journal for the Study of Judaism Supplements 108. Leiden: Brill, 2006.

Buber, Martin. *Two Types of Faith*. Translated by Norman P. Goldhawk. New York: Macmillan, 1951.

Buhl, Frants. *De messianske Forjaettelser i det gamle Testamente*. Copenhagen: Gyldendal, 1894.

Bultmann, Rudolf. *Theology of the New Testament*. 2 vols. Translated by Kendrick Grobel. New York: Scribner, 1951–1955. [Translation of *Theologie des Neuen Testaments*. 3 vols. Tübingen: Mohr Siebeck, 1948–1953.]

Burger, Christoph. *Jesus als Davidssohn*. Forschungen zur Religion und Literatur des Alten und Neuen Testaments 98. Göttingen: Vandenhoeck & Ruprecht, 1970.

Burkitt, F. C. "Josephus and Christ." *Theologisch tijdschrift* 47 (1913): 135–44.

Burridge, Kenneth. *Mambu: A Melanesian Millennium*. London: Methuen, 1960.

Cameron, Averil. "Jews and Heretics—A Category Error?" Pages 345–60 in *The Ways That Never Parted*. Edited by Adam H. Becker and Annette Yoshiko Reed. Texte und Studien zum antiken Judentum 95. Tübingen: Mohr Siebeck, 2003.

Carleton Paget, James. "Egypt." Pages 183–97 in *Redemption and Resistance: The Messianic Hopes of Jews and Christians in Antiquity*. Edited by Markus Bockmuehl and James Carleton Paget. London: T. & T. Clark, 2007.

———. "Some Observations on Josephus and Christianity." *Journal of Theological Studies* n.s. 52 (2001): 539–624.

———. "The Definition of the Term 'Jewish Christian'/'Jewish Christianity' in the History of Research." Pages 289–324 in *Jews, Christians, and Jewish Christians in Antiquity*. Wissenschaftliche Untersuchungen zum Neuen Testament 251. Tübingen: Mohr Siebeck, 2010.

———. *The Epistle of Barnabas: Outlook and Background*. Wissenschaftliche Untersuchungen zum Neuen Testament 2.64. Tübingen: Mohr Siebeck, 1994.

Carmignac, J. J. "Les citations de l'Ancien Testament et spécialement des Poèmes du Serviteur dans les Hymnes de Qumrân." *Revue de Qumran* 2 (1960): 357–94.

Carrier, Richard. "Origen, Eusebius, and the Accidental Interpolation in Josephus, *Jewish Antiquities* 20.200." *Journal of Early Christian Studies* 20 (2012): 489–514.

Castelli, David. *Il Messia secondo gli Ebrei.* Florence: Le Monnier, 1874.

Cazelles, Henri. "L'enfantement de la Sagesse en Prov. VIII." Pages 511–15 in vol. 1 of *Sacra Pagina.* Edited by Joseph Coppens. Bibliotheca ephemeridum theologicarum lovaniensium 12. Gembloux: Duculot, 1959.

Cerrato, J. A. *Hippolytus between East and West.* Oxford Theological Monographs. Oxford: Oxford University Press, 2002.

Charlesworth, James H. "From Jewish Messianology to Christian Christology." Pages 225–64 in *Judaisms and Their Messiahs at the Turn of the Christian Era.* Edited by Jacob Neusner, William Scott Green, and Ernest Frerichs. Cambridge: Cambridge University Press, 1987.

———. "From Messianology to Christology: Problems and Prospects." Pages 3–35 in *The Messiah: Developments in Earliest Judaism and Christianity.* Edited by James H. Charlesworth. Minneapolis: Fortress, 1992.

———. "Introduction: Messianic Ideas in Early Judaism." Pages 1–8 in *Qumran Messianism: Studies on the Messianic Expectations in the Dead Sea Scrolls.* Edited by James H. Charlesworth, Hermann Lichtenberger, and Gerbern S. Oegema. Tübingen: Mohr Siebeck, 1998.

———. "Messianology in the Biblical Pseudepigrapha." Pages 21–52 in *Qumran Messianism: Studies on the Messianic Expectations in the Dead Sea Scrolls.* Edited by James H. Charlesworth, Hermann Lichtenberger, and Gerbern S. Oegema. Tübingen: Mohr Siebeck, 1998.

———. "The Concept of the Messiah in the Pseudepigrapha." *ANRW* 19.1:188–218. Part 2, *Principat,* 19.1. Edited by H. Temporini and W. Haase. Berlin: De Gruyter, 1979.

———, ed. *The Messiah: Developments in Earliest Judaism and Christianity.* Minneapolis: Fortress, 1992.

Chazan, Robert. *Barcelona and Beyond: The Disputation of 1263 and Its Aftermath.* Berkeley: University of California Press, 1992.

Chester, Andrew. *Messiah and Exaltation: Jewish Messianic and Visionary Traditions and New Testament Christology.* Wissenschaftliche Untersuchungen zum Neuen Testament 207. Tübingen: Mohr Siebeck, 2007.

Childs, Brevard. *Biblical Theology of the Old and New Testaments: Theological Reflection on the Christian Bible.* Minneapolis: Fortress, 1992.

Chilton, Bruce. "Jesus ben David: Reflections on the Davidssohnfrage." *Journal for the Study of the New Testament* 14 (1982): 88–122.

Chin, Catherine M. *Grammar and Christianity in the Late Roman World.* Philadelphia: University of Pennsylvania Press, 2008.

Clements, R. E. "The Messianic Hope in the Old Testament." *Journal for the Study of the Old Testament* 43 (1989): 3–19.

Clifford, Hywel. "Moses as Philosopher-Sage in Philo." Pages 151–68 in *Moses in Biblical and Extra-Biblical Traditions*. Edited by Axel Graupner and Michael Wolter. Beihefte zur Zeitschrift für die alttestamentliche Wissenschaft 372. Berlin: De Gruyter, 2007.

Cohen, Shaye J. D. *From the Maccabees to the Mishnah*. 2d ed. Louisville, Ky.: Westminster John Knox, 2006.

———. *The Beginnings of Jewishness: Boundaries, Varieties, Uncertainties*. Berkeley: University of California Press, 1999.

———. "The Rabbi in Second-Century Judean Society." Pages 922–90 in vol. 3 of *Cambridge History of Judaism*. Edited by William Horbury, W. D. Davies, and John Sturdy. New York: Cambridge University Press, 1999.

Cohn, Naftali S. *The Memory of the Temple and the Making of the Rabbis*. Philadelphia: University of Pennsylvania Press, 2013.

Cohn-Sherbok, Dan. *The Jewish Messiah*. London: T. & T. Clark, 1997.

Collins, John J. "A Messiah before Jesus?" Pages 15–36 in *Christian Beginnings and the Dead Sea Scrolls*. Edited by John J. Collins and Craig A. Evans. Grand Rapids: Baker, 2006.

———. "An Essene Messiah? Comments on Israel Knohl, *The Messiah before Jesus*." Pages 37–44 in *Christian Beginnings and the Dead Sea Scrolls*. Edited by John J. Collins and Craig A. Evans. Grand Rapids: Baker, 2006.

———. *Between Athens and Jerusalem: Jewish Identity in the Hellenistic Diaspora*. 2d ed. Grand Rapids: Eerdmans, 2000.

———. *Beyond the Qumran Community: The Sectarian Movement of the Dead Sea Scrolls*. Grand Rapids: Eerdmans, 2010.

———. "Gabriel and David: Some Reflections on an Enigmatic Text." Pages 99–112 in *Hazon Gabriel: New Readings of the Gabriel Revelation*. Edited by Matthias Henze. Atlanta: SBL, 2011.

———. "Messiahs in Context: Method in the Study of Messianism in the Dead Sea Scrolls." *Annals of the New York Academy of Sciences* 722 (1994): 213–27.

———. "Mowinckel's *He That Cometh* in Retrospect." Pages xv–xxviii in *He That Cometh: The Messiah Concept in the Old Testament and Later Judaism*, by Sigmund Mowinckel. Grand Rapids: Eerdmans, 2005.

———. "Review of Philip R. Davies, *The Damascus Covenant*." *Journal of Biblical Literature* 104 (1985): 530–33.

———. "Teacher and Servant." *Revue d'histoire et de philosophie religiuses* 80 (2000): 37–50.

———. *The Dead Sea Scrolls: A Biography*. Princeton: Princeton University Press, 2013.

———. *The Scepter and the Star: Messianism in Light of the Dead Sea Scrolls*. 2d ed. Grand Rapids: Eerdmans, 2010.

———. "The Time of the Teacher: An Old Debate Renewed." Pages 212–29 in *Studies in the Hebrew Bible, Qumran, and the Septuagint Presented to Eugene Ulrich*. Edited by Peter W. Flint, Emanuel Tov, and James C. VanderKam. Vetus Testamentum Supplements 101. Leiden: Brill, 2006.

Conder, Claude Reignier. *Judas Maccabaeus and the Jewish War of Independence.* New ed. London: Watt, 1894.

Conzelmann, Hans. *The Theology of St. Luke.* New York: Harper & Row, 1960. [German original 1953.]

Coppens, Joseph. *La relève apocalyptique du messianisme royal.* 3 vols. Bibliotheca ephemeridum theologicarum lovaniensium 50, 55, 61. Leuven: Peeters, 1979–1983.

———. *Le messianisme et sa relève prophétique: Les anticipations vétérotestamentaires: Leur accomplissement en Jésus.* Bibliotheca ephemeridum theologicarum lovaniensium 38. Gembloux: Duculot, 1974.

———. *Le messianisme royal: Ses origines, son développement, son accomplissement.* Lectio divina 54. Paris: Cerf, 1968.

Costa, José. "Le Messie judéo-chrétien et les rabbins." Pages 203–27 in *Aux origines des messianismes juifs.* Edited by David Hamidović. Vetus Testamentum Supplements 158. Leiden: Brill, 2013.

Cotton, Hannah M. "The Bar Kokhba Revolt and the Documents from the Judaean Desert." Pages 133–52 in *The Bar Kokhba War Reconsidered.* Edited by Peter Schäfer. Texte und Studien zum antiken Judentum 100. Tübingen: Mohr Siebeck, 2003.

Cross, Frank Moore. "The Judaean Royal Theology." Pages 241–73 in *Canaanite Myth and Hebrew Epic.* Cambridge, Mass.: Harvard University Press, 1973.

———. "The Priestly Tabernacle in the Light of Recent Research." Pages 169–80 in *Temples and High Places in Biblical Times.* Edited by Avraham Biran. Jerusalem: Hebrew Union College, 1981.

Dahl, Nils A. "Eschatology and History in Light of the Qumran Texts." Pages 49–64 in *Jesus the Christ.* Edited by Donald H. Juel. Minneapolis: Fortress, 1991.

———. "Messianic Ideas and the Crucifixion of Jesus." Pages 382–403 in *The Messiah: Developments in Earliest Judaism and Christianity.* Edited by James H. Charlesworth. Minneapolis: Fortress, 1992.

———. "Sigmund Mowinckel, Historian of Religion and Theologian." *Scandinavian Journal of the Old Testament* 2 (1988): 8–22.

———. "Sources of Christological Language." Pages 113–36 in *Jesus the Christ.* Edited by Donald H. Juel. Minneapolis: Fortress, 1991.

———. "The Crucified Messiah." Pages 27–47 in *Jesus the Christ.* Edited by Donald H. Juel. Minneapolis: Fortress, 1991.

———. "The Messiahship of Jesus in Paul." Pages 15–25 in *Jesus the Christ.* Edited by Donald H. Juel. Minneapolis: Fortress, 1991.

Daley, Brian E. "'Faithful and True': Early Christian Apocalyptic and the Person of Christ." Pages 106–26 in *Apocalyptic Thought in Early Christianity.* Edited by Robert J. Daly. Grand Rapids: Baker, 2009.

Dalferth, I. U. "Wittgenstein: The Theological Reception." Pages 273–302 in *Religion and Wittgenstein's Legacy.* Edited by D. Z. Phillips and Mario von der Ruhr. Surrey: Ashgate, 2005.

Dalley, Stephanie. "Anointing in Ancient Mesopotamia." Pages 19–25 in *The Oil of Gladness: Anointing in Christian Tradition*. Edited by Martin Dudley and Geoffrey Rowell. London: SPCK, 1993.

Dalman, Gustaf. *Der leidende und sterbende Messias der Synagoge im ersten nach-christlichen Jahrtausend*. Schriften des Institutum Judaicum in Berlin 4. Berlin: Reuther, 1888.

Dan, Joseph. "Armilus: The Jewish Antichrist and the Origins and Dating of the Sefer Zerubbavel." Pages 73–104 in *Toward the Millennium: Messianic Expectations from the Bible to Waco*. Edited by Peter Schäfer and Mark R. Cohen. Studies in the History of Religions 77. Leiden: Brill, 1998.

Danker, F. W., W. Bauer, W. F. Arndt, and F. W. Gingrich. *Greek–English Lexicon of the New Testament and Other Early Christian Literature*. 3d ed. Chicago: University of Chicago Press, 1999.

Davies, Philip R. *The Damascus Covenant: An Interpretation of the "Damascus Document."* Journal for the Study of the Old Testament Supplements 25. Sheffield: JSOT Press, 1983.

———. "The Teacher of Righteousness and the End of Days." *Revue de Qumran* 13 (1988): 313–17.

Davies, W. D. "From Schweitzer to Scholem: Reflections on Sabbatai Svi." *Journal of Biblical Literature* 95 (1976): 529–58.

Davila, James R. "Heavenly Ascents in the Dead Sea Scrolls." Pages 461–85 in vol. 2 of *The Dead Sea Scrolls after Fifty Years: A Comprehensive Assessment*. Edited by Peter W. Flint and James C. VanderKam. 2 vols. Leiden: Brill, 1998.

———. *The Provenance of the Pseudepigrapha: Jewish, Christian, or Other?* Journal for the Study of Judaism Supplements 105. Leiden: Brill, 2005.

Dawson, David. *Allegorical Readers and Cultural Revision in Ancient Alexandria*. Berkeley: University of California Press, 1992.

Day, John, ed. *King and Messiah in Israel and the Ancient Near East*. London: T. & T. Clark, 2013. [First pub. Sheffield: Sheffield Academic, 1998.]

———. "The Canaanite Inheritance of the Israelite Monarchy." Pages 72–90 in *King and Messiah in Israel and the Ancient Near East*. Edited by John Day. London: T. & T. Clark, 2013. [First pub. Sheffield: Sheffield Academic, 1998.]

———. "The Daniel of Ugarit and Ezekiel and the Hero of the Book of Daniel." *Vetus Testamentum* 30 (1980): 174–84.

Dehart, Paul. *The Trial of the Witnesses: The Rise and Decline of Postliberal Theology*. Hoboken, N.J.: Wiley, 2008.

de Hoop, Raymond. *Genesis 49 in Its Literary and Historical Context*. Oudtestamentische Studiën 39. Leiden: Brill, 1998.

De Jonge, Marinus. "Jewish Expectations about the 'Messiah' according to the Fourth Gospel." *New Testament Studies* 19 (1973): 246–70.

———. "The Use of the Word 'Anointed' at the Time of Jesus." *Novum Testamentum* 8 (1966): 132–48.

———. "Variety and Development in Johannine Christology." Pages 193–222 in *Jesus, Stranger from Heaven and Son of God*. Society of Biblical Literature Sources for Biblical Study 11. Missoula, Mont.: Scholars Press, 1977.

Delitzsch, Franz. *Messianische Weissagungen in geschichtlicher Folge*. Leipzig: Faber, 1890.

Delling, Gerhard. "Philons Enkomion auf Augustus." *Klio* 54 (1972): 171–92.

Denzey, Nicola. "Bardaisan of Edessa." Pages 159–84 in *A Companion to Second-Century Christian "Heretics."* Edited by Antti Marjanen and Petri Luomanen. Leiden: Brill, 2008.

Dequeker, L. "1 Chronicles XXIV and the Royal Priesthood of the Hasmoneaons." Pages 94–106 in *Crises and Perspectives: Studies in Ancient Near Eastern Polytheism, Biblical Theology, Palestinian Archaeology, and Intertestamental Literature*. Leiden: Brill, 1986.

de Vaux, Roland. *Ancient Israel: Its Life and Institutions*. Translated by John McHugh. London: Darton, Longman & Todd, 1980.

———. "The King of Israel, Vassal of Yahweh." Pages 152–66 in *The Bible and the Ancient Near East*. Translated by Damian McHugh. London: Darton, Longman & Todd, 1972.

Dimant, Devorah. "The History of the Qumran Community in Light of New Developments." Pages 221–46 in *History, Ideology and Bible Interpretation in the Dead Sea Scrolls*. Forschungen zum Alten Testament 90. Tübingen: Mohr Siebeck, 2014.

Dix, G. H. "The Messiah ben Joseph." *Journal of Theological Studies* 27 (1926): 130–43.

Dixon, Edward P. "Descending Spirit and Descending Gods: A 'Greek' Interpretation of the Spirit's 'Descent as a Dove' in Mark 1:10." *Journal of Biblical Literature* 128 (2009): 759–80.

Docherty, Susan E. *The Use of the Old Testament in Hebrews: A Case Study in Early Jewish Bible Interpretation*. Wissenschaftliche Untersuchungen zum Neuen Testament 2.260. Tübingen: Mohr Siebeck, 2009.

Doyle, Arthur Conan. *Memoirs of Sherlock Holmes*. New York: Burt, 1894.

Drijvers, H. J. W. "Adam and the True Prophet in the Pseudo-Clementines." Pages 314–23 in *Loyalitätskonflikte in der Religionsgeschichte*. Edited by Christoph Elsas and Hans Kippenberg. Würzburg: Königshausen & Neumann, 1990.

———. *Bardaisan of Edessa*. Studia semitica neerlandica 6. Assen: Van Gorcum, 1966.

Drummond, Andrew. "Fasces." Pages 587–88 in *Oxford Classical Dictionary*. 3d ed. Edited by S. Hornblower and A. Spawforth. Oxford: Clarendon, 1996.

Drummond, James. *The Jewish Messiah: A Critical History of the Messianic Idea among the Jews from the Rise of the Maccabees to the Closing of the Talmud*. London: Longman, 1877.

Duling, Dennis C. "The Promises to David and Their Entrance into Christianity: Nailing Down a Likely Hypothesis." *New Testament Studies* 20 (1973): 55–77.

Dunn, Geoffrey D. *Tertullian's Adversus Ioudaeos: A Rhetorical Analysis*. Patristic Monograph Series 19. Washington, DC: Catholic University of America Press, 2008.

Dunn, James D. G. *Christology in the Making*. London: SCM, 1980.

_____. *Jesus Remembered*. Grand Rapids: Eerdmans, 2003.

_____, ed. *Jews and Christians: The Parting of the Ways, A.D. 70 to 135*. Grand Rapids: Eerdmans, 1999.

_____. *The Partings of the Ways: Between Judaism and Christianity and Their Significance for the Character of Christianity*. 2d ed. London: SCM, 2006.

Dupont-Sommer, André. "La grotte aux manuscrits du désert de Juda." *Revue de Paris* (July 1949): 79–90.

_____. *The Dead Sea Scrolls: A Preliminary Survey*. Translated by E. Margaret Rowley. Oxford: Blackwell, 1952. [Translation of *Aperçus préliminaires sur les manuscrits de la mer Morte*. Paris: Maisonneuve, 1950.]

_____. *The Essene Writings from Qumran*. Translated by Geza Vermes. Oxford: Blackwell, 1961. [Translation of *Les Écrits esséniens découverts près de la mer Morte*. Paris: Payot, 1959.]

Dutcher-Walls, Patricia. *Narrative Art, Political Rhetoric: The Case of Athaliah and Joash*. Journal for the Study of the Old Testament Supplements 209. Sheffield: Sheffield Academic, 1996.

Eaton, J. H. "The Origin and Meaning of Habakkuk 3." *Zeitschrift für die alttestamentliche Wissenschaft* 76 (1964): 144–71.

Eck, Werner. "The Bar Kokhba Revolt: The Roman Point of View." *Journal of Roman Studies* 89 (1999): 76–89.

Eckardt, Regine, Klaus von Heusinger, and Christoph Schwarze, eds. *Words in Time: Diachronic Semantics fom Different Points of View*. Trends in Linguistics Studies and Monographs 143. Berlin: De Gruyter, 2003.

Edmondson, Jonathan, Steve Mason, and James Rives, eds. *Flavius Josephus and Flavian Rome*. Oxford: Oxford University Press, 2005.

Ehrman, Bart D. *The Orthodox Corruption of Scripture*. New York: Oxford University Press, 1993.

Engnell, Ivan. *Studies in Divine Kingship in the Ancient Near East*. Uppsala: Almqvist & Wiksell, 1943.

Eshel, Esther "Self-Glorification Hymn." Page 1215 in *Eerdmans Dictionary of Early Judaism*. Edited by John J. Collins and Daniel C. Harlow. Grand Rapids: Eerdmans, 2010.

_____. "The Identification of the 'Speaker' of the Self-Glorification Hymn." Pages 619–35 in *The Provo International Conference on the Dead Sea Scrolls: Technological Innovations, New Texts, and Reformulated Issues*. Edited by Donald W. Parry and Eugene Ulrich. Studies of the Texts of the Desert of Judah 30. Leiden: Brill, 1999.

Eshel, Hanan. *The Dead Sea Scrolls and the Hasmonean State*. Grand Rapids: Eerdmans, 2008.

Eskola, Timo. *Messiah and the Throne: Jewish Merkabah Mysticism and Early Christian Exaltation Discourse*. Wissenschaftliche Untersuchungen zum Neuen Testament 2.142. Tübingen: Mohr Siebeck, 2001.

Evans, Craig A. "Mishna and Messiah 'in Context': Some Comments on Jacob Neusner's Proposals." *Journal of Biblical Literature* 112 (1993): 267–89.

Eyal, Regev. *The Hasmoneans: Ideology, Archaeology, Identity*. Journal of Ancient Judaism Supplements 10. Göttingen: Vandenhoeck & Ruprecht, 2013.

Falasca-Zamponi, Simonetta. *Fascist Spectacle: The Aesthetics of Power in Mussolini's Italy*. Berkeley: University of California Press, 1997.

Feldman, Louis H. "Introduction." Pages 17–49 in *Josephus, the Bible, and History*. Edited by Louis H. Feldman and Gohei Hata. Leiden: Brill, 1988.

———. "Josephus's Biblical Paraphrases as a Commentary on Contemporary Issues." Pages 124–201 in *The Interpretation of Scripture in Early Judaism and Christianity*. Edited by Craig A. Evans. Journal for the Study of the Pseudepigrapha Supplements 33. Sheffield: Sheffield Academic, 2000.

———. "Josephus's Portrait of David." *Hebrew Union College Annual* 60 (1989): 129–74.

———. "On the Authenticity of the Testimonium Flavianum Attributed to Josephus." Pages 14–30 in *New Perspectives on Jewish-Christian Relations*. Edited by Elisheva Carlebach and Jacob J. Schechter. Brill Reference Library of Judaism 33. Leiden: Brill, 2012.

———. *Philo's Portrayal of Moses in the Context of Ancient Judaism*. Christianity and Judaism in Antiquity Series 15. South Bend, Ind.: University of Notre Dame Press, 2007.

———. "Prophets and Prophecy in Josephus." *Journal of Theological Studies* n.s. 41 (1990): 386–422.

Figal, Günter. "On the Silence of Texts: Toward a Hermeneutic Concept of Interpretation." Pages 1–11 in *For a Philosophy of Freedom and Strife: Politics, Aesthetics, Metaphysics*. Translated by Wayne Klein. Albany, N.Y.: SUNY Press, 1998. [German original 1994.]

Firestone, Reuven. *Holy War in Judaism: The Fall and Rise of a Controversial Idea*. New York: Oxford University Press, 2012.

Fishbane, Michael. *Biblical Interpretation in Ancient Israel*. Oxford: Clarendon, 1985.

———. "Inner-Biblical Exegesis: Types and Strategies." Pages 3–18 in *The Garments of Torah: Essays in Biblical Hermeneutics*. Bloomington, Ind.: Indiana University Press, 1989.

———. "Midrash and Messianism: Some Theologies of Suffering and Salvation." Pages 57–72 in *Toward the Millennium: Messianic Expectations from the Bible to Waco*. Edited by Peter Schäfer and Mark R. Cohen. Studies in the History of Religions 77. Leiden: Brill, 1998.

———. "The 'Measures' of God's Glory in the Ancient Midrash." Pages 53–74 in *Messiah and Christos: Studies in the Jewish Origins of Christianity*. Edited by Ithamar

Gruenwald, Shaul Shaked, and Gedaliahu G. Stroumsa. Texte und Studien zum antiken Judentum 32. Tübingen: Mohr Siebeck, 1992.

Fitzmyer, Joseph A. *The One Who Is to Come*. Grand Rapids: Eerdmans, 2007.

Flanagan, James W. "Chiefs in Israel." *Journal for the Study of the Old Testament* 20 (1981): 47–73.

Fleming, Daniel E. "The Biblical Tradition of Anointing Priests." *Journal of Biblical Literature* 117 (1998): 401–14.

Fletcher-Louis, Crispin H. T. *All the Glory of Adam: Liturgical Anthropology in the Dead Sea Scrolls*. Studies of the Texts of the Desert of Judah 42. Leiden: Brill, 2002.

Flusser, David. "Bericht des Josephus über Jesus." Pages 216–25 in vol. 1 of *Entdeckungen im Neuen Testament*. Neukirchen-Vluyn: Neukirchener, 1987.

———. "Jesus, His Ancestry, and the Commandment of Love." Pages 153–76 in *Jesus' Jewishness: Exploring the Places of Jesus within Early Judaism*. Edited by James H. Charlesworth. New York: Crossroad, 1991.

———. "Jewish Messianism Reflected in the Early Church." Pages 258–88 in vol. 2 of *Judaism of the Second Temple Period*. Translated by Azzan Yadin. 2 vols. Grand Rapids: Eerdmans, 2007–2009.

———. "Josippon." Pages 296–98 in vol. 10 of *Encyclopedia Judaica*. Edited by Cecil Roth and Geoffrey Wigoder. 16 vols. New York: Macmillan, 1971–1972.

———. "Judaism in the Second Temple Period." Pages 6–43 in vol. 2 of *Judaism of the Second Temple Period*. Translated by Azzan Yadin. 2 vols. Grand Rapids: Eerdmans, 2007–2009.

———. "Messianology and Christology in the Epistle to the Hebrews." Pages 246–79 in *Judaism and the Origins of Christianity*. Jerusalem: Magnes, 1988.

Foster, Paul. "Justin and Paul." Pages 108–25 in *Paul and the Second Century*. Edited by Michael F. Bird and Joseph R. Dodson. Library of New Testament Studies 412. London: T. & T. Clark, 2011.

Franklin, Arnold E. *This Noble House: Jewish Descendants of King David in the Medieval Islamic East*. Philadelphia: University of Pennsylvania Press, 2013.

Fredriksen, Paula. *From Jesus to Christ*. 2d ed. New Haven: Yale University Press, 2000.

———. "How Later Contexts Affect Pauline Content, or: Retrospect is the Mother of Anachronism." Pages 17–51 in *Jews and Christians in the First and Second Centuries: How to Write Their History*. Edited by Peter J. Tomson and Joshua Schwartz. Compendia rerum iudaicarum ad Novum Testamentum 13. Leiden: Brill, 2014.

Frey, Jörg. "Critical Issues in the Investigation of the Scrolls and the New Testament." Pages 517–45 in *The Oxford Handbook of the Dead Sea Scrolls*. Edited by Timothy H. Lim and John J. Collins. Oxford: Oxford University Press, 2010.

Freyne, Sean. "The Herodian Period." Pages 29–43 in *Redemption and Resistance: The Messianic Hopes of Jews and Christians in Antiquity*. Edited by Markus Bockmuehl and James Carleton Paget. London: T. & T. Clark, 2007.

Fried, Lisbeth S. "Cyrus the Messiah? The Historical Background to Isaiah 45:1." *Harvard Theological Review* 95 (2002): 373–93.

Frost, S. B. *Old Testament Apocalyptic: Its Origins and Growth.* London: Epworth, 1952.

Fuller, R. H. *The Foundations of New Testament Christology.* New York: Scribner, 1965.

Fuller, Russell. "The Sequence of Malachi 3:22–24 in the Greek and Hebrew Textual Traditions: Implications for the Redactional History of the Minor Prophets." Pages 371–80 in *Perspectives on the Formation of the Book of the Twelve.* Edited by Rainer Albertz, James D. Nogalski, and Jakob Wöhrle. Beihefte zur Zeitschrift für die alttestamentliche Wissenschaft 433. Berlin: De Gruyter, 2012.

Fuhrmann, Christopher J. *Policing the Roman Empire: Soldiers, Administration, and Public Order.* New York: Oxford University Press, 2012.

Gafni, Isaiah M. "The Political, Social, and Economic History of Babylonian Jewry, 224–638 CE." Pages 792–820 in vol. 4 of *Cambridge History of Judaism.* Edited by Steven T. Katz. New York: Cambridge University Press, 2006.

Gager, John G. *Kingdom and Community: The Social World of Early Christianity.* Englewood Cliffs, N.J.: Prentice-Hall, 1975.

———. "Messiahs and Their Followers." Pages 37–46 in *Toward the Millennium: Messianic Expectations from the Bible to Waco.* Edited by Peter Schäfer and Mark R. Cohen. Studies in the History of Religions 77. Leiden: Brill, 1998.

———. *Reinventing Paul.* New York: Oxford University Press, 2000.

Gagg, R. P. "Jesus und die Davidssohnfrage." *Theologische Zeitschrift* 7 (1951): 18–30.

Galsterer, H. "A Man, a Book, and a Method: Sir Ronald Syme's *Roman Revolution* after Fifty Years." Pages 1–20 in *Between Republic and Empire: Interpretations of Augustus and His Principate.* Edited by Kurt A. Raaflaub and Mark Toher. Berkeley: University of California Press, 1990.

García Martínez, Florentino. "Old Texts and Modern Mirages: The 'I' of Two Qumran Hymns." *Ephemerides theologicae lovanienses* 78 (2002): 321–39. [Repr., pages 105–25 in *Qumranica Minora I: Qumran Origins and Apocalypticism.* Edited by Eibert J. C. Tigchelaar. Studies of the Texts of the Desert of Judah 63. Leiden: Brill, 2007.]

Gaston, Lloyd. *Paul and the Torah.* Vancouver: University of British Columbia Press, 1987.

Gero, Stephen. "With Walter Bauer on the Tigris: Encratite Orthodoxy and Libertine Heresy in Syro-Mesopotamian Christianity." Pages 287–307 in *Nag Hammadi, Gnosticism, and Early Christianity.* Edited by Charles W. Hendrick and Robert Hodgson. Cascade, OR: Wipf & Stock, 2005.

Giblet, Jean. "Prophétisme et attente d'un messie prophète dans l'Ancien Testament." Pages 85–129 in *L'Attente du Messie.* Edited by Lucien Cerfaux. Bruges: Desclée de Brouwer, 1958.

Gillingham, S. E. "The Messiah in the Psalms." Pages 209–37 in *King and Messiah in Israel and the Ancient Near East.* Edited by John Day. London: T. & T. Clark, 2013. [First pub. Sheffield: Sheffield Academic, 1998.]

Ginsberg, H. L. "Messiah." Pages 1407–8 in vol. 11 of *Encyclopedia Judaica.* Edited by Cecil Roth and Geoffrey Wigoder. 16 vols. New York: Macmillan, 1971–1972.

Gladigow, Burkhard. "Die sakralen Funktionen der Liktoren: Zum Problem von institutioneller Macht und sakraler Präsentation." *ANRW* 1.2:295–314. Part 1,

Von den Anfängen Roms bis zum Ausgang der Republik. Edited by H. Temporini and W. Haase. Berlin: De Gruyter, 1972.

Goodblatt, David. "Did the Tannaim Support Bar-Kokhba?" *Cathedra* 29 (1983): 6–12 (in Hebrew).

———. *The Monarchic Principle: Studies in Jewish Self-Government in Antiquity.* Texte und Studien zum antiken Judentum 38. Tübingen: Mohr Siebeck, 1994.

Goodenough, E. R. *The Politics of Philo Judaeus: Practice and Theory.* New Haven: Yale University Press, 1939.

Goodman, Martin. "Current Scholarship on the First Revolt." Pages 15–24 in *The First Jewish Revolt: Archaeology, History, and Ideology.* Edited by Andrea M. Berlin and J. Andrew Overman. New York: Routledge, 2002.

———. "Messianism and Politics in the Land of Israel, 66–135 C.E." Pages 149–57 in *Redemption and Resistance: The Messianic Hopes of Jews and Christians in Antiquity.* Edited by Markus Bockmuehl and James Carleton Paget. London: T. & T. Clark, 2007.

———. *State and Society in Roman Galilee, A.D. 132–212.* 2d ed. London: Valentine Mitchell, 2000.

Gordon, Robert P. "Messianism in Ancient Bible Translations in Aramaic and Syriac." Pages 262–73 in *Redemption and Resistance: The Messianic Hopes of Jews and Christians in Antiquity.* Edited by Markus Bockmuehl and James Carleton Paget. London: T. & T. Clark, 2007.

Goren, Yuval. "Micromorphologic Analysis of the Gabriel Revelation Stone." *Israel Exploration Journal* 58 (2008): 220–29.

Gorgulho, L.- B. "Ruth et la 'Fille de Sion,' mère du Messie." *Revue thomiste* 63 (1963): 501–14.

Goulder, Michael. *St. Paul versus St. Peter: A Tale of Two Missions.* Louisville, Ky.: Westminster John Knox, 1995.

Graetz, Heinrich. *History of the Jews.* 6 vols. Edited and translated by Bella Löwy. Philadelphia: Jewish Publication Society, 1891–1898. [Translation of *Geschichte der Juden von den ältesten Zeiten bis auf die Gegenwart.* 11 vols. Leipzig: Leiner, 1861–1875.]

———. "Stages in the Evolution of the Messianic Belief." Pages 151–71 in *The Structure of Jewish History, and Other Essays.* Translated by Ismar Schorsch. Moreshet 3. New York: Jewish Theological Seminary, 1975.

Graham, William Creighton. Review of Hugo Gressmann, *Der Messias. Journal of Religion* 10 (1930): 410–12.

Grant, Robert M. *Irenaeus of Lyons.* London: Routledge, 1997.

———. *Jesus after the Gospels: The Christ of the Second Century.* Louisville, Ky.: Westminster John Knox, 1990.

———. "The Problem of Theophilus." *Harvard Theological Review* 43 (1950): 180–96.

———. "Theophilus of Antioch to Autolycus." *Harvard Theological Review* 40 (1947): 227–56.

Gray, Rebecca. *Prophetic Figures in Late Second Temple Jewish Palestine: The Evidence from Josephus.* New York: Oxford University Press, 1993.

Green, William Scott. "Introduction: Messiah in Judaism: Rethinking the Question." Pages 1–14 in *Judaisms and Their Messiahs at the Turn of the Christian Era.* Edited by Jacob Neusner, William Scott Green, and Ernest Frerichs. Cambridge: Cambridge University Press, 1987.

Greenstone, Julius H. *The Messiah Idea in Jewish History.* Philadelphia: Jewish Publication Society, 1906.

Gressmann, Hugo. *Der Messias.* Edited by Hans Schmidt. Forschungen zur Religion und Literatur des Alten und Neuen Testaments 26. Göttingen: Vandenhoeck & Ruprecht, 1929.

———. "Die ammonitischen Tobiaden." *Sitzungsberichte der Preußischen Akademie der Wissenschaften* 39 (1921): 663–71.

———. *Der Ursprung der israelitisch-jüdischen Eschatologie.* Forschungen zur Religion und Literatur des Alten und Neuen Testaments 6. Göttingen: Vandenhoeck & Ruprecht, 1905.

Griffith, Terry. *Keep Yourselves from Idols: A New Look at 1 John.* Journal for the Study of the New Testament Supplements 233. Sheffield: Sheffield Academic, 2002.

Grillmeier, Aloys. *Christ in Christian Tradition*, vol. 1. Translated by J. S. Bowden. London: Mowbray, 1965.

Gruen, Erich S. *Diaspora: Jews amidst Greeks and Romans.* Cambridge, Mass.: Harvard University Press, 2002.

Grypeou, Emmanouela, and Helen Spurling. *The Book of Genesis in Late Antiquity.* Jewish and Christian Perspectives 24. Leiden: Brill, 2013.

Gunkel, Hermann. *An Introduction to the Psalms.* Translated by James D. Nogalski. Macon, Ga.: Mercer University Press, 1998. [Translation of *Einleitung in die Psalmen.* Gottingen: Vandenhoeck & Ruprecht, 1933.]

Habicht, Christian. "Messianic Elements in the Pre-Christian Greco-Roman World." Pages 47–56 in *Toward the Millennium: Messianic Expectations from the Bible to Waco.* Edited by Peter Schäfer and Mark R. Cohen. Studies in the History of Religions 77. Leiden: Brill, 1998.

Hague, W. V. "The Eschatology of the Apocryphal Scriptures I: The Messianic Hope." *Journal of Theological Studies* 12 (1911): 57–98.

Hahn, Ferdinand. *The Titles of Jesus in Christology: Their History in Early Christianity.* Translated by Harold Knight and George Ogg. London: Lutterworth, 1969. [Translation of *Christologische Hoheitstitel: Ihre Geschichte im frühen Christentum.* Forschungen zur Religion und Literatur des Alten und Neuen Testaments 83. Göttingen: Vandenhoeck & Ruprecht, 1963.]

Häkkinen, Sakari. "Ebionites." Pages 247–78 in *A Companion to Second-Century Christian "Heretics."* Edited by Antti Marjanen and Petri Luomanen. Leiden: Brill, 2008.

Halpern, Baruch. *David's Secret Demons: Messiah, Murderer, Traitor, King.* Grand Rapids: Eerdmans, 2001.

———. "The New Names of Isaiah 62:4: Jeremiah's Reception in the Restoration and the Politics of 'Third Isaiah.'" *Journal of Biblical Literature* 117 (1998): 623–43.

———. "The Rise of Abimelek ben-Jerubbaal." *Hebrew Annual Review* 2 (1978): 79–100.

Hamburger, Jacob. *Real-Encyclopädie des Judentums*. 3d ed. 3 vols. Strelitz, 1905.

Hammerstein, Franz von. *Das Messiasproblem bei Martin Buber*. Stuttgart: Kohlhammer, 1958.

Hanson, Paul D. "Messiahs and Messianic Figures in Proto-Apocalypticism." Pages 67–75 in *The Messiah: Developments in Earliest Judaism and Christianity*. Edited by James H. Charlesworth. Minneapolis: Fortress, 1992.

Harkins, Angela Kim. *Reading with an "I" to the Heavens: Looking at the Qumran Hodayot through the Lens of Visionary Traditions*. Ekstasis 3. Berlin: De Gruyter, 2012.

———. "Who Is the Teacher of the Teacher Hymns? Re-examining the Teacher Hymns Hypothesis Fifty Years Later." Pages 449–67 in vol. 1 of *A Teacher for All Generations: Essays in Honor of James C. VanderKam*. Edited by Eric F. Mason. 2 vols. Journal for the Study of Judaism Supplements 153. Leiden: Brill, 2012.

Harnack, Adolf. "Der jüdische Geschichtsschreiber Josephus und Jesus Christus." *Internationale Monatsschrift für Wissenschaft, Kunst und Technik* 7 (1913): 1037–68.

Harper, Joshua L. *Responding to a Puzzled Scribe: The Barberini Text of Habakkuk 3 Analyzed in the Light of the Other Greek Versions*. Library of Hebrew Bible/Old Testament Studies 608. London: T. & T. Clark, 2015.

Harrington, Daniel. "The Reception of Walter Bauer's *Orthodoxy and Heresy in Earliest Christianity* in the Last Decade." *Harvard Theological Review* 73 (1980): 289–98.

Hata, Gohei. "Is the Greek Version of Josephus' Jewish War a Translation or a Rewriting of the First Version?" *Jewish Quarterly Review* 66 (1975–1976): 89–108.

Hauptman, Judith. *Rereading the Mishnah: A New Approach to Ancient Jewish Texts*. Texte und Studien zum antiken Judentum 109. Tübingen: Mohr Siebeck, 2005.

Hay, David. *Glory at the Right Hand: Psalm 110 in Early Christianity*. Society of Biblical Literature Monograph Series 18. Nashville: Abingdon, 1973.

Hays, Richard B. *The Conversion of the Imagination: Paul as Interpreter of Israel's Scripture*. Grand Rapids: Eerdmans, 2005.

Hayward, C. T. R. "The Date of Targum Pseudo-Jonathan: Some Comments." *Journal of Jewish Studies* 40 (1989): 7–30.

Head, Peter M. "On the Christology of the Gospel of Peter." *Vigiliae Christianae* 46 (1992): 209–24.

Hecht, Richard D. "Philo and Messiah." Pages 139–68 in *Judaisms and Their Messiahs at the Turn of the Christian Era*. Edited by Jacob Neusner, William Scott Green, and Ernest Frerichs. Cambridge: Cambridge University Press, 1987.

Heinemann, Joseph. "The Messiah of Ephraim and the Premature Exodus of the Tribe of Ephraim." *Harvard Theological Review* 68 (1975): 1–15. [Hebrew original in *Tarbiz* 40 (1970–1971): 450–61.]

Helderman, J. "Das Evangelium Veritatis in der neueren Forschung." *ANRW* 25.5:4054–4106. Part 2, *Principat*, 25.5. Edited by H. Temporini and W. Haase. Berlin: De Gruyter, 1988.

Hendel, Ronald. "The Messiah Son of Joseph: Simply 'Sign.'" *Biblical Archaeology Review* 35 (2009): 8.

Hengel, Martin. "Jesus, the Messiah of Israel." Pages 1–72 in *Studies in Early Christology*. Edinburgh: T. & T. Clark, 1995. [German original 1993.]

———. "'Sit at My Right Hand!' The Enthronement of Christ at the Right Hand of God and Psalm 110:1." Pages 119–225 in *Studies in Early Christology*. Edinburgh: T. & T. Clark, 1995. [German original 1993.]

———. *The Zealots*. Translated by David Smith. Edinburgh: T. & T. Clark, 1989. [German original 1961.]

Hengstenberg, Ernst Wilhelm. *Christology of the Old Testament, and a Commentary on the Messianic Predictions*. Translated by Theodore Meyer and James Martin. 4 vols. Edinburgh: T. & T. Clark, 1854–1858. [Translation of *Christologie des Alten Testaments und Commentar über die messianischen Weissagungen der Propheten*. 3 vols. Berlin: Oehmigke, 1829–1835.]

Henze, Matthias, ed. *A Companion to Biblical Interpretation in Early Judaism*. Grand Rapids: Eerdmans, 2012.

Herman, Geoffrey. *A Prince without A Kingdom: The Exilarch in the Sasanian Era*. Texte und Studien zum antiken Judentum 150. Tübingen: Mohr Siebeck, 2012.

Hezser, Catherine. "The Mishnah and Ancient Book Production." Pages 167–92 in *The Mishnah in Contemporary Perspective, Part One*. Edited by Alan J. Avery-Peck and Jacob Neusner. Leiden: Brill, 2002.

———. *The Social Structure of the Rabbinic Movement in Roman Palestine*. Texte und Studien zum antiken Judentum 66. Tübingen: Mohr Siebeck, 1997.

Hiers, Richard H. "The Problem of the Delay of the Parousia in Luke-Acts." *New Testament Studies* 20 (1974): 145–55.

Higgins, A. J. B. "Jewish Messianic Belief in Justin Martyr's *Dialogue with Trypho*." *Novum Testamentum* 9 (1967): 298–305.

———. Review of Sigmund Mowinckel, *He That Cometh*. *Scottish Journal of Theology* 10 (1957): 304–9.

Hill, C. E. "Cerinthus, Gnostic or Chiliast? A New Solution to an Old Problem." *Journal of Early Christian Studies* 8 (2000): 135–72.

———. *From the Lost Teaching of Polycarp*. Wissenschaftliche Untersuchungen zum Neuen Testament 186. Tübingen: Mohr Siebeck, 2006.

———. *Regnum Caelorum: Patterns of Millennial Thought in Early Christianity*. 2d ed. Grand Rapids: Eerdmans, 2001.

Hill, David. "Jesus and Josephus' 'Messianic Prophets.'" Pages 143–54 in *Text and Interpretation: Studies in the New Testament Presented to Matthew Black*. Edited by Ernest Best and R. McL. Wilson. Cambridge: Cambridge University Press, 1979.

Hillers, Delbert R. *Lamentations*. Anchor Bible. New York: Doubleday, 1972.

Himmelfarb, Martha. *A Kingdom of Priests: Ancestry and Merit in Ancient Judaism*. Philadelphia: University of Pennsylvania Press, 2006.

———. "Sefer Zerubbabel and Popular Religion." Pages 621–34 in vol. 2 of *A Teacher for All Generations: Essays in Honor of James C. VanderKam*. Edited by Eric F. Mason. 2 vols. Journal for the Study of Judaism Supplements 153. Leiden: Brill, 2012.

———. "The Messiah Son of Joseph in Ancient Judaism." Pages 771–90 in vol. 2 of *Envisioning Judaism: Studies in Honor of Peter Schäfer*. Edited by Ra'anan S. Boustan, Klaus Herrmann, Reimind Leicht, Annette Yoshiko Reed, and Giuseppe Veltri. 2 vols. Tübingen: Mohr Siebeck, 2013.

———. "The Mother of the Messiah in the Talmud Yerushalmi and Sefer Zerubbabel." Pages 369–89 in vol. 3 of *The Talmud Yerushalmi and Graeco-Roman Culture*. Edited by Peter Schäfer. Texte und Studien zum antiken Judentum 93. Tübingen: Mohr Siebeck, 2002.

Hirshman, Marc. *A Rivalry of Genius: Jewish and Christian Biblical Interpretation in Late Antiquity*. Translated by Batya Stein. Albany, N.Y.: SUNY Press, 1996.

Hodge, Caroline Johnson. *If Sons Then Heirs: A Study of Kinship and Ethnicity in the Letters of Paul*. New York: Oxford University Press, 2007.

Hoenig, Sidney B. "Menahem, Hillel's First Associate." *Bitzaron* 52 (1964–1965): 87–96 (in Hebrew).

Hoffmann, Matthias Reinhard. *The Destroyer and the Lamb: The Relationship between Angelomorphic and Lamb Christology in the Book of Revelation*. Wissenschaftliche Untersuchungen zum Neuen Testament 2.203. Tübingen: Mohr Siebeck, 2005.

Hogeterp, Albert L. A. *Expectations of the End: A Comparative Traditio-Historical Study of Eschatological, Apocalyptic, and Messianic Ideas in the Dead Sea Scrolls and the New Testament*. Studies on the Texts of the Desert of Judah 83. Leiden: Brill, 2009.

Holleman, Joost. *Resurrection and Parousia: A Tradition–Historical Study of Paul's Eschatology in 1 Corinthians 15*. Novum Testamentum Supplements 84. Leiden: Brill, 1996.

Holtzmann, Heinrich Julius. "Die Messiasidee zur Zeit Jesu." *Jahrbuch für deutsche Theologie* (1867): 389–411.

Hooke, S. H. Review of Sigmund Mowinckel, *He That Cometh*. *New Testament Studies* 4 (1958): 227–30.

Horbury, William. "Herod's Temple and 'Herod's Days.'" Pages 83–122 in *Messianism among Jews and Christians*. London: T. & T. Clark, 2003.

———. *Jewish Messianism and the Cult of Christ*. London: SCM, 1998.

———. *Jewish War under Trajan and Hadrian*. Cambridge: Cambridge University Press, 2014.

———. *Messianism among Jews and Christians*. London: T. & T. Clark, 2003.

———. "Messianism among Jews and Christians in the Second Century." *Augustinianum* 28 (1988): 71–88. [Repr., pages 275–88, *Messianism among Jews and Christians.* London: T. & T. Clark, 2003.]

Horner, Timothy J. *Listening to Trypho: Justin Martyr's Dialogue with Trypho Reconsidered.* Contributions to Biblical Exegesis and Theology 28. Leuven: Peeters, 2001.

Horsley, Richard A. "Messianic Figures and Movements in First-Century Palestine." Pages 276–95 in *The Messiah: Developments in Earliest Judaism and Christianity.* Edited by James H. Charlesworth. Minneapolis: Fortress, 1992.

Horsley, Richard A., and John S. Hanson. *Bandits, Prophets, and Messiahs: Popular Movements at the Time of Jesus.* Minneapolis: Winston, 1985.

Horster, Marietta. "Living on Religion: Professionals and Personnel." Pages 331–41 in *A Companion to Roman Religion.* Edited by Jörg Rüpke. Oxford: Blackwell, 2011.

Hunt, Alice. *Missing Priests: The Zadokites in Tradition and History.* Library of Hebrew Bible/Old Testament Studies 452. London: T. & T. Clark, 2006.

Hurwitz, Siegmund. *Die Gestalt des sterbenden Messias.* Studien aus dem C. G. Jung-Institut 8. Zurich: Rascher, 1958.

Idel, Moshe. *Messianic Mystics.* New Haven: Yale University Press, 1998.

Ilan, Tal. "King David, King Herod and Nicolaus of Damascus." *Jewish Studies Quarterly* 3 (1998): 195–240.

Iricinschi, Eduard. "If You Got It, Flaunt It: Religious Advertising in the *Gospel of Philip.*" Pages 253–72 in *Heresy and Identity in Late Antiquity.* Edited by Eduard Iricinschi and Holger M. Zellentin. Texte und Studien zum antiken Judentum 119. Tübingen: Mohr Siebeck, 2008.

Irmscher, Johannes, and Georg Strecker. "The Pseudo-Clementines." Pages 483–541 in vol. 2 of *New Testament Apocrypha.* Edited by Edgar Hennecke and Wilhelm Schneemelcher. Translated by R. McL. Wilson. 2 vols., rev. ed. Cambridge: Clarke, 1992.

Ishida, Tomoo. *The Royal Dynasties in Ancient Israel.* Beihefte zur Zeitschrift für die alttestamentliche Wissenschaft 142. Berlin: De Gruyter, 1977.

Jackson-McCabe, Matt. "What's in a Name? The Problem of 'Jewish Christianity.'" Pages 7–38 in *Jewish Christianity Reconsidered: Rethinking Ancient Groups and Texts.* Edited by Matt Jackson-McCabe. Minneapolis: Fortress, 2007.

Jacobs, Andrew S. "Jews and Christians." Pages 169–85 in *The Oxford Handbook of Early Christian Studies.* Edited by Susan Ashbrook Harvey and David C. Hunter. Oxford: Oxford University Press, 2008.

Jacobs, Martin. *Die Institution des jüdischen Patriarchen.* Texte und Studien zum antiken Judentum 52. Tübingen: Mohr Siebeck, 1995.

Jacobson, David, and Niko Kokkinos, eds. *Herod and Augustus.* IJS Studies in Judaica 6. Leiden: Brill, 2009.

Jaffé, Dan. "Croyances et conceptions messianiques dans la literature talmudique: entre rationalisme et utopie." Pages 173–202 in *Aux origines des messianismes juifs*. Edited by David Hamidović. Vetus Testamentum Supplements 158. Leiden: Brill, 2013.

Japhet, Sara. "Sheshbazzar and Zerubbabel against the Background of the Historical and Religious Tendencies of Ezra-Nehemiah, Part 1." Pages 53–84 in *From the Rivers of Babylon to the Highlands of Judah: Collected Studies on the Restoration Period*. Winona Lake, Ind.: Eisenbrauns, 2006.

Jastrow, Marcus. *A Dictionary of the Targumim, the Talmud Babli and Yerushalmi, and the Midrashic Literature*. New York: Putnam's, 1903.

Jeremias, Gert. *Der Lehrer der Gerechtigkeit*. Studien zur Umwelt des Neuen Testaments 2. Göttingen: Vandenhoeck & Ruprecht, 1963.

Jeremias, Joachim. *Jerusalem in the Time of Jesus*. Philadelphia: Fortress, 1969.

Jeselsohn, David. "The Jeselsohn Stone: Discovery and Publication." Pages 1–9 in *Hazon Gabriel: New Readings of the Gabriel Revelation*. Edited by Matthias Henze. Atlanta: SBL, 2011.

Johnson, Marshall D. *The Purpose of the Biblical Genealogies*. 2d ed. Cambridge: Cambridge University Press, 1969.

Joosten, Jan. "Reflections on the Original Language of the Psalms of Solomon." Pages 31–37 in *The Psalms of Solomon: Language, History, Theology*. Edited by Eberhard Bons and Patrick Pouchelle. Early Judaism and Its Literature 40. Atlanta: Society of Biblical Literature, 2015.

Juel, Donald H. *Messianic Exegesis: Christological Interpretation of the Old Testament in Early Christianity*. Philadelphia: Fortress, 1988.

Kalmin, Richard. "Midrash and Social History." Pages 133–59 in *Current Trends in the Study of Midrash*. Edited by Carol Bakhos. Journal for the Study of Judaism Supplements 106. Leiden: Brill, 2006.

Kamesar, Adam. "Biblical Interpretation in Philo." Pages 65–91 in *The Cambridge Companion to Philo*. Edited by Adam Kamesar. Cambridge: Cambridge University Press, 2009.

Kapelrud, A. S. "König David und die Söhne des Saul." *Zeitschrift für die alttesta-mentliche Wissenschaft* 67 (1955): 198–205.

Karrer, Martin. *Der Gesalbte: Die Grundlagen des Christustitels*. Forschungen zur Religion und Literatur des Alten und Neuen Testaments 151. Göttingen: Vandenhoeck & Ruprecht, 1990.

Kasher, Aryeh. *King Herod: A Persecuted Persecutor*. With Eliezer Witztum. Translated by Karen Gold. Berlin: De Gruyter, 2007.

———. *The Jews in Hellenistic and Roman Egypt*. Texte und Studien zum antiken Judentum 7. Tübingen: Mohr Siebeck, 1985. [Hebrew original 1978.]

Kaufmann, Yehezkel. "The Messianic Idea: The Real and the Hidden Son of David." *Jewish Bible Quarterly* 22 (1994): 141–50. [First pub. 1961.]

Kelley, Nicole. *Knowledge and Religious Authority in the Pseudo-Clementines: Situating the Recognitions in Fourth-Century Syria*. Wissenschaftliche Untersuchungen zum Neuen Testament 2.213. Tübingen: Mohr Siebeck, 2006.

Kerr, Fergus. "The Reception of Wittgenstein's Philosophy by Theologians." Pages 253–72 in *Religion and Wittgenstein's Legacy*. Edited by D. Z. Phillips and Mario von der Ruhr. Surrey: Ashgate, 2005.

Kessler, Rainer. "The Unity of Malachi and Its Relation to the Book of the Twelve." Pages 223–36 in *Perspectives on the Formation of the Book of the Twelve*. Edited by Rainer Albertz, James D. Nogalski, and Jakob Wöhrle. Beihefte zur Zeitschrift für die alttestamentliche Wissenschaft 433. Berlin: De Gruyter, 2012.

Kingsbury, Jack Dean. "The Title 'Son of David' in Matthew's Gospel." *Journal of Biblical Literature* 95 (1976): 591–602.

Kinlaw, Pamela E. *The Christ Is Jesus: Metamorphosis, Possession, and Johannine Christology*. Atlanta: SBL, 2005.

Kister, Menahem. "Divine and Heavenly Figures in the Dead Sea Scrolls." Paper presented at the Fourteenth International Orion Symposium. Jerusalem, 2013.

Kittel, Gerhard, and Gerhard Friedrich, eds. *Theological Dictionary of the New Testament*. Translated by Geoffrey W. Bromiley. 10 vols. Grand Rapids: Eerdmans, 1964–1976.

Kittel, Harald, Armin Paul Frank, and Norbert Greiner, eds. *Übersetzung, Translation, Traduction*, vol. 2. Handbücher zur Sprach- und Kommunikationswissenschaft 26.2. Berlin: De Gruyter, 2007.

Klausner, Joseph. *The Messianic Idea in Israel: From Its Beginning to the Completion of the Mishnah*. Translated from the 3d Hebrew ed. by W. F. Stinespring. New York: Macmillan, 1955.

Klijn, A. F. J., and G. J. Reininck. *Patristic Evidence for Jewish–Christian Sects*. Leiden: Brill, 1973.

Kneebone, Emily. "Josephus' Esther and Diaspora Judaism." Pages 165–82 in *The Romance between Greece and the East*. Edited by Tim Whitmarsh and Stuart Thomson. Cambridge: Cambridge University Press, 2013.

Knight, John Allan. *Liberal versus Postliberal: The Great Divide in Twentieth-Century Theology*. New York: Oxford University Press, 2013.

Knohl, Israel. "'By Three Days, Live': Messiahs, Resurrection, and Ascent to Heaven in Hazon Gabriel." *Journal of Religion* 88 (2008): 147–58.

———. *Messiahs and Resurrection in "The Gabriel Revelation."* London: Continuum, 2009.

———. "On 'the Son of God,' Armilus, and Messiah Son of Joseph." *Tarbiz* 68 (1998): 13–38 (in Hebrew).

———. "Studies in the Gabriel Revelation." *Tarbiz* 76 (2007): 303–28 (in Hebrew).

———. "The Apocalyptic and Messianic Dimensions of the Gabriel Revelation in Their Historical Context." Pages 39–59 in *Hazon Gabriel: New Readings of the Gabriel Revelation*. Edited by Matthias Henze. Atlanta: SBL, 2011.

———. "The Messiah Son of Joseph: 'Gabriel's Revelation' and the Birth of a New Messianic Model." *Biblical Archaeology Review* 34 (2008): 58–62, 78.

———. *The Messiah before Jesus: The Suffering Servant of the Dead Sea Scrolls*. Translated by David Maisel. Berkeley: University of California Press, 2000.

Koester, Helmut. *Synoptische Überlieferung bei den Apostolischen Vätern.* Texte und Untersuchungen zur Geschichte der altchristlichen Literatur 65. Berlin: Akademie Verlag, 1957.

König, Eduard. *Die messianische Weissagungen des Alten Testaments vergleichend, geschichtlich und exegetisch behandelt.* 3d ed. Stuttgart: Belser, 1925.

Kraemer, Joel L. "On Maimonides' Messianic Posture." Pages 109–42 in vol. 2 of *Studies in Medieval Jewish History and Literature.* Edited by Isadore Twersky. Cambridge, Mass.: Harvard University Press, 1984.

Kraft, Robert A. "Barnabas' Isaiah Text and the 'Testimony Book' Hypothesis." *Journal of Biblical Literature* 79 (1960): 336–50.

———. "Para-mania: Beside, Before, and Beyond Bible Studies." *Journal of Biblical Literature* 126 (2007): 5–27.

———. "The Epistle of Barnabas: Its Quotations and Their Sources." Ph.D. diss., Harvard University, 1961.

———. "Was There a 'Messiah–Joshua' Tradition at the Turn of the Era?" IOUDAIOS, 1992.

Krochmal, Nachman. *The Writings of Nachman Krochmal.* Edited by Simon Rawidowicz. London: Ararat, 1961 (in Hebrew).

Kugel, James L. "Early Interpretation: The Common Background of Later Forms of Biblical Exegesis." Pages 9–106 in James L. Kugel and Rowan A. Greer, *Early Biblical Interpretation.* Philadelphia: Westminster, 1986.

———. *How to Read the Bible: A Guide to Scripture, Then and Now.* New York: Free Press, 2007.

———. *The Bible As It Was.* Cambridge, Mass.: Harvard University Press, 1999.

Kugel, James L., and Rowan A. Greer. *Early Biblical Interpretation.* Philadelphia: Westminster, 1986.

Kuhn, K. G. "The Two Messiahs of Aaron and Israel." Pages 54–64 in *The Scrolls and the New Testament.* Edited by Krister Stendahl. New York: Crossroad, 1957. [Repr., 1992.]

Kutsch, Ernst. *Salbung als Rechtsakt im Alten Testament und im Alten Orient.* Beihefte zur Zeitschrift für die alttestamentliche Wissenschaft 87. Berlin: Töpelmann, 1963.

Laato, Antti. *A Star is Rising: The Historical Development of the Old Testament Royal Ideology and the Rise of the Jewish Messianic Expectations.* University of South Florida International Studies in Formative Christianity and Judaism 5. Atlanta: Scholars Press, 1997.

———. *Josiah and David Redivivus: The Historical Josiah and the Messianic Expectations of Exilic and Postexilic Times.* Coniectanea biblica: Old Testament Series 33. Stockholm: Almqvist & Wiksell, 1992.

———. *The Servant of YHWH and Cyrus: A Reinterpretation of the Exilic Messianic Programme in Isaiah 40–55.* Coniectanea biblica: Old Testament Series 35. Stockholm: Almqvist & Wiksell, 1992.

————. *Who Is Immanuel? The Rise and the Foundering of Isaiah's Messianic Expectations.* Åbo: Åbo Academy Press, 1988.

Lake, Kirsopp, and H. J. Cadbury. *The Beginnings of Christianity: The Acts of the Apostles*, vol. 4. London: Macmillan, 1933.

Lampe, G. W. H. *Patristic Greek Lexicon.* Oxford: Clarendon, 1969.

Lane, William L. "Times of Refreshment: A Study of Eschatological Periodization in Judaism and Christianity." Th.D. diss., Harvard Divinity School, 1962.

Lapin, Hayim. *Rabbis as Romans: The Rabbinic Movement in Palestine, 100–400 CE.* New York: Oxford University Press, 2012.

Lawee, Eric. "The Messianism of Isaac Abarbanel." Pages 1–39 in *Jewish Messianism in the Early Modern Period.* Edited by Matt Goldish and Richard Popkin. Dordrecht: Kluwer, 2001.

Le Donne, Anthony. *The Historiographical Jesus: Memory, Typology, and the Son of David.* Waco: Baylor University Press, 2009.

Legaspi, Michael C. *The Death of Scripture and the Rise of Biblical Studies.* New York: Oxford University Press, 2010.

Lenowitz, Harris. *The Jewish Messiahs: From the Galilee to Crown Heights.* New York: Oxford University Press, 1998.

Levenson, Jon D. "The Davidic Covenant and Its Modern Interpreters." *Catholic Biblical Quarterly* 41 (1979): 205–19.

Levey, Samson H. *The Messiah: An Aramaic Interpretation.* Monographs of the Hebrew Union College 2. Cincinnati: Hebrew Union College Press, 1974.

Lévi, Israël. "Le ravissement du Messie à sa naissance." *Revue des Études Juives* 74 (1922): 113–26.

Levin, Yigal. "Jesus, 'Son of God' and 'Son of David': The 'Adoption' of Jesus into the Davidic Line." *Journal for the Study of the New Testament* 28 (2006): 415–42.

Levine, Baruch A. *Numbers 21–36.* Anchor Bible. New York: Doubleday, 2000.

Levy, Jacob. *Neuhebräisches und chaldäisches Wörterbuch über die Talmudim und Midraschim*, vol. 3. Leipzig: Brockhaus, 1883.

Libero, Loretana de. "Fasces." Page 359 in vol. 5 of *Brill's New Pauly.* Edited by Hubert Cancik, Helmuth Schneider, and Manfred Landfester. 22 vols. Leiden: Brill, 2011.

Liddell, H. G., R. Scott, and H. S. Jones. *A Greek–English Lexicon.* 9th ed. with revised supplement. Oxford: Clarendon, 1996.

Liebes, Yehuda. "Appendix: Messianism in Maimonides." Pages 61–64 in *Studies in Jewish Myth and Jewish Mysticism.* Translated by Batya Stein. Albany, N.Y.: SUNY Press, 1993.

Lieu, Judith. "History and Theology in Christian Views of Judaism." Pages 79–96 in *The Jews among Pagans and Christians in the Roman Empire.* Edited by Judith Lieu, John North, and Tessa Rajak. New York: Routledge, 1992.

————. "Messiah and Resistance in the Gospel and Epistles of John." Pages 97–108 in *Redemption and Resistance: The Messianic Hopes of Jews and Christians in*

Antiquity. Edited by Markus Bockmuehl and James Carleton Paget. London: T. & T. Clark, 2007.

———. Review of William Horbury, *Jewish Messianism and the Cult of Christ. Journal of Theological Studies* n.s. 50 (1999): 671–74.

———. *The Theology of the Johannine Epistles.* Cambridge: Cambridge University Press, 1991.

Lightfoot, J. B. *Saint Paul's Epistle to the Galatians.* London: Macmillan, 1865.

Limor, Ora, and Guy G. Stroumsa, eds. *Contra Iudaeos: Ancient and Medieval Polemics between Christians and Jews.* Texts and Studies in Medieval and Early Modern Judaism 10. Tübingen: Mohr Siebeck, 1996.

Lindbeck, George. *The Nature of Doctrine: Religion and Theology in a Postliberal Age.* Philadelphia: Westminster, 1984.

Litwa, M. David. *Iesus Deus: The Early Christian Depiction of Jesus as a Mediterranean God.* Minneapolis: Fortress, 2014.

Liver, Joseph. "The Doctrine of the Two Messiahs in Sectarian Literature in the Time of the Second Commonwealth." *Harvard Theological Review* 52 (1959): 149–85.

Logan, Alastair H. B. "Post-Baptismal Chrismation in Syria: The Evidence of Ignatius, the Didache, and the Apostolic Constitutions." *Journal of Theological Studies* n.s. 49 (1998): 92–108.

Longenecker, Richard N. *The Christology of Early Jewish Christianity.* London: SCM, 1970.

———. "The Melchizedek Argument of Hebrews." Pages 161–85 in *Unity and Diversity in New Testament Theology.* Edited by Robert Allison Guelich. Grand Rapids: Eerdmans, 1978.

Lowrie, Michèle. "Horace and Augustus." Pages 77–90 in *The Cambridge Companion to Horace.* Edited by Stephen Harrison. Cambridge: Cambridge University Press, 2007.

Lowy, S. "The Confutation of Judaism in the Epistle of Barnabas." *Journal of Jewish Studies* 11 (1960): 1–33.

Lucass, Shirley. *The Concept of the Messiah in the Scriptures of Judaism and Christianity.* Library of Second Temple Studies 78. London: T. & T. Clark, 2011.

Lust, Johan. "Msgr. J. Coppens: The Old Testament Scholar." *Ephemerides theologicae lovanienses* 57 (1981): 241–65.

———. "The Greek Version of Balaam's Third and Fourth Oracles: The ΑΝΘΡΩΠΟΣ in Num 24:7 and 17: Messianism and Lexicography." Pages 69–86 in *Messianism and Septuagint: Collected Essays.* Edited by K. Hauspie. Bibliotheca ephemeridum theologicarum lovaniensium 178. Leuven: Peeters, 2004.

Luttikhuizen, Gerard P. "The Suffering Jesus and the Invulnerable Christ in the Gnostic *Apocalypse of Peter.*" Pages 187–99 in *The Apocalypse of Peter.* Edited by Jan. N. Bremmer and Istvan Czachesz. Studies on Early Christian Apocrypha 7. Leuven: Peeters, 2003.

Luz, Ulrich. *Matthew 1–7: A Commentary.* Translated by James E. Crouch. Edited by Helmut Koester. Hermeneia. Minneapolis: Fortress, 2007.

Mack, Burton L. *A Myth of Innocence: Mark and Christian Origins.* Minneapolis: Fortress, 1988.

———. "Why Christos? The Social Reasons." Pages 365–74 in *Redescribing Christian Origins.* Edited by Ron Cameron and Merrill P. Miller. Atlanta: SBL, 2004.

———. "Wisdom Makes a Difference: Alternatives to 'Messianic' Configurations." Pages 15–48 in *Judaisms and Their Messiahs at the Turn of the Christian Era.* Edited by Jacob Neusner, William Scott Green, and Ernest Frerichs. Cambridge: Cambridge University Press, 1987.

MacRae, George. "Messiah and Gospel." Pages 169–85 in *Judaisms and Their Messiahs at the Turn of the Christian Era.* Edited by Jacob Neusner, William Scott Green, and Ernest Frerichs. Cambridge: Cambridge University Press, 1987.

Magness, Jodi. *The Archaeology of the Holy Land: From the Destruction of Solomon's Temple to the Muslim Conquest.* New York: Cambridge University Press, 2012.

Marcus, Joel. "Are You the Messiah-Son-of-God?" *Novum Testamentum* 31 (1989): 125–41.

———. "Birkat Ha-Minim Revisited." *New Testament Studies* 55 (2009): 523–51.

———. "The Once and Future Messiah in Early Christianity and Chabad." *New Testament Studies* 47 (2001): 381–401.

———. *The Way of the Lord: Christological Exegesis of the Old Testament in the Gospel of Mark.* London: T. & T. Clark, 2004.

Marks, Richard G. *The Image of Bar Kokhba in Traditional Jewish Literature: False Messiah and National Hero.* University Park, Pa.: Penn State University Press, 1993.

Markschies, Christoph. "Kerinth: Wer war er und was lehrte er?" *Jahrbuch für Antike und Christentum* 41 (1998): 48–76.

Marshall, Anthony J. "Symbols and Showmanship in Roman Public Life: The Fasces." *Phoenix* 38 (1984): 120–41.

Marshall, John W. *Parables of War: Reading John's Jewish Apocalypse.* Études sur le christianisme et le judaïsme 10. Waterloo, Ont.: Wilfrid Laurier University Press, 2001.

Martin, Dale B. "Paul and the Judaism/Hellenism Dichotomy: Toward a Social History of the Question." Pages 29–61 in *Paul beyond the Judaism/Hellenism Divide.* Edited by Troels Engberg-Pedersen. Louisville, Ky.: Westminster John Knox, 2001.

Martyn, J. Louis. *History and Theology in the Fourth Gospel.* 3d ed. Louisville, Ky.: Westminster John Knox, 2003.

———. *Theological Issues in the Letters of Paul.* London: T. & T. Clark, 2005. [First pub. 1997.]

Mason, Eric F. *You Are a Priest Forever: Second Temple Jewish Messianism and the Priestly Christology of the Epistle to the Hebrews.* Studies on the Texts of the Desert of Judah 74. Leiden: Brill, 2008.

Mason, Rex. "The Messiah in the Postexilic Old Testament Literature." Pages 338–64 in *King and Messiah in Israel and the Ancient Near East.* Edited by John Day. London: T. & T. Clark, 2013. [First pub. Sheffield: Sheffield Academic, 1998.]

Mason, Steve. *A History of the Jewish War, A.D. 66–74*. Cambridge: Cambridge University Press, 2016.

Matthews, Elaine. "Names, personal, Greek." Pages 1022–24 in *Oxford Classical Dictionary*. Edited by Simon Hornblower and Antony Spawforth. 3d ed. Oxford: Clarendon, 1996.

McCant, J. W. "The Gospel of Peter: Docetism Reconsidered." *New Testament Studies* 30 (1984): 258–73.

McCarter, P. Kyle. "The Apology of David." *Journal of Biblical Literature* 99 (1980): 489–504.

Meeks, Wayne A. "Moses as God and King." Pages 354–71 in *Religions in Antiquity: Essays in Memory of Erwin Ramsdell Goodenough*. Edited by Jacob Neusner. Leiden: Brill, 1968.

———. Review of William Horbury, *Messianism among Jews and Christians*. *Jewish Quarterly Review* 95 (2005): 336–40.

———. *The Prophet–King: Moses Traditions and the Johannine Christology*. Novum Testamentum Supplements 14. Leiden: Brill, 1967.

Meier, John P. "From Elijah-like Prophet to Royal Davidic Messiah." Pages 45–83 in *Jesus: A Colloquium in the Holy Land*. Edited by James D. G. Dunn and Doris Donnelly. London: Continuum, 2001.

Mendelson, Alan. "Philo's Dialectic of Reward and Punishment." *Studia Philonica Annual* 9 (1997): 104–25.

Merrills, Andy. "Isidore's *Etymologies*: On Words and Things." Pages 301–24 in *Encyclopaedism from Antiquity to the Renaissance*. Edited by Jason König and Greg Woolf. Cambridge: Cambridge University Press, 2013.

Meyer, Rudolf. *Der Prophet aus Galiläa: Studie zum Jesusbild der drei ersten Evangelien*. Darmstadt: Wissenschaftliche Buchgesellschaft, 1970.

Michel, Otto. "Studien zu Josephus: Simon bar Giora." *New Testament Studies* 14 (1967–1968): 402–8.

Mildenberg, Leo. *The Coinage of the Bar Kokhba War*. Zurich: Schweizerische Numismatische Gesellschaft, 1984.

Milgrom, Jacob. *Numbers*. Philadelphia: Jewish Publication Society, 1990.

———. "The Antiquity of the Priestly Source: A Reply to Joseph Blenkinsopp." *Zeitschrift für die alttestamentliche Wissenschaft* 111 (1999): 10–22.

Miller, Eric. "The Self-Glorification Hymn Reexamined." *Henoch* 31 (2009): 307–24.

Miller, J. M. "Saul's Rise to Power." *Catholic Biblical Quarterly* 36 (1974): 157–74.

Miller, Merrill P. "How Jesus Became Christ: Probing a Thesis." *Continuum* 2 (1993): 243–70.

———. "The Anointed Jesus." Pages 375–416 in *Redescribing Christian Origins*. Edited by Ron Cameron and Merrill P. Miller. Atlanta: SBL, 2004.

———. "The Problem of the Origins of a Messianic Conception of Jesus." Pages 301–36 in *Redescribing Christian Origins*. Edited by Ron Cameron and Merrill P. Miller. Atlanta: SBL, 2004.

Mimouni, Simon C. "Jésus: Messie Fils de David et Messie Fils d'Aaron." Pages 145–72 in *Aux origines des messianismes juifs*. Edited by David Hamidović. Vetus Testamentum Supplements 158. Leiden: Brill, 2013.

Mitchell, David C. "A Dying and Rising Josephite Messiah in 4Q372." *Journal for the Study of the Pseudepigrapha* (2008): 181–205.

———. "Firstborn Shor and Rem: A Sacrificial Josephite Messiah in 1 Enoch 90.37–38 and Deuteronomy 33.17." *Journal for the Study of the Pseudepigrapha* 15 (2006): 211–28.

———. "Messiah bar Ephraim in the Targums." *Aramaic Studies* 4 (2006): 221–41.

———. "Messiah ben Joseph: A Sacrifice of Atonement for Israel." *Review of Rabbinic Judaism* 10 (2007): 77–94.

———. "Rabbi Dosa and the Rabbis Differ: Messiah ben Joseph in the Babylonian Talmud." *Review of Rabbinic Judaism* 8 (2005): 77–90.

———. "The Fourth Deliverer: A Josephite Messiah in 4Q175." *Biblica* 86 (2005): 545–53.

Mitchell, J. B. *Chrestos: A Religious Epithet, Its Import and Influence*. London: Williams & Norgate, 1880.

Moffitt, David M. *Atonement and the Logic of Resurrection in the Epistle to the Hebrews*. Novum Testamentum Supplements 141. Leiden: Brill, 2011.

Momigliano, Arnaldo. "What Josephus Did Not See." Translated by Joanna Weinberg. Pages 108–19 in *On Pagans, Jews, and Christians*. Middletown, Conn.: Wesleyan University Press, 1987.

Moore, George Foot. *Judaism in the First Centuries of the Christian Era*. 3 vols. Cambridge, Mass.: Harvard University Press, 1927–1930.

Moore, Stephen, and Yvonne Sherwood. *The Invention of the Biblical Scholar: A Critical Manifesto*. Minneapolis: Fortress, 2011.

Mor, Menahem. *The Second Jewish Revolt: The Bar Kokhba War, 132–136 C.E.* Brill Reference Library of Judaism 50. Leiden: Brill, 2016.

Morgan, Michael L., and Steven Weitzman, eds. *Rethinking the Messianic Idea in Judaism*. Bloomington: Indiana University Press, 2014.

Mortensen, Beverly P. "Pseudo-Jonathan's Temple, Symbol of Judaism." Pages 129–37 in *Targum and Scripture: Studies in Aramaic Translation and Interpretation in Memory of Ernest G. Clarke*. Edited by Paul V. M. Flesher. Leiden: Brill, 2002.

Mowinckel, Sigmund. *He That Cometh: The Messiah Concept in the Old Testament and Later Judaism*. Translated by G. W. Anderson. Grand Rapids: Eerdmans, 2005. [First pub. Abingdon, 1956. Translation of *Han som kommer* (Copenhagen: Gad, 1951).]

———. "Die Vorstellungen des Spätjudentums vom heiligen Geist als Fürsprecher johanneische Paraklet." *Zeitschrift für die neutestamentliche Wissenschaft und die Kunde der älteren Kirche* 32 (1933): 97–130.

———. *The Psalms in Israel's Worship*. Translated by D. R. Ap-Thomas. 2 vols. Grand Rapids: Eerdmans, 2004. [First pub. Oxford: Blackwell, 1962.]

Bibliography

Mroczek, Eva. "The Hegemony of the Biblical in the Study of Second Temple Literature." *Journal of Ancient Judaism* 6 (2015): 2–35.

Muilenburg, James. Review of Sigmund Mowinckel, *He That Cometh. Journal of Biblical Literature* 76 (1957): 243–46.

Munier, Charles. "Initiation chrétienne et rites d'onction (IIe–IIIe siècles)." *Recherches de science religieuse* 64 (1990): 115–25.

Myllykoski, Matti. "Cerinthus." Pages 213–46 in *A Companion to Second-Century Christian "Heretics."* Edited by Antti Marjanen and Petri Luomanen. Leiden: Brill, 2008.

Najman, Hindy. "A Written Copy of the Law of Nature: An Unthinkable Paradox." *Studia Philonica Annual* 15 (2003): 54–63.

———. "The Law of Nature and the Authority of the Mosaic Law." *Studia Philonica Annual* 11 (1999): 55–73.

———. "The Vitality of Scripture within and beyond the 'Canon.'" *Journal for the Study of Judaism* 43 (2012): 497–518.

Nasrallah, Laura Salah. *Christian Responses to Roman Art and Architecture: The Second-Century Church amid the Spaces of Empire.* New York: Cambridge University Press, 2010.

Neugebauer, Fritz. "Die Davidssohnfrage und der Menschensohn." *New Testament Studies* 21 (1974): 81–108.

Neusner, Jacob. *History of the Jews in Babylonia*, vol. 3. Leiden: Brill, 1968.

———. *Judaism: The Evidence of the Mishnah.* Brown Judaic Studies 129. Atlanta: Scholars Press, 1988.

———. *Messiah in Context: Israel's History and Destiny in Formative Judaism.* Philadelphia: Fortress, 1984.

———. "Mishnah and Messiah." Pages 265–82 in *Judaisms and Their Messiahs at the Turn of the Christian Era.* Edited by Jacob Neusner, William Scott Green, and Ernest Frerichs. Cambridge: Cambridge University Press, 1987.

———. "Preface." Pages ix–xiv in *Judaisms and Their Messiahs at the Turn of the Christian Era.* Edited by Jacob Neusner, William Scott Green, and Ernest Frerichs. Cambridge: Cambridge University Press, 1987.

———. *The Rabbinic Traditions about the Pharisees before 70.* 3 vols. Leiden: Brill, 1971.

———. *There We Sat Down: Talmudic Judaism in the Making.* Nashville: Abingdon, 1978.

Neusner, Jacob, William Scott Green, and Ernest Frerichs, eds. *Judaisms and Their Messiahs at the Turn of the Christian Era.* Cambridge: Cambridge University Press, 1987.

Newsom, Carol A. *The Self as Symbolic Space: Constructing Identity and Community at Qumran.* Studies of the Texts of the Desert of Judah 52. Leiden, Brill, 2004.

Nickelsburg, George W. E. *Jewish Literature between the Bible and the Mishnah.* Philadelphia: Fortress, 1981.

Niebuhr, Karl-Wilhelm. "Jesus Christus und die vielfältigen messianischen Erwartungen Israels: Ein Forschungsbericht." *Jahrbuch für biblische Theologie* 8 (1993): 337–46.

Niebuhr, Reinhold. "Martin Buber: 1878–1965." *Christianity and Crisis* 25 (1965): 146–47.

Niehoff, Maren. *Philo on Jewish Identity and Culture.* Texte und Studien zum antiken Judentum 86. Tübingen: Mohr Siebeck, 2001.

Niemann, Hermann Michael. "Choosing Brides for the Crown-Prince: Matrimonial Politics in the Davidic Dynasty." *Vetus Testamentum* 56 (2006): 225–38.

Niese, Benedikt. *De Testimonio Christiano quod est apud Iosephum ant. Iud. XVIII, 63 sq. disputatio.* Marburg: Friedrich, 1894.

Nodet, Etienne. "The Sabbath and War." Pages 63–92 in *A Search for the Origins of Judaism: From Joshua to the Mishnah.* Sheffield: Sheffield Academic, 1997. [French original 1992.]

Norden, Eduard. "Josephus und Tacitus über Jesus Christus und eine messianische Prophetie." *Neue Jahrbücher für das klassische Altertum* 16 (1913): 637–66.

Norderval, Øyvind. "Simplicity and Power: Tertullian's *De Baptismo.*" Pages 947–72 in vol. 2 of *Ablution, Initiation, and Baptism: Late Antiquity, Early Judaism, and Early Christianity.* Edited by David Hellholm, Tor Vegge, Øyvind Norderval, and Christer Hellholm. 3 vols. Beihefte zur Zeitschrift für die neutestamentliche Wissenschaft 176. Berlin: De Gruyter, 2011.

Noth, Martin. "Office and Vocation in the Old Testament." Pages 229–49 in *The Laws in the Pentateuch and Other Essays.* Translated by D. R. Ap-Thomas. Edinburgh: Oliver & Boyd, 1966.

Novak, David. "Maimonides' Concept of the Messiah." *Journal of Religious Studies* 9 (1982): 42–50.

Novenson, Matthew V. *Christ among the Messiahs: Christ Language in Paul and Messiah Language in Ancient Judaism.* New York: Oxford University Press, 2012.

———. "Jewish Messiahs, the Pauline Christ, and the Gentile Question." *Journal of Biblical Literature* 128 (2009): 357–73.

———. "The Messiah ben Abraham in Galatians: A Response to Joel Willits." *Journal for the Study of Paul and His Letters* 2 (2012): 163–70.

———. "Why Does R. Akiba Acclaim Bar Kokhba as Messiah?" *Journal for the Study of Judaism* 40 (2009): 551–72.

Oegema, Gerbern. *The Anointed and His People: Messianic Expectations from the Maccabees to Bar Kokhba.* Journal for the Study of the Pseudepigrapha Supplements 27. Sheffield: Sheffield Academic, 1998. [Translation of *Der Gesalbte und sein Volk: Untersuchungen zum Konzeptualisierungsprozess der messianischen Erwartungen von den Makkabäern bis Bar Koziba.* Schriften des Institutum Judaicum Delitzschianum 2. Göttingen: Vandenhoeck & Ruprecht, 1994.]

Oesterley, W. O. E. *The Evolution of the Messianic Idea: A Study in Comparative Religion.* New York: Dutton, 1908.

Olson, Ken. "A Eusebian Reading of the Testimonium Flavianum." Pages 97–114 in *Eusebius of Caesarea: Tradition and Innovations*. Edited by Aaron Johnson and Jeremy Schott. Hellenic Studies Series 60. Cambridge, Mass.: Harvard University Press, 2013.

———. "Eusebius and the Testimonium Flavianum." *Catholic Biblical Quarterly* 61 (1999): 305–22.

O'Neill, J. C. "The Mocking of Bar Kokhba and of Jesus." *Journal for the Study of Judaism* 31 (2000): 39–41.

Oppenheimer, Aharon. "Betar als Zentrum vor dem Bar-Kochba-Aufstand." Pages 303–19 in *Between Rome and Babylon*. Texte und Studien zum antiken Judentum 108. Tübingen: Mohr Siebeck, 2005.

———. "Leadership and Messianism in the Time of the Mishnah." Pages 152–68 in *Eschatology in the Bible and in Jewish and Christian Tradition*. Edited by Henning Graf Reventlow. Journal for the Study of the Old Testament Supplements 243. Sheffield: Sheffield Academic, 1997.

Osborn, Eric. *Tertullian: First Theologian of the West*. Cambridge: Cambridge University Press, 1997.

Pagels, Elaine. "Ritual in the Gospel of Philip." Pages 280–91 in *The Nag Hammadi Library after Fifty Years*. Edited by John D. Turner and Anne McGuire. Nag Hammadi and Manichaean Studies 44. Leiden: Brill, 1997.

Pomykala, Kenneth E. *The Davidic Dynasty Tradition in Early Judaism: Its History and Significance for Messianism*. Early Judaism and Its Literature 7. Atlanta: Scholars Press, 1995.

Puech, Émile. *La croyance des Esséniens en la vie future: Immortalité, résurrection, vie éternelle?* 2 vols. Etudes bibliques 21–22. Paris: Gabalda, 1993.

———. "Préséance sacerdotale et Messie-Roi dans la Règle de la Congrégation (1QSa ii 11–22)." *Revue de Qumran* 16 (1995): 351–65.

Pummer, Reinhard. *The Samaritans in Flavius Josephus*. Texte und Studien zum antiken Judentum 129. Tübingen: Mohr Siebeck, 2009.

Quinn, Esther C. *The Quest of Seth for the Oil of Life*. Chicago: University of Chicago Press, 1962.

Rabin, Chaim. "The Translation Process and the Character of the Septuagint." *Textus* 6 (1968): 1–26.

Rajak, Tessa. "Cio che Flavio Giuseppe Vide: Josephus and the Essenes." Pages 219–40 in *The Jewish Dialogue with Greece and Rome: Studies in Cultural and Social Interaction*. Leiden: Brill, 2001.

———. "Hasmonean Kingship and the Invention of Tradition." Pages 39–60 in *The Jewish Dialogue with Greece and Rome: Studies in Cultural and Social Interaction*. Leiden: Brill, 2001.

———. "Jewish Millenarian Expectations." Pages 164–88 in *The First Jewish Revolt: Archaeology, History, and Ideology*. Edited by Andrea M. Berlin and J. Andrew Overman. New York: Routledge, 2002.

———. *Josephus: The Historian and His Society*. London: Duckworth, 1983.

———. "Talking at Trypho: Christian Apologetic as Anti-Judaism in Justin's Dialogue with Trypho the Jew." Pages 59–80 in *Apologetics in the Roman Empire: Pagans, Jews, and Christians*. Edited by Mark Edwards, Martin Goodman, and Simon Price. Oxford: Oxford University Press, 1999.

———. *Translation and Survival: The Greek Bible of the Ancient Jewish Diaspora*. Oxford: Oxford University Press, 2009.

Rappaport, Uriel. "John of Gischala: From Galilee to Jerusalem." *Journal of Jewish Studies* 33 (1982): 479–93.

Rasimus, Tuomas. *Paradise Reconsidered in Gnostic Mythmaking*. Nag Hammadi and Manichaean Studies 68. Brill, 2009.

Reed, Annette Yoshiko. "'Jewish Christianity' after the 'Parting of the Ways': Approaches to Historiography and Self-Definition in the Pseudo-Clementine Literature." Pages 188–231 in *The Ways that Never Parted*. Edited by Adam H. Becker and Annette Yoshiko Reed. Texte und Studien zum antiken Judentum 95. Tübingen: Mohr Siebeck, 2003.

———. "Messianism between Judaism and Christianity." Pages 23–62 in *Rethinking the Messianic Idea in Judaism*. Edited by Michael L. Morgan and Steven Weitzman. Bloomington: Indiana University Press, 2014.

———. "The Modern Invention of 'Old Testament Pseudepigrapha.'" *Journal of Theological Studies* n.s. 60 (2009): 403–36.

Reed, Annette Yoshiko, and Adam H. Becker. "Introduction." Pages 1–34 in *The Ways that Never Parted*. Edited by Adam H. Becker and Annette Yoshiko Reed. Texte und Studien zum antiken Judentum 95. Tübingen: Mohr Siebeck, 2003.

Reimer, David J. "Old Testament Christology." Pages 380–400 in *King and Messiah in Israel and the Ancient Near East*. Edited by John Day. London: T. & T. Clark, 2013. [First pub. Sheffield: Sheffield Academic, 1998.]

Reinhartz, Adele. "Rabbinic Perceptions of Simeon bar Kosiba." *Journal for the Study of Judaism* 20 (1989): 171–94.

———."The Johannine Community and Its Jewish Neighbors: A Reappraisal." Pages 111–38 in *What Is John? Readers and Readings of the Fourth Gospel*. Edited by Fernando F. Segovia. Atlanta: Scholars Press, 1996.

Renan, Ernest. *Histoire du Peuple d'Israël*. 5 vols. Paris: Calmann Lévy, 1887–1893.

Rendsburg, Gary A. "Linguistic and Stylistic Notes to the Hazon Gabriel Inscription." *Dead Sea Discoveries* 16 (2009): 107–16.

Richardson, H. Neil. Review of Sigmund Mowinckel, *He That Cometh*. *Journal of Bible and Religion* 26 (1958): 135–37.

Ringgren, Helmer. "Mowinckel and the Uppsala School." *Scandinavian Journal of the Old Testament* 2 (1988): 36–41.

———. *The Messiah in the Old Testament*. Studies in Biblical Theology 18. Chicago: Allenson, 1956.

Roberts, J. J. M. *Nahum, Habakkuk, and Zephaniah*. Old Testament Library. Louisville, Ky.: Westminster John Knox, 1991.

———. "The Davidic Origin of the Zion Tradition." Pages 313–30 in *The Bible and Ancient Near East*. Winona Lake, Ind.: Eisenbrauns, 2002.

———. "The Old Testament's Contribution to Messianic Expectations." Pages 39–51 in *The Messiah: Developments in Earliest Judaism and Christianity*. Edited by James H. Charlesworth. Minneapolis: Fortress, 1992.

———. "Zion in the Theology of the Davidic–Solomomic Empire." Pages 331–47 in *The Bible and Ancient Near East*. Winona Lake, Ind.: Eisenbrauns, 2002.

Robinson, J. A. T. *Jesus and His Coming: The Emergence of a Doctrine*. London: SCM, 1957.

———. "The Most Primitive Christology of All?" *Journal of Theological Studies* n.s. 7 (1956): 177–89.

Rocca, Samuel. "Josephus and the Psalms of Solomon on Herod's Messianic Aspirations: An Interpretation." Pages 313–33 in *Making History: Josephus and Historical Method*. Edited by Zuleika Rodgers. Journal for the Study of Judaism Supplements 110. Leiden: Brill, 2007.

Rokeah, David. *Justin Martyr and the Jews*. Jewish and Christian Perspectives 5. Leiden: Brill, 2002.

Römer, Thomas. "Les interrogations sur l'avenir de la dynastie davidique aux époques babylonienne et perse et les origines d'une attente messianique dans les textes de la Bible hébraïque." Pages 47–59 in *Aux origines des messianismes juifs*. Edited by David Hamidović. Vetus Testamentum Supplements 158. Leiden: Brill, 2013.

Rooke, Deborah W. "Kingship as Priesthood: The Relationship between the High Priesthood and the Monarchy." Pages 198–206 in *King and Messiah in Israel and the Ancient Near East*. Edited by John Day. London: T. & T. Clark, 2013. [First pub. Sheffield: Sheffield Academic, 1998.]

———. *Zadok's Heirs: The Role and Development of the High Priesthood in Ancient Israel*. Oxford: Clarendon, 2000.

Rorty, Richard. "The Historiography of Philosophy: Four Genres." Pages 49–75 in *Philosophy in History*. Edited by Richard Rorty, J. B. Schneewind, and Quentin Skinner. Cambridge: Cambridge University Press, 1984.

Rose, Wolter H. *Zemah and Zerubbabel: Messianic Expectations in the Early Postexilic Period*. Journal for the Study of the Old Testament Supplements 304. Sheffield: Sheffield Academic, 2000.

Rösel, Martin. "Jakob, Bileam und der Messias." Pages 151–76 in *The Septuagint and Messianism*. Edited by M. A. Knibb. Bibliotheca ephemeridum theologicarum lovaniensium 195. Leuven: Peeters, 2006.

Rosenthal, Keith. "Rethinking the Messianological Vacuum: The Prevalence of Jewish Messianism during the Second Temple Period." Ph.D. diss., Graduate Theological Union, 2006.

Rost, Leonhard. *The Succession to the Throne of David.* Translated by M. D. Rutter and D. M. Gunn. London: Bloomsbury, 2015. [Translation of *Die Überlieferung von der Thronnachfolge Davids.* Stuttgart: Kohlhammer, 1926.]

Roth, Cecil. "The Disputation of Barcelona (1263)." *Harvard Theological Review* 43 (1950): 117–44.

Rowley, H. H. "The Herodians in the Gospels." *Journal of Theological Studies* 41 (1940): 14–27.

Runia, David T. "God and Man in Philo of Alexandria." *Journal of Theological Studies* n.s. 39 (1988): 48–75.

———. *Philo of Alexandria and the Timaeus of Plato.* Philosophia Antiqua 44. Leiden: Brill, 1986.

Sabugal, S. "El titulo Messias-Christos en el contexto del relato sobre l'actividad de Jesús in Samaría." *Augustinianum* 12 (1972): 79–105.

Saebo, Magne. "On the Relationship between 'Messianism' and 'Eschatology' in the Old Testament: An Attempt at a Terminological and Factual Clarification." Pages 197–231 in *On the Way to Canon: Creative Tradition History in the Old Testament.* Journal for the Study of the Old Testament Supplements 191. Sheffield: Sheffield Academic, 1998.

Salters, R. B. *Lamentations.* International Critical Commentary. London: T. & T. Clark, 2010.

Salvesen, Alison. "The Trappings of Royalty in Ancient Hebrew." Pages 119–41 in *King and Messiah in Israel and the Ancient Near East.* Edited by John Day. London: T. & T. Clark, 2013. [First pub. Sheffield: Sheffield Academic, 1998.]

Samely, Alexander. *Rabbinic Interpretation of Scripture in the Mishnah.* Oxford: Oxford University Press, 2002.

Sanders, E. P. *Jewish Law from Jesus to the Mishnah: Five Studies.* London: SCM, 1990.

Sandnes, Karl Olav. "Seal and Baptism in Early Christianity." Pages 1441–81 in vol. 2 of *Ablution, Initiation, and Baptism: Late Antiquity, Early Judaism, and Early Christianity.* Edited by David Hellholm, Tor Vegge, Øyvind Norderval, and Christer Hellholm. 3 vols. Beihefte zur Zeitschrift für die neutestamentliche Wissenschaft 176. Berlin: De Gruyter, 2011.

Savignac, J. de. "Le Messianisme de Philon d'Alexandrie." *Novum Testamentum* 4 (1960): 319–24.

Schäfer, Peter. "Bar Kokhba and the Rabbis." Pages 1–22 in *The Bar Kokhba War Reconsidered.* Edited by Peter Schäfer. Texte und Studien zum antiken Judentum 100. Tübingen: Mohr Siebeck, 2003.

———. *Der Bar Kokhba-Aufstand: Studien zum zweiten jüdischen Krieg gegen Rom.* Texte und Studien zum antiken Judentum 1. Tübingen: Mohr Siebeck, 1981.

———. "Diversity and Interaction: Messiahs in Early Judaism." Pages 15–35 in *Toward the Millennium: Messianic Expectations from the Bible to Waco.* Edited by Peter Schäfer and Mark R. Cohen. Studies in the History of Religions 77. Leiden: Brill, 1998.

——. *Jesus in the Talmud*. Princeton: Princeton University Press, 2007.

——. "Rabbi Aqiva and Bar Kokhba." Pages 113–30 in *Approaches to Ancient Judaism*, vol. 2. Edited by William S. Green. Chico, Calif.: Scholars Press, 1980.

——. "Rabbis and Priests, or: How to Do Away with the Glorious Past of the Sons of Aaron." Pages 155–72 in *Antiquity in Antiquity: Jewish and Christian Pasts in the Greco-Roman World*. Edited by Gregg Gardner and Kevin L. Osterloh. Texte und Studien zum antiken Judentum 123. Tübingen: Mohr Siebeck, 2008.

——, ed. *The Bar Kokhba War Reconsidered*. Texte und Studien zum antiken Judentum 100. Tübingen: Mohr Siebeck, 2003.

——. *The Hidden and Manifest God: Some Major Themes in Early Jewish Mysticism*. Translated by Aubrey Pomerance. Albany, N.Y.: SUNY Press, 1992.

——. *The History of the Jews in Antiquity: The Jews of Palestine from Alexander the Great to the Arab Conquest*. Luxembourg: Harwood, 1995. [Translation of *Geschichte der Juden in der Antike*. Stuttgart: Katholisches Bibelwerk, 1983.]

——. *The Jewish Jesus: How Judaism and Christianity Shaped Each Other*. Princeton: Princeton University Press, 2012.

——. *The Origins of Jewish Mysticism*. Tübingen: Mohr Siebeck, 2009.

Schäfer, Peter, and Mark R. Cohen, eds. *Toward the Millennium: Messianic Expectations from the Bible to Waco*. Studies in the History of Religions 77. Leiden: Brill, 1998.

Schalit, Abraham. *König Herodes: Der Mann und Sein Werk*. Berlin: De Gruyter, 1969.

Schall, Anton. *Studien über griechische Fremdwörter im Syrischen*. Darmstadt: Wissenschaftliche Buchgesellschaft, 1960.

Schaper, Joachim. "The Persian Period." Pages 3–14 in *Redemption and Resistance: The Messianic Hopes of Jews and Christians in Antiquity*. Edited by Markus Bockmuehl and James Carleton Paget. London: T. & T. Clark, 2007.

Schiffman, Lawrence H. "Messianism and Apocalypticism in Rabbinic Texts." Pages 1053–72 in vol. 4 of *Cambridge History of Judaism*. Edited by Steven T. Katz. New York: Cambridge University Press, 2006.

——. *Reclaiming the Dead Sea Scrolls*. Philadelphia: Jewish Publication Society, 1994.

——. "The Eschatological Community of the *Serekh Ha-ʿEdah*." *Proceedings of the American Academy for Jewish Research* 51 (1984): 105–29.

——. *The Halakhah at Qumran*. Leiden: Brill, 1975.

Schneider, Gerhard. "Die Davidssohnfrage." *Biblica* 53 (1972): 65–90.

Schnelle, Udo. *Antidocetic Christology in the Gospel of John*. Translated by Linda Maloney. Minneapolis: Fortress, 1992.

——. "Salbung, Geist, und Taufe im 1. Johannesbrief." Pages 629–54 in vol. 1 of *Ablution, Initiation, and Baptism: Late Antiquity, Early Judaism, and Early Christianity*. Edited by David Hellholm, Tor Vegge, Øyvind Norderval, and Christer Hellholm. 3 vols. Beihefte zur Zeitschrift für die neutestamentliche Wissenschaft 176. Berlin: De Gruyter, 2011.

Schniedewind, William M. *Society and the Promise to David*. New York: Oxford University Press, 1999.

Schofield, Alison, and James C. VanderKam. "Were the Hasmoneans Zadokites?" *Journal of Biblical Literature* 124 (2005): 73–87.

Scholem, Gershom. *The Messianic Idea in Judaism and Other Essays on Jewish Spirituality.* New York: Schocken, 1971.

———. "Toward an Understanding of the Messianic Idea in Judaism." Pages 1–36 in *The Messianic Idea in Judaism and Other Essays on Jewish Spirituality.* New York: Schocken, 1971. [Translation of "Zum Verständnis der messianischen Idee im Judentum." *Eranos Jahrbuch* 28 (1959): 173–239. Repr. in pages 7–74 of *Judaica,* vol. 1. Frankfurt: Suhrkamp, 1963.]

Schreiber, Stefan. *Gesalbter und König: Titel und Konzeptionen der königlichen Gesalbtenerwartung in frühjüdischen und urchristlichen Schriften.* Beihefte zur Zeitschrift für die neutestamentliche Wissenschaft 105. Berlin: De Gruyter, 2000.

Schürer, Emil. "Josephus." *Realenzyklopädie für die protestantische Theologie und Kirche* 9 (1901): 377–86.

———. *The History of the Jewish People in the Age of Jesus Christ.* Revised and edited by Geza Vermes, Fergus Millar, and Matthew Black. 3 vols. Edinburgh: T. & T. Clark, 1973–1987. [Translation of *Geschichte des jüdischen Volkes im Zeitalter Jesu Christi.* 3d and 4th ed. Leipzig: Hinrich, 1901–1909.]

Schwartz, Daniel R. *2 Maccabees.* Commentaries on Early Jewish Literature. Berlin: De Gruyter, 2008.

Schwartz, Dov. "The Neutralization of the Messianic Idea in Medieval Jewish Rationalism." *Hebrew Union College Annual* 64 (1993): 37–58 (in Hebrew).

Schweitzer, Albert. *The Quest of the Historical Jesus: A Critical Study of Its Progress from Reimarus to Wrede.* Translated by W. Montgomery. New York: Macmillan, 1961. [German original 1906.]

Schwemer, Anna Maria. "Jesus Christus als Prophet, König und Priester: Das munus triplex und die frühe Christologie." Pages 165–230 in *Der messianische Anspruch Jesu und die Anfänge der Christologie.* Wissenschaftliche Untersuchungen zum Neuen Testament 138. Edited by Martin Hengel and Anna Maria Schwemer. Tübingen: Mohr Siebeck, 2001.

Scott, Ernest F. "What Did the Idea of Messiah Mean to the Early Christians?" *Journal of Religion* 1 (1921): 418–20.

Scott, Ian W. "Is Philo's Moses a Divine Man?" *Studia Philonica Annual* 14 (2002): 87–111.

Scott, James. "Historical Development of the Messianic Idea." *The Old Testament Student* 7 (1888): 176–80.

Scott, James C. *Domination and the Arts of Resistance: Hidden Transcripts.* New Haven: Yale University Press, 1992.

Secunda, Shai. *The Iranian Talmud: Reading the Bavli in Its Sasanian Context.* Philadelphia: University of Pennsylvania Press, 2014.

Segal, Alan F. "Conversion and Messianism: An Outline for a New Approach." Pages 296–340 in *The Messiah: Developments in Earliest Judaism and Christianity*. Edited by James H. Charlesworth. Minneapolis: Fortress, 1992.

———. Review of Jacob Neusner et al., eds., *Judaisms and Their Messiahs at the Turn of the Christian Era*. *Jewish Social Studies* 50 (1988–1992): 117–18.

———. *Two Powers in Heaven: Early Rabbinic Reports about Christianity and Gnosticism*. Leiden: Brill, 1977.

Segelberg, Eric. "The Antiochene Background of the Gospel of Philip." *Bulletin de la Société d'Archéologie Copte* 18 (1965–1966): 205–23.

———. "The Antiochene Origin of the Gospel of Philip." *Bulletin de la Société d'Archéologie Copte* 19 (1967–1968): 207–10.

Shinan, Avigdor. "Dating Targum Pseudo-Jonathan: Some More Comments." *Journal of Jewish Studies* 41 (1990): 57–61.

Shukster, Martin B., and Peter Richardson. "Temple and Bet Ha-midrash in the Epistle of Barnabas." Pages 17–32 in *Anti-Judaism in Early Christianity*, vol. 2. Edited by Stephen G. Wilson. Études sur le christianisme et le judaïsme 3. Waterloo, Ont.: Wilfrid Laurier University Press, 1986.

Simpson, J., and E. Weiner, eds. *Oxford English Dictionary*. 2d ed., 20 vols. Oxford: Clarendon, 1989.

Skarsaune, Oskar. "Jews and Christians in the Holy Land, 135–325 C.E." Pages 158–70 in *Redemption and Resistance: The Messianic Hopes of Jews and Christians in Antiquity*. Edited by Markus Bockmuehl and James Carleton Paget. London: T. & T. Clark, 2007.

———. *The Proof from Prophecy: A Study in Justin Martyr's Proof-Text Tradition*. Leiden: Brill, 1987.

Slingerland, H. Dixon. "Chrestus: Christus?" Pages 133–44 in *New Perspectives on Ancient Judaism*, vol. 4: *The Literature of Early Rabbinic Judaism*. Edited by Alan J. Avery-Peck. Lanham, Md.: University Press of America, 1989.

Smith, D. Moody. *John among the Gospels*. 2d ed. Columbia: University of South Carolina Press, 2001.

Smith, Geoffrey S. *Guilt by Association: Heresy Catalogues in Early Christianity*. New York: Oxford University Press, 2014.

Smith, Jonathan Z. *Drudgery Divine: On the Comparison of Early Christianities and the Religions of Late Antiquity*. Chicago: University of Chicago Press, 1994.

———. "Manna, Mana Everywhere and /_/_/." Pages 117–44 in *Relating Religion*. Chicago: University of Chicago Press, 2004.

Smith, Morton. "Ascent to the Heavens and Deification in 4QMa." Pages 181–88 in *Archaeology and History in the Dead Sea Scrolls*. Edited by Lawrence H. Schiffman. Sheffield: JSOT Press, 1990.

———. "Historical Method in the Study of Religion." Pages 3–11 in vol. 1 of *Studies in the Cult of Yahweh*. Edited by Shaye J. D. Cohen. 2 vols. Leiden: Brill, 1996.

———. *Jesus the Magician*. San Francisco: Hampton Roads, 2014. [First pub. 1978.]

——. "Messiahs: Robbers, Jurists, Prophets, and Magicians." Pages 39–46 in vol. 2 of *Studies in the Cult of Yahweh*. Edited by Shaye J. D. Cohen. 2 vols. Leiden: Brill, 1996.

——. "Two Ascended to Heaven: Jesus and the Author of 4Q491." Pages 290–301 in *Jesus and the Dead Sea Scrolls*. Edited by James H. Charlesworth. New York: Doubleday, 1991.

——. "Were the Maccabees Priests?" Pages 320–25 in vol. 1 of *Studies in the Cult of Yahweh*. Edited by Shaye J. D. Cohen. 2 vols. Leiden: Brill, 1996.

——. "What Is Implied by the Variety of Messianic Figures?" *Journal of Biblical Literature* 78 (1959): 66–72.

Sobosan, H. G. "The Role of the Presbyter: An Investigation into the *Adv. Haer.* of St. Irenaeus." *Scottish Journal of Theology* 27 (1974): 129–46.

Soggin, J. A. "Charisma und Institution im Königtum Sauls." *Zeitschrift für die alttestamentliche Wissenschaft* 75 (1963): 54–65.

Sommer, Benjamin D. *The Bodies of God and the World of Ancient Israel*. New York: Cambridge University Press, 2009.

Stähelin, Johann Jakob. *Die messianischen Weissagungen des Alten Testaments*. Berlin: Reimer, 1847.

Stanton, Graham N. *A Gospel for a New People: Studies in Matthew*. Edinburgh: T. & T. Clark, 1992.

——. "Messianism and Christology: Mark, Matthew, Luke, and Acts." Pages 78–96 in *Redemption and Resistance: The Messianic Hopes of Jews and Christians in Antiquity*. Edited by Markus Bockmuehl and James Carleton Paget. London: T. & T. Clark, 2007.

——. "The Gospel Traditions and Early Christological Reflection." Pages 191–204 in *Christ, Faith, and History: Cambridge Studies in Christology*. Edited by S. W. Sykes and J. P. Clayton. Cambridge: Cambridge University Press, 1972.

Stanton, V. H. *The Jewish and the Christian Messiah*. Edinburgh: T. & T. Clark, 1886.

Staveley, E. S. "The Fasces and Imperium Maius." *Historia* 12 (1963): 458–84.

Steeg, Jules. *Le Messie d'après les Prophètes*. Strasbourg: Treuttel et Wurtz, 1867.

Stemberger, Günter. "Die Messiasfrage in den christlich-jüdischen Disputationen des Mittelalters." *Jahrbuch für biblische Theologie* 8 (1993): 239–50.

Stendahl, Krister. "Quis et Unde? An Analysis of Mt. 1–2." Pages 94–105 in *Judentum, Urchristentum, Kirche*. Edited by Walther Eltester. Beihefte zur Zeitschrift für die neutestamentliche Wissenschaft 26. Berlin: Töpelmann, 1964.

——. *The School of St. Matthew and Its Use of the Old Testament*. Lund: Gleerup, 1954.

——. "The Scrolls and the New Testament: An Introduction and a Perspective." Pages 1–17 in *The Scrolls and the New Testament*. Edited by Krister Stendahl. New York: Crossroad, 1957. Repr., 1992.

Steppa, Jan-Eric. "The Reception of Messianism and the Worship of Christ in the Post-Apostolic Church." Pages 79–116 in *The Messiah in Early Judaism and Christianity*. Edited by Magnus Zetterholm. Minneapolis: Fortress, 2007.

Stern, Menahem. "A. Schalit's Herod." *Journal of Jewish Studies* 11 (1960): 49–58.

Stone, Michael E. "The Angelic Prediction in the Primary Adam Books." Pages 111–32 in *Literature on Adam and Eve: Collected Essays*. Edited by Gary A. Anderson, Michael E. Stone, and Johannes Tromp. Studia in Veteris Testamenti pseudepigrapha 15. Leiden: Brill, 2000.

———. "The Concept of the Messiah in IV Ezra." Pages 295–312 in *Religions in Antiquity: Essays in Memory of Erwin Ramsdell Goodenough*. Edited by Jacob Neusner. Leiden: Brill, 1968.

Stout, Jeffrey. "What Is the Meaning of a Text?" *New Literary History* 14 (1982): 1–12.

Strack, H. L., and Günter Stemberger. *Introduction to the Talmud and Midrash*. Translated by Markus Bockmuehl. Minneapolis: Fortress, 1996.

Strack, H. L., and Paul Billerbeck. *Kommentar zum Neuen Testament aus Talmud und Midrasch*. 6 vols. Munich: Beck, 1922–1961.

Strauss, D. F. *The Life of Jesus, Critically Examined*. Translated by George Eliot. London: Sonnenschein, 1892. [Translation of *Das Leben Jesu, kritisch bearbeitet*. 2 vols. Tübingen: Osiander, 1835–1836.]

Strauss, Mark L. *The Davidic Messiah in Luke-Acts: The Promise and Its Fulfillment in Lukan Christology*. Journal for the Study of the New Testament Supplements 110. Sheffield: Sheffield Academic, 1995.

Strecker, Georg. *The Johannine Letters*. Translated by Linda Maloney. Hermeneia. Minneapolis: Fortress, 1996.

Stromberg, Jacob. "Deutero-Isaiah's Restoration Reconfigured." Pages 195–218 in *Continuity and Discontinuity: Chronological and Thematic Development in Isaiah 40–66*. Edited by Lena-Sofia Tiemeyer and Hans M. Barstad. Forschungen zur Religion und Literatur des Alten und Neuen Testaments 255. Göttingen: Vandenhoeck & Ruprecht, 2014.

Stroumsa, Gedaliahu G. "Form(s) of God: Some Notes on Metatron and Christ." *Harvard Theological Review* 76 (1983): 269–88.

———. "Jewish Myth and Ritual and the Beginnings of Comparative Religion: The Case of Richard Simon." Pages 27–48 in *Religions and Cultures*. Edited by Adriana Destro and Mauro Pesce. Binghamton, N.Y.: Global Publications, 2001.

Stuckenbruck, Loren T. "Messianic Ideas in the Apocalyptic and Related Literature of Early Judaism." Pages 90–113 in *The Messiah in the Old and New Testaments*. Edited by Stanley E. Porter. Grand Rapids: Eerdmans, 2007.

Stuhlmacher, Peter. "Der messianische Gottesknecht." *Jahrbuch für biblische Theologie* 8 (1993): 131–54.

Sukenik, Eliezer L. *Hidden Scrolls: First Survey*. Jerusalem: Bialik Institute, 1948 (in Hebrew).

Syme, Ronald. *The Roman Revolution*. Oxford: Clarendon, 1939.

Tabor, James D. "Are You the One? The Textual Dynamics of Messianic Self-Identity." Pages 179–90 in *Knowing the End from the Beginning: The Prophetic, the Apocalyptic, and Their Relationships*. Edited by Lester L. Grabbe and Robert D. Haak. Library of Second Temple Studies 46. London: T. & T. Clark, 2003.

Talmon, Shemaryahu. "Kingship and the Ideology of the State." Pages 9–38 in *King, Cult and Calendar in Ancient Israel: Collected Studies*. Jerusalem: Magnes, 1986.

———. "The Concept of *Masiah* and Messianism in Early Judaism." Pages 79–115 in *The Messiah: Developments in Earliest Judaism and Christianity*. Edited by James H. Charlesworth. Minneapolis: Fortress, 1992.

Taubes, Jacob. "The Price of Messianism." *Journal of Jewish Studies* 33 (1982): 595–600.

Taylor, Joan E. *The Essenes, the Scrolls, and the Dead Sea*. Oxford: Oxford University Press, 2012.

Telford, W. R. *The Theology of the Gospel of Mark*. Cambridge: Cambridge University Press, 1999.

Temkin, Owsei. *Hippocrates in a World of Pagans and Christians*. Baltimore: Johns Hopkins University Press, 1991.

Thiessen, Matthew. *Contesting Conversion: Genealogy, Circumcision, and Identity in Ancient Judaism and Christianity*. New York: Oxford University Press, 2011.

Thomassen, Einar. "Baptism among the Valentinians." Pages 895–915 in vol. 2 of *Ablution, Initiation, and Baptism: Late Antiquity, Early Judaism, and Early Christianity*. Edited by David Hellholm, Tor Vegge, Øyvind Norderval, and Christer Hellholm. 3 vols. Beihefte zur Zeitschrift für die neutestamentliche Wissenschaft 176. Berlin: De Gruyter, 2011.

———. "How Valentinian Is the Gospel of Philip?" Pages 251–79 in *The Nag Hammadi Library after Fifty Years*. Edited by John D. Turner and Anne McGuire. Nag Hammadi and Manichaean Studies 44. Leiden: Brill, 1997.

Thompson, Stephen E. "The Anointing of Officials in Ancient Egypt." *Journal of Near Eastern Studies* 53 (1994): 15–25.

Tishby, Isaiah. "The Messianic Idea and Messianic Trends at the Beginning of Hasidism." *Zion* 32 (1967): 1–45 (in Hebrew).

Toher, Mark. "Herod, Augustus, and Nicolaus of Damascus." Pages 65–82 in *Herod and Augustus*. Edited by David Jacobson and Niko Kokkinos. IJS Studies in Judaica 6. Leiden: Brill, 2009.

Torrey, Charles C. "The Messiah Son of Ephraim." *Journal of Biblical Literature* 66 (1947): 253–77.

Treat, Jay Curry. "Barnabas, Epistle of." Pages 611–14 in vol. 1 of *Anchor Bible Dictionary*. Edited by David Noel Freedman. 6 vols. New York: Doubleday, 1992.

Tromp, Johannes. "The Sinners and the Lawless in *Psalm of Solomon* 17." *Novum Testamentum* 35 (1993): 344–61.

Turner, John D. *Sethian Gnosticism and the Platonic Tradition*. Leuven: Peeters, 2001.

Urbach, E. E. *The Sages: Their Concepts and Beliefs*. Translated by Israel Abrams. 2 vols. Jerusalem: Magnes, 1979.

Utzschneider, Helmut. "Tabernacle." Pages 267–301 in *The Book of Exodus: Composition, Reception, and Interpretation*. Edited by Thomas B. Dozeman, Craig A. Evans, and Joel N. Lohr. Vetus Testamentum Supplements 164. Leiden: Brill, 2014.

van den Hoek, A. W. *Clement of Alexandria and His Use of Philo in the Stromateis*. Vigiliae Christianae Supplements 3. Leiden: Brill, 1988.

van der Horst, Pieter Willem. "Jesus and the Jews according to the Suda." *Zeitschrift für die neutestamentliche Wissenschaft und die Kunde der älteren Kirche* 84 (1993): 268–77.

VanderKam, James C. *The Dead Sea Scrolls Today.* Grand Rapids: Eerdmans, 1994.

———. *From Joshua to Caiaphas: High Priests after the Exile.* Minneapolis: Fortress, 2004.

VanderKam, James C., and Peter Flint. *The Meaning of the Dead Sea Scrolls.* London: T. & T. Clark, 2002.

van der Kooij, Arie. "The Greek Bible and Jewish Concepts of Royal Priesthood and Priestly Monarchy." Pages 255–64 in *Jewish Perspectives on Hellenistic Rulers.* Edited by Tessa Rajak, Sarah Pearce, James Aitken, and Jennifer Dines. Berkeley: University of California Press, 2007.

van der Woude, A. S. *Die messianische Vorstellungen der Gemeinde von Qumran.* Studia semitica neerlandica 3. Assen: van Gorcum, 1957.

van Os, Bas. "Baptism in the Bridal Chamber: The Gospel of Philip as a Valentinian Baptismal Instruction." Ph.D. diss., University of Groningen, 2007.

———. "Was the Gospel of Philip Written in Syria?" *Apocrypha* 17 (2006): 87–94.

van Unnik, W. C. "The Authority of the Presbyters in Irenaeus' Works." Pages 248–60 in *God's Christ and His People: Studies in Honour of Nils Alstrup Dahl.* Edited by Jacob Jervell and Wayne A. Meeks. Oslo: Universitetsforlaget, 1978.

———. "Three Notes on the Gospel of Philip." *New Testament Studies* 10 (1964): 465–69.

Veijola, Timo. "Solomon: Bathsheba's Firstborn." Pages 340–57 in *Reconsidering Israel and Judah: Recent Studies on the Deuteronomistic History.* Edited by Gary N. Knoppers and J. Gordon McConville. Sources for Biblical and Theological Study 8. Winona Lake, Ind.: Eisenbrauns, 2000.

Verheyden, Joseph. "Epiphanius on the Ebionites." Pages 182–208 in *The Image of the Judaeo-Christians in Ancient Jewish and Christian Literature.* Edited by Peter J. Tomson and Doris Lambers-Petry. Wissenschaftliche Untersuchungen zum Neuen Testament 158. Tübingen: Mohr Siebeck, 2003.

Vermes, Geza. *Jesus the Jew: A Historian's Reading of the Gospels.* London: Collins, 1973.

———. "Jewish Literature and New Testament Exegesis: Reflections on Method." Pages 74–88 in *Jesus and the World of Judaism.* London: SCM, 1983.

———. *Scripture and Tradition in Judaism.* 2d ed. Leiden: Brill 1973.

Vernes, Maurice. *Histoire des idées messianique depuis Alexandre jusqu'à l'empereur Hadrien.* Paris: Sandoz et Fischbacher, 1874.

Vielhauer, Philipp, and Georg Strecker. "Introduction: Apocalyptic in Early Christianity." Pages 569–602 in vol. 2 of *New Testament Apocrypha.* Edited by Edgar Hennecke and Wilhelm Schneemelcher. Translated by R. McL. Wilson. Rev. ed., 2 vols. Cambridge: Clarke, 1992.

Vieyra, M. "Rites de purification hittites." *Revue de l'histoire des religions* 119 (1939): 121–53.

Vogel, K.- H. "Imperium und Fasces." *Zeitschrift der Savigny-Stiftung für Rechtsgeschichte* 67 (1950): 62–111.

von Balthasar, Hans Urs. *Herrlichkeit: Eine theologische Ästhetik.* 3 vols. Einsiedeln: Johannes Verlag, 1961–1969.

von Gall, A. F. *ΒΑΣΙΛΕΙΑ ΤΟΥ ΘΕΟΥ.* Heidelberg: Winter, 1926.

von Hofmann, Johann Christian Konrad. *Weissagung und Erfüllung im alte und im neue Testamente.* 2 vols. Nördlingen: Becksche, 1841–1844.

von Rad, Gerhard. "Royal Ritual in Judah." Pages 222–31 in *The Problem of the Hexateuch and Other Essays.* Translated by N. W. Porteous. Edinburgh: Oliver & Boyd, 1965.

Waddell, James. *The Messiah: A Comparative Study of the Enochic Son of Man and the Pauline Kyrios.* Jewish and Christian Texts in Contexts 10. London: T. & T. Clark, 2011.

Warren, Minton. "On Latin Glossaries, with Especial Reference to the Codex Sangallensis 912." *Transactions of the American Philological Association* 15 (1884): 124–228.

Waschke, Ernst-Joachim. *Der Gesalbte: Studien der alttestamentliche Theologie.* Beihefte zur Zeitschrift für die alttestamentliche Wissenschaft 306. Berlin: De Gruyter, 2001.

Wasserman, Emma. *The Death of the Soul in Romans 7.* Wissenschaftliche Untersuchungen zum Neuen Testament 2.256. Tübingen: Mohr Siebeck, 2008.

Weber, Ferdinand. *Jüdische Theologie.* 2d ed. Leipzig: Dörffling & Franke, 1897.

Weber, Max. *Ancient Judaism.* Translated and edited by Hans H. Gerth and Don Martindale. New York: Free Press, 1952. [Translation of *Das antike Judentum.* Tübingen: Mohr Siebeck, 1921.]

———. *On Charisma and Institution Building: Selected Papers.* Edited by S. N. Eisenstadt. Chicago: University of Chicago Press, 1968.

———. *The Theory of Social and Economic Organization.* Translated by A. M. Henderson and Talcott Parsons. New York: Oxford University Press, 1947. [Repr., New York: Free Press, 2009. German original 1920.]

Weisman, Z. "Anointing as a Motif in the Making of a Charismatic King." *Biblica* 57 (1976): 378–98.

Werblowsky, R. J. Zwi. "Jewish Messianism in Comparative Perspective." Pages 1–14 in *Messiah and Christos: Studies in the Jewish Origins of Christianity.* Edited by Ithamar Gruenwald, Shaul Shaked, and Gedaliahu G. Stroumsa. Texte und Studien zum antiken Judentum 32. Tübingen: Mohr Siebeck, 1992.

———. "Messianism in Jewish History." Pages 35–52 in *Essential Papers on Messianic Movements and Personalities in Jewish History.* Edited by Marc Saperstein. New York: NYU Press, 1992.

Whealey, Alice. *Josephus on Jesus: The Testimonium Flavianum Controversy from Late Antiquity to Modern Times.* Studies in Biblical Literature 36. New York: Peter Lang, 2003.

White, Marsha C. *The Elijah Legends and Jehu's Coup.* Brown Judaic Studies 311. Atlanta: Scholars Press, 1997.

Wilhite, David E. *Tertullian the African: An Anthropological Reading of Tertullian's Context and Identities.* Berlin: De Gruyter, 2007.

Wilken, Robert L. "Early Christian Chiliasm, Jewish Messianism, and the Idea of the Holy Land." *Harvard Theological Review* 79 (1986): 298–307.

Williams, A. Lukyn. *Adversus Judaeos: A Bird's-Eye View of Christian Apologiae until the Renaissance.* Cambridge: Cambridge University Press, 1935.

Williams, G. "Horace, *Odes* 1.12 and the Succession to Augustus." *Hermathena* 118 (1974): 147–55.

Williams, Michael Allen. *Rethinking "Gnosticism": An Argument for Dismantling a Dubious Category.* Princeton: Princeton University Press, 1996.

Williamson, H. G. M. "Early Post-Exilic Judaean History." Pages 3–24 in *Studies in Persian Period History and Historiography.* Forschungen zum Alten Testament 38. Tübingen: Mohr Siebeck, 2004.

———. "Messianic Texts in Isaiah 1–39." Pages 238–70 in *King and Messiah in Israel and the Ancient Near East.* Edited by John Day. London: T. & T. Clark, 2013. [First pub. Sheffield: Sheffield Academic, 1998.]

———. "The Governors of Judah under the Persians." *Tyndale Bulletin* 39 (1988): 59–82.

———. *Variations on a Theme: King, Messiah, and Servant in the Book of Isaiah.* Carlisle, UK: Paternoster, 1998.

Willitts, Joel. "Davidic Messiahship in Galatians: Clearing the Deck for a Study of the Theme in Galatians." *Journal for the Study of Paul and His Letters* 2 (2012): 143–62.

Winter, Paul. "Appendix: Josephus on Jesus and James." Pages 428–41 in vol. 1 of *The History of the Jewish People in the Age of Jesus Christ.* Revised and edited by Geza Vermes, Fergus Millar, and Matthew Black. 3 vols. Edinburgh: T. & T. Clark, 1973–1987.

Wise, Michael O. "Dating the Teacher of Righteousness and the Floruit of His Movement." *Journal of Biblical Literature* 122 (2003): 53–87.

———. *The First Messiah: Investigating the Savior before Jesus.* San Francisco: Harper, 1999.

———. "The Origins and History of the Teacher's Movement." Pages 92–122 in *The Oxford Handbook of the Dead Sea Scrolls.* Edited by Timothy H. Lim and John J. Collins. Oxford: Oxford University Press, 2010.

———. "מי כמוני באלים: A Study of 4Q491c, 4Q471b, 4Q427 7, and 1QHa 25:35–26:10." *Dead Sea Discoveries* 7 (2000): 173–219.

Wisse, Frederik. "The Nag Hammadi Library and the Heresiologists." *Vigiliae Christianae* 25 (1971): 205–23.

Wittgenstein, Ludwig. *Philosophical Investigations.* Translated by G. E. M. Anscombe. Oxford: Blackwell, 1953.

Wolfson, Elliot R. "Becoming Invisible: Rending the Veil and the Hermeneutic of Secrecy in the Gospel of Philip." Pages 113–36 in *Practicing Gnosis: Essays in*

Honor of Birger A. Pearson. Edited by April DeConick, Gregory Shaw, and John D. Turner. Nag Hammadi and Manichaean Studies 85. Leiden: Brill, 2013.

———. *Open Secret: Postmessianic Messianism and the Mystical Revision of Menahem Mendel Schneerson*. New York: Columbia University Press, 2009.

Wolfson, H. A. *Philo: Foundations of Religious Philosophy in Judaism, Christianity, and Islam*. 2 vols. Cambridge, Mass.: Harvard University Press, 1947.

Wrede, William. "Jesus als Davidssohn." Pages 147–77 in *Vorträge und Studien*. Tübingen: Mohr Siebeck, 1907.

———. *The Messianic Secret*. Translated by J. C. G. Greig. Cambridge: Clarke, 1971. [Translation of *Das Messiasgeheimnis in den Evangelien*. Göttingen: Vandenhoeck & Ruprecht, 1901.]

Wright, Benjamin G. "Eschatology without a Messiah in the Wisdom of Ben Sira." Pages 313–24 in *The Septuagint and Messianism*. Edited by M. A. Knibb. Bibliotheca ephemeridum theologicarum lovaniensium 195. Leuven: Peeters, 2006.

Wünsche, August. *Die Leiden des Messias*. Leipzig: Fues, 1870.

Wyatt, Nicholas. "Royal Religion in Ancient Judah." Pages 61–81 in *Religious Diversity in Ancient Israel and Judah*. Edited by Francesca Stavrakapoulou and John Barton. London: T. & T. Clark, 2010.

Yadin, Yigael. *Bar Kokhba: The Rediscovery of the Legendary Hero of the Second Jewish Revolt against Rome*. New York: Random House, 1971.

Yarbro Collins, Adela. *Crisis and Catharsis: The Power of the Apocalypse*. Philadelphia: Westminster, 1984.

———. "Response to Israel Knohl, *Messiahs and Resurrection in The Gabriel Revelation*." Pages 93–98 in *Hazon Gabriel: New Readings of the Gabriel Revelation*. Edited by Matthias Henze. Atlanta: SBL, 2011.

Yarbro Collins, Adela, and John J. Collins. *King and Messiah as Son of God*. Grand Rapids: Eerdmans, 2008.

York, A. D. "The Dating of Targumic Literature." *Journal for the Study of Judaism* 5 (1974): 49–62.

Yuval, Israel Jacob. *Two Nations in Your Womb: Perceptions of Jews and Christians in Late Antiquity and the Middle Ages*. Berkeley: University of California Press, 2006.

Zeitlin, Solomon "Josephus on Jesus." *Jewish Quarterly Review* 21 (1930–1931): 377–417.

———. "Josippon." *Jewish Quarterly Review* 53 (1963): 273–97.

———. "The Christ Passage in Josephus." *Jewish Quarterly Review* 18 (1927–1928): 231–55.

Zellentin, Holger M. *Rabbinic Parodies of Jewish and Christian Literature*. Texte und Studien zum antiken Judentum 139. Tübingen: Mohr Siebeck, 2011.

———. "Rabbinizing Jesus, Christianizing the Son of David: The Bavli's Approach to the Secondary Messiah Traditions." Pages 99–127 in *Discussing Cultural Influences: Text, Context, and Non-Text in Rabbinic Judaism*. Edited by Rivka Ulmer. Lanham, Md.: University Press of America, 2007.

Zeller, Dieter. "Zur Transformation des χριστός bei Paulus." *Jahrbuch für biblische Theologie* 8 (1993): 155–67.

Zetterholm, Magnus. "Introduction." Pages xxi–xxvii in *The Messiah in Early Judaism
and Christianity*. Edited by Magnus Zetterholm. Minneapolis: Fortress, 2007.

Zimmerman, Johannes. *Messianische Texte aus Qumran: Königliche, priesterliche und prophetische Messiasvorstellungen in den Schriftfunden von Qumran*. Wissenschaftliche
Untersuchungen zum Neuen Testament 2.104. Tübingen: Mohr Siebeck, 1998.

Zwiep, Arie W. *The Ascension of the Messiah in Lukan Christology*. Novum Testamentum
Supplements 87. Leiden: Brill, 1997.

Index of Subjects

Index of Ancient Sources

338

Index of Ancient Sources

Index of Modern Authors

CPSIA information can be obtained
at www.ICGtesting.com
Printed in the USA
BVHW030709180422
634371BV00002B/7

9 780190 053215